Communications
in Computer and Information Science   290

Antonia Mas   Antoni Mesquida   Terry Rout
Rory V. O'Connor   Alec Dorling (Eds.)

Software Process Improvement and Capability Determination

12th International Conference, SPICE 2012
Palma, Spain, May 29-31, 2012
Proceedings

Volume Editors

Antonia Mas
University of the Balearic Islands
Palma de Mallorca, Spain
E-mail: antonia.mas@uib.es

Antoni Mesquida
University of the Balearic Islands
Palma de Mallorca, Spain
E-mail: antoni.mesquida@uib.es

Terry Rout
Software Quality Institute
Griffith University
Brisbane, QLD, Australia
E-mail: t.rout@griffith.edu.au

Rory V. O'Connor
Lero, the Irish Software Engineering
Research Centre
School of Computing
Dublin City University
Dublin, Ireland
E-mail: roconnor@computing.dcu.ie

Alec Dorling
InterSPICE Ltd
Cambridge, UK
E-mail: alec.dorling@interspice.uk.com

ISSN 1865-0929   e-ISSN 1865-0937
ISBN 978-3-642-30438-5   e-ISBN 978-3-642-30439-2
DOI 10.1007/978-3-642-30439-2
Springer Heidelberg Dordrecht London New York

Library of Congress Control Number: Applied for

CR Subject Classification (1998): D.2.9, D.2, K.6, C.2, J.1, K.4.2, K.6.5

© Springer-Verlag Berlin Heidelberg 2012
This work is subject to copyright. All rights are reserved, whether the whole or part of the material is concerned, specifically the rights of translation, reprinting, re-use of illustrations, recitation, broadcasting, reproduction on microfilms or in any other way, and storage in data banks. Duplication of this publication or parts thereof is permitted only under the provisions of the German Copyright Law of September 9, 1965, in its current version, and permission for use must always be obtained from Springer. Violations are liable to prosecution under the German Copyright Law.
The use of general descriptive names, registered names, trademarks, etc. in this publication does not imply, even in the absence of a specific statement, that such names are exempt from the relevant protective laws and regulations and therefore free for general use.

Typesetting: Camera-ready by author, data conversion by Scientific Publishing Services, Chennai, India
Printed on acid-free paper
Springer is part of Springer Science+Business Media (www.springer.com)

Preface

On behalf of the SPICE Organizing Committee we are proud to present the proceedings of the 12th International Conference on Software Process Improvement and Capability dEtermination (SPICE 2012), held in Palma, Spain, during May 29–31, 2012.

The SPICE Project was formed in 1993 to support the development of an international standard for software process assessment. The work of the project has eventually led to the finalization of ISO/IEC 15504 – Process Assessment, and its complete publication represented a climax for the work of the project. As part of its charter to provide ongoing publicity and transition support for the emerging standard, the project organized a number of SPICE Workshops and Seminars, with invited speakers drawn from project participants.

These have now evolved to a sustaining set of international conferences with broad participation from academia and industry with a common interest in model-based process improvement. This was the 12th in the series of conferences organized by the SPICE User Group to increase knowledge and understanding of the International Standard, and of the technique of process assessment.

The conference program featured invited keynote talks, research papers, and industry experience reports on the most relevant topics related to software process assessment and improvement. The technical research papers were selected for presentation following peer review by members of the Program Committee. In addition, a number of tutorials were hosted.

SPICE conferences have a long history of attracting attendees from industry and academia. This confirms that the conference covers topics which are up-to-date, important, and interesting. SPICE 2012 offered a unique forum for industry and academic professionals to discuss their needs and ideas in the area of process assessment and improvement, and related aspects of quality management.

On behalf of the SPICE 2012 conference Organizing Committee, we would like to thank all participants. Firstly all the authors, whose quality work is the essence of the conference, and the members of the Program Committee, who helped us with their expertise and diligence in reviewing all of the submissions. As we all know, organizing a conference requires the effort of many individuals. We wish to thank also all the members of our Organizing Committee, whose work and commitment were invaluable.

May 2012

Antonia Mas
Antoni Mesquida
Terry Rout
Rory V. O'Connor
Alec Dorling

Organization

General Chair

Alec Dorling — InterSPICE, UK

Program Chair

Terry Rout — Griffith University, Australia

Local Organizing Chair

Antonia Mas — University of the Balearic Islands, Spain

Industry Chair

Antoni Mesquida — University of the Balearic Islands, Spain

Proceedings Chair

Rory V. O'Connor — Lero, Dublin City University, Ireland

Tutorial Chair

Timo Varkoi — Tampere University of Technology, Finland

Publicity Chair

Ravindra Joshi — Infiniti, India

Social Networking Chair

Carol Dekkers — Quality Plus Technologies, USA

Program Committee

Beatrix Barafort, Luxembourg
Luigi Buglione, Italy
Aileen Cater-Steel, Australia
Melanie Cheong, Australia
Gerhard Chroust, Austria
Francois Coallier, Canada
Antonio Coletta, Italy
Carol Dekkers, USA
Fabrizzio Fabbrini, Italy
Mario Fusani, Italy
Dennis Goldenson, USA
Christiane Gresse von Wangenheim, Brazil
Victoria Hailey, Canada
John Horch, USA
Linda Ibrahim, USA
Ravindra Joshi, India
Ho-Won Jung, South Korea
Giuseppe Lami, Italy
Jean Pierre Legras, France
Marion Lepmets, Luxembourg
Catriona Mackie, UK
Antonia Mas, Spain
Tom McBride, Australia
Fergal McCaffery, Ireland
Takeshige Miyoshi, Japan
Risto Nevalainen, Finland
Hanna Oktaba, Mexico
Mark Paulk, USA
Alain Renault, Luxembourg
Patricia Rodriguez Dapena, Spain
Clenio Salviano, Brazil
Marty Sanders, Ireland
Jean-Martin Simon, France
Fritz Stallinger, Austria
Robert Treffny, Germany
Han van Loon, Switzerland
Timo Varkoi, Finland

Local Organizing Committee

Antonia Mas — University of the Balearic Islands
Antoni Mesquida — University of the Balearic Islands
José María Gilabert — University of the Balearic Islands
Margalida Barceló Nadal — University of the Balearic Islands
Bartomeu Fluxà — Brújula

The local organizers acknowledge the support of the Office of the Vice-Rector for Research at University of the Balearic Islands.

The conference organizers wish to acknowledge the assistance and support of the SPICE User Group, SPICE 2012 Program Committee and reviewers in contributing to a successful conference.

Table of Contents

Organizational Process Improvement 1

Critical Success Factors in Software Process Improvement: A Systematic Review 1
  Sussy Bayona, Jose A. Calvo-Manzano, and Tomás San Feliu

Integrated Process Improvement Approach: Case Studies in Skype Technologies Ltd. 13
  Anneli Tuisk, André Karpištšenko, and Marion Lepmets

A Case Study on Employee Perceptions of Organization Wide Continuous Process Improvement Activities 26
  Algan Uskarcı and Onur Demirörs

SPI in Small and Very Small Enterprises

Using Composition Trees to Validate an Entry Profile of Software Engineering Lifecycle Profiles for Very Small Entities (VSEs) 38
  Lian Wen and Terry Rout

Gained Experience by Making Intervention to Improve Software Process in Very Small Organizations............................ 51
  Mohammad Zarour, Jean-Marc Desharnais, Abdulrahman Alarifi, Naji Habra, Grégory Cassiers, and Antoine Robaeys

A Hierarchy of SPI Activities for Software SMEs: Results from ISO/IEC 12207-Based SPI Assessments 62
  Paul Clarke, Rory V. O'Connor, and Murat Yilmaz

Process Models 1

Innovation, Knowledge- and Technology Transfer Process Capability Model – innoSPICE^{TM} 75
  Jeremy Besson, Tanja Woronowicz, Antanas Mitasiunas, and Michael Boronowsky

A Case Study on Process Composition Using Enterprise SPICE Model 85
  Amalia Alvarez, Santiago Matalonga, and Tomás San Feliu

Extending ISO/IEC 12207 with Software Product Management: A Process Reference Model Proposal 93
  Fritz Stallinger and Robert Neumann

SPI in Automotive Software and Security

An Experiment on Merging Quality Assessment in Automotive
Domain... 107
   Morayo Adedjouma, Hubert Dubois, François Terrier, and
   Tarek Kitouni

A Process-Oriented Approach for Functional Safety Implementation in
the Automotive Industry.. 118
   Maria Antonieta Garcia, Ernesto Viale, Marco Bellotti, and
   João Carlos Alchieri

Designing a Process Reference Model for Information Security
Management Systems... 129
   Olivier Mangin, Béatrix Barafort, Patrick Heymans, and Eric Dubois

SPI in Medical and Safety Critical Systems

Barriers to Adopting Agile Practices When Developing Medical Device
Software... 141
   Martin McHugh, Fergal McCaffery, and Valentine Casey

Development of a Process Assessment Model for Assessing Medical IT
Networks against IEC 80001-1..................................... 148
   Silvana Togneri MacMahon, Fergal McCaffery, Sherman Eagles,
   Frank Keenan, Marion Lepmets, and Alain Renault

Traceability-Why Do It?.. 161
   Gilbert Regan, Fergal McCaffery, Kevin McDaid, and Derek Flood

Organizational Process Improvement 2

Improving the Tendering Process through the Deployment of
PMBOK®... 173
   Antònia Mas and Antoni Lluís Mesquida

FIRST: Common-Sense Process Scopes for Starting a Process
Improvement Program.. 186
   Luigi Buglione, Fergal McCaffery, Jean Carlo Rossa Hauck, and
   Christiane Gresse von Wangenheim

A Systematic Approach to the Comparison of Roles in the Software
Development Processes.. 198
   Murat Yilmaz, Rory V. O'Connor, and Paul Clarke

Process Models 2

Framework for Usage of Multiple Software Process Models 210
   Stasys Peldzius and Saulius Ragaisis

Self-assessment Model and Review Technique for SPICE:
SMART SPICE 222
   *Sharmistha Kar, Satyabrata Das, Amiya Kumar Rath, and
Subrata Kumar Kar*

Bayesian Network Based Bug-fix Effort Prediction Model 233
   Bharathi V., Udaya Shastry, and Joseph Raj

Short Papers

A State of Art of Software Improvement Implementation Support Tools
in SMEs 239
   *Mirna Muñoz, Antonio De Amescua, Jezreel Mejia,
Jose A. Calvo-Manzano, Gonzalo Cuevas, and
Tomás San Feliu*

Adaptive Process Improvement Approaches 244
   Ravindra Joshi

Improving Risk Management Practices with Success Driver Analysis 249
   Ernest Wallmüller

Software Engineering Process and Quality Assurance Framework for
Automotive Product Engineering Outsourcing 253
   Manfred Schedl, Eugene Nebrat, and Lyudmila Matveeva

Applying Kaizen for Improving Productivity in Automotive Software
Projects 257
   Smitha Bhandary, Balaji Ramachandran, and Basavaraj Betageri

Best Practices for Achieving Automotive SPICE Capability Level 3 261
   Anna Orecka, Sebastian Dawid, and Rafał Dzianach

Development of the Medi SPICE PRM 265
   Valentine Casey and Fergal McCaffery

Concrete, Steel and ISO 15288 269
   Han van Loon

DEFT – A Test Framework to Aid Decision Making 273
   Gerry Crines, Sarah Salahuddin, and Donald Mackinnon

Evaluating Management Sentiment towards ISO/IEC 29110 in Very
Small Software Development Companies 277
   Rory V. O'Connor

Using Process Assessment Models Based on Multiple Process Reference
Models in a Capability Determination Context........................ 282
   Terry Rout

Using Target Process Profiles in the Real World 286
   Han van Loon

Agile Maturity Model: Oxymoron or the Next Level of
Understanding.. 289
   Tomas Schweigert, Risto Nevalainen, Detlef Vohwinkel,
   Morten Korsaa, and Miklos Biro

The Gamification of SPICE 295
   Alec Dorling and Fergal McCaffery

Author Index 303

Critical Success Factors in Software Process Improvement: A Systematic Review

Sussy Bayona, Jose A. Calvo-Manzano, and Tomás San Feliu

Departamento Lenguajes y Sistemas Informáticos e Ingeniería de Software, Universidad Politécnica de Madrid, Facultad de Informática, Spain
sbayonao@hotmail.com, {jacalvo,tsanfe}@fi.upm.es

Abstract. Many methods, models and standards for software process improvement have been developed. However, despite the efforts, they still come up against difficulties in their deployment and the processes are not institutionalized. There is a set of factors that influence the successful deployment of new or modified processes. In this paper we describe the methodology and results from a systematic review of critical success factors in software process improvement and deployment. A total of 28 primary studies were analyzed as a result of the systematic review. Some of the top factors for process improvement and process deployment initiatives are: commitment, alignment with the business strategy and goals, training, communication, resources, skills, improvement management and staff involvement. The obtained results show that is important to take into account organizational, technical and people issues in order to achieve success in improvement initiatives.

Keywords: Critical success factors, Process improvement, Process deployment.

1 Introduction

Several different models and standards have been developed for software process improvement initiatives such as Capability Maturity Model Integration (CMMI) [1], ISO 15504 (SPICE) [2], IDEAL [3], however, organizations have problems when implementing them [4, 5, 6, 7]. Studies have been carried out [8, 9, 10, 11, 12], showing that the effort t that is made in implementing these models and standards can help to produce high-quality software and to increase productivity. Organizations engaged in development define their software process using these reference models. Once processes are well defined and established, they are deployed through the organization. However, organizations have difficulties in the use and adoption of processes.

On the one hand, process deployment is focused on people at all level: persons, groups, organizations, countries and cultures [13]. Issues in process institutionalization arise due to the fact that most of these efforts are mostly focused on technical issues and the issues related to people are ignored. McDermid and others [14] agree that human factors have been ignored in process improvement and this has struck on the efficiency of improvement initiatives. Halland Wilson [15] suggest that experiences, opinions and perceptions of practitioners have an indirect effect on software quality. On the other hand, this situation gets worse when the need of the organization to use these reference models arises from (1) a need to obtain certification, (2) the market pressure or (3) not be aware of improvement. The need to obtain the certification and the market pressure are factors that have been considered demotivators by Hall et al. [16].

According to Niazi et al. [17], the problem of process improvement is not the lack of standards or models, but the lack of an effective and successful strategy to implement the selected model or standards in their current scenario.

Process deployment is a fundamental activity in Software Process Improvement. Process Improvement is defined as a method that is introduced to bring in changes so as to increase the quality of a product, decrease the costs and improve the deviations. Process deployment is defined as *"the process that allows the implementation, adoption, management and institutionalization of the processes generated in Process Engineering, allowing multiple implementations of the process across the organization"* [18].The International Process Research Consortium (IPRC) [13] has included the topic of Process Deployment in a list of research items because intensive research into the human factor and change management is needed. Lepmets and Ras [19] suggest that clarify in goals, tasks, and responsibilities empowers employees to undertake an organizational change.

People in charge of deploying processes across the organization should deal with different problems such as:

- Lack of high level stakeholders and staff commitment [20, 21].
- Lack of high-qualified staff [22, 23].
- Lack of motivation and employee resistance to change [24].
- Lack of a process deployment strategy focused on people [25] to ensure that processes are accepted, used and institutionalized.
- Staff resistance to change and consequently processes are not adopted and used [18].
- Lack of involvement (users of the process, the management, stakeholders) [26].
- Processes deployed are not tailored to organizational needs, and then they must be modified [25].

These reasons allow us to state that process deployment depends strongly on both the social and technical issues [22], [25], [27].

In this paper, we identify through a systematic review, which are the critical success factors to be taken into account when a process deployment strategy is designed. For this purpose, the systematic review technique proposed by Kitchenham [28], [29] is used. A systematic review is a formal and verifiable process that researchers carry out to document the state of knowledge specifically on a topic. This review is more commonly used in other fields such as medicine, to document high-level conclusions that can be obtained from a series of detailed studies. Nevertheless, the systematic review is increasingly extended to other fields such as software engineering [30], [31] [32].

We believe the results of this study will benefit researchers and practitioners. For the industrial readership, the review will provide practitioners with useful information about the critical success factors for process improvement and process deployment. They can use the findings reported in this paper as a reference when developing a process deployment or process improvement strategy.

The rest of this paper is structured as follows: Section 2 describes the methodology of the systematic review which follows the guidelines as presented in [28]. Section 3 presents a report of the systematic review results, while Section 4 discusses the results based on an empirical analysis of the critical success factors in process improvement and process deployment initiatives. Finally, Section 5 draws some conclusions based on the review carried out.

2 Systematic Review Methodology

This section reports the details about each step of the systematic review. According to Kitchenham [29], a systematic review is a means for evaluating and interpreting all available research relevant to a particular research question, topic area, or phenomenon of interest. The systematic review [29] allows: (1) to review the relevant works that have been performed in the study area, (2) to control, evaluate and confirm the results, and (3) to identify research gaps that will lead to new topics of research activity.

The literature systematic review includes the following steps:

- Identify the needs to carry out the systematic review.
- Develop and validate the systematic review protocol.
- Conduct the review (to identify the primary studies, select primary studies, asses the quality of primary studies, extract data and synthesize the data).
- Report the systematic review results.

This section details the procedure followed to identify the critical success factors in the process improvement and process deployment initiatives. The activity "Report the systematic review results" is detailed in Section 3 (general results for process improvement and process deployment initiatives) and Section 4 is related to the critical success factors identified by the systematic review.

2.1 Identify the Needs for a Review

Many methods, models and standards for software process improvement have been developed. However, despite the efforts, they still come up against difficulties in their implementation, due to the fact that most of these efforts are mostly focused on technical issues and the issues related to people are ignored. There is a set of factors that influence the successful deployment of new or modified processes.

The goal of this study is to carry out a systematic review that allows to characterize the critical success factors for successful process improvement and process deployment initiatives.

2.2 Develop and Validate the Systematic Review Protocol

The systematic review protocol describes the steps and the procedures to be followed during a review. It includes the research questions, the source selection criteria, the sources that must be used to perform the search and the methods used to locate and select the studies.

2.2.1 Question Formulation

The systematic review is carried out to identify the initiatives and experience reports related to process improvement and process deployment and their critical success factors. This section aims at defining (1) the problem and (2) the syntax of the research questions (the context in which the review is applied and the questions the study must answer) and its specific semantic described by the remaining items: (3) intervention, (4) effect, (5) outcome measure, (6) population, (7) application and (8) experimental design. Next, each of them is described.

- **Problem:** process improvement and process deployment success is determined by technical, organizational and human factors. So, a study for determining the critical success factors for process improvement and process deployment is necessary.
- **Research questions:** the research questions are showed in Table 1.
- Intervention: current state of the process improvement and deployment determining their critical success factors.
- **Effect:** identify all initiatives and proposals related to process improvement and process deployment and their critical success factors.
- **Outcome measure:** number of critical success factors identified in the process improvement and process deployment initiatives.
- **Population:** the set of research proposals related to process improvement and process deployment and their critical success factors which have been published.
- **Application:** organizations and researchers that have investigated about initiatives of process improvement and process deployment, and their critical success factors.
- **Experimental Design:** None experimental design will be performed.

Table 1. Research questions for the systematic review

ID	Questions	Aim
RQ1	Which are the critical success factors for a successful process improvement initiative?	Identify which are the critical success factors identified in process improvement initiatives and what have a major impact on software process improvement success.
RQ2	Which are the critical success factors for a successful process deployment initiative?	Identify which are the critical success factors identified in process deployment initiatives and what have a major impact on software process deployment success.

2.2.2 Sources Selection

To perform the selection of the sources where searches for primary studies will be performed. This section includes the following activities: (1) sources selection criteria definition, (2) sources identification and (3) sources selection after evaluation.Next, a description of each activity is presented.

2.2.2.1 Sources Selection Criteria Definition
Activity in which the criteria have been established for the identification and selection of the sources (specialized databases).

The source selection criteria are:

- Databases that include journals, papers focused on software engineering empirical studies, human factors in software engineering and software quality.
- Databases with mechanisms of advanced search take into account the terms and synonyms used in the search questions.
- Availability of the complete text papers.
- Papers available in the Website.
- Specialized journals available in the library of the Universidad Politécnica de Madrid (UPM).
- Papers written in English.

2.2.2.2 Sources Identification
The sources include specialized digital sources of software engineering literature, such as Science @ Direct, IEEE Explore, ACM Digital library, SpringerLink, Institute for Scientific Information (ISI) Web Knowledge, Wiley InterScience; articles and conference presentations specialized as Software Engineering Process Group, European Systems & Software Process and Innovation (EUROSPI), as well as reports, articles and presentations by Software Engineering Institute (SEI), CrossTalk, IT Governance and Google Scholar.

The search string used has been: ((process deployment OR software process improvement OR software process implementation OR SPI AND ("critical success factors" OR "key factors" OR "human factors" OR "social factors" OR taxonomy OR catalog OR barriers OR motivators OR demotivators)) AND (CMM OR CMMI OR SPICE OR ISO9000 OR MPS OR IDEAL))

The search mechanisms of the available search engines are different. It has been necessary to design and use different search strings for each database, maintaining the equivalence. The list of sources includes relevant journals such as: *Information and Software Technology, Software Process Improvement and Practice, Journal of Systems and Software, IEEE Transactions on Software Engineering, Software Quality Journal, IEEE Software and Journal of Defense in Software Engineering* among others.The sources have been selected taking into account the defined source search method. First, it was evaluated if the sources fit all the defined source selection criteria. In a previous review search using IEExplore and Google Scholar and the UPM´s library, it was found the same items. And second, the source list was evaluated by three process improvement experts.

2.3 Conduct the Review

This section includes the definition of studies inclusion and exclusion criteria to select the primary studies, the data extraction and summarize the main results. Next, a description of each activity is presented.

2.3.1 Definition of Studies Inclusion and Exclusion Criteria and Selecting Process

Systematic review requires explicit inclusion and exclusion criteria to assess each potential primary study. Table 2 shows the inclusion and exclusion criteria used to determine which piece of literature (paper) founded by the search string, will be used for the data extraction.

Table 2. Inclusion and exclusion criteria definition

Inclusion (I)	Exclusion (E)
I1. Include empirical studies of process improvement and process deployment. Papers related to the critical success factors that determine their success.	E1. Papers that are based only on a particular opinion.
I2. Papers related to the change management and resistance to change in initiatives of process improvement and process deployment.	E2. Short papers.
	E3. Papers that are not relevant for the research questions or are not related specifically to the study.
I3. Papers containing keywords that match with those defined in the search string.	E4. Papers whose full text is not available.
I4. Papers whose title, summary or content is related to the topic.	

2.3.2 Selecting Primary Studies

Using the search engines that counts each of the identified digital sources and submitting the search string elaborated in the review protocol, a total of 1,412 studies were found in the databases, after having eliminated the duplicated studies. Later, each of the studies was reviewed taking into account the previous inclusion criteria, obtaining a total of 232 relevant studies, based on a reading of the title and the abstract of the papers. Finally, a final selection was performed based on a reading of complete papers. The final selected studies consisted of 28 papers. A discussion on the reliability of the selection was performed with the intervention of tree experts in software process improvement in order to avoid the research bias. A previous activity of literature review was performed and the same paper was founded.

2.3.3 Studies Quality Assessment

To evaluate the studies quality, a quality checklist was used as a quality assessment instrument. The quality checklist contains the following questions:

- SQA1: Is primary study relevant to research that is being done by the researcher? To evaluate the quality of the papers with respect their ability and suitability to

answer our research questions. It is assumed that they are reliable and have the sufficient quality to contribute to this systematic review.
- SQA2: Do studies provide the enough information in order to provide enough information to answer the questions of the systematic review? The main propose of studies quality assessment is to assess the impact of the primary studies quality over the conclusions.
- SQA3: Were the critical success factors of the initiatives defined? The critical success factors are clearly identified and defined.

2.3.4 Extract and Synthesize the Data

To extract and synthesize the primary studies data, it was necessary to establish the information inclusion criteria by which the information obtained from the studies has been included. The extraction criteria are described in Table 3.

Table 3. Inclusion criteria for extract the data

Inclusion (In)
In1. Collect information about the reference models for process improvement and process deployment.
In2. Collect the list of critical success factors, their definition and the impact in improvements initiatives.

To extract the relevant data of each paper and to standardize the way information have been represented, a data extraction form was created. The data extraction form was split into different sections to be filled in. For any selected paper, after reading the full text, we proceed to register the relevant information in the form. Keeping the data will allow a more detailed analysis later.

3 Report of the Systematic Review Results

After the systematic review execution, the results are summarized and analyzed. To carry out the summary, studies were classified into two groups: (1) studies related to initiatives for process improvement and (2) studies related to initiatives for process deployment.

3.1 Studies Trends

In order to know the trend of the studies on critical success factors related to the initiatives of process improvement and process deployment, in the last years, the studies were classified, according to process improvement initiatives or process deployment initiatives for a four year period. Figure 1 shows that the studies of critical success factors related to process improvement have a linear trend. This shows that there is an increasing interest on critical success factors related to process improvement. There is a similar interest to perform studies on critical success factors related to process deployment. Both trends indicate there is an increasing interest with respect to critical success factors in the initiatives of process improvement and process deployment. Thus, it is necessary to identify them in order to take them into account in process improvement and process deployment initiatives.

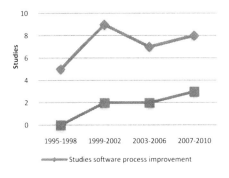

Fig. 1. Studies trend

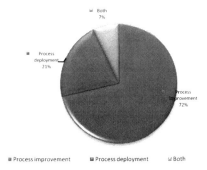

Fig. 2. Studies classification

3.2   Studies Classification

Figure 2 shows that 72 % of the primary studies are related to critical success factors related to process improvement initiatives. However, it is necessary to highlight that only 21% are related to critical success factors related to process deployment and 7 % of the primary studies include both groups. The results show a low percentage of studies related to critical success factors in process deployment.

3.3   Studies by Model

The results of the analysis of the primary studies related to the models and standards used by organizations show that the most used of them are CMM (12), CMMI (8) and ISO 9000 (CMM in studies for the period 1998-2004, CMMI in studies for the period 2002-2010). Ten studies do not specify the reference model or standard used by organizations (studies based on literature review). Some studies can reference more than one reference model.

4   Identified Critical Success Factors

Once each of the primary studies was selected (28 studies) and analyzed, the critical success factors for process improvement and process deployment have been identified. A matrix of the critical success factors identified by author in the studies was elaborated. During the matrix review, it was noticed that different authors were using different names to denominate each factor. Nevertheless, they represent the same concept. The common terms were grouped and named in a new row. Coding in empirical research helps for extracting quantitative data from the qualitative data. The research data from the literature were categorized and coded in order to perform frequency analysis.

4.1 Pareto Analysis

Frequency analysis is a descriptive statistical method that shows the number of occurrences for each critical success factor identified by author. The statistical information such as the number of occurrences and percentages of each variable (factor) can be represented in the shape of frequency distribution. In this case, the frequency distribution has two elements: (1) the critical success factors identified, and (2) number of times the authors make references to each critical success factor. A criterion for determining the importance of the factors founded in the success of improvement and deployment initiatives was established, based on 80-20 rule of Pareto. Pareto analysis is a statistical technique in decision making. Pareto analysis is used when trying to determine which factors in an initiative of process improvement or process deployment will have the most impact.

4.2 Critical Success Factors

The Pareto analysis on critical success factors for process improvement in general compiled from 28 selected papers. For this purpose, each critical success factors mentioned by authors at least once in the literature was listed. The list of critical success factors was reviewed and taking into account their definitions and relations were grouped. Using the new list the frequency of each factor is calculated. From the frequency calculated for each factor the percentage contribution of each factor is computed. Also the cumulative percentage contribution of factors is calculated. It has been found that only 16 critical success factors of 51 are contributing 80% of the total percentage contribution.

Table 4. Critical success factors

	Process improvement	Process deployment
1	Commitment	Commitment
2	Alignment with the business strategy and goals	Alignment with the business strategy and goals
3	Training	Communication
4	Communication	Training
5	Resources	Improvement management
6	Skills	Process definition
7	Improvement management	Resources
8	Staff involvement	Change management
9	Process definition	Culture
10	Change management	Monitoring software process improvement
11	Culture	Roles and responsibilities
12	Monitoring SPI process	Staff involvement
13	Roles and responsibilities	Motivation
14	Politics	Skills
15	Tools	Tools
16	Mentoring	Assessments

Table 4 shows the list of critical success factors for software process improvement (column labeled "Process deployment"). Figure 3 presents a Pareto chart for process improvement critical success factors that indicates the 80 percent of occurrences. This chart is in the form of a bar graph in descending order. The left vertical axis is the frequency of occurrence. The right vertical axis is the cumulative percentage of the total number of occurrences.

Ananalysis of critical success factors compiled related to process deployment from 6 selectedpapers is presented in Table 4 (column labelled "Process deployment").

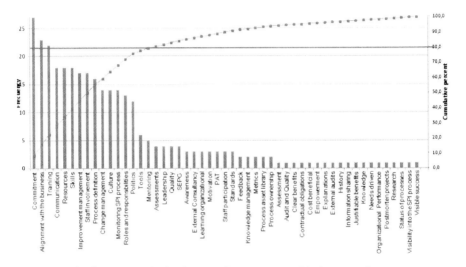

Fig. 3. Pareto analysis of process improvement critical success factors

Identifying the critical success factors allow organizations: (1) to focus their efforts on building their capabilities to conduct successful process improvement initiatives, and (2) identify what strategies need in order to achieve the objectives.

5 Conclusions

This paper presents the results of a systematic review related to the critical success factors for process improvement and process deployment initiatives. In total 28 papers were identified, 22 of them are related to process improvement initiatives and 6 to process deployment initiatives. It shows that there is limited attention paid to study the critical success factors of process deployment. The systematic review has allowed (1) to identify the critical success factors, and (2) to prioritize the most important factors for process deployment. The critical success factors importance is based on the frequency with which these factors have been identified in the primary studies.

From the systematic review results and by applying Pareto analysis it has been found that 16 critical success factors for the success of improvement initiatives are identified as the responsible for process improvement implementation success. The critical success factors are: commitment, alignment with the business strategy and goals, training, communication, resources, skills, staff involvement, improvement management, process definition, monitoring software process improvement process, change management, culture, policies, roles and responsibilities, tools and mentoring. A method that guides technically a software process improvement initiative, must take into account all of these factors.

The critical success factors to process deployment are similar to the ones related to process improvement, but their order in the list is different. For process deployment initiative the factors "process definition" and "improvement management" are number 6 and 5 in the list of critical success factors. This result shows the importance of the process definition to be deployed and the deployment strategy.

The benefits of this study are: (1) a starting point to extend the studies related to critical success factors related to people, (2) to establish a taxonomy of critical success factors for software process deployment and, (3) a guidance to take into account in existing o new process improvement initiatives.

References

1. Chrissis, M., Konrad, B., Shrum, S.: CMMI, Guidelines for Process Integration and Product Improvement, 2nd edn. Addison Wesley (2007)
2. ISO/IEC 15504-2:2003: Information technology- Process assessment -Part 2: Performing an assessment. International Standards Organization, Ginebra, Suiza (2004)
3. McFeeley, R.: IDEAL: A Users Guide for Software Process Improvement. CMU/SEI-96-HB-001, Software Engineering Institute (1996)
4. Sheard, S.: The Frameworks Quagmire. Crosstalk: The Journal of Defense Software Engineering 10(9) (September 1997)
5. Sheard, S.: Evolution of the Frameworks Quagmire. IEEE Computer 34(7), 96–98 (2001)
6. Dyba, T.: An Empirical Investigation of the Key Factors for Success in Software Process Improvement. IEEE Transactions on Software Engineering 31(5), 410–424 (2005)
7. Niazi, M., Babar, M.: Motivators of Software Process Improvement: An Analysis of Vietnamese Practitioners' Views. In: 11th International Conference on Evaluation and Assessment in Software Engineering (EASE), April 2-3. Keele University, UK (2007)
8. Butler, K.: The economics benefits of software process improvement. Cross Talk, 14–17 (1995)
9. Yamamura, G.: Software process satisfied employees. IEEE Software, 83–85 (September/October 1999)
10. Pitterman, B.: Telcordia technologies: the journey to high maturity. IEEE Software 17(4), 89–96 (2000)
11. Mohd, N., Ahmad, R., Hassan, N.: Resistance factors in the implementation of software process improvement project. Journal of Computer Science 4(3), 211–219 (2008)
12. NDIA Systems Engineering Division: The Economics of CMMI (2009), http://www.sei.cmu.edu/library/assets/Economics%20of%20CMMI.pdf
13. Forrester, E. (ed.): International Process Research Consortium: A Process Research Framework. Software Engineering Institute (2006)
14. McDermid, J., Bennet, K.: Software Engineering Research - A critical appraisal. IEEE Proceedings on Software Engineering 146(4), 179–186 (1999)

15. Hall, T., Wilson, D.: Perceptions of software quality: a pilot study. Software Quality Journal 7, 67–75 (1998)
16. Hall, T., Rainer, A., Baddoo, N.: Implementing Software Process Improvement: An Empirical Study. Software Process Improvement and Practice 7, 3–15 (2002)
17. Niazi, M., Wilson, D., Zowghi, D.: A framework for assisting the design of effective software process improvement implementation strategies. Journal of Systems and Software 78, 204–222 (2005)
18. Bayona, S., Calvo-Manzano, J., Cuevas, G., San Feliu, T.: Process Deployment in a Multi-Site CMMI Level 3 Organization: A Case Study. In: Roger, L. (ed.). SCI, vol. 131, pp. 147–153. Springer, Berlin (2008)
19. Lepmets, M., Ras, E.: Motivation and Empowerment in Process Improvement. In: O'Connor, R.V., Pries-Heje, J., Messnarz, R. (eds.) EuroSPI 2011. CCIS, vol. 172, pp. 109–120. Springer, Heidelberg (2011)
20. Lepasaar, M., Varkoi, T., Jaakkola, H.: Models and Success Factors of Process Change. In: Bomarius, F., Komi-Sirviö, S. (eds.) PROFES 2001. LNCS, vol. 2188, pp. 68–77. Springer, Heidelberg (2001)
21. Humphrey, W.: Managing the Software Process. Addison-Wesley, Reading (1989)
22. Arent, J., Norbjerg, J.: Software process improvement as organizational knowledge creation: a multiple case analysis. In: Proceedings of the 33rd Annual Hawaii International Conference on System Sciences, pp. 1–11 (2000)
23. Kasse, T., Mcquaid, P.: Factors affecting process improvement initiatives. Crosstalk the Journal of Defence Software Engineering (2009)
24. Cuevas, G., Amescua, A.: Gestión del proceso software. Centro de Estudios Ramón Areces (2003)
25. Montoni, M., Santos, G., Rocha, A.R., Figueiredo, S., Cabral, R., Barcellos, R., Barreto, A., Soares, A., Cerdeiral, C., Lupo, P.: Taba Workstation: Supporting Software Process Deployment Based on CMMI and MR-MPS.BR. In: Münch, J., Vierimaa, M. (eds.) PROFES 2006. LNCS, vol. 4034, pp. 249–262. Springer, Heidelberg (2006)
26. Christiansen, M., Johansen, J.: ImprovAbility[TK] guidelines for low-maturity organizations. Software. Process: Improvement. Practice 13, 319–325 (2008)
27. Fuggetta, A.: Software Process: A Roadmap. In: Finkelstein, A. (ed.) The Future of Software Engineering, 22nd Int. Conference on Software Engineering, pp. 27–34 (2000)
28. Kitchenham, B., Dybå, T., Jørgensen, M.: Evidence-based software engineering. In: Proceedings of the International Conference on Software Engineering, pp. 273–281 (2004)
29. Kitchenham, B.: Guidelines for performing Systematic Literature Reviews in software engineering, EBSE Technical Report EBSE-2007-01 (2007)
30. Biolchini, J., Gomez, P., Cruz, A., Horta, G.: Systematic review in software engineering. Technical report. Systems Engineering and Computer Science Department, UFRJ, Brasil (2005)
31. Pino, F., Garcia, F., Piattini, M.: Revisión sistemática de mejora de procesos software en micro pequeñas y medianas empresas. REICIS 2(1), 6–23 (2006)
32. Kitchenham, B., Brereton, O., Budgen, D., Turner, M., Bailey, J., Linkman, S.: Systematic literature reviews in software engineering-A systematic literature review. Information and Software Technology 51(1), 7–15 (2009)
33. Muhammad, K.: Literature review on the software process improvement factors in the small organizations. In: 2010 4th International Conference on Proceedings New Trends in Information Science and Service Science (NISS), pp. 592–598 (2010)
34. Zahran, S.: Software Process Improvement - Practical Guidelines for Business Success. Addison Wesley, Harlow (1998)

Integrated Process Improvement Approach: Case Studies in Skype Technologies Ltd.

Anneli Tuisk[1], André Karpištšenko[1], and Marion Lepmets[2]

[1] Skype Technologies Ltd., Tallinn, Estonia
{anneli.tuisk,andre}@skype.net
[2] Public Research Centre Henri Tudor, Luxembourg
marion.lepmets@tudor.lu

Abstract. Software development organizations find support for rapid changes from agile software development methodologies. The agile approaches are also being applied to process improvement to ensure that organizations keep up with the rapidly changing business environment. In this paper we present an approach to process improvement that integrates technology oriented strategy, agile development methods and knowledge-sharing networks, and is capable of meeting high resource and schedule constraints. The approach was continuously developed over the course of two years in a global technology corporation that experienced 55% revenue and 62% employee growth during that period. Two organization-wide process improvements are discussed as the detailed case studies of this approach. The approach enabled a new team to take ownership of new process areas and implement improvements with high employee involvement and empowerment.

Keywords: Software process improvement, agile methods, technology orientation, knowledge-sharing networks.

1 Introduction

Volatile business environments create pressure on all the dimensions of IT project constraints and although up front benefits' estimation and later tracking of those benefits is desirable, it is done in less than 25% of companies [1]. For a successful software process improvement, the improvement approach should integrate the organizational characteristics and the development methods.

According to Salo and Abrahamsson [2], Software Process Improvement (SPI) aims to provide the means for improving the capabilities of software development teams and organizations. ISO/IEC 15504 defines process improvement as actions taken to change organization's processes so that they more effectively and efficiently meet the organization's business goals [3].

SPI has been extensively studied in the past few decades [2] with the first reference to improving the programming process appearing in 1951 [4]. The traditional SPI approaches support the ideology of creating and improving a universal and repeatable software development process for an organization, controlled largely by management [5].

The emergence of agile methodologies begun in the mid-1990s with software methodologies and techniques such as Extreme programming (XP) [6], Scrum [7], and eXtreme testing [8, 9]. Agile approaches seek to provide adaptable processes to support context-specific development, increased customer satisfaction, lower defect rates, faster development, and responsiveness to rapidly changing requirements [10]. The principles of agile software development request that "at regular intervals, the team reflects on how to become more effective, then tunes and adjusts its behavior accordingly" [11]. Thus, the ideologies of agile software development emphasize the need for process adaptation within ongoing projects and seek to move process control from the organizational level to practitioners [2, 5] proposing an iterative improvement approach within agile software development teams. The central idea is to empower and encourage development teams to adapt and improve their daily working practices iteratively and in a face-to-face manner.

In this paper we present a process improvement approach integrating technology orientation, agile methods and knowledge-sharing networks that is illustrated by two case studies in Skype Technologies Ltd. (Skype) - a global technology corporation with a major development center located in Estonia.

2 Motivation for Developing an Integrated Process Improvement Approach

Despite the participation of several companies in SPICE trials during the international SPICE project [12] and the reported SPI case studies in software organizations [13-19], Estonian companies have still remained critical of the process model implementation and even more so towards process assessment with international standards. Even though the processes are analyzed and changed, the improvements are rarely systematically implemented and their progress measured [20].

As Tersine pointed out in [21], every improvement is a change, but not every change is an improvement. A change in circumstance or condition is frequently the impetus for the improvements, and the subsequent improvements create their own level of change. It is also argued that focusing on people will improve software productivity and quality [22]. That is exactly what agile methods provide and why they have become so popular. At the same time, agile methods generally lack practices and guidance for implementing and supporting an agile approach across the organization. It is argued that an agile implementation will not "stick" without an organizational context that supports process definitions that are described in process models [23]. As Boehm and Turner put it in [24], "agility without discipline is the unencumbered enthusiasm of a startup company before it has to turn a profit". The discipline of plan driven methods approach development with standard and well-defined processes that organizations improve continuously. Plan-driven methods are characterized by heavy upfront planning, focus on predictability and documentation, while Scrum, one of the agile methods, relies on tacit knowledge within a team as opposed to documentation [10].

We suggest an integrated process improvement approach that was developed over a couple of years in Skype. This approach, illustrated on Figure 1, is based on an organization that is strategically technology oriented, and applies agile process improvement methods and knowledge-sharing networks.

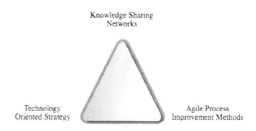

Fig. 1. Cornerstones of the integrated process improvement approach

In the next section we will elaborate on each of these principles. We will first describe the characteristics of the organization that play a major role in the development of the integrated process improvement approach. We will then describe the two case studies that formed this approach over time through improving two organization-wide processes. The integrated improvement approach will then be summarized and ideas on further works provided.

2.1 Technology Orientation

Technology orientation implies that software reuse is applied to shorten process change cycles. In the context of this paper, technology orientation means introduction of external reference implementations of best practices. The aim is to reduce the overall costs of ownership that can be achieved through appropriate selection method [25]. Inherent uncertainty and incompleteness of information in such decisions can be reduced by building the necessary level of understanding of requirements through pilot projects. Early feedback from pilot teams will help filter out potential dead-end solutions. Choice of the teams for pilot projects must be a conscious decision since feedback from the teams will be used during the organization-wide deployment phase to implement the system.

Whether the candidate process needs to be changed is evaluated with interviews that can also be used as a means to identify potential technological solutions for the processes. Informal requirements gathered during the interviews, high-level business requirements and constraints are then mapped to available technological choices to do the initial filtering. Depending on project constraints, a number of technologies can then be piloted and finally chosen.

2.2 Agile Process Improvement Methods

Most process changes in today's organizations will materialize in enterprise systems – best practices in IT portfolio management (ITPM) and software development can provide the necessary inspiration for process change. Iterative development and continuous performance feedback have proved to be the key success factors for phasing ITPM into organizations [1].

Dealing with changes or emergent requirements is at the core of agile software development methodologies and Scrum has proved to be suitable to the needs of product-leader and customer-intimate companies [26]. Thus instead of relying on detailed process assessments and improvement plans, relying on strict time boxing, frequent communications and prioritized backlogs allows for better monitoring of changes. An agile process improvement approach allows the change of the organization to happen gradually – transitions from piloting phase to customization/configuration (depending on the technology) phase and to deployment and maintenance phase will be continuous, reducing the chances of process improvement failure. The iterative nature of agile methods will ensure that significant unmet requirements and resistance will quickly surface and can be tackled efficiently by the team and the knowledge-sharing network. In short, agile process improvement methods allow for better risk management and transparency with a team organized approach to delivery. As Skype was already using Scrum in project management, the approach was natural and logical path to follow.

Agile process improvement teams will create a high level of employee involvement and lower the pressure on senior management. Since adjustments to roadmap and requirements are continuous, monitoring of the changes will allow process improvement initiator to focus their attention on the most critical issues. Early feedback of failures gives additional opportunity to stop ongoing changes with limited waste of time and resources. As the process change becomes closer to organization-wide roll out, the nature of team tasks will become more operational. To ensure focus on timely resolution of operational tasks the team roles should be crystallized through responsibility assignment matrix that has been well established for role clarification in business setting [27] before the launch. Additionally migration and training plans have to be created and followed in parallel with follow-up incremental tool improvements as the organization adapts to the new solution.

2.3 Knowledge-Sharing Networks

While technological aspects are important for successful process improvement, deployment depends on involvement of people to ensure that the change is actually carried through, and that all cultural aspects and business requirements are considered. Support of process change from top management is usually suggested as the most effective means to involve people and ensure organization-wide coherency [28, 29]. However top management support can become sporadic if the business priorities do not allow for sufficient time or when the changes are made in operational and support processes. CIOs who are usually responsible for technological solutions in these areas are struggling to get the necessary involvement in business decisions [30], thus process changes must rely on alternative employee involvement methods. With the advent of enterprise social networks and adoption of instant messaging services, building knowledge-sharing networks that span the entire organization has become a low-cost opportunity. These virtual networks can be used to shorten the feedback cycle for agile process change teams the same way as businesses rely on virtual networks for customer feedback.

Knowledge-sharing networks consisting of employees, contractors and vendor representatives (called super-users) provide means to maintain productivity and quality advantages after process improvement deployment [31]. Pilot teams formed during technology evaluation are crucial components in building confidence and engagement across the entire organization, thus the early choice of volunteers must consider whether they have sufficient respect and authority across the organization. In growing the knowledge-sharing network beyond pilot teams, actual organizational map is required since the goal of super-users is to ensure that there is a two-way communication between process change team and the entire organization across all offices. In case of strong resistance by some groups, continuously seeking for high involvement from the group's influencers could help in finding solutions to the groups' concerns.

Change team has to involve super-users by giving regular status updates and ensure that concerns of the super-users are resolved. Knowledge-sharing networks do not disperse after organization-wide rollout, as continuous changes will be required. In the maintenance phase of the process change, super-users also serve as the first line of support inside the teams, strengthening IT self-service in the organization and lowering the needs for support budgets. Separate, advanced trainings for the super-users can be used to create a stronger sense of community and to spread the necessary detailed knowledge across the organization.

3 Case Studies in Skype Technologies Ltd.

The integrated process improvement approach was continuously developed over the course of two years in Skype (founded in 2003) that experienced 55% revenue and 62% employee growth during the two-year period. Skype grew from 518 employees and contractors to 839 in that period of time. It also suffered from not having a formal CIO organization yet, thus top management support to process improvement was limited - the changes had to be implemented globally by a team without a formal structure to support the change. Additionally, high employee growth in Skype and diverse product portfolio had resulted in an organization without clear chain-of-command and with highly varying processes and maturity of the teams.

The approach described in previous sections was used for taking ownership for previously unmaintained process areas and implementing improvements as a part of related tools migrations. Processes that were improved:

- Task and issue management: 3 months of preparation and piloting followed by 3 months of customization, migration and deployment. Finished in mid-2009.
- Collaboration and knowledge management: 3 months of preparation and piloting followed by 6 months of configuration, migration and deployment. During the period the team had to recover from losing two project managers due to organizational restructuring. Eventually temporary contractors were used to deliver the change. Finished in mid-2010.

3.1 Case Study A – Task and Issue Management Process Improvement

The organization had outgrown its task and issue management (IM) processes and needed a solution suitable for its size. Activities, roles, responsibilities and rights were not clearly defined in the IM process, which caused several projects to not have clear owners after the public release. This resulted in no-one taking responsibility for operational issues of particular functionalities, thereby information sharing was delayed, decisions made late and similar problems kept reoccurring.

The goal of the improvement was to allow the organization to take responsibility for tasks and issues as well as allow for prioritization and better scheduling. The target process needed to provide an overview and visibility of open issues, and give instructions on how to handle them from initial submission until closure.

The initial mapping of the process area was done by Tuisk in [32]. Although a formal process assessment was not conducted, semi-structured interviews were prepared to map the extent of the problems. These interviews were based on ISO/IEC 12207 [33], Capability Maturity Model Integration v1.3 (CMMI) [34], Corrective Maintenance Maturity Model (CM3) [35] and Information Technology Infrastructure Library (ITIL) [36, 37], which provided guidance for defining issue management procedures to software development organizations. In the current paper, the term Issue Management is used as it is the term applied in Skype, while the process is called problem resolution management in ISO/IEC 12207 [33] and problem management in both CM3 [35] and ITIL [37].

Technology orientation was visible as potential technological solutions were identified in parallel by the change team and at the interviews. This allowed evaluation of what needs to be changed in the old IM process and how well existing tools resolve the issues.

In total, 14 people were interviewed in focus groups, four persons maximum in one group. During the interviews, two main topics were focused on – how the IM process works inside the group as well as between the groups. Also, problems related to the existing tool were discussed. In order to analyze interview results, two methods were used. First, the affinity diagram [38] was used in order to analyze IM problems by dividing them into logical groups. Second, comparison was done between interview results and models described in existing standards to find out areas covered by interviews and those that were missing.

The results of the analysis indicated that in addition to defining the IM process, there was also a need to define the feature request (FR) process, which is handled in the organization as the sub-process of the IM process. Similarly to IM, FR is the term used in Skype, which also known as change management in ITIL [36] and modification management in CM3 [35]. Feature requests had to become prioritized by the product managers so that the Quality Assurance (QA) who received a lot of the feature requests for resolution or feedback would know the importance of these issues from the release perspective.

While the IM process had to be universal for the entire organization, flexibility was required to tailor it to individual team needs. For easier understanding, the process was divided into four phases – problem reporting, problem control, problem analysis and problem resolution. In each phase, a set of activities was defined, which would be necessary to perform in order to move on to the next phase. Specific roles and responsibilities were described. In addition, defining the FR process must result in an organization-wide understanding as to what a FR is and what the lifecycle is from submission through to closure. The research results described above were not immediately followed up with improvement, however after the IM and FR processes were described, the change team scheduled to look more closely into the tool related problems defined during the analysis phase. This introduced a delay of one year from initial interviews to the time when the change was started. Due to the fact that the existing tool did not serve its main purpose, an evaluation was carried out as a first step and a new tool was selected which best met the organization needs.

The knowledge-sharing networks were employed as the project managers whose involvement in super-users group was later crucial for the success of migration, started to evaluate the strongest candidate solution in pilot projects in parallel with building an understanding of IM and FR processes. This enabled fast introduction of project portfolio management best practices that later evolved into product centric development approach. The migration plan included 5000 open issues across the projects, which were reviewed and approved beforehand by the relevant stakeholders. It was decided that the remainder of the 105450 closed issues would not be migrated but rather kept in the old IM tool for archive purposes. The team also faced the challenge to solve issues relating to managing multiple projects and multiple release vehicles. Due to the fact the new chosen tool offered a high level of customization, the problems were solved with custom configurations and development. Together with the migration decision, it was essential to establish a strong super-user community as the change affected two thirds of the organization, in particular, the software development organization. In addition to the super-user community, active training sessions were provided before and after the migration.

Besides training, it was essential to provide feedback-based custom development in order to enable better adoption of the new IM tool. *Agile process improvement methods* were thus applied – two weeks sprints with a clear focus to solve problems based on user feedback that guaranteed the satisfaction of the users with a relatively short adoption period. Initially the IM tool was used as a project-oriented development tool, which resulted in significant project creation and custom development. As the organization became product-oriented and started to adopt agile methods across the organization, major customizations could be removed.

To conclude, there were several elements that contributed to the success of this process improvement: 1) Clear scope and goal for the change; 2) Prior understanding of existing informal processes; 3) Evaluation of new technological solutions; 4) Early pilot projects; 5) Frequent communication with all stakeholders; 6) Establishing active knowledge sharing network; 7) Phased training sessions; 8) Continuous improvements after company-wide rollout; and 9) Agile approach to process improvement.

3.2 Case Study B – Improvement of Collaboration Infrastructure

In this case study, the infrastructure supporting collaboration within the organization was analyzed and improved in the organization. The implementation of suitable solutions for improving document management (DM), specification management (SM) and knowledge management (KM) processes is described in particular. Completely e-mail and instant messaging based processes were left out of scope.

According to Curtis et al. [39], collaboration involves the exchange of information between two or more parties. In a web-based collaborative software development project, the collaboration consists of many tasks that involve different individuals working together without the barrier of time and space limitations [40]. Large companies with many offices located in different parts of the world imply the existence of distributed teams and the need for an enterprise wide collaboration tool. The tool enables teams to reduce the distance gap, provide a better communication and share their knowledge. In addition, it is vital for people to access one central place in order to gain knowledge in real time situations. One option to share the knowledge is to use wikis.

In Case Study B, a wiki was used by the organization as the main collaboration tool since 2005. The organization was using a wiki solution for four purposes - as a basic information source, for specification management, document management and knowledge management. Although the existing collaboration tool served its main purpose to provide basic information about teams, processes, rules and various documents for employees, it did not offer functionality required for larger teams. Since the use of wiki had been continuously degrading due to lack of new employee training, no knowledge management processes and limited functionality, the need for changing the tool and related processes was raised.

Technology orientation and *agile process improvements* were applied by involving pilot projects in order to gather feedback and gain confidence about the suitability of the possible candidate tools. Two strong development teams agreed to be volunteers to use main candidate tool for their everyday collaboration in terms of projects and communication. Later on, these development teams became also the first super-users who helped to support the change of the wiki platform. In addition, a small experimental development project was launched with the purpose to become acquainted with the technological capabilities of the system and with a new system integration partner. The piloting was done during a three-month period before the actual decision was made whether to migrate to the new platform or to seek new alternatives. Interviews were conducted to understand how the wiki was used in the organization, what its main problems were and which tool could solve these problems and provide a better fit to the needs of the organization. Prior to interviews, a questionnaire was sent to prepare the interviews and drive a semi-structured discussion. In total, 56 people were interviewed and the selection contained people from each high-level organizational unit and five different office locations. Due to time pressures from top management, a strong technological candidate had been identified beforehand that aligned well with technical infrastructure as it was developed by the same vendor that was deployed in Case Study A and allowed for a short delivery schedule. In order to analyze interview results, the same methods were used, except that for technical solutions counter-arguments were searched instead of alternative solutions. No strong counter arguments were identified during the interview process although a wealth of alternatives was listed. The tool comparison analysis later served as means to motivate platform change in discussions with user groups who preferred the existing solution.

The knowledge-sharing networks were used to create an active dialogue with each team in order to provide them with the detailed migration information and to hear out and eliminate their worries. In addition, each team was asked to find at least one person who could be involved in the super-user's community where the latest ideas, technical solutions and information were discussed. Eventually the community self-organized and people began helping each other when questions arose. In addition to forming a super-user's community, active training sessions were provided both before and after the release. This resulted in growing awareness and attraction, especially to people with less technical skills. One month later, after the official release of the new solution, a survey was done to gather people's feedback about the new platform. Based on the results, almost half of the respondents were happy with the new tool, while 19% of the respondents had very few contact with the tool and therefore did not have any strong opinion at all. 18% of the respondents wished to return to the old wiki, which was an indication for the team that some more work was needed. Reflecting half a year later, the migration is well received, however some lessons are still to be learnt. First, the amount of resistance should be gauged earlier and attention to this should be given during the whole project lifecycle. Second, up front manual work to resolve routine requirements (e.g. relating to user permissions) is preferable to fixing them afterwards with duplicated effort. Third, whatever system is under construction, dedicated resources and ownership should be assigned for the entire length of the project.

During the analyses, the understanding of the extent to which the system fulfills the requirements gradually improved. The existing wiki served well the purpose of a basic information source, thus the new solution had to replicate the experience to its best abilities. However knowledge management (KM) was barely mentioned in the organization even though wiki is considered as the main knowledge repository throughout the organization. One reason why KM was not explicitly sensed is in the way people use the tools. This notion is also supported by McAfee [41] who emphasizes the fact that a lot of people do not help to produce the platform, they just want to use it. This might also be the case in the organization, where the wiki usage is too complicated and therefore it is easier to let someone do the work, and just search for the information when needed. Hasan and Pfaff [42] offer a solution here - management should begin to talk explicitly about KM, which creates presumption and obligation for employees to provide latest up to date information by using an organization wide collaboration tool. Effective knowledge management is a powerful asset and an excellent method for individuals and teams to share perspectives, ideas, experience and information [36].

Another interesting finding was the importance of KM, which encompassed approximately one third of organizational need in terms of the collaboration tool. Before the tool change, there was a general understanding that the main aim of the wiki is to support document management (DM) and specification management (SM). However, according to Rus and Lindvall [43], DM is a basic KM activity toward supporting an organization's implementation to share documented knowledge. Furthermore, based on Hasan and Pfaff [42] it is also possible to conclude that SM and DM are actually the input for the creation of KM platform. Thus the organizations understanding of its needs evolved during the project and this guided the maintenance iteration priorities.

There were many elements that supported the successful improvement of these processes; the most important ones being: 1) Clear goal and limited scope for the change; 2) Continuously building an understanding of existing informal processes; 3) Evaluation of technological solution with counter-arguments; 4) Early pilot projects; 5) Communication with all stakeholders; 6) Dedicated, continuous cooperation with resistant groups; 7) Establishing active knowledge sharing network; 8) Phased migration; 9) Frequent training sessions; 10) Continuous improvements after company-wide rollout; and 11) Agile approach to process improvement.

4   Discussion

The migrations to new platforms allowed the organization to take ownership of task and issue management, document management, specification management and knowledge management processes. The change team was able to deploy improvements without formal authority and the team's changes were welcomed across the organization.

The new technological platforms and active knowledge sharing networks facilitated continuous improvements of related processes, e.g. introduction of project portfolio management practices shortly after taking ownership of issue and task management; and introduction of internal communications portal with the collaboration platform change. The solutions and improvement approach were sustainable enough to allow later changes from project teams to agile product teams and facilitated introduction of higher maturity product, and release and deployment management processes. One of the key success factors of the integrated approach was the ability to configure and customize processes and tools to individual project/product team needs. High empowerment ensured a continuous inflow of improvement ideas even after the initial changes were done.

As any research, this also has its limitations. Not all aspects of the organizational change have been analyzed due to time constraints in implementing the tools. A further analysis should be conducted in order to realize the impact organization's restructuring had on the success of implementing the tools that took place at the same time.

5 Conclusions

In this paper we described two case studies in a global software organization. The organization is strategically technology oriented, and applies agile software development methods where process improvements are based largely on knowledge sharing networks. The key success elements of the two case studies illustrate that when process improvement approach is selected based on the organization's characteristics, there is little resistance to change and rapid feedback provides for a faster implementation of improvements.

The integrated process improvement approach enabled to take ownership of new process areas and implement improvements with high employee involvement and empowerment. The key characteristic of the approach resides in fast feedback cycle allowing for better risk management.

The integrated approach presented in this paper could be applied in several additional process improvements for increasing its validity. A more rigorous improvement impact analysis on organization's efficiency would provide for additional future work.

Acknowledgments. We are grateful for everyone at Skype and the partner companies who were involved in making the improvements a success.

References

1. Jeffery, M., Leliveld, I.: Best Practices in IT Portfolio Management. MIT Sloan Management Review (2004)
2. Salo, O., Abrahamsson, P.: An Iterative Improvement Process for Agile Software Development. Software Process: Improvement and Practice 12, 81–100 (2007)
3. ISO/IEC 15504-4:2004 - Information technology - Process assessment - Part 4: Guidance on use for process improvement and process capability determination (2004)
4. Wilkes, M.V., Wheeler, D.J., Gill, S.: The Preparation of Programs for an Electronic Digital Computer. Addison-Wesley (1951)
5. Lycett, M., Macredie, R.D., Patel, C., Paul, R.J.: Migrating agile methods to standardized development practice. Computer 36, 79–85 (2003)
6. Beck, K.: Embracing Change with Extreme Programming. Computer 32, 70–77 (1999)
7. Schwaber, K.: Scrum Development Process. In: Springer (ed.) Tenth Annual Conference on Object-Oriented Programming Systems, Languages, and Applications - Workshop on Business Object Design and Implementation, Austin, Texas, USA, pp. 117–134 (1995)
8. Jeffries, R.E.: eXtreme Testing: Why Aggressive Software Development Calls for Radical Testing Efforts. Software Testing & Quality Engineering, 23–26 (March/April 1999)
9. Salo, O.: Enabling Software Process Improvement in Agile Software Development Teams and Organisations. Faculty of Science, PhD, p. 153. University of Oulu, Oulu (2006)
10. Boehm, B., Turner, R.: Using risk to balance agile and plan-driven methods. Computer 36, 57–66 (2003)
11. Agile Alliance: Manifesto for Agile Software Development (2001), http://goo.gl/ruvK

12. Software Quality Institute: SPICE Phase 2 Trials Interim Report (1998), http://goo.gl/WpXV8
13. Lepasaar, M.: Software Process Improvement in Small Software Organizations. Department of Computer Engineering, MSc. Thesis at Tallinn University of Technology, Tallinn (2001)
14. Klesment, K.: Joint influence of software process improvement, quality management and culture based on the example of organization N. Department of Informatics, MSc Thesis at Tallinn University of Technology, Tallinn (2004)
15. Seeba, A.: Unified Software Development Process and a Case Study of It's Application. Department of Computer Science, MSc Thesis at University of Tartu, Tartu (2001)
16. Valter, K.: Designing change management process based on international process standards and models. Department of Computer Science, BSc. Thesis at Tallinn University of Technology, Tallinn (2008)
17. Karpištšenko, A., Altermann, A.: Conducting first-time software process improvement work in a small software development company. Department of Quality Sciences, MSc Thesis at Chalmers University of Technology, Gothenburg (2000)
18. Piho, G.: About implementation of XP in small Estonian software organizations. Institute of Informatics, MSc Thesis at Tallinn University, Tallinn (2003)
19. Lepmets, M., Nael, M.: Balancing Scrum Project Management Process. In: Sillitti, A., Martin, A., Wang, X., Whitworth, E. (eds.) XP 2010. LNBIP, vol. 48, pp. 391–392. Springer, Heidelberg (2010)
20. McBride, T., Lepmets, M.: The Many Forms of Process Improvement - Results of an International Survey. In: Software Quality Days, p. 7. Springer, Vienna (2012)
21. Tersine, R.J.: The primary drivers for continuous improvement: the reduction of the triad of waste. Journal of Managerial Issues (2004)
22. Dingsøyr, T., Dyba, T., Abrahamsson, P.: A Preliminary Roadmap for Empirical Research on Agile Software Development. In: Agile 2008 Conference, Toronto, pp. 83–94 (2008)
23. Glazer, H., Dalton, J., Anderson, D., Konrad, M., Shrum, S.: CMMI or Agile: Why Not Embrace Both! (2008), http://goo.gl/FP5TC
24. Boehm, B., Turner, R.: Balancing Agility and Discipline - A Guide for the Perplexed, Boston (2004)
25. Land, R., Blankers, L., Chaudron, M., Crnkovic, I.: COTS Selection Best Practices in Literature and in Industry. In: Mei, H. (ed.) ICSR 2008. LNCS, vol. 5030, pp. 100–111. Springer, Heidelberg (2008)
26. Paulk, M.C., Davis, N., Maccherone, L.: On Empirical Research Into Scrum (2009), http://goo.gl/vNNT2
27. Smith, M.L., Erwin, J.: Role & Responsibility Charting, RACI (2010), http://goo.gl/bSibx
28. Bergman, B., Klefsjö, B.: Quality from Customer Needs to Customer Satisfaction. Studentlitteratur, Lund (2003)
29. Trkman, M., Trkman, P.: A wiki as internet: a critical analysis using the Delone and McLean model. Online Information Review 33, 1087–1102 (2009)
30. Bass, L., Berenbach, B.: Leadership and Management in Software Architecture Workshop 2009 report. ACM Sigsoft Software Engineering Notes 34, 25–27 (2009)
31. Dyer, J.H., Nobeoka, K.: Creating and managing a high performance knowledge-sharing network: the Toyota case. Strategic Management Journal 21, 345–367 (2000)
32. Tuisk, A.: Developing the Issue Management Process for Skype Technologies. Department of Technology Management and Economics, MSc. Thesis at Chalmers University of Technology, Gothenburg (2008)

33. ISO/IEC 12207: Information technology – Software life cycle processes. ISO/IEC 12207 (2008)
34. CMMI v1.3: CMMI® for Development, Version 1.3. Software Engineering Institute (2010)
35. Kajko-Mattson, M., Forssander, S., Olsson, U.: Corrective Maintenance Maturity Model: Maintainers Education and Training. In: International Conference on Software Engineering, pp. 610–619. IEEE Computer Society Press, Los Alamitos (2001)
36. Rance, S., Rudd, C., Lacy, S., Hanna, A.: ITIL Service Transition. TSO, London (2011)
37. Steinberg, R., Rudd, C., Lacy, S., Hanna, A.: ITIL Service Operation. TSO, London (2011)
38. Gaffney, G.: What is an Affinity Diagramming? Information & Design (1999)
39. Curtis, C., Whited, V., Kancler, D., Burneka, C.: Analyzing Requirements for and Designing a Collaborative Tool based on Functional and User Input. In: International Symposium on Collaborative Technologies and Systems, pp. 220–225 (2006)
40. Wu, L., Sahraoui, H.: Supporting Web Collaboration for Cooperative Software Development. In: IEEE/WIC/ACM International Conference on Web Intelligence, pp. 740–743 (2004)
41. McAfee, A.P.: Enterprise 2.0: The Dawn of Emergent Collaboration (2006), `http://goo.gl/VLwN7`
42. Hasan, H., Pfaff, C.C.: The Wiki: an environment to revolutionise employees' interaction with corporate knowledge. In: 18th Australia Conference on Computer-Human Interaction: Design: Activities, Artefacts and Environments, vol. 206, pp. 377–380 (2006)
43. Rus, I., Lindvall, M.: Knowledge Management in Software Engineering. IEEE Software 19, 26–38 (2002)

A Case Study on Employee Perceptions of Organization Wide Continuous Process Improvement Activities

Algan Uskarcı and Onur Demirörs

Informatics Institute, Middle East Technical University, Ankara, Turkey
algan.uskarci@gmail.com, demirors@ii.metu.edu.tr

Abstract. Staged models for software process improvement have been extensively used by organizations. However the relationship between these models and organization wide continuous process improvement has not been studied extensively. This study builds upon a previous study that aims to fill in this gap by analyzing the software process improvement activities within a software company that has CMMI level-3 certification. The employees' perception regarding the organization wide continuous process improvement activities are analyzed and improvement opportunities for staged models are discussed.

Keywords: Software process improvement, Staged models, employee participation.

1 Introduction

Software process improvement (SPI) frameworks such as CMMI (Capability Maturity Model Integration) [1] and ISO-15504 [2] have been used for nearly 20 years for process improvement activities. Organizations utilizing these frameworks evaluate their processes based on the reference models and identify improvement opportunities.

In model based improvement, the natural course of action for an organization is to first determine its current status (i.e. capability level) based on the model. After that, the organization performs a gap analysis in order to determine the deviation between the current capability level and the targeted capability level. Once the deviation is determined the quest for process improvement takes the form of tasks performed to fill the gap. The benefits and difficulties of applying specific models have been discussed in a number of studies [3] [4] [5] [6].

One of the less frequently discussed difficulties related with model based improvement is the continuity of process improvement. Although the models suggest in the contrary, as the nature of the models are discrete (in the form of capability levels) improvements can happen in discrete steps. In other words, the process improvement life in an organization between the capability level assessment checkpoints is the subject of research.

To be able to understand the continuity of the model based process improvement as well as the contribution characteristics of the employees, we performed a case study in two phases.

In the first phase we have explored the answers of the following questions in [7]:

- How do the staged models enforce continuous process improvement?
- How do the staged models enforce organization wide commitment?
- How do the staged models enforce process wide improvement?

For this purpose we analyzed the process improvement activities of a CMMI level-3 software and electronics company operating in the defense industry sector in Turkey. We have specifically studied the commitment of the company employees to process improvement activities in various aspects. The process improvement database maintained by the company was analyzed for this purpose.

The second phase of the case study builds on the findings of the previous phase by analyzing the opinions of the employees of the target company in order to answer the following question:

- How is software process improvement contribution related to an employee's education, experience and role within the organization?

A questionnaire was created and distributed to the employees of the company. The findings obtained by the questionnaire are analyzed and improvement opportunities for staged models are discussed.

In the second section of this paper we have summarized the related work performed by different researchers. A summary of our previous work regarding the target company conducted in the first phase of our case study is presented in the third section. The statistical analysis of the results of the questionnaire obtained from the target company is presented in the fourth section. Finally we have summarized our findings and conclusions in the last section together with plans for future work.

2 Continuity of Process Improvement

Although continuity of model based improvement has not been studied frequently, a range of research is focused on employee commitment for software process improvement activities. For example a study [8] realized by conducting focus groups for 13 different companies identified de-motivating factors that affect software practitioners regarding software process improvement. The results are presented based on the grouping of practitioners in three as developers, project managers and senior managers. It is concluded that common de-motivators for SPI activities are lack of resources, commercial pressures, the actual process constraints, implementation issues and personnel factors. Another study [9] presented findings obtained by a survey of Irish very small enterprise (VSE) employees. The questionnaires used include questions related to the involvement and commitment of both the people and the managers in the SPI activities. The results indicate that VSE's commitment towards SPI is very high and positive. However the analysis regarding the commitment is only a small part of the study and the main focus is on the overall SPI activities for VSEs. Unfortunately, these studies do not relate their findings with staged models but present them on a more generalized level for software process improvement.

3 Case Study

In order to explore the first set of questions presented in the first section, we searched the process asset library of the target company [7]. The total number of employees of the company is more than 200 with the software group comprising of about 100 employees. The main areas of interest for the software group are avionics software and command & control software. The company has been maintaining an internal Process and Technology Improvement (PTI) suggestion database since December 2006. The PTI DB is important in the sense that it is the major tool that can be used by employees for contributing to the software process improvement activities. All the employees of the company have the right to record any suggestion in the database. The entries are evaluated by the Software Engineering Process Group (SEPG) of the company and the suggestions which are deemed beneficial are integrated into the process assets of the company in the form of process baselines. The total number of entries in the database was 845 as of February 2011. The submission characteristics of the improvement database are analyzed yielding the following findings.

3.1 Submitter Characteristics

The submitters are analyzed according to their roles within the company and their seniority. Although there are more than 20 role types in the company these roles are divided into four groups as follows:

- CM: Software Configuration Managers
- QA: Quality Assurance Engineers
- Support: Contract, documentation, process and project management specialists
- SW: Software developers, software engineers and software test engineers

The employees are classified based on their work experience as junior (0-5 Years), senior (5-10 Years) and manager (10+ Years).

Two different characteristics are presented as average submission count per employee (**Table 1**) and the ratio of employees with at least one submission (**Table 2**).

Table 1. Submission Count per Employee

	Junior	Senior	Manager	Average
CM	15.67	60	-	26.57
QA	14.87	-	24	15.44
Support	11	-	-	11
SW	0.37	4.55	22.46	4.78
Average	4.82	6.96	22.57	7.45

Table 2. Employee Particiaption

	Junior	Senior	Manager	Average
CM	100%	100%	-	100%
QA	93.3%	-	100%	93.8%
Support	85.7%	-	-	85.7%
SW	19.6%	68.2%	69.2%	39.5%
Average	43.4%	69.6%	71.4%	52.2%

The discrepancies between the ratios of different groups are explained by the fact that the configuration managers and quality engineers are usually employed at maturity level assessment activities within the company thus gaining a higher level of understating of the processes within the company. Furthermore, their duties usually include ensuring that the activities within the company are performed in accordance with the defined processes. These two factors might form the basis for their high level of contribution to process improvement activities.

The software developers and engineers, which form the majority of the company, have a much lower contribution to process improvement, although the processes are enforced in the first place to mold the way that they produce their software products. Therefore it is observed that the initiative has not been successful in enforcing organization wide process improvement commitment. The current situation is a *process-wise oligarchy* where a minority manages the processes for a majority who use them. It might not be the goal of the company to establish a *process-wise democracy* where every employee has equal commitment and voice in the process improvement; however, it was concluded that the organization wide process improvement commitment is not enabled for the organization.

3.2 Date Characteristics

The monthly submission count to the improvement database was also analyzed for the period December 2006 to February 2011. It was observed that the submission rates reach peak values in May and June of 2007. This situation results from the fact that the company underwent their first SCAMPI Class A appraisal for CMMI in June 2007. The submission rates decrease significantly after the assessment is completed successfully. A small increase is also observed in March 2010 when the company underwent SCAMPI Class B appraisal in preparation of the next formal CMMI assessment in June 2010. A minor increase is also observed for that month when SCAMPI Class A appraisal is conducted. It was observed that process improvement suggestions are concentrated before the maturity level assessment periods. This results in half of the database entries being submitted in only 5 months over a period of 5 years. Therefore it is not possible to state that the maturity model based approaches enforced continuous process improvement for the organization.

3.3 Content Characteristics

The content of the improvements submitted is classified by the CMMI process areas in the database. It was observed that the improvements are spread over 21 of 22 process areas. However it is evident that the distribution of suggestions to these process areas is not balanced. The ratio of the highest submission count process area (CM: Configuration Management) to lowest (OPP: Organizational Process Performance) is nearly 43.

Another aspect of the content wise analysis of the improvement database is the classification of the suggestions according to the process asset categorization of the target company. It was observed that an internally defined classification schema is much more balanced than the externally defined CMMI process area distribution.

4 Employee Perception

To be able to understand the perception of process improvement among employees and to explore the quality of the employees who participate in process improvement work, we prepared an online questionnaire and announced to the employees of the target organization. The questionnaire consists of two parts. The first part contains 15 questions with 5-level Likert scale answers (Coded as 1 for Strongly Agree to 5 for Strongly Disagree). These questions aim to document the opinion of the employees regarding the process improvement activities and the improvement database used within the company. The questions of the first part of the questionnaire are given in **Table 3** together with the associated codes which will be used for the rest of this study.

The second part of the questionnaire consists of 8 questions which obtain personal information about the employee as presented in **Table 4**. The unit of measurement for the three questions regarding experience duration is months. The role variable is measured in the nominal scale with values SW, QA, CM and Support. A total of 42 people submitted answers for the questionnaire. Among these answers 35 were complete.

Table 3. Questionnaire Part I

Code	Question
SPIRequired	Process improvement activities are required and important for the success of organizations.
SPIContinous	Process improvement activities shall be performed continuously independent of maturity level assessments.
ProcessesMature	Processes of my organization do not need to be improved.
AllParticipate	All members of the organization shall participate in process improvement activities.
SmallTeam	A small dedicated team shall perform process improvement activities while minimally disturbing the rest of the organization.

Table 3. (*Continued*)

RoleBased	Participation ratio in process improvement activities shall be based on the employee's role.
SeniorityBased	Participation ratio in process improvement activities shall be based on the employee's seniority and experience.
HeavyWorkload	I cannot spare time for process improvement activities because of my heavy workload.
NotJustified	The gains obtained from process improvement activities is not high enough to justify the effort dedicated to them.
SPIKnowledge	I have adequate knowledge about what I can do for the improvement of my organization's processes.
PTIKnowledge	I have adequate knowledge about the Process and Technology Improvement Database (PTI DB).
PTIBeneficial	PTIDB is beneficial in continuous process improvement activities.
PTISufficient	PTIDB is sufficient in continuous process improvement activities.
PTIContent	I know the possible content of suggestions that I can submit to PTIDB.
PTIEvaluation	I think that the suggestions I have submitted/plan to submit to the PTIDB are evaluated in an adequate way.

Table 4. Questionnaire Part II

Code	Question
Sex	Sex
University	University
Department	Department
TargetExp	Employment duration in target company
MaturityExp	Employment duration in an organization with a maturity level certificate (CMMI, ISO 15504 etc.) other than the target company
NonMaturityExp	Employment duration in an organization without a maturity level certificate (CMMI, ISO 15504 etc.) other than the target company
Role	Role
PTISubmission	PTIDB Submission Count

4.1 Factor Analysis

A factor analysis [10] is performed on the questionnaire results to identify the underlying approaches of target company employees. As a first step the variables of the first part of the questionnaire were subjected to a factor analysis. However the results did not converge to logically coherent factors. As an improvement the PTISubmission variable from the second part of the questionnaire was also added to the analysis. The improvement submission count is a strong indicator of an employee's commitment to the process improvement activities. Therefore, its inclusion in the variable list has improved the underlying logic of the factors.

The Kaiser–Meyer–Olkin measure verified the sampling adequacy for the analysis, KMO = .523 and Bartlett's test of sphericity χ^2 (120) = 172.378, p = .001, indicated that correlations between items were sufficiently large. Finally, it was decided that three components explaining 48.38% of the variance might yield a meaningful grouping based on the analysis of the Scree plot. The analysis with three components is presented in **Table 5**. It should be noted that orthogonal rotation has been applied to the results and weights less than 0.4 are not shown.

The first component is deemed to indicate the *unknowledgeable* attitude. Employees with this attitude do not feel that they have adequate information about Software Process Improvement or PTI DB; they do not appreciate the benefits of the PTI DB, they think that current processes are already mature, and they have low PTI submission counts.

The second component indicates an attitude favoring continuous process improvement activities. This attitude includes the thought that the processes are not mature and improvement activities should be performed independent of the roles or workload of employees. Furthermore these activities should not only consist of the PTI DB usage. Therefore this attitude covers the *proponents* of continuous process improvement.

The third component indicates an attitude which can be named *unbelievers* since this attitude is based on the thought that PTI DB is not beneficial and the entries in the DB are not handled adequately. Furthermore, this approach includes the thought that a small team should be responsible for the process improvement activities and excessive effort should not be allocated to it.

Table 5. Components Obtained by the Factor Analysis

	Unknowledgeable	Proponent	Unbeliever
SPIRequired		-.708	
SPIContinous		-.709	
ProcessesMature	-.404	.557	
AllParticipate			
SmallTeam			-.460
RoleBased		.662	
SeniorityBased	.447		
HeavyWorkload		.490	
NotJustified			.638
SPIKnowledge	.763		
PTIKnowledge	.821		
PTIBeneficial	.487		.504
PTISufficient		.716	
PTIContent	.824		
PTIEvaluation			.726
PTISubmission	-.643		

Employee Perceptions of Organization Wide Continuous Process Improvement Activities   33

4.2   Reliability Analysis

A reliability analysis is performed by calculating Cronbach's Alpha for each factor [10]. The questions with negative weight are reversed for the purpose of the reliability analysis. The findings of the analysis are presented at **Table 6**.

Table 6. Reliability Analysis Results

Components	Cronbach's Alpha	Cronbach's Alpha Based on Standardized Items	Number of Items
Unknowledgeable	.264	.778	7
Proponent	.684	.725	6
Unbeliever	.400	.472	4

Unknowledgeable. Although Cronbach's α is low, the value based on standardized items is satisfactorily high. This is due to the inclusion of PTISubmission which has a different scale than the other variables in the factor analysis. Cronbach's α is increased if PTISubmission is deleted, which suggests that the inclusion of PTISubmission decreases reliability despite increasing the logical foundation of the factors determined.

Proponent. Cronbach's α is satisfactorily high for this factor, and the deletion of none of the items increases Cronbach's α significantly. Therefore this factor is deemed to be reliable.

Unbeliever. Cronbach's α is not high for this factor. The deletion of SmallTeam increases the reliability, albeit by a small amount (Cronbach's α after deletion is 0.539).

4.3   Multiple Regression Analysis

The next step we performed is the determination of the relationship between the factors and the experience of the employees obtained in three categories represented by the TargetExp, MaturityExp and NonMaturityExp variables by performing multiple regression analysis [10].

Unknowledgeable. The experience in the target company (sig. = .000) and any other company with a maturity level certification (sig. = .008) significantly affects the unknowledgeable attitude in employees. The experience in any other type of company is not significant (sig. = .394) and therefore was dropped from the model. The experience in the target company is more effective than the experience in other certified organizations (coefficients -0.560 to -0.356). The model consisting of the experience levels explain nearly 50% of the variance in the unknowledgeable attitude.

Proponent. The employee being a proponent of process improvement is not related to his/her experience. The regression model eliminated all the experience types without reaching a significant model during our analysis.

Unbeliever. Interestingly, the employee believing in PTI DB is not related to his/her experience. The regression model eliminated all the experience types without reaching a significant model.

4.4 Comparison of Means

Our research question also asks about the relationship of software process improvement contribution and the role and education of the employee. Unfortunately the survey data collected was uneven with respect to these variables. For example there was only 1 employee with CM role while there were 29 employees with SW role. Therefore a statistical study more advanced than comparing the means could not be accomplished.

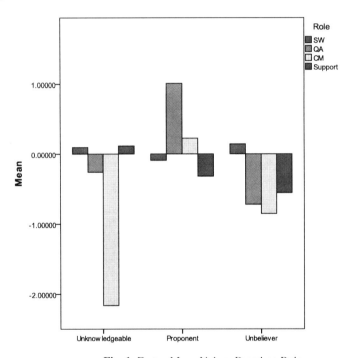

Fig. 1. Factor Mean Values Based on Role

Role. The mean values for the factors based on the employee roles are presented in **Fig. 1**. The members of the quality and configuration management believe that they are knowledgeable about the process improvement activities and tools, while software engineers and support personnel believe that they are not knowledgeable. The quality assurance and configuration management staff is also the proponents of process improvement activities within the organization. All groups except the software engineers believe in the benefits of the PTI DB.

Education. Although the target company specializes in software, employees come from a variety of educational backgrounds. The undergraduate departments of the employees who have participated in the survey are summarized in **Table 7** and the mean values for the factors based on the employee education are presented in **Fig. 2**. The highest values belong to CE and ME graduates. However it is not possible to obtain reliable data from these sources since both CE and ME have only one graduate employed in the target company. Therefore it is very possible that these high values are dependent on the specific person participating in the survey. Nevertheless an interesting result is that CENG and EEE graduates, which are the largest groups, have opposite approaches for all three factors.

Table 7. Educational Background of Employees

Undergraduate Degree	Abbreviation	No. of Employees
Chemical Engineering	CE	1
Computer Engineering	CENG	21
Electrical-Electronics Engineering	EEE	9
Mechanical Engineering	ME	1
Statistics	STAT	3

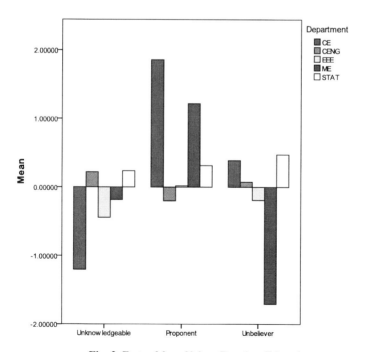

Fig. 2. Factor Mean Values Based on Education

5   Conclusion

Our research question was to identify the possible relationships between software process improvement contribution and an employee's education, experience and role within the organization. We have been able to identify three attitudes forging the contribution of an employee, namely the employee's perceived lack of knowledge (unknowledgeable factor), his/her support of SPI (proponent factor) and the belief in effectiveness of the PTI DB of the target company (believer factor). Ideally it is desired that an employee has satisfactory knowledge regarding software process improvement activities of his/her organization, support these activities and has belief in the methods and tools used by the organization for process improvement.

In our previous study we have observed that the submission count of the employees and therefore their commitment to process improvement increases with the experience of the employee. In this study we have determined that the experience of an employee in this maturity certified organization significantly affects his/her self image regarding knowledge level. However this experience does not make him/her a proponent of SPI activities or alter his/her thoughts on the effectiveness of PTI DB. Therefore it can be concluded that with increasing experience in this maturity-certified organization employees feel that they gain adequate information about software process improvement, and they appreciate the need for improving the current processes within the organizations. Naturally, the experience in the target organization raises the awareness of the employee regarding the tools and methods used in the organization for process improvement. However, we have seen that experience explains only half of the variance regarding knowledge. Therefore, there is room for improving the perceived knowledge of employees with varying experiences. This improvement might even be incorporated into the models used for process improvement by the target company.

The relationships regarding the employee's role and education could not be analyzed exhaustively due to the uneven distribution of answers from the conducted survey. Our previous study has shown that configuration managers and quality assurance engineers have much higher contribution to process improvement suggestions than software engineers. This study has verified these results by showing that configuration managers and quality assurance engineers see themselves more knowledgeable than the software engineers. They are also proponents and believers of software process improvement activities within the organization. Therefore, our claim of the existence of a *process wise oligarchy* within the company still holds. As we have explained in our previous study, discrepancies between different groups may be explained by the fact that the configuration managers and quality assurance engineers are usually employed at maturity level assessment activities within the company. The majority of the appraisal teams formed during previous assessments were formed of the members of the configuration management, quality assurance and support groups. This situation enables the members of these groups to attain a higher level of understating of the processes within the company. In order to overcome this, the assessment procedures might encourage employees with different roles to be part of the assessment team. A rotation of these employees with each assessment will eventually raise the overall level of awareness within the company with respect to processes and improvement activities.

The analysis regarding educational background faced challenges since the most significant outcomes belonged to groups with only one member. Nevertheless it is interesting that computer engineering and electrical-electronics engineering graduates, which are largest groups, have opposite approaches for all three factors. It should also be noted that electrical-electronics engineers have higher outcomes for desired properties.

The overall results show some of the problems faced in a company employing a staged model with respect to the contribution of employees to the process improvement activities. We are currently extending our research to similar companies in order to be able to generalize our findings. A questionnaire that is not specific to a single company is in preparation and will be distributed to the software industry employees of Turkey. It is expected that these studies will help in determining improvement opportunities for staged models.

References

1. Software Engineering Institute. CMMI Version 1.3 Information Center, http://www.sei.cmu.edu/cmmi/tools/cmmiv1-3/ (retrieved January 25, 2010)
2. International Organization for Standardization. ISO/IEC 15504-1:2004, Geneva (2004)
3. Goldenson, D.R., Gibson, D.L.: Demonstrating the Impact and Benefits of CMMI: An Update and Preliminary Results. Software Engineering Institute (2003)
4. Wilkie, F.G., McFall, D., McCaffery, F.: An Evaluation of CMMI Process Areas for Small- to Medium-sized Software Development Organisations. Software Process: Improvement and Practice 10(2), 189–201 (2005)
5. Huang, D., Zhang, W.: CMMI in Medium & Small Enterprises: Problems and Solutions. In: The 2nd IEEE International Conference on Information Management and Engineering, pp. 171–174 (2010)
6. Tosun, A., Bener, A., Turhan, B.: Implementation of a Software Quality Improvement Project in an SME: A Before and After Comparison. In: 35th Euromicro Conference on Software Engineering and Advanced Applications, pp. 203–209 (2009)
7. Uskarci, A., Demirors, O.: Do Staged Models Enable Organization Wide Continuous Process Improvement? In: 2011 IEEE International Conference on Quality and Reliability (ICQR), pp. 20–24 (2011)
8. Baddoo, N., Hall, T.: De-Motivators for Software Process Improvement: An Analysis of Practitioners' Views. The Journal of Systems and Software 66, 23–33 (2003)
9. Basri, S., O'Connor, R.V.: Organizational Commitment towards Software Process Improvement: An Irish Software VSEs Case Study. In: 2010 International Symposium in Information Technology (ITSim), pp. 1456–1461 (2010)
10. Field, A.: Discovering Statistics Using SPSS, 3rd edn. Sage Publications, London (2009)

Using Composition Trees to Validate an Entry Profile of Software Engineering Lifecycle Profiles for Very Small Entities (VSEs)

Lian Wen[1,2] and Terry Rout[1]

[1] Institute for Integrated and Intelligent Systems, Griffith University
[2] School of Information and Communication Technology, Griffith University
170 Kessels Rd, Qld 4111, Australia
{l.wen,t.rout}@griffith.edu.au

Abstract. ISO/IEC TR 29110-5-1 provides a Software Engineering life cycle reference model for Very Small Entities on small software projects (less than 6 people month). This paper uses Composition Trees (CT) as a formal notation to model part of this process, and compares it with its counterpart process (which is also modeled in a CT) from ISO/IEC 12207. The outcome of the comparison is a Comparison Composition Tree (CCT). This CCT shows clearly the similarity and difference between the VSE Entry Profile and ISC12207. This information may help people to validate and understand the VSE Profile. This paper also proposes this approach can be used as a general approach for people to develop, study, and implement software processes.

Keywords: Composition Trees, Very Small Entity, Software Process.

1 Introduction

Model-based process improvement has been widely applied to support the design, implementation and improvement of processes for the development of complex products [27], especially in the domain of systems and software engineering. Significant benefits have been shown to derive from the application of model-based improvement [8], and it is common for acquirers to require demonstration of some degree of implementation of effective processes as part of an evaluation of supplier capability. A wide range of techniques have been applied for the definition and specification of industrial processes, having widely differing degrees of formality.

In the domains of software and system engineering, a range of Standards and related products have been developed specifying processes to be employed in the product life cycle – see, for example, ISO/IEC 12207:2008 [10], ISO/IEC 15288:2008 [11] and the Capability Maturity Model Integration suite [3]. These Standards are predominantly descriptive and prescriptive in nature. We have highlighted in a previous paper [25] the problems that can arise in comparing similar processes defined in different contexts, in some cases using different modeling approaches.

In seeking a solution to these problems in process modeling, similar problems can be identified with the requirement specifications for software systems. Ambiguous language, incomplete descriptions, repetition and redundancies in the way specifications are expressed inevitably lead to sub-optimal project outcomes (systems that do not meet the user's needs). Behavior Engineering [1, 4] successfully addresses the problems faced by software developers seeking to translate a set of user requirements into a complete and consistent requirements specification.

Behavior Engineering uses a formally-grounded graphical notation with the capability to represent a wide range of system behaviors in unambiguous terms. Its strength is its ability to accommodate complexity and detail, ease of use, and in particular for this project its ability to expose defects.

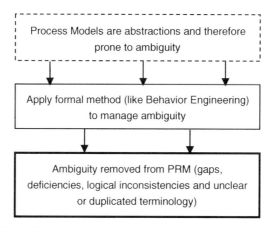

Fig. 1. Use of formal method to remove ambiguity from abstract model

Previous research indicates that BE notations can be useful verification tools for process modeling [22]. In our previous paper we refined this concept by proposing a detailed scheme to model a software process based on its purpose and process outcomes in a Composition Tree (CT) [6], which is one of the key parts of the BE notations. The graphic version of a process model is more intuitive, less ambiguous and easier to verify than the original natural language described process.

The application of Behavior Engineering to process modeling offers significant benefits, in terms of clarifying process descriptions and specifically in helping to establish process-related risk associated with process tailoring. In the current investigations, we report on the application of the technique to analysis of tailoring of process models for Very Small Enterprises.

2   Lifecycle Profiles for Very Small Entities

Very Small Enterprises (VSEs) are defined as those having 25 or fewer personnel. It has been widely recognized that enterprises in this class make a very significant contribution to the IT industry [18]. However, it is also acknowledged that most VSEs do not find the process models typically available and useful for their purposes, primarily because of associated high bureaucratic overheads. Actions have been taken to develop specific models more suitable for the use of VSEs, generally by tailoring existing approaches; the most widely recognized of these is the development of the ISO/IEC 29110 [13] series of Standards.

ISO/IEC 29110 specifies process models for VSEs as "standard lifecycle profiles", following the approach described in ISO/IEC 10000-1 [9]. The Profiles are designed for use both for internal, model-based improvement within the VSE, and for use in the assessment of overall organizational capability [16]. ISO/IEC 29110 provides for the definition of a range of profiles, tailored from processes specified in the source Standard, ISO/IEC 12207 [10], and designed for enterprises engaged in different classes of development.

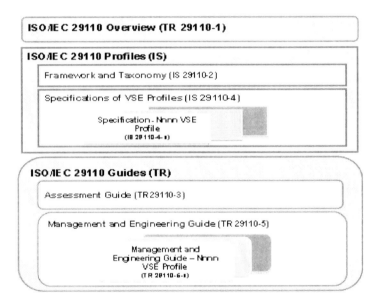

Fig. 2. ISO/IEC 29110 set of Documents [13]

The document set for ISO/IEC 29110 is based around a three-tiered structure, shown in Fig. 2. At the top level, there is an overview of the approach [13]. Normative elements of the standard suite comprise a Framework and Taxonomy for specifying profiles [14], and an envisaged set of Profile Specifications [15]; these specify the structure and content of profiles to be developed for specified classes of users. The detailed Profiles are set out in the Management and Engineering Guides [17]; these are implementations of tailored process descriptions, based on the source Standards, and employing the relevant Specifications. Multiple different profiles are to be established for different classes of VSEs and projects; in the initial phase of development, a set of "Generic Profiles" have been developed and published.

In the profile specifications, ISO/IEC 29110 follows the approach defined in ISO/IEC 24774:2007 - *Software and systems engineering -- Life cycle management -- Guidelines for process description* [12], which outlines a standard format for any process reference model, including those intended for process implementation and process assessment. This general purpose standard outlines the elements used to describe a process; title, purpose statement, outcomes, activities and tasks.

- The **title** conveys the scope of the process as a whole, expressed as a short noun phrase that summarize the scope of the process, identify the principal concern of the process, and distinguishes it from other processes within the scope of a process model.
- The **purpose** describes the goal of performing the process. It is expressed as a high level goal for performing the process, preferably stated in a single sentence. The implementation of the process should provide measurable, tangible benefits to the stakeholders through the expected outcomes
- The **outcomes** express the observable results expected from the successful performance of the process. Outcomes are expressed in terms of a positive, observable objective or benefit. The list of outcomes associated with a process shall be prefaced by the text, 'As a result of successful implementation of this process:'. The outcomes should be no longer than two lines of text, about twenty words. The number of outcomes for a process should fall within the range 3 to 7. Outcomes should express a single result. The use of the word 'and' or 'and/or' to conjoin clauses should be avoided.
- The **activities** are a list of actions that may be used to achieve the outcomes. Each activity may be further elaborated as a grouping of related lower level actions;
- The **tasks** are specific actions that may be performed to achieve an activity. Multiple related tasks are often grouped within an activity.

In ISO/IEC 29110-5-1 [17], a Profile is specified for VSEs undertaking software development of a generic class, tailored from ISO/IEC 12207. The Profile contains two identified Processes, each comprising a set of high-level tasks; the tasks and processes are derived by tailoring and assembling process components from ISO/IEC 12207 [10]. The impact of the tailoring is not immediately obvious, and the implications of the application of these profiles in an organization are not clear. For this reason, we have undertaken an analysis of the available profiles, using Behavior Engineering approach, and applied Composition Trees to specifically determine the impact of the tailoring.

3 Using Composition Trees to Model and Compare Software Processes

3.1 Composition Trees

A Composition Tree (CT) is originally used to describe the composition of a component based software intensive system [6]. It provides useful summary information including states, attributes and relationships about the system and other entities under the system. The CT notation is then adapted to model software processes [25] and manufacture processes [26].

Similar to the way of constructing a Behavior Tree from the functional requirements [5], A Composition Tree can also be constructed through translating the individual functional requirements one by one. In this sub section, we use a small example to show what a CT looks like (in Fig. 3). Detailed and formal introduction of CT can be found somewhere else [1, 25].

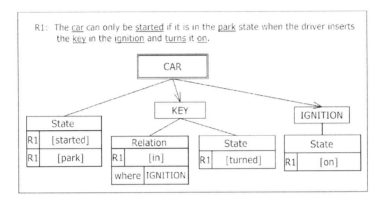

Fig. 3. The Composition Tree (CT) generated from translating requirement 1 (R1). *Within the CAR system, there are two components: KEY and IGNITION. The CAR has two possible states: [started] and [park], while the KEY has one state of [turned] and one state [on] for the component IGNITION. There is a relation [in] between the KEY and the IGNITION.*

The process to translate all the requirements into one CT has following advantages:

- All information is integrated together so it is easy to indentify the requirement defects. For example, the incompleteness and inconsistency in the original requirements.
- A CT arranges the information about one component in one place. It will be easier for people to design and implement the components than the original requirements with the information of one component may be scattered all around the requirements.
- The more specific graphic notation is less ambiguous than the more flexible natural language.
- A CT removes the entire alias so it will use a consistent vocabulary for the system.

The advantages of using CT in Software and System Engineering has been demonstrated elsewhere [6], further details are not provided in this paper.

3.2 Using Composition Trees to Model Software Processes

According to ISO/IEC 24774:2007 [12], the standard elements to describe a process include the title, the purpose, outcomes, activities and tasks. Apart from the title, which is only the name of a process, purpose and outcomes are more static elements, so they may be more suitable to be modeled by composition trees.

Fig. 4 is the CT for the purpose of the Configuration Management Process defined in ISO/IEC 12207. The CT for the whole process and the detailed translation steps can be found in [25].

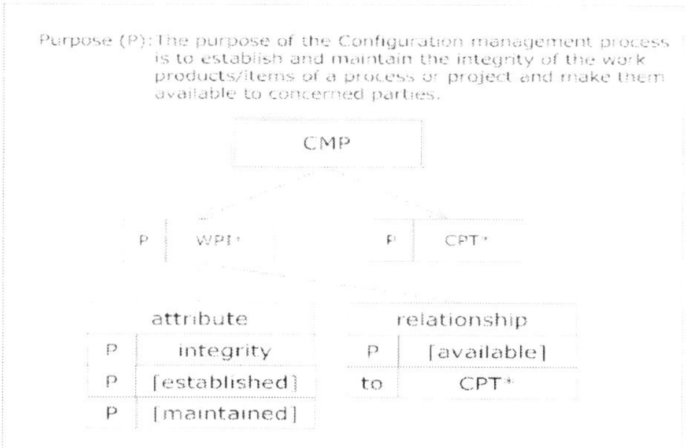

Fig. 4. The Composition Tree constructed from the purpose of the Configuration Management Process

CMP stands for Configuration Management Process; WPI means Work Product/Item; CPT means Concerned Parts. "*" means this component may have multiple instances

3.3 Comparing Composition Trees

One special advantage to model software processes in composition trees is that we can define formal algorithm to compare the two composition trees. Therefore, it provides a simple method to identify the similarity and difference between two related processes. While it could be more challenge if we try to compare two processes simply based on their natural language descriptions.

The comparison implements a label matching tree merging algorithm which has been used for comparing different versions of Behavior Trees [24].

A critical task in tree merging algorithm is to identify the matching nodes. For CTs, the way to identify the same nodes is based on the name of the component and its state, etc. Therefore, before applying the merging algorithm, the first step is to identify the same component and/or the same state which may be called by different names in the two compared trees and to establish a mapping between them.

The second step is to compare and merge the two trees. To simplify the discussion, we may call the first tree as the old tree and the second tree as the new tree. In this way, the comparison procedure will create a merged tree that is called a Comparison Composition Tree (CCT). A CCT shows all the information of both trees and also highlights the difference in an easy to read way. To achieve this purpose, a display style convention is used in this paper as in Fig. 5.

Under this display style convention, in a CCT, a piece of information which exists in both the old tree and the new tree is called unchanged and will be drawn in normal style; a piece of information if only exists in the old tree will be called old and will be drawn in dotted lines; a piece of information if only exists in the new tree will be called new and will be drawn in bolded lines.

Fig. 5. The display style convention for a CCT

4   Comparing the VSE Entry Profile with ISO/IEC 12207

In this section, we compare one of the process objectives defined in the VSE Entry Profile [17] with their more comprehensive counterparts defined in ISO/IEC 12207 [10] through their CT modeling. Because the comparison models show the similarities and differences in a clear, simple, and easy to read way, they can be useful for people to validate the profile for its usefulness regarding to the VSE.

The Entry Profile of VSE defines only two processes: Project Management (PM) process and Software Implementation (SI) process, while ISO/IEC 12207:2008 has defined 43 processes. Each process in VSE Entry Profile has a number of objectives with each objective includes certain elements which are covered by one or more processes defined in ISO/IEC 12207.

In this paper, we firstly investigate the object 1 (O1) in the PM process from the VSE Entry Profile. PM.O1 mainly focuses on the project plan that is mostly defined in the Project Planning Process in ISO/IEC 12207.

According to ISO/IEC 29110-5-1 [17], PM.O1 is:

The Project Plan for the execution of the project is developed according to the Statement of Work and reviewed and accepted by the Customer. The tasks and resources necessary to complete the work are sized and estimated.

The CT of PM.O1 is shown in Fig. 6:

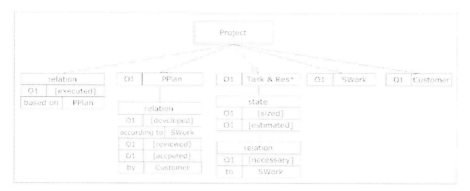

Fig. 6. The Composition Tree (CT) modeling of the first object in the Project Management process in the VSE Entry Profile

PPlan: Project Plan   **Task & Res**: Task and resource.
SWork: Statement of Work   **O1**: Object one of the project management process

Fig. 6 shows that: the Project is executed based on the Project Plan (PPlan); the Project includes a Project Plan, multiple Tasks and Resources (the '*' sign means plural), Statement of Work (SWork) and a Customer; the Project Plan is developed according to the Statement of Work (SWork), and the Project Plan is reviewed and accepted by the Customer; the Tasks and Resources are sized and estimated, they are also necessary to the Statement of Work.

Compared the graphic notation with the natural language description of PM.O1, it is easier to identify the relationship between different concepts is the CT notation.

Secondly, we identify that the counterpart process in ISO/IEC 12207 is the Project Planning Process. The purpose and outcomes of the Project Planning Process are:

Purpose: *The purpose of the Project Planning Process is to produce and communicate effective and workable project plans.*

This process determines the scope of the project management and technical activities, identifies process outputs, project tasks and deliverables, establishes schedules for project task conduct, including achievement criteria, and required resources to accomplish project tasks.

Outcomes:

a) *the scope of the work for the project is defined;*
b) *the feasibility of achieving the goals of the project with available resources and constraints are evaluated;*
c) *the tasks and resources necessary to complete the work are sized and estimated;*
d) *interfaces between elements in the project, and with other project and organizational units, are identified;*
e) *plans for the execution of the project are developed; and*
f) *plans for the execution of the project are activated.*

We draw the Composition Tree model of the Project Planning Process in Fig. 7. This model is built based on the process purpose and the process outcomes. This composition tree uses the following abbreviations:

Task & Res: task and resources; OUnit: Other project & organizational unit.

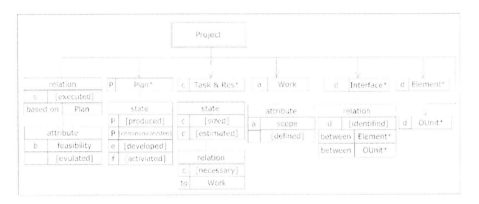

Fig. 7. The Composition Tree for the Project Planning Process in ISO/IEC 12207
This model is based on the process purpose and process outcomes.

Finally, we compare the two composition trees based on the algorithm introduced in the previous section. Before the comparison, we need to identify the mapping terms between the two composition trees. The mapping terms are listed in Table 1.

Table 1. - The mapping terms between PM.O1 and the Project Planning Process

#	PM.O1	Project Planning Process	Comments
1	PPlan	Plan*	For an Entry Profile in VSE, a simple Project Pan is sufficient; while for a more general project, multiple plans would be required.
2	SWork	Work	For an Entry Profile, the work is materialized as a Statement of Work.

The composition tree for the Project Planning Process in ISO/IEC 12207 is called the old tree (shown in Fig. 7); the composition tree for PM.O1 is called the new tree (shown in Fig. 6). Then we apply the tree merging algorithm to create the Comparison Composition Tree (CCT) as in Fig. 8.

In Fig. 8, the information exists in both ISO/IEC 12207 and the VSE is displayed in the normal style, the information is called unchanged. The information exists only in ISO/IEC 12207 is called old, that means this information has been removed from the VSE, and it is displayed in gray boxes. The information exists only in the VSE is called new, and it is displayed in bold boxes.

The CCT highlights the difference between the PM.O1 of VSE Entry Profile and its counterpart process defined in ISO/IEC 12207. The difference helps people to understand the rationality behind the design of the Profile. In next section, we will go through the details of CCT and illustrate this point.

5   Discussion

In the previous section, we have created the CCT of the ISO/IEC 12207 Project Planning Process and the PM.O1 of the VSE Entry Profile in Fig. 8. In this section, we will go through the details of the CCT to examine what information can be directly retrieved from the CCT and how it could be used to justify the rationality of the VSE Entry Profile.

To read the CCT, we go through all branches one by one from the leftmost.

The leftmost branch shows that for both ISO/IEC 12207 and the VSE Profile, the Project should be executed based on plan. However, the VSE Profile does not mention that the feasibility of the project should be evaluated. The reason for this point being removed from the VSE Profile is that the VSE Profile is designed for small project team (up to 25 people in the organization) and with small projects. The feasibility of the project is easy to be evaluated and it should have been evaluated earlier, so it is not necessary to be a formal part of the planning process.

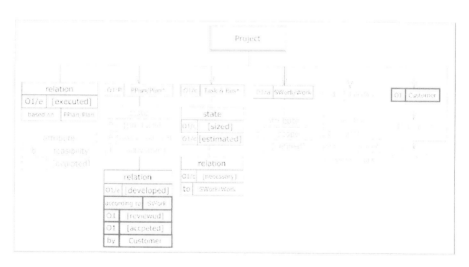

Fig. 8. The Comparison Composition Tree (CCT) generated from merging the composition tree of the Project Planning Process in ISO/IEC 12207 and the PM.O1 from the VSE Entry Profile

The second branch in the CCT is about the plan document(s). An obvious difference is that the VSE Profile only has one Project Plan while ISO/IEC 12207 may have multiple plans for the project. This difference is easy to understand as the VSE Profile handles very small projects, one project plan should be efficient.

The second difference in the second branch is that the VSE Profile doesn't mention that the Project Plan should be *produced, communicated* and *activated*. Of course, the plan should be created, communicated and activated even for small projects. The reason for it is not mentioned in the VSE Profile is these requirements are too obvious to be formally addressed. However, for large projects which involve many stakeholders and many different kinds of plans, the requirements should be explicitly addressed.

The third difference in the second branch is that the VSE Entry Profile mentions that the Project Plan should be *reviewed* and *accepted* by the Customer, while this point is not mentioned in the Project Planning Process in ISO/IEC 12207. The reason is that ISO/IEC 12207 builds a much large and complex process groups to handle the procedures to create, verify and accept any formal documents, therefore, it doesn't need to repeat it in the Project Planning Process for this point.

There is no much difference in the third branch.

The first interesting point in the fourth branch is that the VSE Entry Profile uses the Statement of Work while ISO/IEC 12207 uses a more general term Work. The difference can be explained that for a small project, the work is already well expressed in the Statement of Work. However, for large projects, it may not have a formal statement of work at the planning stage, so it use a more general term Work. The second point is that as ISO/IEC 12207 uses a more general term Work, it also need to define the scope of the work in the planning process, but this is not required if we already have a Statement of Work in the VSE Profile.

The fifth branch only exists in ISO/IEC 12207. The branch expresses that the interfaces between different *Elements* and other *Project and Organization Units* are identified. As the VSE Profile only deals with small projects; they are usually small and simple, so the identification of the interfaces between different internal and/or external parts is usually not an issue.

The last branch in the CCT shows that Customer appears only in the VSE Profile while the Elements and OUnits only appear in the ISO/IEC 12207 Project Planning Process. The reasons have already been discussed in the previous paragraphs.

In this section, we go through the details of the CCT. We find that the CCT uses a clear and easy to read way to highlight the difference and similarity between the PM.O1 and the Project Planning Process. This information helps to understand, reason and validate the VSE Profile

6 Conclusions and Further Research Topics

This paper investigates Composition Trees as a formal graphic language to present software processes defined in a VSE Profile; and then comparing it with software processes defined in ISO/IEC 12207 by generating a CCT. The CCT shows the similarities and differences between processes defined in the two standards in a clear, precise and easy to read way. This comparison helps people who make standards to reason and then improve their new standards; it also help software engineering practitioners to understand and implement the VSE Profile in their projects and then eventually adapt additional elements from more comprehensive standards such as ISO/IEC 12207 into their practices. Even though the research is for the Entry Profile of VSE, the method can also be used for other profiles in VSE or other standards.

So far the research is still at its preliminary stage and the research results are very promising. Some possible further research directions include adding more elements such as work products, activities and tasks in the CT models, integrating multiple processes in one CT, and developing suitable software tools to support this approach.

References

1. Behavior Engineering Web Site, http://www.behaviorengineering.org/
2. Box, G.E.P.: Robustness in the strategy of scientific model building. In: Launer, R.L., Wilkinson, G.N. (eds.) Robustness in Statistics. Academic Press, New York (1979)
3. Chrissis, M.B., Konrad, M., Schrumm, S.: CMMI for Development®: Guidelines for Process Integration and Product Improvement, 3rd edn. Addison-Wesley (2011)
4. Dromey, R.G.: Climbing Over the 'No Silver Bullet' Brick Wall. IEEE Software 23(2), 118–120 (2006)
5. Dromey, R.G.: Formalizing the Transition from Requirements to Design. In: Mathematical Frameworks for Component Software, Models for Analysis and Syn., pp. 173–206 (2006)
6. Dromey, R.G.: System Composition: Constructive Support for the Analysis and Design of Large Systems. In: SETE 2005, Brisbane, Australia (2005)
7. Feiler, P.H., Humphrey, W.S.: Software Process Development and Enactment. Software Engineering Institute, Pittsburgh, CMU/SEY-92-TR-04, p. 11 (1992)
8. Gibson, D., Goldenson, D., Kost, K.: Performance Results of CMMI-Based Process Improvement, Technical Report CMU/SEI-2006-TR-004 (2006)
9. ISO/IEC TR 10000-1:1998, Information technology – Framework and taxonomy of International Standardized Profiles: General principles and documentation framework
10. ISO/IEC 12207:2008, Information technology – Software engineering – Software life cycle processes
11. ISO/IEC 15288:2008, Information technology - System engineering – System life cycle process
12. ISO/IEC TR 24774. Software and systems engineering – Life cycle management – Guidelines for process description (2007)
13. ISO/IEC TR 29110-1:2011, Software engineering – Lifecycle profiles for Very Small Entities (VSEs) – Part 1: Overview
14. ISO/IEC 29110-2:2011, Software engineering – Lifecycle profiles for Very Small Entities (VSEs) – Part 2: Framework and taxonomy
15. ISO/IEC TR 29110-3:2011, Software engineering – Lifecycle profiles for Very Small Entities (VSEs) – Part 3: Assessment guide
16. ISO/IEC 29110-4-1:2011, Software engineering – Lifecycle profiles for Very Small Entities (VSEs) – Part 4-1: Profile specifications: Generic profile group
17. ISO/IEC TR 29110-5-1-2:2011, Software engineering – Lifecycle profiles for Very Small Entities (VSEs): Management and engineering guide: Generic profile group: Basic profile
18. Laporte, C.Y., Alexandre, S., O'Connor, R.: A Software Engineering Lifecycle Standard for Very Small Enterprises. In: O'Connor, R.V., Baddoo, N., Smolander, K., Messnarz, R. (eds.) EuroSPI 2008. CCIS, vol. 16, pp. 129–141. Springer, Heidelberg (2008)
19. Podorozhny, R.M., Perry, D.E., et al.: Artifact-based functional comparison of software processes. In: 4th IWSPSM, pp. V.29.1–V.29.10 (May 2003)

20. Scacchi, W.: Process Models in Software Engineering. In: Marciniak, J.J. (ed.) Encyclopedia of Software Engineering, 2nd edn. John Wiley and Sons, Inc., New York (2001)
21. Sheard, S.A.: The frameworks quagmire, a brief look. In: Proceedings of the 7th Annual International INCOSE, Symposium, INCOSE 1997 (1997)
22. Tuffley, D., Rout, T.: Behavior Engineering as a Process Model Verification Tool. In: Proceedings of the 10th International SPICE Conference (2010)
23. Varkoi, T.: Process Assessment in Very Small Entities - An ISO/IEC 29110 based method, 7th QUATIC (2010)
24. Wen, L., Dromey, R.G.: From Requirements Change to Design Change: A Formal Path. In: Proceedings of the 2nd IEEE International Conference on SEFM, pp. 104–113 (2004)
25. Wen, L., Tuffley, D., Rout, T.: Using Composition Trees to Model and Compare Software Process. In: O'Connor, R.V., Rout, T., McCaffery, F., Dorling, A. (eds.) SPICE 2011. CCIS, vol. 155, pp. 1–15. Springer, Heidelberg (2011)
26. Wen, L., Tuffley, D.: Formalizing Manufacturing Process Modeling using Composition Trees. Advanced Materials Research 399-401, 1852–1855 (2012)
27. Wynn, D.C.: Model-Based Approaches to Support Process Improvement in Complex Product Development, PhD Thesis, University of Cambridge (2007)

Gained Experience by Making Intervention to Improve Software Process in Very Small Organizations

Mohammad Zarour[1], Jean-Marc Desharnais[2], Abdulrahman Alarifi[1], Naji Habra[3], Grégory Cassiers[3], and Antoine Robaeys[3]

[1] King AbdulAziz City of Science and Technology
Computer Research Center, Department of Software Engineering
Saudi Arabia P.O Box 6086 Riyadh 11442
{mzarour,alarifi}@kacst.edu.sa
[2] École de Technologie Supérieure, Montréal, Québec, Canada
desharnaisjm@gmail.com
[3] University of Namur – Facultés Universitaires N.D. de la Paix
Rue Grandgagnage, 21 5000 Namur – Belgique
nha@info.fundp.ac.be,
{gregory.cassiers,antoine.robaeys}@gmail.com

Abstract. Many research have been accomplished in assessing software process in small enterprises; in this paper we introduce our experience in conducting SPI initiatives with very small enterprises VSE using the OWPL assessment method. Interventions to these enterprises have been made to help them improving their software processes. The lessons learned by applying the micro-evaluation approach have been discussed at the end of the intervention process. In this intervention we have assessed four different VSE.

Keywords: Software process improvement (SPI), Process model, OWPL, small organizations, Micro-Evaluation.

1 Introduction

Researchers and practitioners have the perception that software process improvement (SPI) is an important process to achieve better software quality and productivity. Since the mid of eighties, many organizations have conducted assessment process to explore the strengths and weaknesses as well as possible improvements in their software development process. A large portion of these organizations stopped progress at that point and did not embark in any improvement effort and even did not embark in a reassessment process.

SPI is vital for all types of software organizations regardless of their size or type of products they produce. Very Small Enterprises (VSE), defined by ISO as having less than 25 employees [1], plays a great roll in the overall IT industry sector. A study conducted in Montreal area [1] showed that 78% of organizations in the IT sector are VSE and these organizations hire about 29% of the total number of employees in this sector.

Despite of the importance of VSE in the IT sector in any country, most of them still did not embark in software process improvement. VSE are facing several problems due to the high cost of assessment and improvement processes in terms of cost in time and resources.

Although several well-known software process improvement models, like CMMI, ISO 15504, ISO 9001 and others, are currently available, small and very small enterprises , due to their lack of resources in terms of time, cost and personnel, find the use of such models very complex [2]. The complexity of these models is due to their comprehensiveness, high level of detailed and the high cost associated with their implementation. This has pushed toward a new trend in research community to tailor these models to fit the needs of small and very small organizations. The result of this trend is a set of tailored assessment methods dedicated for small and very small organizations that are used to assess many organizations.

This paper provides our experience in conducting an action research where we made a direct intervention to four VSE (in Montreal) in order to apply SPI initiative. The use of micro-evaluation assessment method has been discussed by several researchers; see for example [3-6], but without being involved in applying the suggested improvements. This work continues the previous work done in this field [4, 7-11] to deeply understand the needs and problems of small and very small enterprises as well as explore the improvements possibilities for micro-evaluation assessment method of the OWPL[1] model.

2   Assessment Execution

Many assessments have been conducted for VSEs. Usually the assessments end by sending the final report to the assessed organizations which specifies the strengths, weaknesses and the suggested recommendations.

Recently, several organizations from those already assessed (in Montreal) have been contacted to explore the possibility of making intervention to apply our action research and participate in improving the software process based on the recommendations mentioned in the delivered report at the end of the assessment process. Four (4) organizations have shown interest to embark in our SPI intervention initiative.

2.1   Process Assessment Model

The micro-evaluation assessment method is based on the OWPL model. This model has been constructed by CETIC institute in Belgium to fit small enterprises and help them improve their software practices. OWPL focuses on simplifying the practices of CMM and SPICE, which become ISO 15504 standard, to become applicable to small and very small enterprises [12].

---

[1] *OWPL* stands for Observatoire Wallon des Pratiques Logicielles (Walloon Observatory for Software Practices).

2.2 Process Assessment Process

The assessment process has been conducted using micro-evaluation questionnaire. This process is divided into several phases: training, collecting data, analyzing data and then reporting.

In the training phase, undergraduate software engineering students have been trained in how to conduct the assessment and provided with necessary information about the assessment process and the related underlying model. This phase is carried out by one SPI expert (co-author) and a trained post-graduate student. In the second phase, students start collecting data from the companies through an interview that lasts for an hour. An Excel sheet paper is used as a tool to record the enterprise sponsor responses. In the third phase, the collected data are analyzed and rated based on the 5 levels scale of the micro-evaluation. In the reporting phase, a final report identifying strengths, weaknesses, risks and possible suggestions is defined and sent to the enterprise sponsor.

3 Context

We have started our intervention process by contacting the companies and arranging for the first meeting asking them to review the evaluation report sent to them previously. Our SEPG team participate in the four different meetings to explore the possible improvements, discuss and decide which process areas are more crucial for each enterprise and then develop and implement the suggested solutions.

The selection of the problems to be solved is made taking into consideration three main criteria:

1. The problem could be realized in the short term.
2. The problem must be interesting to the enterprise and bring benefits to it.
3. The problem must generate costs that can be supported by the enterprise.

For each of the four companies our SEPG team has built an action plan by analyzing the weaknesses reported in the micro-evaluation assessment report delivered previously for each enterprise, the set of recommendations in each report are also studied well for each enterprise from our team.

In the following subsections we introduce a brief description of the companies participated in our SPI intervention process.

3.1 Enterprise A

This enterprise provides consultations and development of specialized applications. The enterprise has a total of 10 employees and produces software for different sectors like manufacturing companies, hiring services companies and charity organizations. The mission of this enterprise is to contribute to the improvement of the effectiveness and the efficiency of management processes while developing real business software.

The enterprise's weakness points indicated in the action plan has been discussed with the person in charge in the enterprise; he emphasized their need to manage the requirements and also manage the large number of change requests. Based on this discussion our team has reached an agreement with enterprise sponsor to help them improve the requirements management and the change management.

3.2 Enterprise B

This Enterprise works in the field of dynamic and autonomous robotics. Their objective is to incorporate technologies and knowledge from all engineering branches into a project that will captivate all of its members. It is composed of 15 persons who work in different domains such as software, electricity and mechanics.

The corresponding action plan deals with several weakness points which exist in the VSE e.g. change management, quality management, risk management and development process. Having the action plan in hand, our team met the persons in charge for the VSE and discussed the different problems mentioned in the action plan in order to choose the most critical one to start with. This discussion emphasized the quality problem as the most important, mainly how to manage code review and the unit test problems.

3.3 Enterprise C

This VSE works in the agricultural field. It devotes approximately 60% of their activities in the management of a regrouping of agricultural producers with non lucrative goal in agro environment and approximately 40% of their activities in the web conception. The team is composed of 9 employees: mostly data processing specialists and analysts, plus administrative employees.

The corresponding action plan deals with several weakness points which exist in the enterprise, e.g. requirement management, documentation, project management and development process. Having the action plan in hand, our SEPG team met the persons in charge for the enterprise and discussed its contents to choose one of the problems that we can resolve based on our selection criteria. This discussion emphasized the importance of the requirements management problem, that is to say, the requirements specifications and formalization problems and their possible changes

3.4 Enterprise D

This VSE is an IT-specific department in charge of developing software for managing employees. This department has a total of three employees two of them working as programmers and the third as project manager. Their main goal is to facilitate the task for those managing human resources.

The corresponding action plan has focused on the critical weakness points in the enterprise. We have discussed these problems with the project leader of the enterprise and decided to help them improving the project estimation because the project manager doesn't have a formal way that allows him to know and follow the effort, the duration and the costs of his project and he was much concerned with this problem.

4   Process Improvement and Intervention

Enterprise A: Our intervention for this enterprise has two main axes: the requirement management and the change management as follows:

Requirement management (RM): We started our work to improve RM by searching the web for open source software that deals with requirement management; we found software developed by Hydro-Quebec to manage requirements called GenSpec; this software is based on international standards and solves well known problems in requirement engineering. After approval and encouragement of Hydro-Quebec, the software has been studied by SEPG team and used it to represent a sample of software requirements provided by Enterprise A, the description, demo and results have been documented in a report. Another meeting is arranged with the sponsor of the enterprise along with another person on the enterprise to present the GenSpec software and discuss its uses for the enterprise. The enterprise sponsor was interested in the software and its features. An agreement has been achieved with the enterprise to use this software to improve the SR process. The software and the report have been delivered to the enterprise to be installed and used. After a week, one of our SEPG members made a visit to the enterprise for a one day training and troubleshooting where he demonstrated the use of software and provided help to apply the software.

Change management: we have provided the enterprise with a change management process adapted to the context of the enterprise that allows formalizing the way that change requests are recorded, managed and resolved.

Our solution consists of two complementary parts: the first part is the development of templates to be used by the clients and the enterprise to track the requests and their application status. In the other part; we developed software, we call it ModeX, to record and manage the requests and make links between the change request and the requirements, this link would help the project manager to merge several requests that concern certain requirement and so can be applied and tested together.

Enterprise B: Based on the results of the previous meeting with the enterprise's representatives is been decided that this enterprise is suffering from several quality problems mainly in managing code review and unit test, after exploring the availability of suitable open source software, the team has decided to develop our own software to manage the code review. This task has been assigned to one of the SEPG members who developed the software using Java and MySQL technology. The software has been introduced to the enterprise sponsor and started the use of the software. With regarding to the unit test, the JTest tool provided by the Java IDE has been used to perform such tests.

Enterprise C: This enterprise shares the same interests with enterprise A, so we introduced our solution provided for enterprise A to this enterprise. The enterprise's sponsor showed his interest in the GenSpec software, as well as, the proposed change management process, then, we reached an agreement to install and use the proposed solutions. Based on this agreement, one of our team members took an appointment from the person in charge to install the GenSpec software which has been used in the enterprise's current project. For the change management software it has been sent to the enterprise by Email once completed to be installed and used too.

Enterprise D: After agreeing to improve the estimation process, we realized that there was almost no existing process and the documentation needed to make estimation was unavailable. We recommended informally to create the necessary documentation, if possible, to make a first estimation. Unfortunately the enterprise was not able to produce the necessary documentation in the time frame of our research.

This experience shows the difficulty for a VSE to realize some objectives because the basic processes to realize them are not available.

5 Cost and Benefits

The direct benefits of applying an assessment process in the VSE is the increase in the awareness and understanding of software processes and possible improvements, the assessment process also shows the strengths and weaknesses of the assessed processes. Our intervention process in VSE not only has achieved these benefits, but it has deepened the perception and showed practically the benefits of applying process improvement for at least three of them. Our solutions and demonstrations showed the enterprises sponsors how they can deal with the difficulties they are facing in their processes.

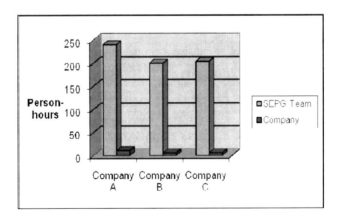

Fig. 1. Intervention cost by enterprise

The cost of the intervention process is measured in person-hours spent in each activity; the intervention activities have been divided into three parts: planning, developing and implementing. Figure 1 shows the number of person-hours spent by the SEPG team members and the enterprise sponsor for each enterprise. Note that enterprise 4 is excluded from the calculations since there was no intervention being made. As shown in Figure 1 the SEPG team has spent the majority of the time for each intervention process for each enterprise. Since our goal is not providing or recommending solutions only but we worked in realizing and implementing these solutions and because of that our SEPG team spent the majority of the time in providing the solutions.

The next figure shows that the SEPG team has spent most of the time in the development activity, this activity includes the development of new software and studying some other software that are already exist.

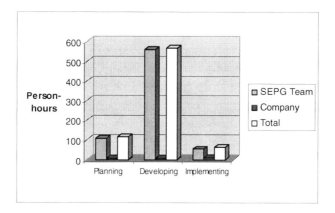

Fig. 2. Intervention cost by activity

Stambollian et. al. [12] have studied the application of the micro-assessment method to assess software process in VSE, the study showed the strengths and weaknesses of this method, and discussed what improvements can be added to get more accurate data and represent the current status more precisely. By analyzing the assessment result and review the questionnaire for the three organizations, we agree on the comments and weaknesses mentioned in Stambollian's et al. article, namely.

1. The questionnaire contains few questions, sometimes covering far too much terrain, which makes the scope of the evaluation too vague
2. Some of the *Micro-Evaluation*'s questions are redundant
3. The questions from the "Customer management" axis of the *Micro-Evaluation* are evidently not adapted to organizations that do not have direct clients (the concept of "client" not having the same definition for those who function on government funding, or for those who produce "off-the-shelf" or "R&D" software, for example). That said, the questions of this axis are mostly centered on managing needs and software requirements anyway, thus eliminating the need to include the "client" concept in this axis.

4. The levels of formalism and objectivity of the acquired answers from a *Micro-Evaluation* assessment are quite low. A solution must be found to increase these levels, to provide more accurate, reliable and objective results.

We also agree that these weaknesses should be resolved to achieve better representation for the assessed organization information. At the end of the intervention process, a small questionnaire has been sent by Email for the three companies involved in the improvement process to explore their opinions about the effort already done and the degree of satisfaction with the results. The responses have been sent back by Email, where the general feeling is that the companies are very interested in the solutions presented to them and that they are satisfied by the work done. They mentioned that they need some time to implement and test these solutions before judging the degree of usefulness of these solutions. Enterprise A has given a quick judgment on the GenSpec software indicating that it fits partially to their needs; we hope that enterprise A will continue using a variation of GenSpec that fit totally their needs, and explore its features and capabilities before giving the final decision later on. Hence, we are agreed to conduct a reassessment process after a reasonable amount of time (about 6 months).

6 Reassessment Process

After the specified period for the implementation and testing of the proposed solutions which is six months, the three organizations have been contacted to make reassessment to measure the progress and benefits resulted from the SPI initiatives. Two of the three organizations namely A and B have committed with the agreement to conduct a reassessment process while the third one organization C does not undertake this process for unknown reasons. The reassessment process has been conducted solely for the process areas that have undertaken an SPI process using the same assessment method. While the achieved improvements do not increase the capability level of each organization to a higher level, the main contribution is to open the eyes of the organization's project leaders and developers on possible solutions to their current problems. Our experience and lessons learned through this empirical study is summarized in the next section.

7 Lessons Learned

Based on the intervention process which took about 4 months, and the reassessment process held 6 months later, we noticed the following:

1. The processes that have been improved are not necessarily the ones found to be the weakest by the OWPL assessment method. The enterprise may decide to improve certain process even if it is not the weakest, which depends on its importance from the enterprise's point of view.

2. The data gathering approach is done in a hybrid method that combines the interview approach with questionnaire approach with fixed number of questions. This provide a convenient method to acquire the data where the interviewer uses a predefined set of questions most of them are open-ended questions, the interviewer can discuss the questions with the interviewee and get a complete answer to the question.
3. The use of supporting tools during the assessment process for managing documents would increase the overhead on the assessment process itself, since our experience with this type of organizations (VSE) showed that the amount of documents to be reviewed is not a problem that needs management tools, keeping in mind that the data are directly extracted from the interviewee.
4. Supporting tools would be useful to analyze the collected data after the assessment process and draw results. On our case an Excel sheet is used as a tool to help analyzing data and drawing figures to draw final results.
5. The reassessment process showed that no significant improvements have been really achieved for processes in question. This result can be referred to the fact that the solutions have not been fully implemented and also the proposed solutions require farther enhancements.
6. Although the primary goal has not been remarkably achieved, as mentioned above, the proposed solutions give a great insight to the different organizations on how to improve their processes by their own methods; this has been indicated explicitly by companies A and B.
7. The commitment from both managers and developers in VSE is one of the critical issues facing successful SPI process and this is conforms the findings of other researches as [13] and [14].
8. The process of developing a software as a solution to the current weakness point undertaking an improvement process is better done by the organization itself (if there is no ready to use software) since the developed software may needs farther improvement and maintenance which may not be provided by the SEPG team or research group.
9. The experience with VSE D shows the difficulty for a VSE to realize some objectives because the basic processes to realize them are not available.

8 Recommendations

As a result of our findings and the lessons learned, we recommend taking the following points into considerations to achieve both successful SPI process and improved OWPL assessment method:

1. The OWPL assessment method should be improved by adding some more specific (close-ended) questions that help giving more precise information, e.g. identify exactly which process area is more critical for the assessed organization.

2. The data gathering process is conducted via interview and questionnaire techniques. The use of some other techniques during this process that ensure participation of people affected by the SPI process, as suggested in [15], would help increase the degree of personnel commitment and increase the probability of achieving successful SPI initiative.
3. The implication of the sponsors and the personnel who are affected by the intervention process should be taken in consideration from the beginning.

9 Conclusions

The micro-evaluation assessment method used as a tool to evaluate the current status of the organizations showed good results that reflect the real situation in the organizations, but this tool needs farther improvement to achieve better image of the organizations by having more precise data.

The main achievement of the intervention process is giving the different sections in the organizations better understanding on how to deal and solve the weakness points in the assessed process areas.

10 Future Work

The next phase of this research is to work on improving the OWPL assessment method to overcome its weaknesses and give more precise information.

Acknowledgment. The authors would like to thank the sponsor's of the companies that participated in our intervention process and agreed to apply our solutions on their ongoing projects.

References

1. Laporte, C.Y., Alexandre, S., O'Connor, R.: A Software Engineering Lifecycle Standard for Very Small Enterprises. In: O'Connor, R.V., Baddoo, N., Smolander, K., Messnarz, R. (eds.) EuroSPI 2008. CCIS, vol. 16, pp. 129–141. Springer, Heidelberg (2008)
2. Habra, N., et al.: Software Process Improvement in Small Organizations Using Gradual Evaluation Schema. In: International Conference on Product Focused Software Process Improvement, Oulu, Finland (1999)
3. Alexandre, S., Renault, A., Habra, N.: OWPL: A Gradual Approach for Software Process Improvement in SMEs. In: 32nd EUROMICRO Conference on Software Engineering and Advanced Applications, pp. 328–335 (2006)
4. Desharnais, J.M., et al.: Initiating Software Process Improvement with a light model for Small Enterprise: Our Experience. In: 3rd International Workshop on Quality of Information and Communication Technologies, Havana - Cuba (2007)
5. Laporte, C., et al.: Initiating Software Process Improvement in Small Enterprises: Experiments with Micro-Evaluation Framework. In: SWDC-REK International Conference on Software Development, Rekjavick, Iceland (2005)

6. Habra, N., et al.: Software Process Improvement for Small Structures: First Results of a Micro-Assessment Framework. In: European Conference on Software Process Improvement SPI 1999, Barcelona, Spain (1999)
7. Habra, N., et al.: OWPL Micro Assessment. In: Software Quality Workshop, 24th International Conference on Software Engineering ICSE, ACM, USA (2002)
8. Habra, N., Renault, A.: OWPL Une Méthodologie et des Modèles Légers pour Initier une Démarche d'Amélioration des Pratiques Logicielles APL. In: Ingénierie des Systèmes d'Information (2004)
9. Desharnais, J.M., Zarour, M., April, A.: Very Small Enterprises (VSE) Quality Process Assessment. In: 3rd International Workshop on Quality of Information and Communication Technologies, Havana - Cuba (2007)
10. Zarour, M., Desharnais, J.-M., Abran, A.: A Framework to Compare Software Process Assessment Methods Dedicated to Small and Very Small Organizations. In: International Conference on Software Quality - ICSQ 2007, USA (2007)
11. Zarour, M., et al.: Design and Implementation of Lightweight Software Process Assessment Methods: Survey of Best Practices. In: Proceedings of the 10th Software Process Improvement & Capability Determination Conference (SPICE 2010), Pisa, Italy (2010)
12. Stambollian, A., et al.: OWPL: A Light Model & Methodology for Initiation Software Process Improvement. In: SPICE 2006, Luxembourg (2006)
13. Niazi, M., Wilson, D., Zowghi, D.: Critical Success Factors for Software Process Improvement Implementation: An Empirical Study. Software Process Improvement and Practice 11(2) (2006)
14. Dangle, K.C., et al.: Software process improvement in small organizations: a case study. IEEE Software 22(6), 68–75 (2005)
15. Moe, N.B., Dybå, T.: Improving by Involving: A Case Study in a Small Software Company. In: Richardson, I., Runeson, P., Messnarz, R. (eds.) EuroSPI 2006. LNCS, vol. 4257, pp. 159–170. Springer, Heidelberg (2006)

A Hierarchy of SPI Activities for Software SMEs: Results from ISO/IEC 12207-Based SPI Assessments

Paul Clarke[1], Rory V. O'Connor[2,3], and Murat Yilmaz[1]

[1] Lero Graduate School in Software Engineering, Dublin City University, Ireland
{pclarke,myilmaz}@computing.dcu.ie
[2] Dublin City University, Ireland
[3] Lero, The Irish Software Engineering Research Centre
roconnor@computing.dcu.ie

Abstract. In an assessment of software process improvement (SPI) in 15 software small- and –medium-sized enterprises (software SMEs), we applied the broad spectrum of software specific and system context processes in ISO/IEC 12207 to the task of examining SPI in practice. Using the data collected in the study, we developed a four-tiered pyramidal hierarchy of SPI for software SMEs, with processes in the higher tiers undergoing SPI in more companies than processes on lower level tiers. The development of the hierarchy of SPI activities for software SMEs can facilitate future evolutions of process maturity reference frameworks, such as ISO/IEC 15504, in better supporting software development in software SMEs. Furthermore, the findings extend our body of knowledge concerning the practice of SPI in software SMEs, a large and vital sector of the software development community that has largely avoided the implementation of established process maturity and software quality management standards.

Keywords: Software development process, SPI, software SMEs.

1 Introduction

Software process maturity frameworks such as ISO/IEC 15504 [1] and the Capability Maturity Model Integrated (CMMI) [2] provide structured and proven paths to improved process maturity. Software process maturity is "the extent to which a specific software process is explicitly defined, managed, measured, controlled and effective" [3], with higher levels of process maturity being associated with higher product quality, reduced production costs [4], and with increased predictability of the process results [5], [6]. Although process maturity reference frameworks can deliver benefits to any type of software development organisation, evidence from earlier studies suggests their adoption would appear to be mostly concentrated in large organisations [7], [8]. Some earlier research has investigated the reasons for non-adoption of process maturity reference frameworks in the software SME sector, with the finding that software SMEs view process maturity frameworks as being infeasible (i.e. overly time-consuming or costly to implement) rather than non-beneficial [9-11].

Although software SMEs tend to not implement process maturity frameworks, they nonetheless require a software development process in order to produce and maintain software products. The software process can be implemented in a formal or informal manner, but in order to best address the needs of the organisation "it is reasonable to assume that the optimal process is not static but is organization-dependent and time-dependent, and will have to be modified as the context in which the organization operates evolves" [12]. With organisational context regularly changing, companies need to continually adapt their software development processes in order to maximise the efficiency and effectiveness of their software development efforts. However, despite the obvious theoretical benefits of adopting a strong software development process focus, evidence from recent studies suggests that in practice, software SMEs can adopt a low process priority [13], tending only to implement SPI in response to negative business events [14]. Given this gap between the theory and practice, it is the view of the authors of this paper that we need to develop a much greater understanding of SPI as practiced in software SMEs.

In order to develop a better understanding of SPI as practiced in software SMEs, we designed a study that investigates SPI across the broadest possible range of software development processes. As we shall present in this paper, our study permits the development of a hierarchy of process areas in terms of their importance for SPI in software SMEs. The development of this classification extends our knowledge of SPI as practiced in software SMEs, and provides valuable information that can assist future evolutions of process reference frameworks in addressing the needs of software SMEs.

The remainder of this paper is structured as follows: Section 2 provides an overview of our study, including details of the approach to data collection and the participating organisations; Section 3 presents a hierarchy of SPI as practiced in software SMEs, along with some recommendations for future research directions and field studies. Finally, Section 4 discusses the importance of the findings along with some concluding remarks.

2 Study Overview

The study presented in this paper is primarily concerned with examining the extent of SPI implemented in software SMEs over a 12 month period. In order to examine the extent of SPI implemented in an organisation, it is possible to utilise the process assessment vehicles associated with process maturity reference frameworks. For example, an ISO/IEC 15504 assessment could be conducted at the commencement of the 12 months under investigation, hence establishing the process maturity at the start of the period under investigation. At the end of the period of investigation, a second process assessment could be conducted, this time establishing the process maturity at the end of the year. A comparative analysis of the two process assessment results could thereafter being employed so as to determine the amount of SPI conducted during the elapsed period of time.

While two process assessments, followed by a finite difference analysis, could be employed in order to determine the amount of SPI implemented in an organisation, there are a number of reasons why this approach is considered unsuited to the needs of this study. Firstly, this study is concerned with examining SPI in software SMEs, a sector that has traditionally declined to implement process maturity reference frameworks. Secondly, process assessments are concerned with collecting data in relation to process maturity. Although this study is interested in examining the extent of SPI implemented in software SMEs, it is not concerned with the degree process maturity in the participating organisations and therefore, the collection of process maturity data would represent an inefficient approach to collecting the data required for this research. A third reason for not employing process assessments in this research relates to the time requirement for the discharge of two process assessments. Gaining access to participating organisations is a difficult challenge for researchers and the research team felt that the large amount of time required to conduct two process assessments might act as a further disincentive for the candidate software SMEs who might consider participating in this study.

Given the limitations of process assessments as outlined above, we formulated a new, more efficient approach to examining the amount SPI implemented in software SMEs, an approach that does not require the collection of process maturity data and a subsequent finite difference analysis. Conceptually, our new approach requires that an organisation is asked to identify the instances of SPI as implemented in their organisations over the past 12 months. In order for such an approach to be reliable, it is important that as a basis, the instrument of inquiry is developed from a recognised, comprehensive process reference framework. Although a number of candidate reference frameworks exist, it is the view of the authors that no single framework offers greater scope than ISO/IEC 12207 [15].

2.1 ISO/IEC 12207 Software Development Process Reference Framework

ISO/IEC 12207 identifies a comprehensive set of software development processes – covering not just the core activities related to software developed (which ISO/IEC 12207 terms *Software specific processes*) but also including the additional related processes required for the housing of software development activities in the broader processes that are required for conducting business (which ISO/IEC 12207 terms *System context processes*). In total, there are 43 individual processes identified in ISO/IEC 12207, with these processes being broken down into over 400 process tasks (refer to Figure 1).

As well as offering a broad set of core and supporting software development processes, ISO/IEC 12207 is also considered to be suited to the needs of this study because of the consensual nature of the development and maintenance of the process reference framework. This consensual nature is exemplified by the approach adopted by the International Organization for Standardisation (ISO) when drafting, accepting and evolving standards – whereby 75% of the participating national bodies must approve a standard prior to publication [15]. In addition to the rigorous and consensual nature of the ISO's standard acceptance criteria, ISO/IEC 12207 has also been developed in collaboration with the Institute of Electrical and Electronic Engineers (IEEE) Computer Society, hence further ensuring that ISO/IEC 12207 is comprehensive in nature and generally accepted by the broader software development community.

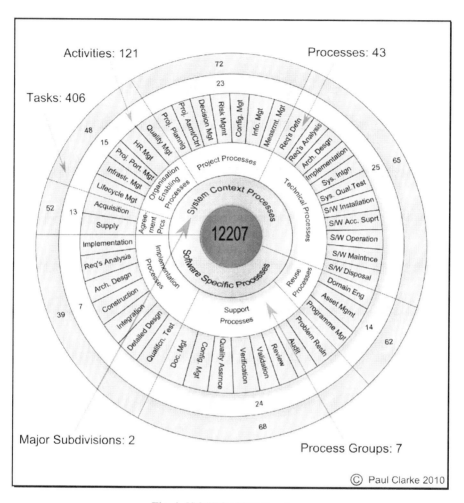

Fig. 1. ISO/IEC 12207 Topology

In addition to the reasons cited above for adopting ISO/IEC 12207 for this study, a further important consideration relates to the independence of ISO/IEC 12207. Since a number of software SMEs will participate in this study, and considering that they may all adopt different process development methodologies, it is important that the chosen software development process reference framework is independent of any particular, prescribed software development approach. Since ISO/IEC 12207 provides a "meta-model that defines common software engineering activities independently of a particular life-cycle model" [16], it is considered to offer an ideal reference framework for the type of study that we wanted to conduct. While ISO/IEC 12207 is well suited to the requirements of this study, the standard does not natively present in a form that permits the investigation of the amount of SPI implemented in a software development organisation. Therefore, this study developed a systematic method for converting ISO/IEC 12207 to a survey instrument suited to the task of investigation the amount of SPI conducted in a company over a period of time.

2.2 Technique for Converting ISO/IEC 12207 to a SPI Survey Instrument

In order to adapt ISO/IEC 12207 [15] for the purpose of investigating the amount of SPI implemented in software SMEs over a period of time, it is necessary to first fully analyse the standard, becoming intimately familiar with all of the details that are contained within the standard. These details are first extracted to a master list of questions that can be employed in order to determine the amount of SPI in an organisation over a period of time. Since ISO/IEC 12207 incorporates a large degree of cross-referencing of processes, the next step in the survey instrument development is to remove instances of duplication in the questions. Following the removal of duplications, the list of questions is further distilled in order to meet practical considerations – for example, the time required to discharge the survey instrument.

Subsequent survey instrument development steps include a reordering of the questions so as to ensure that the survey instrument has a suitable flow, and the engagement of external expert reviewers. In the case of the independent expert review, current and former editors of ISO/IEC 12207 along with other experts familiar with ISO/IEC 12207, are engaged so as to examine multiple aspects of the draft SPI survey instrument, including content, scope and look and feel. Following feedback from the independent expert reviewers, a number of updates were made to the SPI survey instrument. Thereafter, the survey instrument was subject to a pilot phase with an industry partner, after which the survey instrument was again updated based on the industry feedback. Extensive details on the conversion of ISO/IEC 12207 to the SPI survey instrument are available in an earlier published work [17].

In its final form, the SPI survey instrument contained 63 questions that took the general form of: *"Over the past year, has there been any modification in the approach to...[some aspect of the software development process]?"* In responding to the questions, the interviewees were asked to rate the degree of process modification according to a four point Likert scale, as follows: 0 = no modification; 1 = minor modification; 2= major modification; and 3 = significant modification.

Having systematically developed our SPI survey instrument from ISO/IEC 12207, the next step in the study was to secure the engagement of participating software SMEs, followed by a discharge of the survey instrument in order to collect SPI data from the participating organisations.

2.3 SPI Data Collection

The SPI survey instrument was deployed to a total of 15 participating companies between March and July 2011. Each of the participating organisations satisfied the

European Commission definition of an SME [18]. Within each of the participating organisations, a suitable participant was identified; most commonly, the interviewee held the job title of Software Development Manager, Engineering Manager or Director of Engineering – in all cases, the interviewee was identified as the most appropriate person in the organisation to address the broad scope of inquiry covered by the SPI survey instrument. The participating software SMEs varied in terms of the headcount: 3 of the participating companies had less than 10 staff; 4 companies had between 10 and 19 staff; the remaining 8 companies had between 20 and 129 staff.

Predominately, the participating organisations were primarily located in Ireland. However, in some cases, the organisations were mostly located outside of Ireland, in places such as the US and Chile. Where possible, the interviews were conducted face-to-face with telephone interviews being employed in a small number of cases (for example, where the interviewee was based in a remote location). The interviews required approximately 2 hours to complete, giving a total interview time of ~30 hours. Irrespective of whether the interview was conducted face-to-face or via telephone, the interview was (with the consent of the interviewee) recorded and later, the interview recording was carefully examined to ensure that the responses of the interviewee were accurately and complete documented in electronic form.

In addition to generally being extremely busy, candidate organisations were somewhat cautious about revealing information regarding the internal workings of the company. In order to assuage such concerns, a number of procedures were implemented: (1) each of the participating organisations was allocated a random pseudonym such that the identity of the organisations was not divulged; (2) all recordings, be they stored on portable or fixed devices, were securely encrypted; and (3) the researchers developed a bi-lateral non-disclosure agreement that could be employed to further reinforce the confidence of the participating organisation regarding the privacy and security of the data.

Following the completion of the interviews in the 15 participating organisations, the researchers collected a large volume of data in relation to SPI as practiced in software SMEs. The next step in to apply the study data towards the development a hierarchy of SPI activities for software SMEs.

3   Hierarchy of SPI Activities for Software SMEs

An analysis of the SPI reported in this study permits the development of a hierarchy of SPI processes, as implemented in practice in software SMEs. Since the SPI survey instrument was developed from ISO/IEC 12207 (refer to Section 2), it is possible to map each of the questions in the survey instrument back to the originating process in ISO/IEC 12207. Using this mapping, we constructed a hierarchy of ISO/IEC 12207 processes in terms of the processes being targets for SPI, i.e. processes that constitute the top tier of the pyramidal hierarchy underwent SPI in a greater number of organisations than processes that are on the second tier of the hierarchy; with processes on the second tier of the hierarchy undergoing SPI in a greater number of organisations than processes that are on the third tier, etc. The resulting hierarchy is presented in Figure 2.

From the SPI hierarchy pyramid presented in Figure 2, it can be seen that there are nine key software processes that undergoing SPI most frequently in software SME. Some of these processes have been reported in earlier studies, while others have not. For example, earlier related studies demonstrated that software SMEs derived both short- and long-term benefits from SPI in areas such as requirements analysis, configuration management and project planning [19-23]. However, no earlier published study indicated that infrastructure management, installation, and supply were key process improvement targets for software SMEs. This is perhaps owing to the broad nature of the inquiry in this study. Earlier studies may have focused just on the software specific processes as identified in ISO/IEC 12207. However, the infrastructure management, installation, and supply processes are all system lifecycle processes and therefore, broader in scope than the purely software specific process grouping.

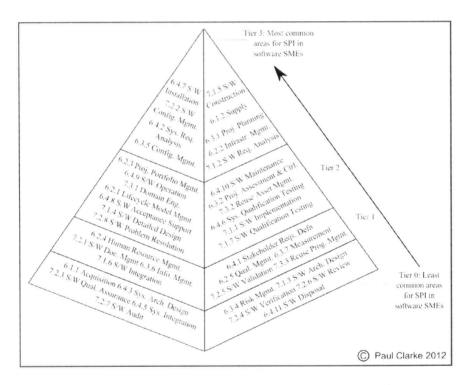

Fig. 2. ISO/IEC 12207 based SPI hierarchy for software SME [1]

---

[1] There are 43 individual processes identified in ISO/IEC 12207. The Implementation Process (6.4.4) is wholly defined by the Software Implementation Process (7.1.1) and is therefore not separately included in the hierarchy. Following feedback from independent expert reviewers, the Decision Management Process (6.3.3) was not included in the survey instrument – it was the view of the reviewers that this process was beyond the scope of software SMEs. Therefore, the resulting hierarchy presented in Figure 2 has 41 individual processes included.

In the lowest tier of the SPI hierarchy, Tier 0, there are ten key software processes. As with the processes in the highest tier of the pyramid, a number of these processes have been identified in earlier studies, while others have not been. For example, earlier related studies have highlighted that software SMEs can adopt a low process focus [13], electing only to implement process improvements in response to negative business events [14]. Therefore, it is not surprising to discover that the software quality assurance, software review, risk management, and software audit processes are all to be found on the lowest tier of the hierarchy – though clearly, for the software process and SPI community, this is certainly disappointing.

On the lowest tier of the SPI hierarchy pyramid, we also find a number of additional processes that do not appear to have been identified in earlier published studies – though it should be noted that earlier related works were not necessarily concerned with identifying the low priority processes for SPI in software SMEs. The additional low priority processes identified in this study are: acquisition, system and software architecture design, system integration, software verification and software disposal. Of these processes, the inclusion of the software architecture and system architecture design processes is of considerable interest. The feedback from the study participants indicates quite strongly that software SMEs do not necessarily make a distinction between architectural and detailed design efforts. Essentially, the responses from participants indicate that the architecture and detailed design processes are effectively bundled into a single activity. Therefore, this represents a good example of where the ISO/IEC 12207 process reference listing is beyond the scope of software SMEs. While ISO/IEC 12207 does permit that the process selection can be tailored for different settings, it does not permit that two separate processes can be merged into a single process. Therefore, the general infrastructure of the ISO/IEC 12207 framework is perhaps over-extended for the purposes of software SMEs. This finding also has implications for ISO/IEC 15504 which utilises ISO/IEC 12207 as the underlying process reference framework, a finding which we discuss further in section 3.1.

3.1 Recommendations for Future SPI Assessments and Studies

Taking the data from this study, it is possible to develop a number of recommendations for future SPI assessments and studies:

Recommendation 1: In order to maximize the effectiveness of future SPI studies and assessments in software SMEs, it is considered beneficial to treat architectural and design activities as a single activity (rather than as two separate activities as identified in ISO/IEC 12207).

Recommendation 2: In order to maximize the effectiveness of future SPI studies and assessments in software SMEs, where there is strong overlap between system lifecycle and software specific processes (e.g. requirements analysis and configuration management processes), researchers should consider merging the system life cycle and software processes into a single thread of inquiry.

Recommendation 3: Future SPI studies seeking to identify the high priority process improvements for software SMEs should consider omitting those processes that are in Tier 0 of the SPI hierarchy pyramid (ref. Fig. 2).

In the case of Recommendation 1, the evidence of this study indicates that software SMEs rarely differentiate between architectural and design considerations. Future assessments and studies of SPI in software SMEs should not necessarily remove either the design or architecture activities but rather, should merge them into a single thread of investigation. In the case of Recommendation 2, although we find considerable evidence of important SPI occurring to the system life cycle processes of ISO/IEC 12207, SMEs can find it difficult to distinguish between system life cycle level activities and core software specific activities. As indicated by our independent expert reviewers, this can particularly be the case where there is a software specific process that has a corresponding parent system level process; for example, the system requirements analysis process and the software requirements analysis processes. We therefore recommend that where there is a strong overlap between a system life cycle process and a software specific process, these two processes can be merged into a single spoke of inquiry. In relation to Recommendation 3, since our study (along with earlier studies [13], [14]) has indicated that software SMEs can have a low process priority, future studies examining the key processes for SPI in software SMEs should consider omitting processes on Tier 0 of the SPI hierarchy (ref. Figure 2).

3.2 Recommendations for Versions of Process Reference Frameworks

We have one further important recommendation, this time regarding future versions of process maturity frameworks. As a research community, we need to start developing new thinking regarding the utility of reference frameworks and quality management standards for the software SME sector. Furthermore, framework authors and those responsible for writing software process standards should consider extending existing process reference and process assessment models to more accurately reflect and support software development as practiced in software SMEs. Although software SMEs are a large and vital component of the overall software development landscape, they have to-date failed to embrace established process maturity and quality management frameworks. Whatever the reason for the failure to adopt these approaches, it seems unlikely at this stage that software SMEs will ever implement these approaches to any great extent. Given the extensive wealth of knowledge, wisdom and experience incorporated into existing process maturity and quality management standards, it is very disappointing that they are not more widely adopted in software SMEs. In an earlier published work, the authors of this paper highlighted the importance of further integration of the dynamic capability concept into process maturity and quality management standards [24]. Dynamic capability relates to the ability to adapt a process in response to changes in the environment and is considered to be representative of an evolutionary mechanism, as espoused in the *evolutionary* theory of the firm [25].

The dynamic capability concept is not entirely absent in existing process maturity frameworks, it is in fact the embodiment of the highest level of process maturity, the *optimising* level. That the concept of optimising is an existing component of process maturity frameworks is considered by the authors to be hugely positive, however, that an organisation should only optimise of the highest maturity level is considered a drawback. The need to optimise, adapt and evolve is a continuous consideration and one for which it may be difficult to fully prescribe a maturity framework – since all successful organisations and organisms are considered successful if they respond to their particular set (as opposed to some general set) of environmental challenges and changes. As Prof. Harvey Fineberg states: *"Evolution... doesn't necessarily favour the biggest or the strongest or the fastest and not even the smartest. Evolution favours those creatures best adapted to their environment, that is the sole test of survival and success"* [26]. Companies, like creatures, must also evolve relative to their particular environment.

Therefore, our fourth recommendation is that we develop new thinking in terms of how process maturity and quality management standards can better assist software SMEs, and to this end, we recommend greater integration of dynamic capability concepts. Naturally, increased integration of dynamic capability into existing process maturity and quality management standards should benefit organisations of all sizes, not just software SMEs.

Recommendation 4: In order to benefit software SMEs, future evolutions of process maturity frameworks and quality management standards should further integrate dynamic capability concepts.

4 Conclusion

In our study of 15 software SMEs, we find that the software quality assurance, software audit, software review and risk management processes are in receipt of very little process improvement focus. The collective lack of attention on these three processes highlights a major impediment for the adoption of process maturity frameworks and quality management frameworks (such as ISO 9000 [27]) in software SMEs. The evidence of this study suggests that software SMEs do not embrace some of the most basic principles of process maturity and quality management frameworks. Such basic principles include the adoption of a process focus, the explicit awareness of process activities (preferably in documented form), the reflection on the efficacy of the adopted software process, and the improvement of the software process in line with recommended process improvement paths. There is therefore a significant gap in the fundamental process thinking promoted by process maturity and quality management frameworks, and the reality of process implementation in software SMEs.

Despite the noted gap in process thinking between software SMEs and process maturity and quality management frameworks, there is some encouragement to be taken from the fact that some process areas were reported as having experienced relatively high levels of SPI. These areas include configuration management, requirements analysis, infrastructure management and project planning. We are therefore presented with something of a conundrum: on the one hand software SMEs appear unwilling to embrace a strong software process focus while on the other hand they do appear to be quite capable of realising instances of software process improvements.

It is the view of the authors of this paper that as a research community, we should work to find new ways to maximize the ability of software SMEs to realise software process improvements. This view is based on the premise that some SPI is better than no SPI at all. Software SMEs have largely failed to implement long-established process maturity and quality management frameworks; with the result that we have good reason to believe that they will continue to avoid adopting such approaches to software processes and SPI. However, as with organisations of all sizes, it is important to continually optimise business processes in software SMEs (incl. the software development process) and consequently, there is an unavoidable need for SPI. Perhaps the extensive knowledge and experience encapsulated in established process maturity and quality management frameworks can be reoriented such that the principle of process optimisation is more central to the basic demands of the frameworks (rather than being a highest maturity level activity alone). Developments in this direction may encourage software SMEs to consider the implementation of software process and SPI frameworks and in so doing would help to improve the competitive advantage and success prospects of software SMEs. Since most software development companies are SMEs, this would appear to be a worthy pursuit.

Acknowledgments. This work is supported, in part, by Science Foundation Ireland grant 03/CE2/I303_1 to Lero, the Irish Software Engineering Research Centre (www.lero.ie).

References

1. ISO/IEC: 15504-1 information technology - process assessment - part 1: Concepts and vocabulary. ISO/IEC, Geneva, Switzerland (2004)
2. SEI: CMMI for development, version 1.2. Software Engineering Institute, CMU/SEI-2006-TR-008, Pittsburgh, PA, USA (2006)
3. Paulk, M.C., Curtis, B., Chrissis, M.B., et al.: Capability maturity model for software. Version 1.1 edn. Software Engineering Institute, Carnegie Mellon University, CMU/SEI-93-TR-24, Pittsburgh, Pennsylvania, USA (1993)
4. Harter, D.E., Slaughter, S.A.: Quality Improvement and Infrastructure Activity Costs in Software Development: A Longitudinal Analysis. Management Science 49(6), 784–800 (2003)
5. Ferguson, P., Leman, G., Perini, P., et al.: Software process improvement works! CMU/SEI-99-TR-027. Software Engineering Institute, Carnegie Mellon University, Pittsburgh, Pennsylvania, USA (1999)
6. Harrison, W., Settle, J., Raffo, D.: Assessing the Value of Improved Predictability due to Process Improvements. In: 3rd International Workshop on Economics-Driven Software Engineering Research (EDSER-3). IEEE Computer Society, Los Alamitos (2001)

7. Gibson, D., Goldenson, D., Kost, K.: Performance results of CMMI-Based Process Improvement. Software Engineering Institute, Carnegie Mellon University, CMU/SEI-2006-TR-004, Pittsburgh, Pennsylvania, USA (2006)
8. Herbsleb, J., Goldenson, D.: A systematic survey of CMM experience and results. In: Proceedings of the 18th International Conference on Software Engineering (ICSE 1996), pp. 323–330. IEEE Computer Society, Los Alamitos (1996)
9. Saastamoinen, I., Tukiainen, M.: Software Process Improvement in Small and Medium Sized Software Enterprises in Eastern Finland: A State-of-the-Practice Study. In: Dingsøyr, T. (ed.) EuroSPI 2004. LNCS, vol. 3281, pp. 69–78. Springer, Heidelberg (2004)
10. Staples, M., Niazi, M., Jeffery, R., Abrahams, A., Byatt, P., Murphy, R.: An Exploratory Study of Why Organizations do Not Adopt CMMI. Journal of Systems and Software 80(6), 883–895 (2007)
11. Khurshid, N., Bannerman, P.L., Staples, M.: Overcoming the First Hurdle: Why Organizations Do Not Adopt CMMI. In: Wang, Q., Garousi, V., Madachy, R., Pfahl, D. (eds.) ICSP 2009. LNCS, vol. 5543, pp. 38–49. Springer, Heidelberg (2009)
12. Poulin, L.A.: Achieving the Right Balance between Process Maturity and Performance. IEEE Canadian Review 56, 23–26 (2007)
13. Baddoo, N., Hall, T.: De-Motivators for Software Process Improvement: An Analysis of Practitioners' Views. Journal of Systems and Software 66(1), 23–33 (2003)
14. Coleman, G., O'Connor, R.: Investigating Software Process in Practice: A Grounded Theory Perspective. Journal of Systems and Software 81(5), 772–784 (2008)
15. ISO: Amendment to ISO/IEC 12207-2008 - systems and software engineering – software life cycle processes. ISO, Geneva, Switzerland (2008)
16. Tilley, T., Cole, R., Becker, P., Eklund, P.: A Survey of Formal Concept Analysis Support for Software Engineering Activities. In: Ganter, B., Stumme, G., Wille, R. (eds.) Formal Concept Analysis. LNCS (LNAI), vol. 3626, pp. 250–271. Springer, Heidelberg (2005)
17. Clarke, P., O'Connor, R.: Harnessing ISO/IEC 12207 to Examine the Extent of SPI Activity in an Organisation. In: Riel, A., O'Connor, R., Tichkiewitch, S., Messnarz, R. (eds.) EuroSPI 2010. CCIS, vol. 99, pp. 25–36. Springer, Heidelberg (2010)
18. European Commission: Commission Recommendation of 6 may 2003 Concerning the Definition of Micro, Small and Medium-Sized Enterprises. 2003/361/EC. Official Journal of the European Union, L (124), 36–41 (2003)
19. Sanders, M. (ed.): The SPIRE handbook. better, faster, cheaper software development in small organisations. Centre for Software Engineering Limited, DCU, Dublin, Ireland (1998)
20. Sanders, M., Richardson, I.: Research into Long-Term Improvements in Small- to Medium-Sized Organisations using SPICE as a Framework for Standards. Software Process: Improvement and Practice 12(4), 351–359 (2007)
21. Cater-Steel, A., Rout, T.: SPI long-term benefits: Case studies of five small firms. In: Oktaba, H. (ed.) Software Process Improvement for Small and Medium Enterprises - Techniques and Case Studies. Information Science Reference, London (2008)
22. Fleck, D.: A Process for Very Small Projects. In: Proceedings of the 22nd Annual Pacific Northwest Software Quality Conference, pp. 107–115. PNSQC/Pacific Agenda, Portland, Oregon (2004)
23. Montoni, M., Rocha, A.R.: A Methodology for Identifying Critical Success Factors That Influence Software Process Improvement Initiatives: An Application in the Brazilian Software Industry. In: Abrahamsson, P., Baddoo, N., Margaria, T., Messnarz, R. (eds.) EuroSPI 2007. LNCS, vol. 4764, pp. 175–186. Springer, Heidelberg (2007)

24. Clarke, P., O'Connor, R.V.: An Approach to Evaluating Software Process Adaptation. In: O'Connor, R.V., Rout, T., McCaffery, F., Dorling, A. (eds.) SPICE 2011. CCIS, vol. 155, pp. 28–41. Springer, Heidelberg (2011)
25. Nelson, R.R., Winter, S.: An evolutionary theory of economic change. The Balknap Press of Harvard University Press, Cambridge (1982)
26. Fineberg, H.: Are we ready for neo-evolution?, http://www.ted.com/talks/harvey_fineberg_are_we_ready_for_neo_evolution.html
27. ISO: ISO/IEC 9003:2004 - software engineering - guidelines for the application of ISO 9001:2000 to computer software. ISO, Geneva, Switzerland (2004)

Innovation, Knowledge- and Technology Transfer Process Capability Model – innoSPICE™

Jeremy Besson[1], Tanja Woronowicz[2], Antanas Mitasiunas[1], and Michael Boronowsky[2]

[1] Vilnius University, 3 Universiteto Street, Vilnius, LT-01315, Lithuania
[2] Bremen University, TZI, Am Fallturm 1, Bremen, 28359, Germany
`contact.jeremy.besson@gmail.com, worono@tzi.de, antanas.mitasiunas@maf.vu.lt, mb@tzi.de`

Abstract. The constant technological improvement of products, services, processes and work environment is a critical factor for the development of our economy and society. It strongly depends on the ability to develop knowledge and technology, to transfer it from the point of generation to the site of adaptation and application and to put the technology into use for the benefit of the acquirers and transferors. So far, there is no widely accepted, reliable, predictable and efficient method to evaluate to what extent an organization performs such activities, i.e., innovation, knowledge- and technology transfer (IKaTT). To cope with this problem, we propose to adopt a process-oriented point of view where outcome quality is achieved by the means of process quality. This paper introduces a SPICE conformant innovation, knowledge and technology transfer process capability model that reuses the existing capability dimension of ISO/IEC 15504 to assess knowledge and technology development, transfer and innovation.

Keywords: Knowledge & technology transfer (IKaTT), innovation, capability model, SPICE.

1 Introduction

A key challenge for developing a sustainable and growing economy is the continuous improvement of products, services, processes and work environment. It strongly depends on our ability to develop new technologies, to transfer them from the point of generation to the site of adaptation and application and to put the technologies into practical use for the benefit of the acquirers and transferors. Even if, nowadays, technology is part of our daily-life, we still face critical hindrances to succeeding in transfer activities.

For example, even though universities are important developers of new technologies, their achievements are often only published to the scientific community and not commercialized. SMEs often lack of resources to fully exploit knowledge and technologies for their innovative products. Transfer offices often act in a passive way, i.e., reacting only on demand. They are mainly transfer facilitators rather than transfer drivers. Big companies often close the loop of commercialization internally.

Technology transfer activities take place in quite different ways, depending on traditions, resources and economic structures, but always depending on the active commitment and participation of the involved actors within their organizational structures. Conventionally, innovation, knowledge and technology transfer (IKaTT) is treated as a black box that is studied by comparison of its input and output using statistical data. The proposed approach is a "white box" approach, i.e. it is an attempt to dissect innovation and technology transfer activities into its single processes and performance descriptions. We propose to employ the process-oriented modeling paradigm developed in CMMI [2,3,4], ISO/IEC 15504 [9,10] and iCMM [8].

The main contribution of this work is the development of a conformant ISO/IEC 15504 external process reference model and process assessment model called *innoSPICE*. IKaTT activities that are a priori complex, creative at some extent and organization-dependent, are expressed here in generic process-oriented terms. *innoSPICE* can be used together with the existing capability measurement framework of ISO/IEC 15504 to assess organizations involved in IKaTT activities. *innoSPICE* is based on the results of the European Project BONITA [1] that was financed under the Baltic Sea Region INTERREG 4B program. The process reference model presented in this paper directly originates from the strong practical and theoretical knowledge and experience of BONITA partners in innovation, knowledge and technology transfer. The *innoSPICE* process reference and assessment model have been evaluated in more than 30 research and transfer organizations, ministries, science parks and business development agencies in 13 European countries. During these assessments, the model has proven its applicability and showed that it has already reached an implementation level.

The proposed standards-based *innoSPICE* is applicable to all knowledge intense institutions for generating efficiency gains in the field of innovation and helping investors and research institutions optimize public funds to achieve economic added value. It is the basis for setting up quality management systems in innovation, knowledge- and technology transfer and comes along with important improvements within the innovation cycle:

- **Turning research organizations into knowledge suppliers:** *innoSPICE* supports the identification of relevant partners for research collaborations, securing the quality of the IKaTT-processes. *innoSPICE* is the base to operate the concept of knowledge suppliers. For example, a company that is contracting R&D to a scientific partner might use *innoSPICE* as a proof of competence, similar to how the ISO 15504/SPICE approach is used for suppliers. With a transfer capability assessment, research organizations, on the other hand, can document their interest to be a valuable partner for innovation. This establishes important new aspects of quality for research-intense organizations, and will motivate them to improve for competing as best partners for innovation.
- **Awareness Raising:** *innoSPICE* also documents the need for specific capabilities of organizations in order to perform successful IKaTT activities. This increases the awareness that excellent research does not necessarily lead to innovation, but has to have an active part in the transfer process. The mechanisms of knowledge and

technology transfer and the role and responsibilities of specific organizations become clear and manageable.
- **Self Evaluation:** Offering an instrument for organizations to analyze their own transfer capabilities increases transparency of their own "position" within the economic value chain from idea generation to innovation. Knowing this position is an important element in improving the overall knowledge and technology transfer performance. Following the well-known Plan-Do-Check-Act cycle (Deming Cycle) in management, it is important to enable checking the performance of an organization. The *innoSPICE* model provides a transfer-specific process reference and assessment model that is suitable to assist process improvements. A potential *innoSPICE* certification could prove an organization's capability of the IKaTT-relevant processes and their aspired improvement. This will help develop more mature organizations with improved capabilities that can contribute more to the innovation value chain. Beside this, public R&D organizations might get better support for targeted improvement actions by making challenges more explicit to the funding bodies. Instead of discussing opportunities for organizational improvements on an abstract level, they are identified concretely. This provides a better argumentation for investing in research infrastructures and makes such investments more transparent.
- **Certification of transfer capability:** Moving public innovation and transfer quality management towards standardization will introduce important new opportunities. Certification will be valuable for the evaluation of project funding. On the one hand, a certificate for transfer capability can be established as an evaluation criterion for research consortia when specific transfer results are expected from a program. On the other hand, knowing the transfer capabilities of organizations enables public funding bodies to shift responsibility regarding commercialization and exploitation to the partners without increasing the detailed controlling on micro level. In practice, it has turned out that over-controlling hinders the flexibility to react on transfer opportunities. Funding in research should generally be an investment for sustainable growth, thus it is important that the receivers of research funds can show that they are able to take responsibility of their parts in turning knowledge to innovation. Certification will be an important and objective element to implement these mechanisms.

The paper is organized as following. Section 2 introduces important notions of knowledge and technology development, transfer and innovation. Section 3 presents the *innoSPICE* external process model. The last section briefly concludes.

2 Turning Knowledge- and Technology via Transfer into Innovation

The European Commission states that there is an "urgent need to improve data availability and the breadth and quality of indicators to measure and monitor innovation performance, ranging from technological innovation to other forms of innovation, e.g., public sector innovation" [5]. An innovation is a new or significantly improved product (good or service), process, marketing or organizational method implemented with value to the organization [12,14].

Regarding so-called "science-based technologies", defined as fields with frequent references to scientific knowledge such as biotechnology, information and communication technologies, nanotechnology, new material technology and optical technology, industry-science links have become a key dimension for innovation. Via knowledge and technology transfer, universities and other public research institutes are expected to be not only producers of basic knowledge: the know-how they generate should be transferred into commercial activities whenever relevant. But, as with customer satisfaction in industry or employee motivation, the "transfer capability" and "innovative potential" of a research organization is difficult to report in terms of hard data and facts, and hence, is not easy to manage.

2.1 Understanding Knowledge and Technology Development

The phrase research and development (R&D), according to the Organization for Economic Co-operation and Development [11], refers to "creative work undertaken on a systematic basis in order to increase the stock of knowledge, including knowledge of man, culture and society, and the use of this stock of knowledge to devise new applications". Research often applies to basic experimental research; while development refers to the exploitation of discoveries. A technology can be new for the organization or new to the world, it only needs to have technological characteristics or intended uses that differ significantly from those of previously used technologies. In the public sector, such knowledge and technology-related R&D activities are conducted by units within universities and other public-funded research organizations. For such a technology development organization, it is routine-based and core work and in that sense should be standardized, organized, predictable and evaluated.

Regarding *innoSPICE*, technology development analysis is restricted to the development of new knowledge and technologies that are intended to be transferred or used for innovation. Three phases of the knowledge and technology development may be considered: basic and applied science knowledge, prototypes, and technology.

The following five groups of activities will be considered for knowledge and technology development:

- **Project proposal (D.Project):** Prepare R&D project proposal;
- **Knowledge creation (D.KW):** Create basic and applied science knowledge;
- **Prototyping (D.Proto):** Develop prototypes;
- **Technology development (D.Tech):** Develop new technology related solutions/ products;
- **Technology release and support (D.RelSup):** Provision of the developed technology and customer support.

2.2 Understanding Knowledge- and Technology Transfer

Defining knowledge and technology transfer is an arduous problem. *innoSPICE* understands knowledge and technology transfer as the commercialization of newly developed knowledge and technology as proposed in [12]. In that sense, it has to be proactive, upon-agreement, collaborative and strategic more than opportunist. It is affected and complicated by technological, human, and organizational influences and may change the technology acquirer's way of working. Most of the time, technology is never transferred as-is: it is a raw material. Transferred technology comes with, for example, know-how, process, documentation, training, maintenance, best practices, technology provider employees, technical assistance, et cetera.

It is important to stress the idea that technology transfer is not technology diffusion, dissemination or transplantation. It is goal-oriented, intentional and managed, i.e., not a result of a passive activity, and thus can be defined in process-oriented terms.

The following eight groups of activities will be considered for knowledge- and technology development:

- **Technology transfer concept (T.Concept):** Understand available knowledge/technologies and needs for developing a technology transfer concept;
- **Intellectual property protection (T.IP):** Determine the appropriate intellectual property protection;
- **Technology analysis (T.TechAnal):** Evaluate reasonability and technical viability of the available technologies and analyze the technical aspects of technologies;
- **Technology value evaluation (T.TechVal):** Evaluate the (acquirer's relative) value of a technology;
- **Technology transfer decision (T.Dec):** Decide whether or not to go to the market according to market opportunities;
- **Technology transfer go-to-market (T.Market):** Identify the best route to go-to-market;
- **Technology transfer financing (T.Finan):** Raise financing for commercialization.

2.3 Understanding Knowledge- and Technology Related Innovation

innoSPICE adopts the following definition for innovation: a new or significantly improved product (good or service), process, marketing or organizational method implemented with value to the firm [12,14]. The organization's benefit can be indirect and of any kind, for example: improving the customer satisfaction, improving the daily work of employees and decreasing cost and increasing efficiency. Technology-related innovation is performed by introducing a new technology within the organization. This technology does not need to be new to the world, only new for the organization. The new technology originates from the organization or from outside.

The following three groups of activities will be considered for knowledge- and technology-related innovation:

- **Innovation creation (I.Crea):** Identify and define improvements needs and requirements for the organization and select technologies to be introduced to perform innovation;
- **Innovation deployment (I.Deploy):** Ensure preconditions that the technology deployment will be successful and successfully deploy the introduced technology into its intended environment;
- **Innovation management (I.Mana):** Manage the innovation of the organization within organization to ensure easy adoption of further technology improvements.

2.4 Role of Organizational Structures

To be a continuously successful actor in the IKaTT, involved organizations need adequate organizational structures. Authors in [15] state that the transfer of university technology is not only a one-way transfer process of technological outputs matching a scientific discovery with a market need, but also the building of teams of university and business people working towards the common goal of technological knowledge creation. Organizational and human resource development is, after all, a precondition for improving knowledge and technology transfer in public research organizations. "Despite a long history of extensive discussions in academia and business, innovation is all too often accidental rather than intentional. Organizations do not lack ideas to drive new product or service introductions but structured ways to allocate resources on the right innovation initiative" [13].

The functional organizational design supports knowledge and technology transfer as a core business as well as a subsidiary activity with added value in research environments as stated in [13]:

- Defined processes and metric are essential to create a technology transfer supportive organizational culture;
- Successful implementation of technology transfer supportive organizational processes requires two perspectives: an organizational and an individual perspective;
- The individual dimension includes human resource capability and motivation for technology transfer as personnel added value;
- The organizational dimension includes processes, metrics and value systems leading to a participatory organizational culture.

3 Process-Oriented Knowledge- and Technology Development, Transfer and Innovation Model

innoSPICE defines knowledge and technology development, transfer and innovation activities as a set of ISO/IEC 15504-conformant processes for an external process reference and assessment model. Indeed, ISO/IEC 15504 introduces a concept of capability measurement framework and requirements for external process model. The measurement framework is generic. It defines the capability dimension and how to measure the capability level of any ISO/IEC 15504-conformant process. This framework can be applied to any kind of activity that can be expressed in process-oriented terms. It allows the development of an external IKaTT process capability model as an ISO/IEC 15504-conformant model that reuses the ISO/IEC 15504 capability framework. The innoSPICE external process model consists of processes that satisfy requirements of the Process Reference Model established by ISO/IEC 15504. A set of relevant activities for primary processes category have been defined in the previous sections (see Section 2.1, 2.2 and 2.3).

Therefore, *innoSPICE*'s primary processes are split into three groups:

- Knowledge and Technology development processes;
- Knowledge and Technology Transfer processes;
- Innovation processes.

Organizational and support process categories are reused or adapted from Enterprise SPICE [7], ISO/IEC 15504-5 [10] and P-CMM [6].

According to ISO/IEC 15504-2 [4], processes must be defined by process purpose and outcomes achieved as a result of successful process implementation. In *innoSPICE* technology development (respectively, transfer and innovation) Primary processes are provided in Table 1 (resp. Table 2 and Table 3). For the sake of brevity, only a short description of the processes is provided. It is out of the scope of the paper to provide the full *innoSPICE*' model. There are nine technology development Primary processes, thirteen technology transfer Primary processes, and six innovation Primary processes.

Table 1. Knowledge and Technology development Primary processes

Knowledge Creation Project Proposal Preparation (D.Project)
Knowledge creation project proposals are developed and submitted according to program's objectives, priorities and requirements.
Basic Science Knowledge Creation (D.KW)
Basic science knowledge having commercial potential is developed.
Applied Science Knowledge Creation (D.KW)
Applied science knowledge having commercial potential is developed.
Experimental Science Knowledge Creation (D.KW)
Experimental science knowledge having commercial potential is developed.
Prototype Development (D.Proto)
Prototypes are developed to demonstrate potential use of the technology.
Technology Development (D.Tech)
A solution that can be used in its intended environments is developed.
Technology Release (D.RelSup)
The availability of the product for the intended technology acquirer is controlled.
Technology Acceptance Support (D.RelSup)
The technology acquirer is assisted to take ownership of the technology.
Technology Acquirer Support (D.RelSup)
The technology acquirer is supported to use the acquired technology.

Table 2. Knowledge and Technology Transfer Primary processes

Technology Transfer Concept (T.Concept)
Technology transfer concepts are identified and defined.
Intellectual Property Protection Determination (T.IP)
The appropriate protection for the intellectual property is determined.
Technology Evaluation (T.TechAnal)
The reasonability and technical viability of the available technologies that might be transferred are evaluated.
Technical Analysis (T. TechAnal)
The technical aspects of the technology are refined and developed further.
Technology Value Evaluation (T.TechVal)
The technology value is estimated.
Initial Market Assessment (T.Decision)
Clear contraindications that will severely impede any move to market are assessed.
Market And Competitive Analysis (T.Decision)
The market potential of the technology is evaluated.
Go To Market Estimation (T.Decision)
A go to market strategy is defined.
Commercial Interest Confirmation (T.Decision)
Commercial interest is defined and the most promising route into the market is identified.
Business Case Establishment (T.Decision)
The business case for the innovative technology is built.
Go To Market Strategy Establishment (T.Market)
The market strategy is established.
Business Plan Establishment (T.Market)
The business plan is established.
Financing Sources Raising (C.Finan)
Sources of financing and investors are identified.

Table 3. Innovation Primary processes

Technology Acquirer Needs (I.Creat)
Technology acquirer needs and expectations are understood.
Technology Requirements (I.Creat)
Technology requirements are identified and managed.
New Technologies Selection (I.Creat)
Technologies to be introduced are identified and selected.
Preparation For Innovation Technology Deployment (I.Deploy)
Technology deployment is initiated.
Innovation Technology Deployment (I.Deploy)
The innovative technology is deployed.
Innovation Management (I.Mana)
Innovations are managed in the organization.

4   Conclusion

The paper presents a SPICE-conformant innovation, knowledge and technology transfer process capability model that reuses the existing capability dimension of ISO/IEC 15504 to assess knowledge and technology development, transfer and innovation process capability. It appears that innovation-related knowledge and experiences can effectively be codified into process-oriented terms for process capability assessment and improvement. The *innoSPICE* model follows the a priori expectation that improved processes will lead to subsequent impacts on the organization's performance. The process reference model directly originates from the strong practical and theoretical knowledge and experience of BONITA partners in innovation, knowledge and technology transfer. The *innoSPICE* process reference has been evaluated in more than 30 research and transfer organizations, ministries, science parks and business development agencies in 13 European countries. During these assessments, the model has proven its applicability and showed that it has already reached an implementation level. The next step of this work is to synthesize and present the results of the assessments, as well as the assessment methodology, that have been performed with *innoSPICE* model on the organizations involved in European Project BONITA.

References

1. Woronowicz, T., Boronowsky, M., Mitasiunas, A.: BONITA – Improve Transfer from Universities for Regional Development. In: The Proceedings of the 3rd ISPIM Innovation Symposium held in Quebec City, Canada, December 12-15 (2010) ISBN 978-952-265-004-7
2. CMMI-ACQ, CMMI for Acquisition, Version 1.3. Software Engineering Institute (2010)
3. CMMI-DEV, CMMI for Development, Version 1.3. Software Engineering Institute (2010)
4. CMMI-SVC, CMMI for Services, Version 1.3. Software Engineering Institute (2010)
5. Communication from the Commission to the European Parliament, the Council, the European Economic Committee and the Committee of the Regions, Europe 2020 Flagship Initiative Innovation Union, SEC 1161 (2010)
6. Curtis, B., Hefley, W.E., Miller, S.: The People Capability Maturity Model: Guidelines for Improving the Workforce. Addison Wesley Longman, Reading (2002) ISBN 0-201-60445-0
7. Enterprise SPICE An Integrated Model for Enterprise-wide Assessment and Improvement. Technical Report - Issue 1. The Enterprise SPICE Project Team, 184 psl. (September 2010), http://www.enterprisespice.com/page/publication-1
8. Ibrahim, L., Bradford, B., Cole, D., LaBruyere, L., Leinneweber, H., Piszczek, D., Reed, N., Rymond, M., Smith, D., Virga, M., Wells, C.: FAA-iCMM, The Federal Aviation Administration Integrated Capability Maturity Model for Enterprise-wide Improvement. U.S. Federal Aviation Administration (2001)
9. ISO/IEC 15504-2, Information Technology – Process Assessment – Part 2: Performing an Assessment. International Standards Organization (2003)
10. ISO/IEC 15504-5, Information Technology – Process Assessment – Part 5: An Exemplar Process Assessment Model. International Standards Organization (2006)

11. OECD, Measuring Public Employment in OECD Countries: Sources, Methods and Results, OECD, Paris, France (1997)
12. OECD, EUROSTAT. Oslo Manual, 3rd edn. (2005); Oslo Manual Guidelines for Collecting and Interpreting Innovation Data, 3rd edn., OECD, EUROSTAT, OECD Publishing
13. Peisl, T., Reger, V., Schmied, J.: Innovation Process Design: A Change Management and Innovation Dimension Perspective. In: O'Connor, R.V., Baddoo, N., Cuadrago Gallego, J., Rejas Muslera, R., Smolander, K., Messnarz, R. (eds.) EuroSPI 2009. CCIS, vol. 42, pp. 117–127. Springer, Heidelberg (2009) ISBN 978-3-642-04132-7
14. Rombach, D.H., Achatz, R.: Research Collaborations between Academia and Industry. In: Future of Software Engineering (FOSE 2007). IEEE-CS Press, Washington, DC (2007) ISBN 0-7695-2829-5/07
15. Senoo, D., Fukushima, M., Yoneyama, S., Watanabe, T.: Technology Transfer as Team Building: an empirical analysis of University TLOs in Japan. In: PICMET 2006 Conference, Istanbul, Turkey, July 9-13 (2006)

A Case Study on Process Composition Using Enterprise SPICE Model

Amalia Alvarez[1], Santiago Matalonga[1], and Tomás San Feliu[2]

[1] Universidad ORT Uruguay. Cuareim 1471. 11100 Montevideo, Uruguay
`amalia_a@ort.edu.uy, smatalonga@uni.ort.edu.uy`
[2] Universidad Politécnica de Madrid. Facultad de Informática.
28660 Boadilla del Monte. Madrid. España
`Tomas.sanfeliu@upm.es`

Abstract. Process improvement models include the best practices from relevant disciplines in comprehensive sets. Their purpose is to convey knowledge that will help organizations through their process improvement journey. In this paper we argue that process improvement practitioners do not take advantage of this knowledge. Hence we propose a process to evaluate and extract knowledge form a process model in order to improve an existing process. This paper presents an application of this process using the Enterprise SPICE model to improve an existing training process.

Keywords: Process improvement, Process definition, Process Composition, Enterprise SPICE Model.

1 Introduction

Process improvement models like ISO/IEC 15504[1] or CMMI[2], have grown in popularity and adoption in recent years[3]. These models bring together knowledge and best practices from each of its target domains. Many organizations are convinced about the usefulness of these process models.

Ideally, process models harbor the promise of shortcutting the process improvement journey to high performance[4]. By providing best practices and guidance, process models enable knowledge sharing and knowledge transfer from state of the practice to the organization.

In order to do so, organizations must harness the value of the information contained in those process models. More often than not, organizations fail to understand the intention of the process models guidance and set out looking for solutions to problems already solved by these process models[5].

One of these problems is how to define a process or how to include process elements into a process definition. We understand process composition as the act of harnessing best practices included in references and incorporate them into existing process or into new processes.

This paper presents a case study on process composition. A process for capturing knowledge from process models was defined using Enterprise SPICE model[6], which was also used to improve an existing process.

Enterprise SPICE is an initiative of the SPICE User Group that brings together best practices from several disciplines and several models and standards into a comprehensive improvement model [6].

The enterprise process used as starting point is the ROI+training process[7]. This process links production defects to training interventions. ROI+training support the training department within a software development organization by helping them justify the investments in terms of Return on Investment. The ROI+training process is defined in [7], and its application in the software industry has been published [8].

This paper is organized as follows. Section 2 presents background research on process definition, Enterprise SPICE model, and the ROI+training process. Section 3 presents the case study on process composition using the Enterprise SPICE process model. Finally in Section 4, we present our conclusions.

2 Research Background

2.1 Elements of a Process Description

The most comprehensive research on process definition has been carried a out by [10]. According to [10] a process description has to satisfy criteria that includes a set of information needed for it to be usable by people performing the process. That set of information is organized as process elements.

The basic process elements are: Purpose of the process, Input and Output work products of the process, Activities that should be done, Roles that those Activities should perform, Entry and Exit criteria that state the limits of the process and a Procedure that describes the Tasks needed to perform the activities.

2.2 Enterprise SPICE Overview

The Enterprise SPICE model integrates and harmonizes selected process models and standards into a single enterprise improvement model. By bringing together best practices from several disciplines and several models and standards into a comprehensive improvement model, that provides an efficient and effective mechanism for assessing and improving processes deployed across a typical, large or small, enterprise[6].

In the development of the Enterprise SPICE model the major, essential and widely-recognized process standards and models that cover most of the relevant disciplines that IT enterprises perform [6] were considered.

The result of this work was the Enterprise SPICE Process Reference Model, PRM, and Process Assessment Model, PAM[6], we will refer to it as the "Enterprise SPICE model" to address the all-inclusive PRM and PAM in this paper.

The model is organized in four categories: Governance/Management (GVM), Cycle (LFC), Support (SUP) and Special Applications. Each category has a group of processes that are numbered in a unique way. Process dimensions include Purpose, expected Outcomes, Base Practices (BP), Work Products, Relationship Notes with other processes and Mappings with other references[6]. The code to identify a Base Practice of a process is: PPP.N.BPX, where PPP is the codification of the group of processes, N the number of the process in the group and BPX, the number of Base practice. For instance, GVM.2. BP1, refers to the first Base Practice, of the second process in the Governance/Management category.

2.3 Return on Training Investment

This section details the motivation for the research that leads to the ROI+Training process.

Training investment is of outmost importance for software development organizations. Organizations rely on training for the continuous improvement of their processes or to maintain the set skill of their workforce update to the ever-changing technology [11]. It has been reported that organizations invest over 100 million US dollars per year on training activities[12]. This investment requires organizations to find reliable ways to evaluate the return on their investment in training. Methods of return on investment (ROI) have been proposed as a solution for this problem[13].

The ROI+training process[7] builds on top of these proposals by linking production defects with ROI. We have successfully deployed the ROI+training process in a software factory and found that it brings insight into the training effort[8] and also helps align the training to the organization's business needs[14].

3 Process Composition Using Enterprise SPICE Model

This section details the steps taken by the researchers to improve the ROI+training process definition. Most often new processes are defined by observation and formalization of the activities of people doing their work. For this purpose, several techniques have been developed (i.e. Value-stream mapping [15]). But, when improving an existing process, references models like Enterprise SPICE model or the CMMI[2] can be useful for formalizing and improving processes that are already defined.

The ROI+training process was originally defined in [7] (see Table 1). The goal of the process is to link production defects to return on training investment. ROI+training takes as input defects registered during the software production process, and through causal analysis[16] designs training interventions which are aimed at reducing those defects. Observed reduction is taken as input for return on investment calculation. This process has been piloted at a software factory in Montevideo Uruguay[8].

Table 1. ROI+training original definition

Step	Name
0	Validate Entry Criteria.
	Validate that the organization's measurement infrastructure can support the process
1	Execute the Production Process
	The process needs software defects to take as input.
2	Analyse Defects
	Root cause analysis of defects to select training interventions.
3	Plan Training Interventions.
4	Establish Agreement on Measurement Objectives
	Agree with ROI stakeholders how benefits will be measured.
5	Deliver Training
	Training must be delivered according to the organisation's standard training process.
6	Evaluate Return on Investment
	Calculate ROI by taking into account costs and benefits.
7	Communicate Results
	Communicate the results of the training interventions in terms of ROI.
8	Validate Exit Criteria
	Describes the process takeaways.

3.1 Case Study

Our intention with this case study is to enhance the definition ROI+training process in order to improve its usability and readability. For this purpose we decided to base our discussion by using Enterprise SPICE model as reference model, specifically the Process Improvement process. The Process Improvement process was tailored to suit the case study needs, were some of the best practices suggested by Enterprise SPICE model did not apply. The process followed by the researchers is detailed in Table 2.

1. Identify process improvement opportunities and 2.Analyze process status

After studying the process definition guidelines presented in section 2.1, the following shortcomings were identified on the process definition.

First of all, the purpose of the process is not stated in its definition (Table 1). Hence the process has to be accompanied with a description that clarifies its intention.

Secondly, inputs and outputs of the process are also not defined. This is a major shortcoming, since a process is "a set of integrated activities that uses resources to transform inputs into outputs"[17]. We might even argue that without a clear statement of them, a definition can hardly be called a process definition. In the case of this process, the lack of definition of inputs and outputs makes for confusion on the role of Return of Investment in the process. We claim that it would make for better communication to have ROI as a measure of the process and not as an output. This will allow for comparison between different instances of the process.

Table 2. Process Redefinition Process

Purpose: Improve process definition by taking advantage of documented best practices, in order to improve the capability of the original process so that business can be conducted more efficiently and effectively.	
Inputs • Organization's improvement goals • Process definition • Best practices	Outputs • Improved process

Activities and tasks:
1. Identify process improvement opportunities
2. Analyze process status
3. Plan improvement.
   a. Select best practice reference model
   b. Map best practice chapter to process goals.
4. Implement improvement.
   a. Incorporate best practices into process definition
5. Communicate results of the improvement.
6. Evaluate the results of improvement.	

Finally, there is no reference to the roles that will be executing the activities of the process. Without them there is no clear guidance for the practitioners to assign the task and activities of the process to the resources of their own enterprises.

   3. Plan improvement.

In order to map the best practice chapters to the original process activities we proceed with Crawford slip method with post it notes on a large whiteboard[18].

The resulting process description integrates several best practices from a set of process of the Enterprise SPICE model. These processes and their rationale for inclusion are described below:

- Investment Management (GVM.2). "The purpose of the Investment Management process is to ensure that organizations realize optimal value from strategically aligned business investments at an affordable cost with a known and acceptable level of risk"[6]. Investment management was included to provide guidance on the use of Return on Investment as a financial indicator. It would support steps six and seven of the original process.
- Human Resource Management (GVM.3). "The purpose of the Human Resource Management process is to provide the organization with individuals who possess skills and knowledge to perform their roles effectively and to work together as a cohesive group"[6]. Human resource management was included to provide guidance on establishing developer's knowledge and skills goals. These activities provide guidance for step three of the original process.
- Quality Assurance and Management (SUP.3). "The purpose of the Quality Assurance and Management process is to assure the quality of the product or service and of the processes used, and provide management with appropriate

visibility into all relevant quality aspects."[6]. Quality Assurance and Management was included in order to provide guidance on how to analyze the causes of the defects, and to guide the implementation of corrective actions. These activities support Step two and four of the original process.
- Training (SUP.7). "The purpose of the Training process is to develop and maintain the skills and knowledge of staff so they perform their roles effectively and efficiently"[6]. Training was included to provide guidance on how to plan and provide the training interventions. This process should support steps three and five of the original process.

Table 3. ROI+Training Enhanced Definition

Purpose: Provide specialized training based on causal analysis of production defects. Communicate the results of the training intervention in terms of Return on Investment.	
Inputs • Software defects records classified as "lack of training" • Average cost of a software defect	**Outputs** • Trained individuals • Training records

Activities and tasks:
 	
 1. Determine needed skills and competences
   a. Defect root cause analysis (SUP.3.BP6 "Analyze quality") → **Role**: QM
   b. Identify skills by profile (GVM.3.BP2) → **Role**: HRM
 2. Define training investment evaluation criteria → **Role**: QM
   a. Determine training objectives (GVM.3.BP3)
   b. Establish criteria (GVM.2.BP1) – Establish criteria for selecting and evaluating potential investments.
 3. Evaluate and determine training investment alternatives → **Role**: QM
   a. Develop a strategy for training (SUP.7.BP1)
   b. Identify Investment Proposals (GVM.2.BP2)
   c. Prioritize and evaluate investment proposals (GVM.2.BP4)
   d. Establish the investment portfolio (GVM.2.BP5)
   e. Identify and allocate resources (GVM.2.BP6)
 4. Deliver Training → **Role**: Tr
   a. Establish training plan (SUP.7.BP3)
   b. Establish training mechanism (SUP.7.BP4) * If necessary
   c. Prepare for training execution (SUP.7.BP5)
   d. Train individuals (SUP.7.BP6)
   e. Establish and maintain records (SUP.7.BP7)
 5. Evaluate results → **Role**: QM
   a. Assess training effectiveness (SUP.7.BP8)
   b. Review/evaluate performance (GVM.2.BP7)	

Process Measurement: Return on training investment	

4. Implement improvement.

In this stage the authors started redefining the process. The first insight to improve the definition was the need to clearly determine the process inputs and outputs.

Then, a clear statement that represented the purpose of the process was written.

Finally, the roles that a typical organization should need to implement this process were defined. The improved process definition will include the following three roles: Quality Management (QM), Human Resources Management (HRM) and Trainer (Tr)

5. Communicate results of the improvement.

The resulting process definition is presented in Table 3. Notice the aforementioned division between inputs and outputs, the clear statement of the process´s purpose, and the mapping to the reference model in the description of the activities and tasks, and the roles assignment to activities and tasks.

In order to calculate ROI costs and benefits are necessary. The Trainer will provide cost of preparing and executing the training while the Quality Manager should provide the information about benefits.

6. Evaluate the results of improvement.

Ideally the resulting process should be given to practitioners for their evaluation and acceptance.

4 Conclusions

This paper has shown a method for improving an existing process by taking advantage of the knowledge available in a process improvement model. In this paper we have presented a process to help practitioners "Improve process definition by taking advantage of documented best practices, in order to improve the capability of the original process so that business can be conducted more efficiently and effectively" (Table 2). Furthermore, the tasks and activities encapsulated in this process have been obtained from the best practices of a process improvement model.

In addition to this, we have shown a case study of how to use the knowledge in process improvement models to improve an existing process definition.

The process model we have used as reference is the Enterprise SPICE model. The Enterprise SPICE model is a novel process improvement model that brings together guidance from several models and experiences from the IT sector. To the best of our knowledge, there have been few applications of the Enterprise SPICE model to this date. In this paper we have used it both to design the process for process composition, and as reference to improve an existing process definition.

Future lines of research will include defining guidelines and process assets (like checklists) for supporting the process composition process to help practitioners adopt this process. Successful deployment to an organization will require guidelines that are tailored to the organizations process, roles and technology.

Our intention is to take this process to the enterprise in order to pilot the process in a live organization.

References

1. ISO/IEC, "ISO/IEC 15504-2:2004 Information technology Process assessment Part 2: A model for Process Management" (2004)
2. CMMI Product Team, "CMMI for Development, Version 1.3. Improving processes for developing better products and services," CMU/SEI-2010-TR-033. Software Engineering Institute (2010)
3. El Emam, K., Garro, I.: Estimating the extent of standards use: the case of ISO/IEC 15504. The Journal of Systems & Software 53(2), 137–143 (2000)
4. Womack, J.P., Jones, D.T., Roos, D.: The machine that changed the world, p. 339. Rawson Associates (1990)
5. Humphrey, W.S.: Why don't they Practice what we preach (2007)
6. The Enterprise SPICE Project Team, "Enterprise SPICE ® An Integrated Model for Enterprise-wide Assessment and Improvement" (2010)
7. Matalonga, S.: Un proceso para la evaluación del entrenamiento organizacional. Universidad Politécnica de Madrid (2011)
8. Matalonga, S., San Feliu, T.: Calculating Return on Investment of Training using process variation. IET Software (2011) (accepted)
9. Valdés, G., Visconti, M., Astudillo, H.: The Tutelkan Reference Process: A Reusable Process Model for Enabling SPI in Small Settings. In: O'Connor, R.V., Pries-Heje, J., Messnarz, R. (eds.) EuroSPI 2011. CCIS, vol. 172, pp. 179–190. Springer, Heidelberg (2011)
10. Olson, T.G., Reizer, N.R., Over, J.W.: A Software Process Framework for the SEI Capability Maturity Modelsm, Pittsburg (1994)
11. Hodges, T.: Linking Learning and Performance. Butterworth Heinmann, Masachusetts (2002)
12. Patel, L.: ASTD State of the Industry Report. Asociation for Training and Development (2010)
13. Phillips, J.J.: Return on Investment in Training and Performance Improvement Programs (Improving Human Performance), 2nd edn., p. 344. Butterworth-Heinemann (2003)
14. Matalonga, S., San Feliu, T.: Linking Return on Training Investment with Defects Causal Analysis. In: 20th Conference of Software Engineering Theory and Practice, pp. 42–47 (2008)
15. Hambleton, L.: Treasure chest of Six Sigma growth models, tools & best practices: a desk reference book for innovation and growth. Prentice Hall (2008)
16. Card, D.N.: Learning from Our Mistakes with Defect Causal Analysis. IEEE Software 15(1), 7 (1998)
17. ISO, "ISO 9001:2008(E). Quality Management Systems - Requirements" (2008)
18. Dettmer, W.: Brainpower Networking Using the Crawford Slip Method, p. 178. Trafford, Bloomington (2003)

Extending ISO/IEC 12207 with Software Product Management: A Process Reference Model Proposal

Fritz Stallinger and Robert Neumann

Software Competence Center Hagenberg, Softwarepark 21, Hagenberg, Austria
{fritz.stallinger,robert.neumann}@scch.at

Abstract. Software product management is generally expected to link and integrate business and product related goals with core software engineering and software life cycle activities. Empirical research demonstrates the positive effect of mature software product management practices on key software development performance indicators. Nevertheless, the various frameworks available for software product management have distinct and diverse focus points, are often linked or incorporated with specific development paradigms, or lack integration with or addressing of core software engineering activities. On the other hand, traditional software process improvement approaches generally lack the provision of explicit or detailed software product management activities. – In this paper we build on the results of preceding research on identifying a lack of software product management practices within ISO/IEC 12207 and on deriving key outcomes of software product management activities from selected software product management frameworks. Based on these results we propose a process reference model for software product management that can be integrated with the process reference model as defined in ISO/IEC 12207 for software life cycle processes.

Keywords: software product management, software product line, software process, software life cycle, process reference model, process assessment, process improvement, ISO/IEC 12207, ISO/IEC 15504.

1 Introduction, Goals, and Approach

Software development organizations are increasingly challenged with the need to develop and maintain their software as a product (cf. e.g. [1]). While they traditionally have been used to work in project-oriented ways, this new challenge and the respective transition towards product-oriented development typically implies a change in the whole organization, requires the consideration of the views and needs of additional stakeholders, and generally stresses the importance of business and market considerations. Specific challenges include e.g. the need to cover the expectations of a series of different customers or the need for alignment of the products and services to specific markets, the handling of increased functionality, variability, and complexity, the elaboration and adherence to an appropriate architecture supporting variability and reuse, or the coordination of interdependent or interacting software product components, products, and product portfolios.

Table 1. Key software product management activities, source frameworks, and coverage by ISO/IEC 12207 (adapted from [2])

Key Product Management Activities by Category	van de Weerd et al. [3]	SEI [4]	Pohl et al. [5]	MSF [6]	Coverage by ISO/IEC 12207 [7]
Software Product Management					
Product Portfolio Management	x		x		P
Product Life Cycle Management	x		x		F
Product Roadmapping	x	x	x		N
Release Planning	x			x	N
Product Planning	x	x	x	x	N
Product Controlling		x	x		P
Software Product Management Support					
Market Monitoring	x	x	x	x	N
Customer Interface Management	x	x	x		P
Funding		x			N
Product Innovation			x		N
Cross-functional Communication				x	P
Software Engineering Lifecycle					
Requirements Engineering	x	x			L
Domain and Product Line Scoping	x	x	x		L
Asset Identification	x	x			F

A key goal of transitioning to such a product-oriented development paradigm is to harvest the benefits of pre-defined and ideally pre-developed software products or product components while still satisfying the customers' needs. A mature and well-studied approach therefor is software product line engineering (SPLE) (cf. [8] [5] [9]).

Nevertheless, to exploit the potential of such product- and reuse-focused development approaches, core software engineering activities, like requirements engineering, architecture engineering, or quality assurance, have to be closely linked and aligned with strategic and economic product aspects.

With the term 'product' in this context we refer to applications denoting both software and software-intensive systems; products may also be services or solutions offered to the customer [10]. Product management is commonly defined as the 'planning, organising, executing, and controlling of all tasks, which aim at a successful conception, production, and marketing of the products offered by a company' [5]. In the context of SPLE, product management 'aims to define the products that will constitute the product line as a whole' [9]. Accordingly, product management aims to identify the major commonalities and variabilities among the products and to realize product portfolio planning supported by major economic analyses of the products.

Software product management is generally expected to link and integrate business and product related goals with core software engineering and software life cycle activities and is thus considered a key element in the transition towards product-oriented software engineering.

Empirical research confirms the positive effect of mature software product management practices on key software development performance indicators; e.g. [11] concludes that empowering software product management results in significant improvements in terms of e.g. schedule predictability, quality, and project duration.

Nevertheless, previous research [2] indicated that the various frameworks available for providing product management practices (e.g. [3], [4], [5], [6]) have distinct and diverse foci, are often linked or incorporated with specific development paradigms, and lack completeness or integration with core software engineering activities. On the other hand, traditional software process improvement approaches and respective underlying best practice-based process models like ISO/IEC 12207 on software life cycle processes [7] generally lack the provision of explicit or detailed software product management practices. Table 1 illustrates these results by listing the key software product management activities distilled from four representative frameworks on software product management, software product line engineering, and product-oriented software development together with the tracing of the identified activities to these source frameworks and their coverage by ISO/IEC 12207 measured using an NPLF (not, partly, largely, fully)-scale according to [12].

The long-term vision of our work is to enable and support the transition of software developing organizations towards product-oriented development approaches by providing the necessary guidance for establishing software product management as key intermediary between business-related aspects and proper software engineering activities. The approach chosen aims at establishing software product management within software engineering organizations from a process perspective.

The first major milestone therefor is to provide a best practice reference model for successful product-oriented software engineering conformant to the requirements of ISO/IEC 15504 [12] for process reference models, which integrates the key software product management aspects relevant for organizations aiming to develop and enhance software products. This approach is thus conformant with software process assessment and improvement approaches already well-established in software engineering [12], [7]. In order to facilitate the joint and effective application of software product management improvement endeavors within software engineering improvement initiatives, we pursue to integrate the respective software product management practices with the existing process reference model of ISO/IEC 12207 for software life cycle processes [7].

A first step in this approach (cf. [2] and Table 1) comprised the identification of essential software product management activities through analyses of existing product-oriented models and frameworks and their comparison with ISO/IEC 12207 as the major reference for software engineering life cycle activities. The frameworks analyzed in this step were:

- The framework for software product management by van de Weerd et al. [3].
- The Framework for Software Product Line Practice [4] provided by the Software Engineering Institute (SEI).
- The software product line engineering framework by Pohl et al. [5].
- The Microsoft Solutions Framework [6] which also defines roles and responsibilities including multi-disciplinary roles like product management.

From each framework the topics explicitly associated with product management and those SPLE-related topics considered relevant for product management were analyzed, resulting in the compilation of a set of 14 key product management activities (cf. Table 1). This work highlighted a lack of major software product management activities within ISO/IEC 12207 [7] and derived a first vision of how the standard could be extended to cover software product management best practices.

A second step consisted of the detailed identification and compilation of software product management best practices through analysis of four major software product management and software product line engineering frameworks and their proposal to the software business community (cf. [13]). The means chosen for presentation of the obtained results was the distillation of the identified best practices as first candidates for 'process outcomes' targeting at enabling the integration and harmonization with process-oriented software life cycle best practice models like ISO/IEC 12207 [7].

The work presented in this paper builds on these preceding works. Based on the respective results we derive and propose a process reference model for software product management that can on the one side serve as add-on and be integrated with the process reference model as defined in ISO/IEC 12207 [7] and on the other side be used as a stand-alone reference for software product management best practices.

The remainder of the paper is structured as follows: section 2 presents the proposed process reference model for software product management and provides definitions of the process purposes and process outcomes; section 3 then discusses the mapping of the proposed model with ISO/IEC 12207 and proposes a structure for the integration of the proposed model with the standard; section 4 summarizes the results, provides conclusions, and discusses further work.

2 A Software Product Management Process Reference Model

The analysis of the selected frameworks for software product management as outlined in step 1 above resulted in the identification of 14 key software product management activities. More detailed descriptions of these activities and their traceability to the analyzed frameworks are provided in [2] and [13].

The following subsections - organized by activity categories - shortly characterize the respective key activities and provide – in table form – a proposal for the process purpose definitions and compiled outcomes.

The key software product management activity *Cross-functional Communication*, emphasizing the role of product management as an intermediary between various stakeholders or business functions [6], was not considered as a separate process in the following proposal, but integrated on outcome-level into other processes where appropriate.

2.1 Software Product Management Category

Product Portfolio Management is a strategic function and covers decision making about the set of existing and in-development products offered by an organization, including identification, evaluation, selection, and prioritization of products, as well as decisions on the products' life cycles [5], [3].

Product Life Cycle Management is 'a comprehensive approach for product-related information and knowledge management within an enterprise, including planning and controlling of processes that are required for managing data, documents and enterprise resources throughout the entire product life cycle' [3].

Product Roadmapping deals with long-term plans and expectations and outlines the products in the portfolio as far as they are foreseeable, by determining their major common and variable product features and a schedule of planned release dates [5].

Release Planning covers the definition of product releases by prioritizing and selecting the product requirements to be implemented in each specific release [3].

Product Planning covers both strategic and technical product planning and outlines and determines the product-related goals, strategies, intermediate objectives, and activities to be performed, and the allocation of resources [4]. It includes the selection of product ideas for realization and the definition of the major features of the envisioned product [5].

Product Controlling is concerned with monitoring and guiding product related effort to ensure successful achievement of the product's as well as the organization's goals and objectives [4].

Table 2. Software Product Management Processes

Product Portfolio Management Process
The purpose of the *Product Portfolio Management Process* is to ensure that the business strategy and goals of the organization are properly addressed and achieved by the totality of the organization's products. 1. Life cycle decisions for new or existing products are based on market and trend data and support the product portfolio strategy. 2. The amount of resources required for product-related projects is identified. 3. New product-related projects are defined, evaluated, prioritized, and selected. 4. Justification of existing product-related projects is evaluated and projects are sustained, accelerated, slowed down, or terminated in order to maintain a capable product portfolio. 5. Features provided by the products match the needs and requirements of the customers. 6. The product portfolio is balanced and contains an appropriate and sufficient mix of products across different life cycle stages. 7. Weaknesses in the product portfolio and respective improvement strategies are identified. 8. Interdependencies between products are identified and incorporated into decision making on changes to the product portfolio. 9. Product variability is balanced between the necessities for product variants and their economic implications across all organizational units.

Table 2. (*Continued*)

Product Life Cycle Management Process
The purpose of the *Product Life Cycle Management Process* is to conserve and expand a product's potentials and attractiveness throughout its life cycle or – where necessary - to eliminate it from the product portfolio. 1. Potentials for product improvements are identified based on observation of changes to the external conditions affecting the product. 2. Decisions on product continuation or elimination are unbiased and based on a regular and structured decision process. 3. The product phase out and elimination process is defined and carefully considers constraints like existing contracts, maintenance requirements, or dependencies with other products or product line assets.
Product Roadmapping Process
The purpose of the *Product Roadmapping Process* is to outline the plans and expectations for the products in the product portfolio over a period of time with respect to features, schedules, and dependencies between products. 1. The themes of the products or product line are devised and described in a product roadmap. 2. The major common and variable features of the products or product line are determined and a schedule for their planned availability and market introduction is defined and maintained in a product roadmap. 3. Potential future changes of market needs, technology, legal constraints, standards, etc. are identified and taken into account in the product roadmap.
Product Planning Process
The purpose of the *Product Planning Process* is to specify both the strategic and technical plans for a product. 1. A business case is developed and maintained, at least specifying the goals and measures for tracking the product's success, providing a cost and benefit analysis, and a substantiation of the product's ability to support the business strategy and goals. 2. The strategic goals and objectives for the product, required activities and resources, schedules, and links or dependencies to other products and product plans are specified. 3. The product features and requirements are specified based on market and competitive analysis and on analyzed and prioritized customer and business requirements. 4. Alternatives for obtaining the product and their direct, opportunity, and life time costs are identified and provided to decision makers. 5. Externally available software for use in the product is identified and systematically evaluated according to specified criteria. 6. The use of core assets for realizing the product is specified. 7. Product plans are communicated to relevant stakeholders and updated and revised throughout the product's life cycle.

Extending ISO/IEC 12207 with Software Product Management

Table 2. (*Continued*)

Release Planning Process
The purpose of the *Release Planning Process* is to plan and define product releases and to ensure smooth deployment to the customer and on-going operation of the product.
1. Policies and criteria for release activities are defined in a release strategy.
2. Product requirements are prioritized and selected for implementation in particular releases.
3. For each product release a release definition is developed and validated and approved by relevant stakeholders.
4. For each product release, launch activities are prepared and respective release information communicated to stakeholders.
Product Controlling Process
The purpose of the *Product Controlling Process* is to track the achievement of product goals and objectives and to guide product management decision making.
1. Success criteria and respective indicators and measures for the achievement of the strategic and technical product goals and objectives are defined.
2. Effective use of operationalized measures is ensured and gained information is prepared and reported to relevant stakeholders.
3. The use of core assets, the effort for their incorporation into a product, and the encountered problems are systematically measured and recorded.

2.2 Software Product Management Support Category

Market Monitoring comprises the observation and analysis of the external factors that determine the success of a product in the marketplace [10], [4].

Customer Interface Management comprises the understanding and management of commitments between an organization's producers and its customers [4], referred to as partnering and contracting in [3].

Table 3. Software Product Management Support Processes

Market Monitoring Process
The purpose of the *Market Monitoring Process* is to observe and analyze the external factors of sales and procurement markets that determine or influence product success.
1. Market analysis is performed on a regular basis and relevant market information on customer groups, current and potential competitors, price trends, buying and usage patterns, technology, and barriers to market entry and exit is systematically gathered and monitored.
2. Market analysis is coupled with planning and budgeting cycles and updated on market, product portfolio, or product line changes.
3. Business opportunities for products are identified and quantitatively characterized.
4. Available and future technologies are identified, monitored, and evaluated for their effects on and potentials for product features and capabilities and internal product development.

Table 3. (*Continued*)

Customer Interface Management Process
The purpose of the *Customer Interface Management Process* is to manage the relationships and commitments between an organization and its customers.
1. The roles and responsibilities of business functions involved with customers (e.g. marketing, contracting, or product support) are defined and established.
2. Customers are provided with a central contact point for change requests or support with operational problems of a product.
3. Customer requests are evaluated regarding feasibility of the desired change and desirability to integrate the change into the products or product line.
4. Customers are encouraged to a desired behavior and their expectations are managed by communicating the product strategy and plans for future product developments, providing information and guidance on product features and capabilities, or announcing changed or newly available products.
5. Appropriate capabilities of personnel with customer responsibility are ensured.
6. Customer information, installations, and configurations are tracked and propagated to relevant stakeholders.
7. A customer community is established and their emerging and long-term needs are identified.
Funding Process
The purpose of the *Funding Process* is to plan and establish adequate financing of software development efforts in order to secure the evolution of products or the product line.
1. Appropriate funding sources and models are identified and defined.
2. Funding strategies are identified, evaluated and selected for specific development efforts.
3. Sufficiency and stability of funding is ensured for sustainable development and maintenance of products and core assets.
Product Innovation Process
The purpose of the *Product Innovation Process* is to extend the product portfolio with new or enhanced products that satisfy customer needs.
1. A strategy for product innovation is developed and established.
2. The search for new ideas is performed in a systematic way according to the innovation strategy.
3. Ideas for new products or product enhancements are evaluated and selected for implementation.
4. Technologies are identified and assessed continuously for their immediate benefit and their potential future applicability.

Funding covers the activities to plan and establish adequate financing of software development efforts undertaken in the organization. It includes the identification of appropriate funding sources and the definition of funding requirements and models. The funds must be sufficient with respect to the desired quality of results [4].

Product Innovation aims at the extension of the product portfolio with new or enhanced products that satisfy customer needs. Various strategies and sources for idea generation can be utilized [5].

2.3 Software Engineering Lifecycle Category

Requirements Engineering comprises the elicitation, analysis, specification, verification, and management of user and product requirements in a systematic and repeatable way and aims to ensure their completeness, correctness, consistency, and relevance [4].

Domain and Product Line Scoping determines the relevant entities within the domain, that products will interact with, and the domain's boundaries. It establishes product commonalities and sets limits to their variability [4].

Asset Identification aims to identify and define particular assets and components that cover the commonalities of and are shared by multiple products [3], [4].

Table 4. Software Engineering Lifecycle Processes

Requirements Engineering and Management Process
The purpose of the *Requirements Engineering and Management Process* is to identify, specify, and manage stakeholder and product requirements in a systematic and repeatable way.
1. Incoming requirements from external and internal stakeholders are gathered, consolidated and translated to product requirements, and linked to specific products and core assets.
2. Conflicting stakeholder requirements and necessary trade-offs are identified and respective decisions are documented and linked with the respective product requirements.
3. Anticipated variations over the foreseeable lifetime of the product line or products are gathered with support from market and domain experts and captured as stakeholder and product requirements.
4. Completeness, correctness, consistency, and relevance of the product requirements are ensured.
5. Changes to stakeholder or product requirements are systematically managed.
Domain and Product Line Scoping Process
The purpose of the *Domain and Product Line Scoping Process* is to determine the relevant entities within the domain and the domain boundaries, to establish product commonalities and variability, and to ensure that this information is captured, appropriately represented, and communicated to stakeholders.
1. The concepts, terminology, typical problems and solutions, and the boundaries of the addressed domain are understood, organized, documented and communicated to relevant stakeholders in form of a domain model.
2. The documented domain information enables making informed decisions on proposed products, designs, and the features to be provided by the products.
3. Commonalities and limits to the variability of the product line are established in a scope definition.
4. The context and most important requirements and constraints of the product line are captured and enable derivation of acceptance criteria for developed products.
5. The products and their key features and the assets to be developed for reuse are identified.

Table 4. (*Continued*)

Asset Identification Process
The purpose of the *Asset Identification Process* is to identify and define particular assets that cover the commonalities of and are shared by multiple products in the product line and thus are developed for reuse. 1. The sources for mining existing assets are selected. 2. Existing, internally or externally available assets are identified, understood, organized, and selected - according to specific criteria - for transformation into core assets. 3. For proposed core assets, the total costs of their use across all products are estimated and compared with the costs for individual solutions. 4. Core assets are aligned with the requirements of the product line and current and future products. 5. Core assets realize the commonalities and variability of the product line with minimal tradeoff to product quality. 6. Core assets and their variation mechanisms support the production strategy, i.e. the overall approach to realizing both, core assets and products.

3 Integration of the Reference Model with ISO/IEC 12207

A comparison at outcome level of the suggested processes with ISO/IEC 12207 provides the following observations:

Firstly, the life cycle and engineering related processes *Product Life Cycle Management*, *Domain and Product Line Scoping*, *Requirements Engineering and Management*, and *Asset Identification* are well covered by the standard through its *Life Cycle Model Management Process*, *Domain Engineering Process*, and *Stakeholder Requirements Definition, System Requirements Analysis,* and *Software Requirements Analysis Processes*.

Secondly, processes more specific for product management, which are concerned with project-independent, product-specific, or cross-product topics, are not in the scope of ISO/IEC 12207 and therefore just partly or not at all covered. For some of the processes, namely *Product Roadmapping*, *Release Planning*, *Product Planning*, and *Customer Interface Management*, it would be possible to integrate the respective outcomes into existing processes, mainly into software-specific processes in either the *'Software Specific Processes'* sub-division or in the *'Technical Processes'* group of the *'System Context Processes'* sub-division. Nevertheless, taking into account that there are also outcomes of these processes which could not be integrated into existing processes, it is reasonable to integrate them as part of additional process groups into ISO/IEC 12207. This approach emphasizes product-orientation on the process level and better supports the inherent characteristic of software product management to be vastly independent of particular projects. This enhancement of ISO/IEC 12207 with product management processes involves two additional process groups:

- Firstly, a *'Software Product Management Processes'* group, which incorporates the processes that directly focus on one or more software products and operate independently of specific projects. Processes to include in this process group are *Product Portfolio Management, Product Planning, Product Roadmapping, Release Planning*, and *Product Controlling*.

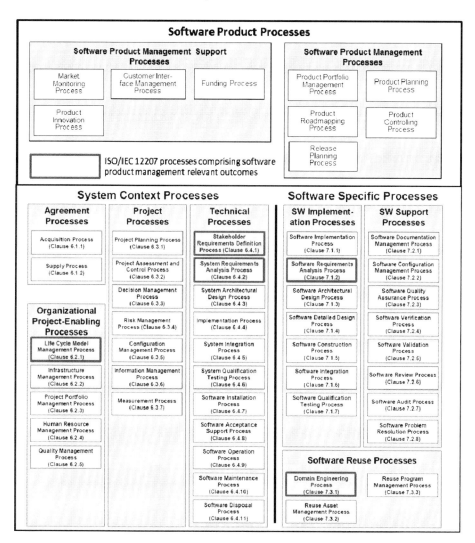

Fig. 1. Software Product Management Enhanced ISO/IEC 12207 Structure

- A second process group of *'Software Product Management Support Processes'* is suggested for addition to ISO/IEC 12207, comprising the processes *Market Monitoring, Product Innovation, Customer Interface Management*, and *Funding*. This process group supports the processes in the *'Software Product Management Processes'* group. These processes on the one hand provide valuable information for any product related process, and on the other hand represent the function of product management as an intermediary between the various stakeholders involved in products and product development. Some of these processes, like *Market Monitoring*, *Funding*, or *Product Innovation* are clearly out of the initial scope of ISO/IEC 12207 but nevertheless relevant for systematic software product management.

Fig. 1 illustrates the resulting overall architecture of ISO/IEC 12207, enhanced with software product management processes.

4 Summary, Conclusions, and Further Work

The paper presented key software product management best practices in form of a proposal for an ISO/IEC 15504 [12] conformant process reference model for software product management (cf. section 2). The outcomes were extracted and distilled from selected software product management and software product line frameworks. Preceding research [2] showed that these practices are currently not fully covered by ISO/IEC 12207.

The reference model has been developed using a bottom-up approach, i.e. identifying key software product management activities first, consolidating them to outcomes, and finally grouping these to appropriate processes and defining meaningful process purposes.

The proposed reference model for software product management can either be applied *'stand-alone'* (as presented in section 2) for evaluation and improvement of core software product management activities, or as *'add-on'* to ISO/IEC 12207. For the latter use, section 3 outlined the appropriate integrated reference model architecture. This extended architecture in particular adds a *'Software Product Management Processes'* group to ISO/IEC 12207 to support and emphasize systematic product management for the software products that are developed as part of an overall system or system product, and a *'Software Product Management Support Processes'* group, which provides the relevant information to successfully execute the software product-related processes.

The suggested enhancements appear satisfactorily suitable. With the suggested additions, previously in ISO/IEC 12207 implicitly implied artifacts like the existence of a release strategy or adequate funding are now appropriately addressed and contribute to the consistency and integrity of ISO/IEC 12207.

An analysis of the outcomes comprising the *software product processes* indicates that they could also be applied to non-software products with only slight changes to their wording and semantics in some of the outcome definitions. It remains to be analyzed, whether currently software-specific product management processes like *Product Portfolio Management* or *Release Planning* are also required on the system product level and how such processes would interplay with the software product-related processes.

Major next steps in our research comprise the validation of the emerging model 1) through analyses against further software product management frameworks (e.g. [14],[15]) that focus more on the role and functions of the software product manager and have at this step been left out of detailed consideration and 2) through application of the model in real-world software product management contexts. A further step consists in the definition of a respective process assessment model and the provision of an assessment method that in particular considers the cross-cutting and interdisciplinary role of software product management.

Acknowledgements. This work has been supported by the *COMET*-Programme of the *Austrian Research Promotion Agency (FFG - Österreichische Forschungsförderungsgesellschaft*) within the projects *Hephaistos* (Integrated Product Engineering, 2008-2011) and *INSPiRE* (INtegrated and Sustainable PRoduct Engineering, 2012-2014).

References

1. Stallinger, F., Neumann, R., Schossleitner, R., Kriener, S.: Migrating Towards Evolving Software Product Lines: Challenges of an SME in a Core Customer-driven Industrial Systems Engineering Context. In: Proceedings of Second International Workshop on Product Line Approaches in Software Engineering (PLEASE 2011), May 22-23, pp. 15–19. ACM, Waikiki (2011) ISBN: 978-1-4503-0584-6
2. Stallinger, F., Neumann, R., Schossleitner, R., Zeilinger, R.: Linking Software Life Cycle Activities with Product Strategy and Economics: Extending ISO/IEC 12207 with Product Management Best Practices. In: O'Connor, R.V., Rout, T., McCaffery, F., Dorling, A. (eds.) SPICE 2011. CCIS, vol. 155, pp. 157–168. Springer, Heidelberg (2011)
3. van de Weerd, I., Brinkkemper, S., Nieuwenhuis, R., Versendaal, J., Bijlsma, L.: Towards a Reference Framework for Software Product Management. In: 14th IEEE International Requirements Engineering Conference, pp. 319–322. IEEE Computer Society, Minneapolis (2006)
4. A Framework: for Software Product Line Practice, Version 5.0, http://www.sei.cmu.edu/productlines/frame_report/index.html
5. Pohl, K., Böckle, G., van der Linden, F.: Software Product Line Engineering – Foundations, Principles, and Techniques. Springer, Berlin (2005)
6. Microsoft Solutions Framework, http://msdn.microsoft.com/de-de/library/bb979125.aspx
7. ISO/IEC 12207:2008: Systems and software engineering — Software life cycle processes. International Standards Organization (2008)
8. Clements, P., Northrop, L.: Software Product Lines: Practices and Patterns. The SEI Series in Software Engineering. Addison-Wesley (2002)
9. van der Linden, F., Schmid, K., Rommes, E.: Software Product Lines in Action. Springer, Berlin (2007)
10. Sabisch, H.: Produkte und Produktgestaltung. In: Kern, W., Schröder, H.-H., Weber, J. (eds.) Handwörterbuch der Produktionswirtschaft, pp. 1439–1450. Schäffer-Poeschel (1996)

11. Ebert, C.: The impacts of software product management. The Journal of Systems and Software 80, 850–861 (2007)
12. ISO/IEC 15504-2: Information Technology – Process Assessment. International Standards Organization (2003)
13. Stallinger, F., Neumann, R.: Towards a Unified Framework for Software Product Management: Identification of Key Outcomes. Technical Report SCCH-TR-1211. Software Competence Center Hagenberg, Hagenberg (2012)
14. Ebert, C.: Software Product Management. Crosstalk 22(1), 15–19 (2009)
15. Kittlaus, H.-B., Clough, P.N.: Software Product Management and Pricing: Key Success Factors for Software Organizations. Springer, Berlin (2009)

An Experiment on Merging Quality Assessment in Automotive Domain

Morayo Adedjouma[1,2], Hubert Dubois[2], François Terrier[2], and Tarek Kitouni[1]

[1] DELPHI France, 64 avenue de la plaine de France, 95572 ROISSY CEDEX, France
[2] CEA LIST, Boîte 94, 91191 Gif-sur-Yvette Cedex, France
{Morayo.Adedjouma,Tarek.Kitouni}@delphi.com,
{Morayo.Adedjouma,Hubert.Dubois,Francois.Terrier}@cea.fr

Abstract. Demands for process oriented development according to Automotive SPICE standard have been constantly issued by automotive companies/suppliers for many years now. Many of them have already set these up for themselves, or accordingly aligned their improvement projects on these recommendations. With the adoption of the new ISO26262 safety standard, their main preoccupation is to check whether what they already achieved for SPICE can still be used and smoothly integrated in a larger framework to meet ISO26262 requirements. This paper discusses our proposal regarding an experiment based on a SPICE-based model assessment for safety engineering with the ISO26262 automotive standard.

Keywords: Quality assessment, software certification, HIS Automotive SPICE, ISO26262.

1 Introduction

With the recent safety-related standard ISO26262 [3], the automotive industry is interested by strategies to master its processes. In the current situation, suppliers have to prove process capabilities to OEM (Original Equipment Manufacturers) through maturity models, and standards such as: CMMI (Capability Maturity Model Integration) [14], ISO/IEC 15504 also called SPICE (Software Process Improvement and Capability Determination) [5], HIS Automotive SPICE [1], [2] (named HIS scope) in automotive domain, etc… These standards are described as being "process-based", as they define a set of practices to be adopted/followed during software development. These processes–define a set of practices to be adhered during the development of software. They provide good strategies to assess organization's software development capability and, based on the resulting assessment, they allow the identification of the processes' strengths, weaknesses and risks, and helps with preventing them. Unfortunately, they do not cover safety aspects, and thus do not satisfy requirements for a consistent safety management. On the other hand, ISO26262 is the new safety standard developed for the automotive industry for addressing this goal. It is a certification system focused on an end-product quality approach based on the construction of well-structured and reasoned safety arguments. Our work is an attempt to develop an instrument to measure the process capability of a specific engineering organization that develops safety systems. It aims at supporting software certification by both end-product quality and the development process approach in the automotive context.

The paper is organized as follows: section 2 presents our goal and the methodology envisaged to allow a full assessment for compliance to both HIS and ISO26262 standards. In section 3, we propose an assessment framework to measure the process capability of a specific engineering organization that develops safety systems. Lastly, section 4 presents an overall assessment of our methodology, and then our conclusions.

2 Certification Representation Model

In [3], an interesting note holds that *"an organization's process definition must address multiple standards at the same time. If a SPICE assessment is performed, then this SPICE assessment and a functional safety audit can be simultaneously performed. There is sufficient commonality in content that can help to avoid duplication of work or process between both standards and to allow synchronization of the planning"*.

2.1 Position Regarding Relevant Works

Much research is oriented towards the determination of a mapping between HIS and ISO 26262 [8], [9], [11]. General evidence shows that there is a high coverage of the HIS scope by the ISO 26262 standard, but a low coverage of the safety standard by the HIS scope. Since, in addition of the requirements defined at process level, as is the case in the HIS scope, the ISO 26262 standard also includes specific requirements to be considered at the product level. According to our study (Fig. 1), we reached the same result as in [16], [7].

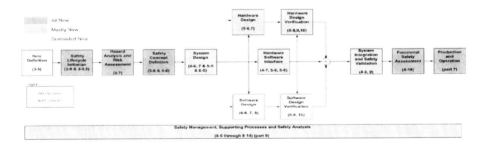

Fig. 1. HIS support in ISO 26262

Some people have opted to extend the HIS standard to ensure compliance with [7] and [8]. These approaches update HIS processes according to some ISO26262 processes that are already partially covered. In addition, they add, at the appropriate level, processes purely dedicated to safety, which is defined as the identification of hazards, the safety case creation, and the classification of safety requirements.

We decided to take another position that we believe more appropriate in the context of certification. How do we ensure good compliance to a standard that has been modified if the modification or the extension has not been approved by the certification body having published the original standard? Thus, in our compliance study, we have chosen not to modify any of the two standards, but to allow a combined assessment method which corresponds to a full compliance to the other two automotive standards. The obtained, enhanced model is an integrated model which focuses on certification and assessment of software, based on both product quality and process development approaches in a wider scope of requirements.

2.2 Extended Metamodel for HIS Scope and ISO26262 Processes

We apply a full algorithm inspired from [4], [6], [12] and [13] in order to identify the extended metamodel corresponding to the ontology of both HIS (for which we listed 16 concepts) and ISO26262 (for which we listed 21 concepts) standards. Let us define the "*similarity concept*" when two similar nodes in different standards correspond to a unique node in the common metamodel (for which we have 27 concepts in total). When a concept of a standard does not have a similar standard in the second instance, the concept is reported in the common metamodel following the transitivity and inheritance rules (see Table 1).

Table 1. Example of some matching concepts

HIS concept	ISO26262 concept	Final Concept
Category	Safety Lifecycle	Category
Workproduct	Workproduct	Workproduct
Outcome	Requirement	Requirement
Base Practice	Requirements Group	RequirementGroup
Capability level	N/A	Capability level
N/A	ASIL	ASIL

We can deduce that the *Workproduct* concept in ISO26262 is similar to the *Workproduct* concept in HIS. It is the same conclusion for the *Requirement* concept in ISO26262 and the *Outcome* concept in HIS, etc… whereas the *ASIL* concept is only present in ISO26262.

The resulting metamodel (Fig. 2) allows the description of two standards in a single way, that is to say with one language (see Fig. 3). It also allows having an assessment framework able to measure both process capability and product quality regarding the safety systems development that will be discussed in the following sections.

110   M. Adedjouma et al.

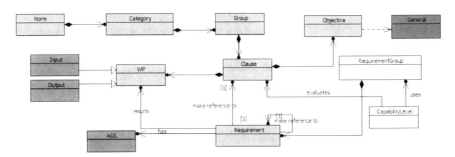

Fig. 2. Extract of the common metamodel after the concepts have been matched. The concepts in red are those from ISO26262 with no matching in HIS. Respectively, the concepts in white are from HIS with no matching found. Those in blue are present in both standards.

Clauses	Requirements	ASIL	Recommendation level	Notes	Examples	Rating
4-7.4.3.5	To ensure the suitability of well trusted design principles or elements in the new item, the results of their application shall be analysed and the underlying assumptions checked before reuse	All		The impact analysis includes the capability and feasibility of the determined diagnostics, environmental constraints, timing constraints, compatibility of the determined resources, and the robustness of the system design		N
4-7.4.3.6	A decision not to re-use well-trusted design principles should be justified.	D				N
4-7.4.3.7	in accordance with 4.3. In order to avoid failures resulting from high complexity, the architectural design shall exhibit the following properties by use of the	(A), (B), C, and D				N
a	modularity	(A), (B), C,				N
b	adequate level of granularity	(A), (B), C,				N
c	simplicity	(A), (B), C,				N
1	Hierarchical design		Highly			L
2	Precisely defined interfaces		recommended			N
3	Avoidance of unnecessary complexity of hardware components and software components		recommended			F
4	Avoidance of unnecessary complexity of interfaces		recommended			N
5	Maintainability during service		recommended			NA
6	Testability during development and operation		Highly			P

Fig. 3. Extract of a set of ISO26262 requirements presented following the common metamodel. A requirement typically has these attributes: *Clauses*, *Requirements*, *ASIL*, *Recommendation level*, Notes, *Examples* and *Rating*. For an HIS requirement, the *ASIL* attributes is always defined with value *"All"*.

3   Integrated Assessment Model

Our framework is based on the Excel format like in [11]. We begin with an analysis about overlapping and the gap existing between the standards of HIS and ISO26262, which identifies how HIS requirements are covered in the safety standard.

3.1   Definition of the Boundaries of the Evaluation Context

Before beginning the audit, it is necessary to define the boundaries of the assessment. The users have an opportunity to select their interested quality factors to be applied in the certification and assessment exercise depending on the organizations requirements:

- What is the system (or subsystem) under evaluation?
- Given that each HIS process may be audited individually, and that the HIS can achieve a different maturity level, that will identify the specific processes that will be subject to evaluation.
- Concerning ISO26262, given the number of requirements to cover increases following the higher severity to be achieved (around 1300 requirements for *ASIL A* and more than 1450 requirements for *ASIL D*, for instance, see Fig. 4), it is necessary to define the ASIL as referred to its system (or subsystem). Moreover, if we do not want to cover the entire standard, the processes (ie. parts) integrated as part of the assessment have to be precised. For instance, if it is the *ASIL A* that is allocated to the system, all requirements that are specifically valid for other severities (*B*, *C*, or *D*) are hidden by a filter defined in the framework. It is the same for methods and tools tables recommended by the standard, which can also be filtered. For generalization, all the HIS requirements have their ASIL put to "*All*".

The certification includes three pillars: product, process and, people. Therefore, we also need to take into consideration the human resources dimension. We have identified a role responsible for each WP. If desired, the assessment can also be filtered by competency.

These different settings can be parameterized in our framework. After having fixed the quality factors, we know exactly how many requirements must be met for the two standards coverage, and also the needed number to be covered for each standard.

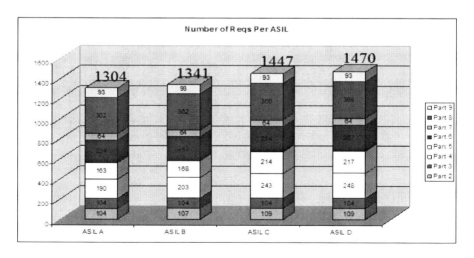

Fig. 4. Intern study realized by DELPHI on number of Requirements as per ASIL in ISO26262 (DIS)

3.2 Assessment Application

We may consider two different cases for the assessment. The first one is to identify which requirements of the safety standard ISO26262 already have a good support, if we suppose a~~n~~ HIS compliance process ready. The second one is to identify which requirements of the safety standard ISO26262 will not be fulfilled assuming the same prerequisite.

Regarding that, for each requirement, some parameters have been added. This results in the addition of new columns (Fig. 5) in the Excel file. Let's consider the example of a requirement *ReqA* of the standard A:

- The column *ISO26262 compliance* (respectively *SPICE compliance*) indicates the level of coverage of *ReqA* in the standard B. Three values are possible: *"OK"* (*ReqA* is completely covered); *"Partially"* (*ReqA* is partially covered), *"NOK"* (*ReqA* is not covered at all).
- The column *Clauses references* indicates the clause(s) reference(s) of the requirement(s) corresponding in the standard B.
- The column *Workproducts References* indicates the associated workproducts reference(s) of the requirement(s) corresponding in the standard B.

Clauses	Requirements	ASIL	Recommendation level	Notes	Examples	Rating	ISO26262 compliance	Clauses References	Workproducts References
ENG.9 - BP.6	**Document the system integration test results.** Document the results of the system integration test. The results should be delivered and communicated to all relevant parties in an appropriate way. [Outcome 5]	All				P	Partially		
	5) test results of system integration testing are recorded.	All				P	Partially	8-9.4.3	8.5.3 Integration testing report(s)
ENG.9 - BP.7	**Ensure consistency and bilateral traceability.** Ensure consistency of system architectural design to the test specification system integration test including test cases. Consistency is supported by establishing and maintaining bilateral traceability between the system architectural design and test specification system integration test including test cases. [Outcomes 6]	All				L	NOK		
	6) consistency and bilateral traceability are established between system architectural design and test specification system integration test including test cases.	All				L	NOK		
ENG.9 - BP.8	**Develop regression testing strategy and perform regression testing.** Develop the strategy for re-testing the system elements if changed hardware items or integrated software are integrated. Perform regression testing as defined in the regression test strategy and document the results. [Outcome 7]	All				N	OK		
	7) a regression strategy is developed and applied for re-testing the system elements when changes are made.	All				N	OK	4-7.4.8.1	7.5.5 System verification report (refined)

Fig. 5. Extract of a requirement specification with his references columns

Note that we rely on the availability of deliverables to assess the maturity level since, in principle, a process is validated only when all its output workproducts are available. Our resulting metamodel allows us to get the information about the (required or optional) output and input workproducts of each process (Fig. 6).Identically, a deliverable is available only if all requirements to which they refer are satisfied (Table 2). We believe that focusing the assessment on the requirement level, and not on the base practice as commonly done, ensures a more detailed assessment. The base practice is defined as an activity that addresses the purpose of a particular process, identifying, at an abstract level, "what" should be done without specifying "how".

An Experiment on Merging Quality Assessment in Automotive Domain   113

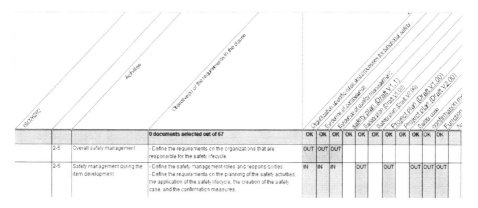

Fig. 6. The input and output workproducts per deliverable and per activity (processes)

Table 2. Example of workproduct declaration in ISO26262 and HIS

	ISO26262	HIS
Workproduct	6.5.3 Safety case, resulting from 6.4.6.	02-00 Contract [Outcome 1-7]

We have defined an Excel spreadsheet for each workproduct with all requirements relating to it. Then, we have as many Excel spreadsheets as available workproducts.

We use the SPICE rating scale [1], [10] generically to assess the satisfaction status of a requirement in the framework, that means the values *"N"*, *"L"*, *"F"*, *"P"* and *"N/A"* (Table 3) for follow-up questions.

Table 3. SPICE rating scale

N	Not achieved	0% - 15%	There is little or no evidence of achievement of the defined attribute in the assessed process.
P	Partially achieved	16% - 50%	There is some evidence of an approach to, and some achievement of, the defined attribute in the assessed process. Some aspects of achievement of the attribute may be unpredictable.
L	Largely achieved	51% - 85%	There is evidence of a systematic approach to, and significant achievement of, the defined attribute in the assessed process. Some weakness related to this attribute may exist in the assessed process.
F	Fully achieved	86% - 100%	There is evidence of a complete and systematic approach to, and full achievement of, the defined attribute in the assessed process. No significant weaknesses related to this attribute exist in the assessed process.

In HIS, as well as in the ISO26262, a requirement may participate in multiple workproducts. Our method avoids redundant work because once a requirement is validated, it will also be validated wherever else it is specified. In addition, each validated requirement automatically validates all relevant requirements, whose references are in column "*Reference*". Let us consider an example of one of the many possible cases: the requirement *ReqA*, which has already its rating value and its reference requirement *ReqB*.

- If the requirement *ReqB* is completely covered by the requirement *ReqA* (equivalent to "*OK*" value), then the rating assigned to the requirement *ReqA* is automatically carried to the requirement *ReqB*.
- If the requirement *ReqB* is partially covered by the requirement *ReqA* (equivalent to "*Partially*" value), then the rating assigned to the requirement *ReqB* is directly below that of the requirement *ReqA*, when it is possible. The table below (Table 4) summarizes the different rating values applied to *ReqB* according to the *ReqA* rating in case of partial coverage.

Table 4. *ReqB* rating values applied following the *ReqA* rating value in case of partial coverage of a requirement *ReqB* by a requirement *ReqA*

ReqA rating	ReqB rating
F	L
L	P
P	N
N	N
N/A	N/A

If the requirement *ReqA* has no corresponding reference in the standard B ("*NOK*" value), then nothing is postponed. The staining tab quickly lets us see that a workproduct is available. The coloration follows the same ones associated to the SPICE rating scale, i.e. green when all clauses are fully achieved (*F*), Yellow when they are largely achieved (*L*), orange when they are partially achieved (*P*), or red when they are not at all achieved (*N*) (Fig. 7), which by transitivity allows us to know the maturity level for each process.

Fig. 7. Staining tab code color following the readiness of the deliverable. Each tab represents the deliverable of a certain process with its rank. For example *4-6 (1)* is the first output deliverable of the subprocess 4-6 (clause 6 of part 4 of ISO26262).

4 Results and Future Works

4.1 Mapping Results

The process can be indifferently started with the HIS requirements or the ISO26262 requirements, as the work done on one affects the other. Nevertheless, it is better to start with the ISO26262 requirements because it has a wider spectrum, and some studies have concluded that covering the ISO26262 standard (regardless of ASIL level) corresponds to cover at least the capability level 2 of the HIS Automotive SPICE standard. The opposite is not true.

After performing the audit of all the requirements of a given standard, it is possible to verify, through a summary sheet, the maturity level for each process being evaluated, derived from rating of Workproducts (Fig. 8).

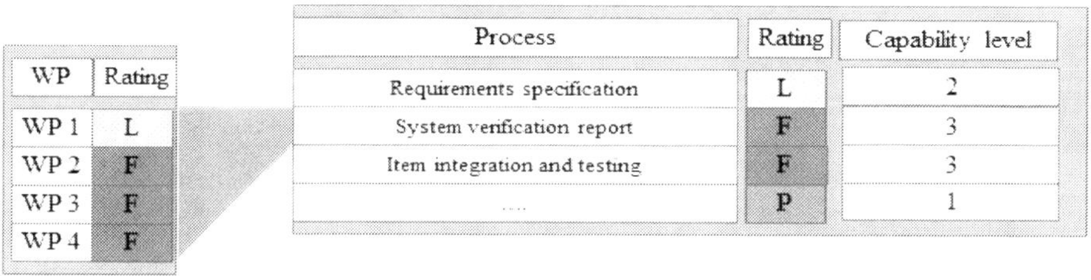

Fig. 8. Method for deriving maturity level of ISO26262 processes

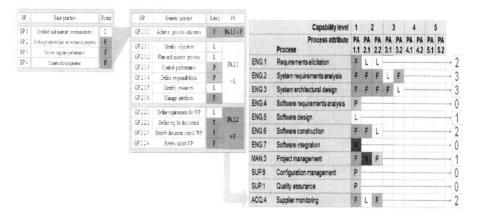

Fig. 9. Maturity level Calculus of SPICE processes. The number in blue (from *0* to *3*) represents the final maturity level achieved by the process derived from rating on their process attributes.

Also, having a partial evaluation of the standard helps greatly, since to perform a complete assessment, it is only necessary to review for each deliverable of this standard, the requirements that have not been automatically validated. These would be those whose reference column contains the *NOK* on the staining tab in red. For a SPICE audit, we have to switch to the terminology given in the standard (meaning *Base Practice, Process Attribute Generic Practice*, etc.) (Fig. 9) that we can find again regarding the matching concept (see Table 1).

We applied it on a trivial industrial case study, considering a subset of the ISO26262 (only activities associated with the specification of functional and technical requirements) and the results are more or less consistent with those expected. The saving of time and effort is undeniable as we avoid some redundancy in the verification requirements. Nevertheless, it should be used carefully; in general, only in the scope of an audit-line evaluation to one project, because, assessing processes in an organizational unit to a certain capability level means much more than requirements conformity. For instance, level 3 in SPICE means having the processes institutionalized in the organization, and a requirement's conformity itself is not enough to be sufficient for judging this fact.

It was also a first solution to evaluate the feasibility, costs and additional efforts that would require the full deployment of the ISO26262 standard on a large scale projects within the organization.

4.2 Future Works

The technology selected for the implementation of our framework is Excel. Nevertheless, given the amount of data and the numerous algorithms implemented, we meet difficulties in maintaining or adding other features. It would be wise to find a more appropriate format to ensure an efficient and effective assessment. A comparison of our common metamodel with SPEM metamodel [15] suggests to us that it would be possible to translate it in this process language with some extensions to develop to cover all our concepts.

Remember also, that the work is still at an experimental stage and therefore needs to be refined to allow a future application in an engineering organization. In addition, the matching between the ISO26262 requirements and HIS, which is the foundation of some features for the assessment, requires a great review of certification experts, although this does not undermine the proposed methodology.

5 Conclusion

Certification is commonly a hard expectation in safety-critical industries like rail, aerospace, automotive, etc. The most well-known process certificate in the automotive domain is the certification based on SPICE, which defines the necessary activities of a general quality management process. However, its application which warrants a better process, is not an assurance of getting higher product quality. At best it offers an increased level of confidence in this quality. The recent definition of the ISO26262 standard focuses on the certification of a product and its (safety-) related artifacts. This work was conducted with the objective to develop a generic methodology in an acceptable certification perspective, where an HIS assessment and a functional safety audit are simultaneously performed. Our main commitment is the definition of a framework that allows a simultaneous assessment of both standards without altering the original text. The proposed solution can be seen as an initial response to the actual automotive needs, and future works are still under development to integrate these results in a more generic process-based language. This will ensure the dissemination of our results.

References

1. Automotive SIG: Automotive SPICE, Process Assessment Model (PAM). Version 2.5 (2010), http://www.automotivespice.com (Status: released May 10, 2010)
2. Automotive SIG: Automotive SPICE, Process Reference Model (PRM). Version 4.5 (2010), http://www.automotivespice.com (Status: released May 10, 2010)
3. International Organization for Standardization: ISO International standard IS0 26262 (all parts) Road vehicles –Funcitonal safety (2011) (Status: 1st edn. November 15, 2011)
4. Kolovos, D.S., Di Ruscio, D., Pierantonio, A., Paige, R.F.: Different models for model matching: An analysis of approaches to support model differencing. In: International 2009 ICSE Workshop on Comparison and Versioning of Software Models, pp. 1–6. IEEE Computer Society (2009)
5. International Organization for Standardization: ISO/IEC International standard 15504 (all parts), Information technology – Process assessment (2004) (Status: release 2004)
6. France, R., Fleurey, F., Reddy, R., Baudry, B., Ghosh, S.: Providing Support for Model Composition in Metamodels Providing Support for Model Composition in Metamodels. In: 11th IEEE International Enterprise Distributed Object Computing Conference, p. 253. IEEE Computer Society, Annapolis (2007)
7. Petry, E.: How to Upgrade SPICE-Compliant Processes for Functional Safety. In: Tutorial, SPICE Conference 2010, Pisa (2010)
8. Lami, G., Fabbrini, F., Fusani, M.: ISO/IEC 15504-10: Motivations for Another Safety Standard. In: Flammini, F., Bologna, S., Vittorini, V. (eds.) SAFECOMP 2011. LNCS, vol. 6894, pp. 284–295. Springer, Heidelberg (2011)
9. Lami, G.: ISO/IEC 15504-10 Safety Extension, Yet Another Safety Standard? In: Report, Automotive SPIN Italia Workshop (2011)
10. Hoermann, K., Mueller, M., Dittmann, L., Zimmer, J.: Automotive SPICE in Practice: Surviving Interpretation and Assessment. Rocky Nook (2008)
11. Messnarz, R., Ross, H.-L., Habel, S., König, F., Koundoussi, A., Unterrreitmayer, J., Ekert, D.: Integrated Automotive SPICE and safety assessments. Software Process: Improvement and Practice 14(5), 279–288 (2009)
12. Chiprianov, V., Kermarrec, Y., Rouvrais, S.: Practical meta-model extension for modeling language profiles: an enterprise architecture modeling language extension for telecommunications service creation. In: 7th Days of Model Driven Engineering, Lille, pp. 85–91 (2011)
13. Barbero, M., Jouault, F., Gray, J., Bézivin, J.: A Practical Approach to Model Extension. In: Akehurst, D.H., Vogel, R., Paige, R.F. (eds.) ECMDA-FA 2007. LNCS, vol. 4530, pp. 32–42. Springer, Heidelberg (2007)
14. CMMI, http://www.sei.cmu.edu/cmmi
15. Object Management Group: OMG Software & Systems Process Engineering MetaModel (SPEM). Version 2.0, OMG document number: formal/2008-04-01 (2008)
16. Petry, E.: Automotive SPICE® & ISO/CD 26262, Their Mutual Relationship. In: Report, Fifth Automotive SPIN Italia Workshop (2009)

A Process-Oriented Approach for Functional Safety Implementation in the Automotive Industry

Maria Antonieta Garcia[1], Ernesto Viale[2], Marco Bellotti[3], and João Carlos Alchieri[4]

[1,4] Federal University of Rio Grande do Norte, Brazil
[1,2] Functional Safety Team, Skytechnology, Italy
[3] Functional Safety Expert Member of TC22/SC3/WG16 "ISO 26262 working group"
{maria.garcia,ernesto.viale}@sky-team.it,
jcalchieri@gmail.com

Abstract. Functional safety had already attracted the attention of the automotive industry, becoming a key issue of electronic control units (ECUs) installed in road vehicles. OEMs and suppliers had initially invested in improvement models, such as SPICE and CMMI, to raise the maturity of their development processes and to ensure a standardized and measurable approach to the design, test and release of ECUs. Next, they had moved to apply draft versions of ISO 26262 as to be up to date with the state-of-the-art in automobiles functional safety. The 15th November 2011, the approved version of ISO 26262 was finally released and now the automotive industry has to gather the challenge of quickly integrating its Automotive SPICE compliant processes and the new functional safety standard. This paper describes a pragmatic Methodology to cope with ISO 26262 based in its integration with Automotive SPICE, in order to optimize costs and time by reusing current processes.

Keywords: Functional Safety, Automotive SPICE, ISO 26262, integration, compliance, assessment.

1 Introduction

The recently released ISO 26262 Road Vehicle – Functional Safety standard, is pushing the automotive industry to urge for compliance.

Achieving functional safety by means of implementing this new standard calls for the development of a new state-of-the-art within the area of functional safety, what implies additional costs to the processes.

In this context emerges the need for compliance projects that optimizes costs and time. With this aim, we propose an approach that attempts to fill the gaps in the existing processes instead of completely reversing an organization's current practices to rebuild processes from scratch, what would be no cost-effective and would generate resistance to change.

Besides, considering that the automotive industry has already reached a very high safety level within the last years, and has also significantly invested in process improvement models (PIM) and dedicated reference standards, i.e. CMMI and Automotive SPICE, the base principle of the Methodology is to systemize and maintain the maturity of the processes, extending it to comprise functional safety as required by ISO 26262.

Indeed, process improvement models are very general and originally do not address functional safety development practices. Even if recently many of those models have published a safety extension, its implementation does not guarantee ISO 26262 compliance.

Within all the previous considerations, the goal of the Methodology is to integrate ISO 26262 and Automotive SPICE, a well-known process reference model (PRM) largely used in the automotive industry, for analyzing the gaps, establishing actions to introduce functional safety and reaching ISO 26262 compliance.

The proposed Methodology is supported by a tool which speeds, simplifies and reduces the effort in implementing the new functional safety standard. The Methodology aims to be fairly general to be applied by any automotive company whose products have safety relevant electronic components.

To the best of our knowledge there is no similar work done on this new standard.

2 Process Improvement Models versus Functional Safety

The knowledge regarding processes is commonly depicted as best practices, collected from the experience of a community of experts and grouped into a framework to enable its systematic implementation customized for specific domains [8].

Process improvement models have emerged with the core objective of aiding the improvement of software development processes, comprehending systems processes but not hardware.

Most models consist of a reference model, that gives guidance on how to construct an infrastructure and a culture that support effective improvement, and an assessment model in order to establish the processes maturity or capability level [1]. The reference model provides a collection of best practices that are efficient, repeatable and at the same time general enough to be applied to the development of almost any software product or service, while the assessment model provides feedback on its successful implementation, resulting in a process maturity or capability certificate.

With the purpose of addressing specific functional safety processes, the main reference models, CMMI and SPICE, have published a safety extension [2][3].

However the reference models still remain generic and not targeted to specific domains, neither detailing how processes may be executed by means of specifying methods and techniques, thus not enough to guarantee ISO 26262 compliance.

Figure Fig. 1 shows the main PRMs original process areas which would need additional safety content to comply with ISO 26262. It also depicts ISO 26262 processes addressed by the PRMs safety extension and demonstrate that although adding functional safety features, the detailed technical solution by means of specific methods remains out of the main PRMs scope.

Indeed, ISO/IEC 15504-10 addresses some key points for safety relevant products development (e.g. safety requirements management, safety planning and monitoring), but the approach requested from ISO 26262 is more rigorous, detailed and complete (e.g. safety integrity level decomposition as a mean to design product architecture).

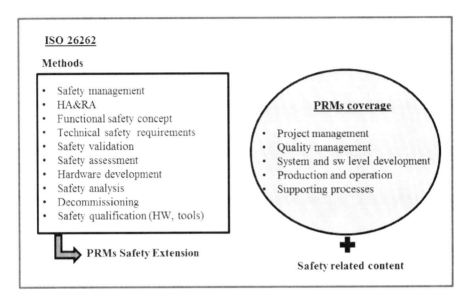

Fig. 1. Process Reference Models' coverage

Furthermore, contrary to the above models, ISO 26262 [7] is a specific standard for functional safety in road vehicles dedicated to electrical and/or electronic (E/E) systems. The standard describes the management of functional safety covering the complete product lifecycle, from system concept, through hardware and software subsystems development, to safety validation at vehicle level, from production and maintenance to product's decommissioning.

In addition it imposes constraints for methods, architectural design and implementation, according to the targeted Automotive Safety Integrity Level (ASIL).

Within the above scenery, the use of process improvement models to support the introduction of ISO 26262 standard demonstrated to be a cost effective and time saving solution, as it enables the use of the already available organizational processes.

3   Challenges in Introducing Functional Safety

The ability to demonstrate an embedded functional safety, has pushed the automotive industry to standardize its E/E systems' safety processes by means of implementing the ISO 26262 standard.

The standard consists of 9 normative parts, composed of more than 600 requirements distributed into 100 work products, and 62 decisional tables. Its great dimension and scope may require Original Equipment Manufacturers (OEM) and suppliers to employ substantial effort and time to achieve compliance and effectiveness of processes applied to its daily work.

Unless an organization intends to implement the standard from scratch, what is very unlikely, an implementation tailored to its demands and focused in updating the current processes is the natural way.

One of the greatest challenges on ISO 26262 implementation regards organizational aspects, as the introduction of functional safety urges for a top-down change process aimed at establishing a safety culture and developing safety competencies. This task requires a strong top management's commitment to institute organizational change across departments and to appoint the necessary functional safety roles with sufficient authority, qualification and knowledge (e.g. the relationship and mutual responsibilities between the Project Manager and the Safety Manager) . Such organizational aspects are out of the scope of this paper.

Another great challenge concerns processes along with its evidences. The synchronization between the new E/E safety lifecycle, as required by ISO 26262 and the current product lifecycle, by changing running processes, introducing new tasks and supporting methods, required particular attention, especially in what regards the tailoring of safety processes and the points of control (e.g. safety requirements reviews, functional safety assessment, bench test and safety validation) to avoid adding extra cost and overload.

The Methodology addresses the above mentioned process issues by integrating Automotive SPICE [5], identified as the running processes, and ISO 26262 standard.

Automotive SPICE [5] was chosen due to its wide diffusion and adoption in the automotive industry, increasing the probability that most organizations have compliant development processes.

4   Building the Method

One of the main objectives of the proposed Methodology was to support the gap analysis execution and to guide processes remediation to achieve ISO 26262 compliance, providing also means for assessing its implementation. The approach used to build the method followed the steps below:

Step 1. Identification of contact points between ISO 26262 and Automotive SPICE. The base principle is to reduce the overhead and to avoid duplicated work, by establishing compliance between their lifecycle, processes and work products, establishing whether they could be assembled by equivalence or affinity.

Step 2. Definition of the integrated Process Reference Model by:
- ✓ Merging lifecycles at system, hardware and software levels;
- ✓ Merging processes (e.g. system integration testing that comprehends vehicle testing);

- ✓ Merging work products (e.g. system requirements specification containing the functional and/or technical safety requirements);
- ✓ Merging methods and techniques (e.g. use of safety analyses to design a safe software and hardware architecture);

Step 3. Definition of the Process Assessment Model, integrating the Functional Safety Assessment, as required by ISO26262-2:2011, and Automotive SPICE PAM (Process Assessment Model) [6].

The integrated PAM allows the evaluation of both processes capabilities and the achieved functional safety.

5 Contact Points between ISO 26262 and Automotive SPICE

The first step to establish the similarities between ISO 26262 and Automotive SPICE was the analysis of their lifecycles to establish the contact points and to insert the confirmation measures required by the standard.

We then performed a clause-by-clause comparison between ISO 26262 and Automotive SPICE. This analysis was done by mapping each work product required by ISO 26262 to the Automotive SPICE process that could address it and its corresponding work product.

Mapping accuracy was ensured by a clear definition of the contents of ISO 26262 work products, making easier to cross-reference the corresponding Automotive SPICE processes and work products.

6 The Integrated Process Reference Model

Considering the fact that, as an improvement model, Automotive SPICE focuses on a general description of the processes, while ISO 26262 requires specific methods to perform it, the Integrated Reference Model proposed in the Methodology:

- ➢ details the common processes down to a level were methods and techniques, required by ISO 26262, can be applied, and
- ➢ allows the specific functional safety processes, to be inserted in the Automotive SPICE framework.

Furthermore, a tailoring effort was done to optimize ISO 26262 features to be embedded in the Integrated Reference Model, even though, the Methodology's application demonstrated it to be really useful when considering methods rather than requirements.

Indeed, from a total of 687 requirements, only 63 are tailorable for a specific ASIL, while from 210 methods, 153 may be tailored according to the ASIL.

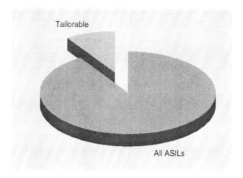

Fig. 2. ISO 26262 tailorable requirements

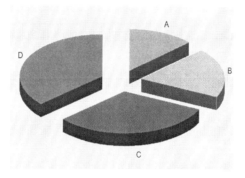

Fig. 3. ISO 26262 tailorable methods

The construction of the Integrated Reference Model has started from the merging of work products, classifying, then, each one as part of an existing process. We then created the additional functional safety specific processes, for the gaps identified in the previous analysis. Finally we defined the set of methods that ensures functional safety as required by ISO 26262 and also meets the company's objectives.

7 The Integrated Process Assessment Model

Automotive SPICE PAM is currently at version 2.5 and has been widely used to assess the capability of software in automotive companies since almost ten years.

Automotive companies are regularly subject to assessments performed either by customers or third part accredited assessors that report an official capability level profile.

Neither ISO 26262 nor IEC 61508 (i.e. general-purpose safety standard from whom ISO 26262, as many sector specific safety standards, is derived) have requirements for Notified Bodies assessment (specific auditing bodies required per standard).

ISO 26262 requires measures to be executed throughout each project, to control how safety requirements have been managed:

a) work product reviews,
b) functional safety audits,
c) functional safety assessments,

Measures of type a (i.e. work product reviews) have the aim to check formality, contents, adequacy and completeness regarding ISO 26262 requirements, of the main project work products (e.g. safety hazard analysis and risk assessment, safety plan).

Automotive SPICE PAM requires for several reviews of the main work products and a specific supporting process (i.e. SUP 4 Joint Review).

Measures of type b (i.e. functional safety audits) have the aim to evaluate the implementation of the processes against the definitions of the activities referenced or specified in the safety plan. The ISO 26262 clause that rules functional safety audits includes two informative notes that make a reference to SPICE assessments highlighting that functional safety assessments have to be performed only according to specific ISO 26262 clauses, but also recommending to integrate SPICE assessments activities and functional safety audits.

Measures of type c (i.e. functional safety assessments) have the aim to evaluate the implementation of the processes against the definitions of the activities referenced or specified in the safety plan and to provide a recommendation to accept or reject the project.

ISO 26262 supplies an informative template of a functional safety assessment agenda, requiring the functional safety assessment to cover all the activities performed by the project throughout the safety lifecycle, at system, hardware and software level, focusing as expected on the safety activities and work products.

Given the above considerations, the Integrated Process Assessment Model of our Methodology:

> lists, defines and describes the base practices of every process of each safety lifecycle phase, according to ISO 26262 framework,
> integrates the base practices from Automotive SPICE PAM, solving possible conflicts and adding recommendations and constraints mainly in the Supporting (e.g. Change and Configuration management), Management (e.g. Measurement) and Process Improvements groups.
> supplies checklists to evaluate functional safety of an E/E product and the capability level of the processes applied throughout the project lifecycle.

8 The Method

As previously stated, we developed a Methodology to aid in introducing functional safety in the development project of an E/E system. It focuses on integrating ISO 26262 requirements into Automotive SPICE implemented processes, with the aim of reducing the onus of creating new processes with all the burdening that it implies.

The method provides a guide for achieving compliance to each single ISO 26262 requirement, linked to the resulting work product(s), and for which an evidence shall be provided.

Traceability is kept to each ISO 26262 subclause and its corresponding process, providing means to establish a compliance level according to requirements coverage as it turns to implemented.

The Gap Analysis is facilitated by a previous mapping between ISO 26262 and Automotive SPICE work products, which shall be further traced to the project specific work products. The already existing work products identified in this first analysis shall be then analyzed to establish compliance. A first level analysis identifies all gaps and its corresponding corrective action. It is important to notice that in this case, there is one corrective action for each gap.

The previously identified gaps are then grouped and addressed by macro corrective actions, divided into strategic and operational corrective actions, for which a priority shall be assigned as well as a person responsible for implementing it and a due date. In this case one macro corrective action may address many gaps. This macro grouping helps to objectively establish the areas where corrective actions are required and how complex may be the interactions to implement it, as it would be very difficult to do so from the analysis of each single gap identified for more than 600 normative requirements. Furthermore it helps to determine the expertise and authority needed for the practical solution.

This classification was made possible by the keywords assigned to the requirements, namely: Process, Work Product, Content and Method. Unless for the corrective actions corresponding to requirements' gaps marked with the 'Process' keyword, all the other are macro grouped into operative corrective actions that require guidelines or templates to be implemented.

Once the macro corrective actions are defined, the above mentioned actions, regarding the update or creation of documents, are further detailed to exhaustive comprise contents and methods, covering each single ISO 26262 requirement.

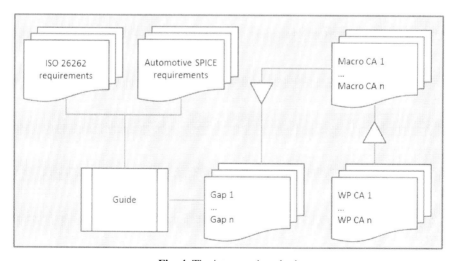

Fig. 4. The integrated method

The Methodology has been evaluated by experts and its efficacy could be demonstrated by the successful implementation of the ISO 26262 standard in OEMs and suppliers' organizations.

The experts evaluation was done by means of a first open feedback on the use of a preliminary version of the tool which supports the Methodology, followed by the tool's update to address the suggested improvements and finally a second feedback.

After the first feedback, some discussion was taken on keywords attribution, what leaded us to add the 'process' keyword, not present in the preliminary version. The guide sentences were re-formulated to clearer address ISO 26262 requirements.

The traceability, cross-referencing ISO 26262, Automotive SPICE and its current implementation, effectively enabled a strong reuse of processes and work products, ensuring compliance to both standards. Indeed, the association of each requirement to a work product enabled the construction of the minimal set, according to what was already produced, and which fully addresses ISO 26262, keeping Automotive SPICE compliance. The work products tailoring, by combination or elimination in case it is out of the company's competence perimeter, was given stronger attention when re-drafting the Methodology as to ensure a better fit to the company's demands.

9 Conclusion and Future Research Directions

The introduction of the new functional safety standard, ISO 26262 in the automotive industry demonstrated to have a huge impact on processes implying a broad range of changes from organizational aspects to the product itself.

Although not demanding a complete organizational reversal in terms of new processes, functional safety specific requirements are embedded in the whole product lifecycle, pervading processes from product concept to its decommissioning, and implying the incorporation of the safety culture into every single aspect of the daily work.

Its impact perimeter requires organizational actions such as clear bounding of responsibilities, authority, competence development and commitment from all organizational units involved in the development and operation of the product.

It also requires operational actions to be taken in a sustainable way to ensure its efficacy and not to overload the processes currently in use.

This paper proposes a method for addressing those operational aspects, in an integrated approach, that ensures ISO 26262 compliance keeping Automotive SPICE compliant processes.

The reuse of processes was made possible due to a accurate tailoring that optimized the standard implementation. This tailoring was facilitated by the integration of ISO 26262 with Automotive SPICE, what provided a solid basis, with a strong definition of processes requirements and organizational aspects.

The results of the Methodology application on pilot projects at companies with different levels of process capability indicate that where Automotive SPICE model is more thoroughly applied, relevant benefits can be achieved not only from effort and elapsed time lowering but also for safety culture diffusion and efficacy of work products development.

Main results arising from Methodology application are the following:

- ➢ fast apportionment of identified corrective actions in few homogeneous macro-classes as, for example, Quality Management System, Control and Measures, and Safety culture communication and diffusion. Each macro-class of corrective actions is assigned to specialized resources (e.g. Quality Assurance staff for QMS procedures to develop or update);
- ➢ guided selection of methods and techniques to be applied on each phase of the lifecycle; the Methodology defines criteria for methods selection (e.g. fault injection for integration testing) and for identifying the minimum set of methods sufficient to ensure the development of a safe product;
- ➢ easier update of current procedures, work instructions and work products templates with safety-specific contents;
- ➢ enhanced control of projects due to the different measures requested by the integrated model: confirmation reviews, verification reviews, safety assessments and safety audits.

The proposed method aimed at unburdening the implementation of ISO 26262, to enable OEMs and suppliers to view the compliance effort as an investment and an opportunity to steadily improve their functional safety processes.

The Proposed approach surely facilitated the achievement of compliance to the standard, even though, the method is in a preliminary stage, requiring further refinements to reach optimal results.

Even if the method speeds up and lightens the introduction of ISO 26262, it cannot be considered a 100% compliance guaranty at the first attempt. Compliance requires experience and experience takes time.

As future work, our intent is to define the ISO 26262 interactions with Automotive SPICE, detailed by capability level, as to ensure a better tailoring of the standard requirements respect to the organization's current operational mode.

We also intend to extend the method to cover other PIMs.

References

[1] Chrissis, M.B., Konrad, M.D., Shrum, S.: CMMI for Development: Guidelines for Process Integration and Product Improvement, 3rd edn. (2011)
[2] +SAFE, V1.2: A Safety Extension to CMMI-DEV, V1.2, CMU/SEI-2007-TN-006 (March 2007)
[3] ISO/IEC TS 15504-10:2011, Information technology -Process assessment - Part 10: Safety extension
[4] ISO/IEC TS 15504-10:2011, Information technology – Process assessment
[5] Automotive SPICE® Process Reference Model v4.5 (May 2010)
[6] Automotive SPICE® Process Assessment Model v2.5 (May 2010)
[7] ISO 26262-1:2011, Road vehicles - Functional safety

[8] Hauck, J.C.R.: Um método de aquisição de conhecimento para customização de modelos de capacidade/maturidade de processos de software, PhD tesis, Federal University of Santa Catarina - Brazil (February 2011)

[9] Schwarz, J., Buechl, J.: Preparing the future for functional safety of automotive e/e-systems. In: Proceedings of the 21st (ESV) International Technical Conference on the Enhanced Safety of Vehicles, Stuttgart, Germany (June 2009)

[10] Burton, S., Habermann, A.: Automotive Systems Engineering und Functional Safety: The Way Forward. In: ERTS 2012 – Embedded Real Time Software and Systems, Toulouse, France (February 2012)

Designing a Process Reference Model for Information Security Management Systems

Olivier Mangin[1], Béatrix Barafort[1], Patrick Heymans[2], and Eric Dubois[1]

[1] Public Research Center Henri Tudor,
29, av. J. F. Kennedy, L-1855 Luxembourg-Kirchberg, Luxembourg
{olivier.mangin,beatrix.barafort,eric.dubois}@tudor.lu
http://www.tudor.lu

[2] PReCISE, University of Namur
INRIA Lille-Nord Europe
Université Lille 1 - LIFL - CNRS, France
patrick.heymans@fundp.ac.be

Abstract. In spite of growing interest for information security, the adoption of the international standard on information security management (ISO/IEC 27001) is still very low. This standard provides requirements to manage an Information Security Management System. We argue that this standard is too complex to be directly implemented by small structures such as SMEs. We thus propose a process model that aims to describe the processes involved in information security management and facilitate adoption. In order to do this, we reuse process model previously derived from ISO/IEC 20000-1, which is also a management system standard but developed for IT Service Management. In this paper, we determine the generic management system requirements and their corresponding processes by mapping the requirements from ISO/IEC 20000-1 and ISO/IEC 27001 standards. At last, we create the information security specific processes with the remaining ISO/IEC 27001 requirements, and we conclude with the possible uses of the process model.

Keywords: Information Security Management, Process Reference Model, ISO/IEC 27001.

1 Introduction

Due to the increasing extent and complexity of *Information Technology* (IT), organizations need support to manage information security. In this context, the *International Organization for Standardization* (ISO) developed the ISO/IEC 2700X standards series for information security matters. The ISO/IEC 27001 [4] is the central document of this family. It provides requirements to establish, monitor, maintain and improve an *Information Security Management System* (ISMS).

Although the interest for this standard is growing, its adoption is still very low, especially in *Small and Medium sized Enterprises* (SMEs). According to Barlette and Fomin [9], the reasons are multiple:

1. It is very difficult to prove the usefulness of information security standards as it is complicated to quantify the increase of information security.
2. SME managers are not aware of legislations concerning insufficient data protection.
3. An important amount of resources (money, time and skills) is needed for efficient implementation.

SMEs with enough resources can hire specialized consultants or buy specific ISMS management tools, but this is a minority. Also, according to Wiedemann [22], such tools (checklists, risk management software) are inadequate as they are *ad hoc* and do not properly cover the standard requirements.

In this context, this article focuses on the design of a *Process Reference Model* (PRM) covering the ISO/IEC 27001 requirements. This PRM will be part of a global framework for facilitating the deployment and maintenance of ISMSs. This framework will be suitable for SMEs by considering their specific issues. This framework is expected to decrease the amount of resource required and to help to quantify information security through the use of metrics. The PRM structures the requirements from the ISO/IEC 27001 standard into reference processes. These processes give a structure to help the persons in charge of the ISMS to deploy processes in their organization. To determine what the PRM should contain, we follow the *ISO/IEC 15504-2* standard [2].

ISO/IEC 15504 is a standard series on Process Assessment. It provides requirements to conduct a process assessment and to design process models; guidelines for process improvement or capability determination; and exemplar process models. The ISO/IEC 15504-2 standard gives organizations the minimum requirements for process assessment and process model design. The process assessment requires two artifacts: the *Process Reference Model* (PRM) and the *Process Assessment Model* (PAM). A PRM describes the various processes in terms of purpose (the high level overall objective for performing the process) and outcomes (demonstrating the successful achievement of process purpose). A PAM is a model suitable for the purpose of assessing process capability, based on one or more Process Reference Models. We do not address the design of the PAM as the process assessment is not in the scope of our research work.

To build this PRM, we propose to reuse an existing PRM that was defined by the ISO project *ISO/IEC 20000-4* [5], namely IT Service Management Process Reference Model. This PRM covers the requirements of the *ISO/IEC 20000-1* standard [3]. This standard defines the requirements for an *IT Service Management System*. This connection is relevant because this standard shares similarities with the ISO/IEC 27001. Indeed, both standards are part of the management system standard family. That is the reason why we propose a mapping between ISO/IEC 27001 and ISO/IEC 20000-1 requirements. This mapping highlights common management system requirements. As these requirements are already linked to a PRM in the ISO/IEC 20000-4, the results of the mapping provide a sound input to the PRM definition based on ISO/IEC 27001 requirements. However, the mapping concerns only the management system requirements, thus, we identified additional information security specific processes based on the remaining requirements. A quick overview of the involved standards is given in Fig. 1. Rectangles represent the standards of the management system family. Ovals represent standards families. Rounded rectangles represent the output of the present article. Rectangles with clipped corners denote the other standards.

To summarize, the purpose of this article is to apply the proposal to design a PRM covering ISO/IEC 27001 requirements. This paper is organized as follows: Section 2 exposes the standardization context. Section 3 discusses related work. Section 4 explains the mapping methodology before the mapping itself presented in Section 5. Section 6 focuses on the remaining processes , i.e. those that are specific to information security. Finally, Section 7 suggests possible uses of the PRM and wraps up the paper.

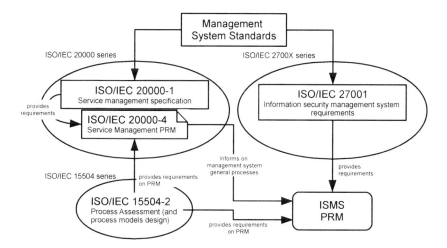

Fig. 1. Overview of the involved standards

2 Standardization Context

According to ISO, a management system refers to what the organization does to manage its processes, or activities, so that its products or services meet the objectives it has set itself. The "*Plan-Do-Check-Act*" (PDCA) cycle is the operating principle of ISO's management system standards. The "Plan" phase aims to establish objectives and make plans (analyze the organization's situation, establish the overall objectives). The "Do" phase intends to implement the plans - do what you planned to. The "Check" phase aims to measure the results. The "Act" phase intends to correct and improve the plans - learn from mistakes and improve plans so as to achieve better results next time. This concept was introduced first with the ISO 9001 standard [1] which provides requirements to establish a quality management system.

Although the ISO/IEC 20000-1 and ISO/IEC 27001 standards are both management system standards, their structure differs. On the one hand, the ISO/IEC 20000-1 standard divides the requirements into 6 main clauses (A clause is a section in a standard document). The first clause considers the service management general requirements while the other five ones consider the service processes. On the other hand, the ISO/IEC 27001 standard follows a different structure. A clause presents the ISMS requirements including the information security specific requirements. The following clauses specify requirements on management system specific activities, namely management responsibility, internal audits, management review and improvement.

In order to harmonize *Management System standards* (MSS), ISO created a group (Technical Management Board / Joint Technical Coordination Group) to improve the alignment between them in 2006. This group started to create a common structure, including common core terms and definitions. The main common identified clauses are *context of organization, leadership & planning, support, operations, performance evaluation,* and *improvement*.

In November 2010, ISO published a PRM based on the ISO/IEC 20000-1 requirements: the ISO/IEC 20000-4 standard [5], with the following scope: *"This Technical Report defines a PRM comprising a set of processes, described in terms of process purpose and outcomes that demonstrate coverage of the requirements of ISO/IEC 20000-1"*. As stated in the Introduction of ISO/IEC 20000-4:

"The PRM specified in this Technical Report describes at an abstract level the processes including the general service management system (SMS) processes implied by ISO/IEC 20000-1[...] Any organization may define processes with additional elements in order to suit it to its specific environment and circumstances. The purposes and outcomes described in this Technical Report are, however, considered to be the minimum necessary to meet ISO/IEC 20000-1 requirements. Some processes cover general strategic aspects of an organization. These processes have been identified in order to give coverage to all the requirements of ISO/IEC 20000-1."

Walker [21] did similar work by proposing a PRM covering ISO 9001 requirements. Although the author gives only few explanations about the identification of the processes, he explains how he linked each atomic requirement to a process outcome. His PRM proposal for ISO 9001 contains a set of management system processes very similar to the ISO/IEC 20000-4 ones.

3 Related Work

To create ISO/IEC 15504 compliant PRM and PAM is a subject of growing interest in the scientific and normative communities. Many initiatives proposed PRM and PAM for various domains such as IT security [7], IT service management [14,15,8,12], knowledge management [11], internal financial control [13], industrial processes [10], regulation compliance [18] and public university research laboratories [19]. In these projects, we noticed that two approaches are used.

The first one [10] consists in extracting processes and their outcomes from subject matter experts in the corresponding community of practice, e.g. through interviews, workshops and surveys. But in very specific domains such as information security, this may be hard to achieve due to limited resources and/or the difficulty to find the adequate experts to consult.

The second approach is based on *Goal Oriented Requirements Engineering* (GORE) techniques [20]. These techniques are one of the major developments of the Requirements Engineering (RE) community. They aim specifically at capturing goals, reasoning on them, and linking them to more operational requirements. Thus, starting from a collection of requirements proposed by a regulation or a standard, the researchers are able to discover underlying goals. Then, the different goals become what the PRM calls the process purpose. In particular, Rifaut and Dubois [18] created a PRM from the Basel II regulation. They started by extracting a flat list of requirements from the regulation. They separated implementation practices (*How*) from business goals (*What*). Then, they used a GORE modeling technique to discover the purpose of the various requirements, and group them according to their high level goal. They used goal diagrams to structure outcomes and indicators. Rifaut and Dubois claim that the usage of GORE techniques demonstrates the full coverage of the regulation and allows keeping traceability between purposes and outcomes. Picard et al. [17] also use a GORE technique to build a process model. They use goal diagrams not only for the process model but also to discuss and validate it. But, at that time, their proposals were just a possible input for the revision of the ISO/IEC 15504-2 standard. This approach was previously used by Barafort *et al.* to propose a PRM and a PAM for ISO/IEC 20000-1 [8].

Our work uses a method similar as the one used by Walker [21] described in section 2. This method is further detailed in the next section.

4 Mapping Methodology

At first, we broke down the ISO/IEC 27001 standard clauses into atomic requirements, which is a recognized best practice in RE. We did not take into account the security controls (from the Annex A). An atomic requirement is a requirement that cannot be further decomposed into multiple requirements. Normative sentences from both standards (ISO/IEC 27001 and ISO/IEC 20000-1) were broken down into atomic requirements. For example, in section 6 *"Internal ISMS Audit"* from ISO/IEC 27001, the requirement *"The audit criteria, scope, frequency and methods shall be defined."* is split into four atomic requirements: *"the audit criteria shall be defined"*, *"the audit scope shall be defined"*, *"the audit frequency shall be defined"* and *"the audit methods shall be defined"*. At the end, the ISO/IEC 20000-1 and ISO/IEC 27001 standards yielded respectively 235 and 273 atomic requirements.

Then, we identified processes from ISO/IEC 20000-4 that are generic to all management systems. The ISO/IEC 20000-4 organizes the processes as sets. Among them, a set is labeled "SMS general processes". This set gathers all processes that refer to management system activities. Only this set will be considered during this mapping as the other processes targeted by the ISO/IEC 20000-4 standard are dedicated to IT Service Management. The processes are: *Organizational Management*, *SMS establishment and maintenance*, *Management review*, *Audit*, *Measurement*, *Improvement*, *Human resource management*, *Risk management*, and *Information item management*. However, ISO/IEC 20000-4 provides high-level traceability between the ISO/IEC 20000-1 subclauses and the corresponding outcomes from the ISO/IEC 20000-4, but it does not refer to the specific requirement inside/of the subclause.

Once the processes were identified, we analyzed the purpose, the outcomes, and the requirements traceability given for each process. Sometimes the purpose and the outcomes were specific to the IT service management domain. We transformed them to match the information security management domain. This transformation consisted mainly in turning "*Service Management System*" (SMS) into "*Information Security Management System*" (ISMS). For example, "*Roles and responsibilities needed to support SMS processes are defined*" became "*Roles and responsibilities needed to support ISMS processes are defined*". We thus created a list of 9 potential processes.

Thanks to the process purpose, the process outcomes and traceability links, we were able to identify the requirements from the ISO/IEC 20000-1 that correspond to a specific process. Then, the work consisted in finding semantically equivalent requirements between those from 20000-1 and those from 27001 to determine management system processes that exist in the latter standard. As both standards use the ISO 9001 management system structure as basis, some requirements were almost identical. But sometimes, this analysis failed to discover the requirements associated with outcomes. We thus looked for synonyms of the keywords in the outcomes in order to discover the requirements.

In parallel, we used a second approach. We used the title of the clauses and the subclauses from both standards (ISO/IEC 20000-1 and ISO/IEC 27001). For example, the "Audit" process from the ISO/IEC 20000-4 PRM refers to the requirements from the "Audit" clause of the ISO/IEC 20000-1. The ISO/IEC 27001 also includes an audit clause under the denomination "Internal ISMS audits". In addition, we checked whether the requirements were semantically equivalent, as described in the previous paragraph, to consolidate the mapping and prevent mapping requirements outside their context.

Moreover, the process outcomes are refined following the recommendations of Medina-Mora *et al.* [16]. The ActionWorkflow Loop requires four phases: a proposal (some conditions of satisfaction are defined), an agreement (the conditions are agreed between stakeholders), a performance (the process is performed), and a satisfaction (the completion of conditions are satisfied). We thus ensure the completeness of the designed processes. Fig. 2 gives an overview of the methodology. As quoted in the ISO/IEC 20000-4 statement of conformity, the ISO/IEC 20000-4 processes meet ISO/IEC 15504-2 requirements concerning process models. As the same approach was used to derived the ISO/IEC 27001 PRM, we consider that the ISO/IEC 27001 PRM processes comply with these requirements.

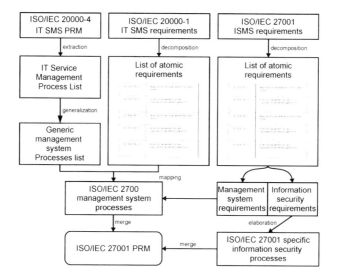

Fig. 2. Overview of the mapping methodology

5 The Mapping

The mapping concerned the nine previously identified processes. Table 1 shows the mapping's output for each of them. Some processes turned out to be easier to map than others. Indeed, the requirements corresponding to *"management review"*, *"improvement"*, *"information item management"* and *"audit"* processes are derived from the ISO 9001 standard. As the mapping for these processes was simple, we just illustrate it through the audit process in the next subsection. But for the *"Organizational Management"* process, the mapping was more complex. Subsection 5.2 will explain why and how the process was adapted to conform to the ISMS context. Note that we did not consider the risk management process as a management system process. This is a core process of information security management and will be treated with the other information security specific processes in Section 6.

5.1 Audit Process

As mentioned previously, the mapping for this process involved similar standard clauses. The sentences do not contain the same words but they have the same meaning. The main information sources are *"Internal audit (4.5.4.2)"* for the ISO/IEC 20000-1 and *"Internal ISMS audits (6)"* for the ISO/IEC 27001.

Table 1. Process candidate overview

Candidate process PRM ISO/IEC 27001	Level of Confidence	Observations
Management review	++	Very similar clause in ISO/IEC 20000-1
Audit	++	Very similar clause in ISO/IEC 20000-1
Improvement	++	Very similar clause with more details. ISO/IEC 27001 considers two kinds of improvements: corrective actions and preventive actions.
Information item management	++	Very similar clause in ISO/IEC 20000-1
Organizational Management	-	Split in two processes: - Organizational Leadership - Resource Management (except human resources dealt with in a specific process)
ISMS establishment and maintenance	+	The process specified by the ISO/IEC 20000-4 is satisfied with the ISO/IEC 27001 context. The given outcomes were specific to IT service management, but we managed to transform them. The degree of confidence is not maximal because it is difficult to verify whether all ISO/IEC 27001 requirements are linked to the process outcomes. And sometimes ISO/IEC 20000-4 process' outcomes were not clear enough.
Measurement	++	Measurement activities are not in a specific clause. They appear more clearly in ISO/IEC 27001 than in ISO/IEC 20000-1
Human resource management	+	There is no Human Resource Management clause in the ISO/IEC 270001. But there is a subclause in both standards.
Risk management	- -	Risk management is much more detailed in ISO/IEC 27001 than in ISO/IEC 20000-1 standard.

+ +: the process defined in ISO/IEC 20000-4 is linked to ISO/IEC 20000-1 requirements which are gathered in a unique clause. The clause and the process have generally a really similar name. Moreover, the clause also exists in ISO/IEC 27001 and its content is very similar to ISO/IEC 20000-1.
+: the process defined in ISO/IEC 20000-4 is linked to ISO/IEC 20000-1 requirements which are gathered in a unique clause. But that clause does not exist in ISO/IEC 27001. Nevertheless, we identified common subclauses and requirements in ISO/IEC 27001.
-: the process defined in ISO/20000-4 contains IT service management specific outcomes. Moreover, its number of outcomes is large. It needs to be transformed into multiple processes to reduce the number of outcomes per process. The new processes will have a smaller and a more understandable scope.
- -: the process defined in ISO/20000-4 is not relevant in the ISO/IEC 27001 context.

These clauses are both based on the ISO 9001 audit clause. For example, in ISO/IEC 20000-1, *"An audit programme shall be planned. This shall take into consideration the status and importance of the processes and areas to be audited, as well as the results of previous audits."* is equivalent to *"An audit programme shall be planned, taking into consideration the status and importance of the processes and areas to be audited, as well as the results of previous audits"* from ISO/IEC 27001. The audit process mentioned in the ISO/IEC 20000-4 standard provides six outcomes. All but one are linked with requirements located in the aforementioned clauses.

For example, the fourth outcome, namely *"nonconformities are recorded"*, is not fully covered by the audit clause. It also refers to the *"Monitor and review the ISMS"* (4.2.3). In order to find requirements that are not located in the expected section, we performed a keyword-based search in the whole document. So, to find audit related requirements, we used the keyword "audit". 25 requirements from the ISO/IEC 27001 requirements list were linked with the audit process.

5.2 Organizational Management Process

According to ISO/IEC 20000-4, this process is *"the umbrella process in the Service Management System"*. The vast majority of the ISO/IEC 20000-1 requirements linked with this process come from the "Management responsibility" subclause.

The purposes of the organizational management process are multiple. It aims to: *"establish the service management objectives in order to satisfy the requirements of customers and interested parties, identify and provide resources in order* to satisfy the requirements of customers and interested parties, and monitor performance of IT service provision in order to satisfy the requirements of customers and interested parties."

We transformed the first part of the purpose to match ISO/IEC 27001 context. It became: "establish the information security management objectives in order to satisfy the business and legal or regulatory requirements, and contractual security obligations". But this is not precise. Even with the link between the requirements and the outcomes, it is difficult to determine whether it covers the ISM (Information Security Management) policy definition or the establishment of ISM processes. The second part of the purpose does not need to be transformed. It concerns resource management and management responsibility. The last part becomes "monitor performance of information security in order to satisfy the business and legal or regulatory requirements, and contractual security obligations". This purpose concerns the measurement, improvement, review, and audit processes.

In addition, we can consider the ISO/IEC TR 24774 [6], a technical report providing guidelines for process description. According to it, *"the number of outcomes for a process should fall within the range 3 to 7"*. This process has 14 outcomes in the ISO/IEC 20000-4 and thus needs simplification. In order to do so, we broke it down into two processes. The first one, resource management, covers all the requirements related to resources, except human resources as they are already covered (see Table 1). The second one, the organizational leadership process, covers all top management responsibility requirements. The two resulting processes are presented in Tables 2 and 3. 23 and 25 requirements from the ISO/IEC 27001 requirements list were linked with the resource management process and organizational management one.

Table 2. Resource Management

Purpose	The purpose of the resource management process is to provide the organization with necessary resources and to maintain their procedures to support information security requirements, business needs and customer requirements.
Outcomes	1. resources required by the organization for information security are identified 2. resources are provided to efficiently manage the ISMS 3. resources are provided to support security controls and legal and regulatory requirements 4. resources are monitored to guarantee their availability and efficiency 5. resource needs are reviewed

6 Determination of Information Security Specific Processes

After this mapping, 55 atomic requirements were still not linked with any process. We inferred that they are information security specific requirements. These requirements are located only in the "Establishing and managing the ISMS" clause of the standard. This clause is divided into four subclauses corresponding to the steps of the PDCA cycle. To elicit processes from these requirements, we gathered the requirements according to their goal as performed in [18]. Then, we transformed these categories into processes, *viz.* *"Scope Management"*, *"Risk Management"* and *"Risk operational treatment"*.

Table 3. Organizational Management

Purpose	The purpose of the organizational management process is to establish the service management objectives, identify and provide resources, and monitor performance of IT service provision, in order to satisfy the requirements of customers and interested parties.
Outcomes	1. the objectives and requirements for ISM are identified and established to satisfy business, financial, regulatory, contractual, and statutory requirements 2. the structure of the organization enables assurance of the information security 3. information security management is planned and implemented with the intent of achieving the ISM objectives 4. roles, competencies, authorities and responsibilities are identified and appointed to enable assurance of information security 5. information security is assured and maintained in accordance with the agreed requirements 6. the importance of meeting information security objectives and conforming to the information security policy is regularly communicated to stakeholders

The *"Scope Management"* process aims to identify all the activities related to the determination of the ISMS' boundaries. These activities cover exclusions and inclusions of business processes in the scope. The scope of the *"Risk management"* process is to identify assets and the risk they face, perform an assessment on the previously identified risks, and determine risk treatment according to the assessment. The *"Risk operational treatment"* process intends to use results of the risk assessment to maintain information security at the agreed level. In order to respect the PRM requirements from ISO/IEC 15504-2 standard, we created outcomes and purpose for each process (see Table 4). After the design of these processes, all the atomic requirements were linked with a process. We used the ActionWorkflow Loop, already introduced in the mapping methodology section, to develop the outcomes.

The Annex A is not considered in the mapping. Indeed, the standard requires to *"select[...] control objectives and controls [...] as suitable to cover the identified*

Table 4. Information Security Specific Processes

Scope management	
Context	The scope of this process is to identify all the activities related to the determination of the boundaries of the ISMS. These activities are covering exclusions and inclusions of different business processes of the organization
Purpose	The purpose of scope management is to establish the scope of the ISMS according to business specificities and top management requirements
Outcomes	1. Business scope and boundaries are defined 2. Organizational scope and boundaries are defined 3. Information communication technology (ICT) scope and boundaries are defined 4. Each scope and boundaries are integrated to obtain the ISMS scope and boundaries 5. Scope is revised according to modification of the organizational structure

Risk management	
Context	The scope of the process is to assess risks faced by the assets that are in the scope of the ISMS
Purpose	The purpose of the process is to identify assets and the risks they face, and determine treatment according to the risk evaluations.
Outcomes	1. A risk assessment approach is selected 2. Risks are identified using the risk assessment approach 3. Risks are analyzed and evaluated 4. Options for treatment of risks are identified and evaluated 5. Control objectives and controls are selected for treatment of risks 6. Risks are updated according to reviews, audits and scope modifications 7. Risk assessment is approved by top management

Risk operational treatment	
Context	The scope of this process is to ensure day-to-day information security assurance
Purpose	The purpose of the process is to maintain information security at its expected level
Outcomes	1. The risk treatment plan is formulated according to the risk assessment 2. Control objectives, controls, and the risk treatment plan are implemented 3. Procedures to detect security events are implemented 4. Procedures to detect security events are monitored and reviewed 5. Risk treatment plan is updated according to security events and modifications of the risk assessment

requirements". As this selection may vary according to the organization's risk assessment, we chose not to include them in the PRM.

7 Conclusion and Perspectives

The method to create the PRM based on the ISO/IEC 27001 requirements is based on a mapping. This mapping with the IT Service Management standard allowed us to extract/find reference management system processes which are also present in the ISMS standard.

The mapping aimed to bring a sound input to the PRM design. Indeed, the management system general processes from ISO/IEC 20000-4 helped to separate management system specific requirements from information security specific ones. The publication of the ISO/IEC 20000-4 and the ISO's efforts to improve MSS alignment provide arguments supporting our methodology. The next step of our work is to validate the model. This validation will concern the representation of the ISO/IEC 27001 standard as a PRM and the adequacy of the PRM. The perspectives are multiple. The PRM aims to help SMEs with the use of the ISO/IEC 27001 standard. It will be the basis for designing a tool for supporting SMEs during ISMS implementation. It will give a list of processes and outcomes required during this task. It will be also useful for verifying day-to-day activities of the ISMS, and discovering what activity is not properly done. For organizations wishing to demonstrate conformity to ISO/IEC 27001 requirements for the purpose of certification, it will help auditors to verify the fulfillment of the requirements.

Acknowledgement. This present project is supported by the National Research Fund, Luxembourg.

References

1. ISO 9001:2008 quality management systems – requirements (2008)
2. ISO/IEC 15504-2:2003 software engineering — process assessment — part 2: Performing an assessment
3. ISO/IEC 20000-1:2011 information technology – service management – part 1: Service management system requirements
4. ISO/IEC 27001:2005 information technology – security techniques – information security management systems – requirements
5. ISO/IEC TR 20000-4:2010 information technology – service management – part 4: Process reference model
6. ISO/IEC TR 24774:2010 systems and software engineering – life cycle management – guidelines for process description
7. Barafort, B., Humbert, J.P., Poggi, S.: Information security management and ISO/IEC 15504: the link opportunity between security and quality. In: SPICE Conference, Luxembourg (2006)

8. Barafort, B., Renault, A., Picard, M., Cortina, S.: A transformation process for building prms and pams based on a collection of requirements – example with ISO/IEC 20000. In: SPICE Conference, Nuremberg, Germany (2008)
9. Barlette, Y., Fomin, V.V.: Exploring the suitability of is security management standards for smes. In: Annual International Conference on System Sciences, Hawaii, USA, vol. 41, p. 308 (2008)
10. Coletta, A.: An industrial experience in assessing the capability of non-software processes using ISO/IEC 15504. Software Process: Improvement and Practice 12(4), 315–319 (2007)
11. Di Renzo, B., Valoggia, P.: Assessment and improvement of firm's knowledge management capabilities by using a KM process assessment compliant to ISO/IEC 15504. A case study. In: SPICE Conference, Seoul, South Korea (2007)
12. Hilbert, R., Renault, A.: Assessing IT service management processes with AIDA experience feedback. In: EuroSPI, Postdam, Germany (2007)
13. Ivanyos, J.: Implementing process assessment model of internal financial control. In: The International SPICE Days, Frankfurt/Main, Germany (2007)
14. Jokela, J.: Long term utilisation of spice in an it service company. In: SPICE Conference, Turku, Finland (2009)
15. Malzahn, D.: A service extension for spice? In: SPICE Conference, Seoul, South Korea (2007)
16. Medina-Mora, R., Winograd, T., Flores, R., Flores, F.: The action workflow approach to workflow management technology. In: ACM Conference on Computer-Supported Cooperative Work, Toronto, Canada, pp. 281–288 (1992)
17. Picard, M., Renault, A., Cortina, S.: How to Improve Process Models for Better ISO/IEC 15504 Process Assessment. In: Riel, A., O'Connor, R., Tichkiewitch, S., Messnarz, R. (eds.) EuroSPI 2010. CCIS, vol. 99, pp. 130–141. Springer, Heidelberg (2010)
18. Rifaut, A., Dubois, E.: Using goal-oriented requirements engineering for improving the quality of ISO/IEC 15504 based compliance assessment frameworks. In: 16th IEEE International Requirements Engineering Conference, Barcelona, Spain, vol. 16, pp. 33–42. IEEE Computer Society (2008)
19. Silva, J.V.L., Nabuco, O.F., Salviano, C.F., Reis, M.C., Maciel Filho, R.: Towards an iso/iec 15504-based process capability model for public university's research laboratory. In: SPICE Conference, Seoul, South Korea, vol. 2007, pp. 12–21 (2007)
20. Van Lamsweerde, A.: Goal-oriented requirements engineering: A guided tour. In: Fifth IEEE International Symposium on Requirements Engineering, Toronto, Canada, pp. 249–262. IEEE (2001)
21. Walker, A.: Towards ISO 9001:201x: Transitioning from process quality to product quality. In: South African Committee for the Certification of Quality System Auditors Conference, vol. 12 (2009)
22. Wiedemann, A.: Evaluation methodology for assessing management system establishment support tools. Open Software Engineering Journal 3, 9–14 (2009)

Barriers to Adopting Agile Practices When Developing Medical Device Software

Martin McHugh, Fergal McCaffery, and Valentine Casey

Regulated Software Research Group, Department of Computing and Mathematics,
Dundalk Institute of Technology & Lero,
Dundalk Co. Louth, Ireland
{martin.mchugh,fergal.mccaffery,val.casey}@dkit.ie

Abstract. Agile methodologies such as XP and Scrum are founded upon the four values and twelve principles of agile software development. A software development project is only considered to be truly agile if these values and principles are followed. However, software developed for use in medical devices must be regulatory compliant and this can make the process of following a single agile methodology such as XP difficult to achieve. This paper outlines how we identified the barriers to agile adoption in the medical device software domain through performing a survey. These barriers include: lack of documentation; maintaining traceability; regulatory compliance; lack of up front planning and the process of managing multiple releases. Based on this research recommendations are also made as to how these barriers can be overcome.

Keywords: Safety Critical, Agile, Plan Driven, XP, Scrum, Barriers, Medical.

1 Introduction

Software is playing an increasingly important role in healthcare [1]. As the reliance on this software is increasing, regulatory controls are evolving to ensure the safe and reliable performance of medical devices, to prevent harm to patients, clinicians and third parties.

Software is developed in accordance with a customer's requirements. Software used as a medical device or as part of a medical device must also be developed in accordance with the regulatory requirements of the region in which the device is being marketed [2]. The generic software development industry has benefited from adopting agile practices [3]. These practices are procedures defined as being highly effective and efficient [4] such as sprint planning, an open office space, daily meetings and product backlogs from Scrum, these have the added benefit of being more cost effective [5]. However, there is a low rate of agile adoption amongst safety critical software developers [6]. The reasons for this are still being investigated. This paper presents research performed to identify the barriers to adopting agile practices when developing medical device software.

As part of this research, a survey was conducted amongst medical device software development organisations in Ireland. This paper also provides recommendations as to how these barriers may be overcome.

The remainder of this paper is structured as follows; in section 2, we present the challenges faced by medical device software developers. In section 3, we outline the survey conducted and present the results. In section 4, we examine each of the barriers identified in section 3 and recommendations are presented as to how these barriers can be overcome. Finally, in section 5, we present our conclusions and outline how this work will contribute to future research.

2 Challenges to Developing Medical Device Software

Software developed for use as a medical device or as part of a medical device in Europe must conform to the latest amendment to the Medical Device Directive (MDD) 2007/47/EC [7] and the guidance of the associated MED DEV [8] document. Software developed as a medical device or part of a medical device in the US must conform to the FDA 21 CFR Part 820 [9] Quality System Regulations and conformance is recommended to one or more of the following Food and Drug Administration (FDA) guidance documents:

- General Principles of Software Validation (GPSV) [10];
- Medical Device Data Systems Rule [11];
- Guidance for the Content of Premarket Submissions for Software Contained in Medical Devices [12];
- Draft Guidance for Industry and Food and Drug Administration - Mobile Device Applications [13];
- Guidance for Industry, FDA Reviewers and Compliance on Off-The-Shelf Software use in Medical Devices [14].

Both the US and European regulations dictate what information a medical device software development organisation must produce in order to achieve regulatory conformance. However, these guidelines do not mandate the usage of a specific lifecycle to produce this necessary information. IEC 62304:2006 – Medical Device Software – Software life cycle processes [15] is harmonised with the MDD [16] and is approved for use by the FDA. IEC 62304 also does not mandate the usage of a specific lifecycle.

Research conducted at Cochlear [17], Abbott Diagnostics [18], Medtronic [19] and a Danish Pharmaceutical Company [20] revealed that medical device software developers are actively seeking an alternative to traditional plan driven methodologies. These case studies revealed that following agile practices can resolve problems associated with plan driven software development.

3   Barriers to Agile Adoption

As part of their on-going research the authors performed a survey of Irish medical device software development organisations. Twenty medical device software development organisations were surveyed with multiple responses being received from each organisation. The survey revealed that 100% of the respondents who are currently marketing medical device software are developing it for use in Europe. In addition, 79% of these are also developing medical device software for use in the US.

The survey identified that 50% of the organisations are developing software in accordance with the V-Model. An important finding was that another 25% of the organisations are developing medical device software in accordance with agile practices. The remaining 25% of organizations are developing software in accordance with other development lifecycles such as the Waterfall, and Iterative & Incremental approaches. Participants were asked as part of this survey, to identify the barriers to adopting agile practices when developing medical device software. The following issues were identified by participants as barriers:

- Lack of Documentation;
- Traceability Issues;
- Regulatory Compliance;
- Lack of Up-Front planning;
- Managing Multiple Releases.

4   Overcoming Identified Barriers

Five barriers to agile adoption have been identified through the survey as outlined in section 3. Each of these barriers was examined and recommendations made as to how these barriers may be overcome.

4.1   Lack of Documentation

The Agile Manifesto [21] has four key values. One of these values is *"Working Software over Comprehensive Documentation"*. This value would appear to be a direct contradiction of the regulatory requirements. The FDA regulations require a medical device software development organisation to fully document requirements prior to development [22]. However, Robert Martin, one of the authors of the Agile Manifesto states [21];

> *"Produce no document unless it's immediate and significant"*.

In terms of achieving regulatory compliance, documentation is significant and as such it would still be produced when following agile practices. Research conducted by Berard [23] examined the misconceptions regarding documentation and agile software development. Agile software developers deliver what is requested by the customer.

Simply put if a customer/regulatory body requires documentation from an agile development team there are no barriers in place to prevent the team from producing this documentation whilst still following agile practices.

4.2 Traceability Issues

In order for medical device software development organisations to achieve regulatory approval they must provide evidence of traceability from the requirements specification to each stage of the development process. The FDA General Principles of Software Validation (GPSV) [10] document mandates that code must be linked to requirements and test cases. Using agile practices, requirements are not fixed before development begins and during development changes to requirements are welcomed. However, once the requirements specifications and changes to the requirements specifications are fully documented, traceability can still be maintained. The FDA General Principles of Software Validation state;

"Most software development models will be iterative. This is likely to result in several versions of both the software requirement specification and the software design specification. All approved versions should be archived and controlled in accordance with established configuration management procedures".

This statement acts as evidence that regulatory bodies acknowledge that requirements can and do change and this is acceptable as long as configuration management procedures are adhered to. This results in requirements that can be used to perform traceability.

Lee et al, [24], present a tool known as *"Echo"* which can be used to capture requirements as part of an agile development project. This tool provides a mechanism to maintain traceability between the requirements and each stage of development whilst developing software in accordance with agile practices.

4.3 Regulatory Compliance

Regulatory controls and development standards provide guidance in the development of a safe and reliable medical device. However, the MDD, the FDA and the IEC 62304 standard do not enforce the use of a specific software development lifecycle. IEC 62304 states;

"(The IEC 62304) standard does not require a particular software development life cycle model"

As a caveat to the previous statement, IEC 62304 also states;

"Whichever life cycle is chosen it is necessary to maintain the logical dependencies between process outputs"

The FDA GPSV states;

> "(the FDA) does not recommend the use of any specific software life cycle model. Software developers should establish a software life cycle model that is appropriate for their product and organization"

The Association of the Advancement of Medical Instrumentation (AAMI), are currently in the process of mapping the principles of the Agile Manifesto to IEC 62304 [25]. As part of this research by the AAMI, each of the 12 agile principles is mapped to a specific stage of development in accordance with IEC 62304. The upcoming release of this document will provide evidence that agile practices can be followed without jeopardising the process of achieving regulatory approval.

4.4 Lack of Up-Front Planning

Plan driven software development lifecycles such as the V-Model place a large emphasis on up-front planning. This up-front planning can provide stability and a point of reference for a development project [2]. However, up-front planning can be difficult to perform following agile practices as requirements changes are welcomed and expected in an agile project [21]. Whilst this is the case, before a project begins agile practices use techniques such as user stories. These are a form of up-front planning [26] and can provide the necessary stability to allow a project to begin.

4.5 Managing Multiple Releases

Software projects developed in accordance with agile practices are divided into iterations. Agile teams attempt to have a potentially shippable system at the end of each iteration [27]. Due to the safety critical nature of medical device software, regulatory requirements prohibit medical device software developers from releasing unfinished software into a live patient environment without being fully tested [10].

However, whilst agile teams typically develop a shippable system during each iteration, this is not a requirement of agile practices. Agile teams can combine components developed during iterations and perform the necessary testing once a number of iterations have been completed. The process of managing multiple releases can be further improved through using third party software tools which are currently available such as "*Subversion*" [28].

5 Conclusions and Future Work

Research into the usage of agile practices when developing medical device software is still at an early stage. There have been reported successes of utilising agile practices when developing medical device software however, these successes have been performed in isolation and are yet to be replicated.

As a result of the survey outlined in this paper, a number of barriers to agile adoption in the development of medical device software have been identified. Through examination of the relevant medical device regulatory requirements, international standards and guidance documents it may be concluded that none of the barriers identified are insurmountable. Each of the barriers were analysed in detail and information has been provided as to how these barriers can be addressed. The research outlined in this paper is part of a larger study and these results will be used to assist with further research into the use of agile practices for medical device software development.

Whilst this research identified the perceived barriers to adopting agile practices within medical device companies, further research will identify the critical success factors to using agile practices when developing medical device software. The research outlined in this paper will also contribute to the development of a software development lifecycle for medical device software that will integrate the stability of following a plan driven software development lifecycle with agile practices.

Acknowledgements. This research is supported by the Science Foundation Ireland (SFI) Stokes Lectureship Programme, grant number 07/SK/I1299, the SFI Principal Investigator Programme, grant number 08/IN.1/I2030 (the funding of this project was awarded by Science Foundation Ireland under a co-funding initiative by the Irish Government and European Regional Development Fund), and supported in part by Lero - the Irish Software Engineering Research Centre (http://www.lero.ie) grant 10/CE/I1855.

References

1. Abraham, C., Nishiharas, E., Akiyama, M.: Transforming healthcare with information technology in Japan: A review of policy, people, and progress. International Journal of Medical Informatics 80(2011), 157–170 (2011)
2. Ge, X., Paige, R.F., McDermid, J.A.: An Iterative Approach for Development of Safety-Critical Software and Safety Arguments. In: Agile 2010, pp. 35–43. IEEE, Orlando (2010)
3. VersionOne, State of Agile Survey - The Stage of Agile Development (2010)
4. http://agilemindstorm.com/agile-glossary/ (accessed February 20, 2012)
5. Turk, D., France, R.: Assumptions Underlying Agile Software Development Processes. Journal of Database Management 16(4), 62–87 (2004)
6. Cawley, O., Wang, X., Richardson, I.: Lean/Agile Software Development Methodologies in Regulated Environments – State of the Art. In: Abrahamsson, P., Oza, N. (eds.) LESS 2010. LNBIP, vol. 65, pp. 31–36. Springer, Heidelberg (2010)
7. European Council, Directive 2007/47/EC of the European Parliament and of the Council of 5 September 2007 (2007)
8. European Commission, Medical Devices Guidance Document - Qualification and Classification of stand alone software MEDDEV 2.1/6 (2012)
9. FDA, Title 21–Food and Drugs Chapter I –Food and Drug Administration Department of Health and Human Services subchapter h–Medical Devices part 820 Quality System Regulation, U.S. Department of Health and Human Services (2007)

10. FDA, General Principles of Software Validation: Final Guidance for Industry and FDA Staff, Centre for Devices and Radiological Health (2002)
11. FDA, Federal Register 73(31), 8637 (February 15, 2011)
12. FDA, Guidance for the Content of Premarket Submissions for Software Contained in Medical Devices, U.S. Department of Health and Human Services (2005)
13. FDA, Draft Guidance for Industry and Food and Drug Administration - Mobile Device Applications, Centre for Devices and Radiological Health (2011)
14. FDA, Guidance for Industry, FDA Reviewers and Compliance on Off-The-Shelf Software use in Medical Devices, U.S. Department of Health and Human Services (1999)
15. AAMI, ANSI/AAMI/IEC 62304, Medical device Software - Software life cycle processes (2006)
16. European Council, Commission communication in the framework of the implementation of the Council Directive 93/42/EEC of 14 June 1993 concerning medical devices (Publication of titles and references of harmonised standards under the directive) (2010)
17. Rottier, P.A., Rodrigues, V.: Agile Development in a Medical Device Company. In: Proceedings of the 11th AGILE Conference, AGILE 2008. Springer, Girona (2008)
18. Rasmussen, R., Hughes, T., Jenks, J.R., Skach, J.: Adopting Agile in an FDA Regulated Environment. In: Agile Conference, AGILE 2009, pp. 151–155. Springer, Chicago (2009)
19. Spence, J.W.: There has to be a better way! [software development]. In: Proceedings to Agile Conference, pp. 272–278. Springer, Denver (2005)
20. Heeager, L.T., Nielsen, P.A.: Agile Software Development and its Compatibility with a Document-Driven Approach? A Case Study. In: 20th Australasian Conference on Information Systems Compatibility of Agile and Document-Driven Approaches, Melbourne (2009)
21. Martin, R.C.: Agile Software Development - Principles, Patterns and Practices. Prentice Hall (2003)
22. Vogel, D.: Agile Methods:Most are not ready for prime time in medical device software design and development. Design Fax Online (July 2006)
23. Berard, E.V.: Misconceptions of the Agile Zealots. In: Software and System Process Improvement Network (2003)
24. Lee, C., Guadagno, L., Jia, X.: An Agile Approach to Capturing Requirements and Traceability. In: Proceedings of the 2nd International Workshop on Traceability in Emerging Forms of Software Engineering (TEFSE 2003), Canada (2003)
25. AAMI, Gudiance on the use of agile practices in the development of medical device software TIR-Master_4-00. Association for the Advancement of Medical Instrumentation (2011)
26. Paetsch, F., Eberlein, A., Maurer, F.: Requirements engineering and agile software development. In: Proceedings of Twelfth IEEE International Workshops on Enabling Technologies: Infrastructure for Collaborative Enterprises, WET ICE 2003, pp. 308–313 (2003)
27. Berczu, S., Cowham, R., Appleton, B.: An Agile Approach to Release Management (2008)
28. http://subversion.apache.org/ (accessed January 12, 2012)

Development of a Process Assessment Model for Assessing Medical IT Networks against IEC 80001-1

Silvana Togneri MacMahon[1], Fergal McCaffery[1], Sherman Eagles[2], Frank Keenan[1], Marion Lepmets[3], and Alain Renault[3]

[1] Regulated Software Research Group, Department of Computing & Mathematics, Dundalk Institute of Technology & Lero, Dundalk Co. Louth, Ireland
{silvana.macmahon,fergal.mccaffery,frank.keenan}@dkit.ie
[2] SoftwareCPR, Saint Paul, MN 55114, USA
seagles@softwarecpr.com
[3] Public Research Centre Henri Tudor, Luxembourg
{alain.renault,marion.lepmets}@tudor.lu

Abstract. Increasingly medical devices are being designed to allow them to exchange information over an IT network. However incorporating a medical device into an IT network can introduce risks which can impact the safety, effectiveness and security of the medical device. Medical devices are stringently tested according to regulation during the design and manufacture process. However until the introduction of IEC 80001-1: Application of Risk Management for IT-Networks incorporating Medical Devices, no standard addressed the risks of incorporating a medical device into an IT network. In order to perform an assessment (which is compliant with ISO/IEC 15504-2) of an IT network against IEC 80001-1, a Process Assessment Model is required. Based on the relationship between IEC 80001-1 and ISO/IEC 20000-1, this paper examines how the TIPA transformation process developed by Public Research Centre Henri Tudor was used to develop a process assessment model (TIPA PAM) for ISO/IEC 20000-1. It also examines how a process assessment model can be developed following that transformation process to assess Medical IT networks against IEC 80001-1.

Keywords: IEC 80001-1, ISO/IEC 15504 – Process Assessment, Service Management, ISO/IEC 20000-1, TIPA, ITIL.

1 Introduction

As Medical Devices are increasingly being designed to be incorporated into hospital IT networks, IEC 80001-1 [1] addresses the risk that this involves. Risks to the safety, effectiveness and security of the system are addressed. These risks are examined in more detail in section 2. The design and production of medical devices is subject to regulation under various standards which are recognised by the regulatory authorities within the region in which the device will be marketed. The incorporation of a medical device into an IT network establishes a Medical IT network. Medical IT networks are increasingly being required to carry diverse traffic from confidential patient information to generic email traffic. Until the introduction of IEC 80001-1, no standard was in place to address the risk that health care can be compromised when a medical device is incorporated into an IT network. IEC 80001-1 seeks to address Life Cycle Risk Management in Medical IT networks and focuses on achieving interoperability of devices on the network without compromising safety, effectiveness or data and system security.

The next section of the paper examines why the IEC 80001-1 standard was developed by looking at the risks that are inherent in the incorporation of Medical Devices into IT networks. Section 3 provides a brief overview of how Process Assessment Model (PAM) may be developed to assess against this standard. In order to develop this assessment model our research has investigated the relationship between IEC 80001-1 and ISO/IEC 20000-1 – Information Technology – Service Management - Part 1: Service management system requirements [2]. Prior to the introduction of IEC 80001-1, ISO/IEC 20000-1 had been published as a generic Service Management Standard. ISO/IEC 20000-1 provides requirements for a service provider to deliver managed service throughout the life cycle. IEC 80001-1 recognises the need for a life cycle approach to risk management of the incorporation of medical devices onto IT networks. As such IEC 80001-1 is similar to ISO/IEC 20000-1, focusing on the specific risks inherent in the Service Management of medical devices within an IT network. Section 4 examines the requirements for process assessment that are defined in ISO/IEC 15004-2 (Process Assessment – Part 2: Performing an assessment). Section 5 describes ISO/IEC 20000 (Parts 1, 2 and 4) while Section 6 examines the relationship between IEC 80001-1 and ISO/IEC 20000 (Parts 1 and 2). On the basis of this relationship our research investigated methodologies that have been developed to assess against ISO/IEC 20000-1 processes. This paper focuses on the TIPA (Tudor IT Service Management Process Assessment) [3] methodology which is compliant with ISO/IEC 15504-2 [4]. Section 7 examines how TIPA uses the requirements contained in ISO/IEC 15504-2 as a guide for its transformation process for the development of Process Reference Models (PRM) and Process Assessment Models (PAM). Section 8 examines how an assessment model could be developed using the TIPA transformation process which could be used to assess medical IT networks against IEC 80001-1. Finally, section 9 contains the conclusions of this research and plans to progress this work further.

2 IEC 80001-1 Overview

2.1 What Is IEC 80001?

Medical Devices are designed and validated in order to ensure that they are safe for their intended use. Increasingly Medical Devices are being produced which are intended to be incorporated into Hospital IT networks. Medical devices are integrated into heterogeneous networks that include other medical devices and other IT components creating a new system in which the medical device has not been validated. New hazards may emerge that are directly related to the interaction of the networked components that were not considered when the device was being designed and validated [5]. Each Healthcare Delivery Organisation (HDO) will approach the integration of a medical device into an IT network in a different way. There are a number of potential problems which are associated with the incorporation of medical devices into hospital IT networks as follows [1]:

- *"Lack of consideration for risk from use of IT networks during evaluation of clinical risk."*
- *"Lack of support from manufacturers of medical devices for the incorporation of their products into IT networks, (e.g. the unavailability or inadequacy of information provided by the manufacturer to the operator of the IT networks)."*
- *"Incorrect operation or degraded performance (e.g. incompatibility or improper configuration) resulting from combining medical devices and other equipment on the same IT networks."*
- *"Incorrect operation resulting from combining medical device software and other software applications (e.g. open email systems or computer games) in the same IT networks."*
- *"Lack of security controls on many medical devices."*
- *"The conflict between the need for strict change control of medical devices and the need for rapid response to the threat of cyber-attack."*

The goal of IEC 80001-1 is to prevent patient harm. The meaning of harm as defined in IEC 80001-1 is extended to address 3 areas – Safety, Effectiveness and (Data & System) Security – therefore covering in addition to physical injury or damage to the health of a patient, any reduction in the effectiveness of the device (in its ability to provide its intended result for the patient) and any breach of data and system security (any degradation of the confidentiality, integrity and availability of information assets) [5].

IEC 80001-1 covers the entire life cycle of the Medical IT network. The standard incorporates the principle that a risk management process should be implemented when creating a medical device network or when removing, maintaining, or changing/modifying equipment on a medical device network. The risk based approach is based on the risk based approach outlined in ISO 14971 [6] which is used by medical devices manufacturers but extends the definition of harm to include reduction in effectiveness and breach of security.

2.2 Roles and Responsibilities

IEC 80001-1 is addressed to Responsible Organisations (defined within the standard as an entity responsible for the use and maintenance of a Medical IT network), Medical Device Manufacturers and to providers of other information technology. This part of the standard outlines the specific roles, responsibilities and activities (of these

Development of a Process Assessment Model for Assessing Medical IT Networks   151

groups) with regard to risk management of the incorporation of medical devices into IT networks to address the safety, effectiveness and data & system security.

The IEC 80001-1 standard acknowledges that the overall responsibility for the Medical IT network belongs to the HDO. Medical device networks are becoming increasingly complex and the clinical users within the HDO may not recognise the risks to patients presented by the incorporation of medical devices onto the IT networks. The HDO must focus on gaining the support and assistance of internal functions and the suppliers of the components and products that will form part of the network in order to gain an understanding of the interactions within the network that present the greatest risk. With the assistance of these parties, the HDO must seek to identify factors over which it has the most control and focus on preventing or mitigating possible hazards based on these factors [5]. The top management of the HDO must establish a risk management policy for the incorporation of medical devices and must appoint a medical IT network risk manager who is appropriately skilled and qualified to administer the policy and who must maintain the medical IT network risk management file. The medical IT risk management file must contain all documentary information (including supplier documentation) as to support the risk management activities of the Medical IT network.

The IEC 80001-1 standard also requires that for a device to be connected to a Medical IT network, the manufacturer of the device must make supporting documents available to the HDO. The documentation must contain instructions for implementing the connection of the device to the medical IT network and should include the purpose of the devices connection to the network, the required characteristics, configuration and technical specification of the network to which the device is being connected, the intended information flow between the medical device, the Medical IT network and any other devices on the network and a list of the hazardous situations that may arise due to the failure of the IT network to meet the characteristics required by the medical device in order to support the connection to the IT network [1] . Should the information provided by the manufacturer be insufficient as to allow the HDO to carry out risk management activities, the HDO must request any additional information required from the medical device manufacturer.

3   Developing Process Models for Assessing against IEC 80001-1

ISO/IEC 15504 is an international standard for process assessment that is widely adopted in the software engineering community. ISO/IEC 15504-2 [4] (ISO/IEC 15504 is also known as SPICE – Software Process Improvement & Capability dEtermination) defines a framework for assessing capability of processes. The SPICE framework is widely used in the safety critical domain in such initiatives as Automotive SPICE and Medi SPICE. For a 15504 compliant process assessment, ISO/IEC 15504-2 requires the use of a PAM which is formulated by reference to one or more external PRMs. It also defines the requirements that process models (PAMs and PRMs) must meet. The ISO/IEC 15504-2 requirements are discussed in detail in the next section.

In order to assess against IEC 80001-1, (in a manner that is compliant with ISO/IEC 15504-2) it is necessary that a PAM is developed. In order to develop this model, we examined how other process models have been developed in order to perform an assessment against similar standards.

Annex D of IEC 80001-1 shows that there is a strong relationship between IEC 80001-1 and ISO/IEC 20000-1 & 2 – Information Technology – Service Management. We discovered that ISO/IEC 15504-8 (Information Technology – Process Assessment – Part 8: An exemplar process assessment model for IT Service Management) had also been developed to assess against ISO/IEC 20000-1.[1] The ISO/IEC 15504 series does not provide guidance today on how to develop PAMs; we can use the TIPA transformation process instead. Within this paper we focus on the TIPA [3] process models and examine how they were developed by using the requirements of ISO/IEC 15504-2 as a framework to assess against ISO/IEC 20000-1 and ITIL [7] - Information Technology Infrastructure Library processes [8]. From this examination, we investigate how to apply the TIPA transformation process[1] to develop a PRM and a PAM for assessing against IEC 80001-1.

4 Process Assessment and ISO/IEC 15504

ISO/IEC 15504 provides a framework for the assessment of processes. ISO/IEC 15504-2 defines a measurement framework for process capability and defines the requirements for performing an assessment, building PRMs, PAMs and verifying conformity of process models and of process assessment. The standard looks at process assessment from the basis of a two dimensional model containing both a process dimension and a capability dimension. The process dimension is provided by reference to an external PRM which characterises processes in terms of their purpose and outcomes. The capability dimension is based on 6 capability levels. The achievement of these capability levels is based on the achievement of the associated process attributes. Further guidelines for process description are outlined in ISO/IEC TR 24774:2010 [9].

ISO/IEC 15504-5 [10] provides an exemplar PAM for software processes which can be used to perform an assessment conformant to ISO/IEC 15504-2. The PAM expands the PRM process definitions by including a set of process performance and process capability indicators. Process performance indicators are called base practices for each process. The PAM also defines a second set of indicators of process performance by associating work products with each process. Process capability indicators are generic practice, generic resource and generic work product.

There are two aspects within process assessment, process capability determination and process improvement. Process capability seeks to assess the current state of a set of processes against the defined capability levels and process attributes. A target capability level will have been determined in advance of the assessment. The results of the assessment are then analysed to determine the strengths, weaknesses, opportunities and threats in the process context and process improvement can be undertaken on this basis.

---

[1] We will use « TIPA transformation process » to make reference to the Transformation Process used to build the TIPA process models, as documented in [14].

5 ISO/IEC 20000 – Service Management Standards

Service Management looks at a lifecycle approach to managing IT services to ensure that the services continually not only provide the required service to the customer but also provide value to the customer in terms of their business goals. ISO/IEC 20000-1 *"requires an integrated process approach when the service provider plans, establishes, implements, operates, monitors, reviews, maintains and improves a service management system (SMS)"* [2].

In order to achieve this integrated process approach, ISO/IEC 20000 advocates a "Plan, Do, Check, Act" approach which is described briefly as follows [2].

- *"**Plan**: establishing, documenting and agreeing the SMS. The SMS includes the policies, objectives, plans andprocesses to fulfil the service requirements."*
- *"**Do**: implementing and operating the SMS for the design, transition, delivery and improvement of the services."*
- *"**Check**: monitoring, measuring and reviewing the SMS and the services against the policies, objectives, plansand service requirements and reporting the results."*
- *"**Act**: taking actions to continually improve performance of the SMS and the services."*

The most important aspect of the integrated methodology and "Plan, Do, Check, Act" approach are detailed in the standard as follows:

- *"understanding and fulfilling the service requirements to achieve customer satisfaction"*
- *"establishing the policy and objectives for service management"*
- *"designing and delivering services based on the SMS that add value for the customer"*
- *"monitoring, measuring and reviewing performance of the SMS and the services"*
- *"continually improving the SMS and the services based on objective measurements"*

ISO/IEC 20000-2 [11] describes the best practices for Service Management within the scope of ISO/IEC 20000-1. This part of the standard provides guidance on the 5 process categories indentified in Part 1 of the standards namely Service Delivery Processes, Control Processes, Release Processes, Resolution Processes and Relationship Processes. Part 4 [12] of the standard (ISO/IEC 20000-4) provides the PRM for IT Service Management based on the requirements of ISO/IEC 20000-1. It should be noted that the TIPA methodology provides an assessment framework to assess against either ISO/IEC 20000-4 or against the processes contained within the widely used Service Management best practice library - ITIL [7]. ITIL was developed in the United Kingdom at the end of the 1980's. Now owned by the Cabinet Office, ITIL has become the world wide 'de facto' standard for IT Service Management [3].

ITIL v3 [7] has been organised into 5 publications which cover – Service Strategy, Service Design, Service Transition, Service Operation and Continual Service Improvement.

ISO/IEC 20000-4 and ITIL are very similar standards – both dealing with a lifecycle approach to Service Management. There is a close relationship between ITILv3 and ISO/IEC 20000 to the extent that ISO/IEC 20000 has become known as the "ITIL standard". With the publication of ISO/IEC 20000-1:2011, there have been steps taken to ensure that ISO/IEC 20000 is more closely aligned with ITIL v3 [13]. Given the alignment between ITILv3 and the ISO/IEC 20000 series, the TIPA methodology is equally effective at assessing ISO/IEC 20000 and ITILv3 processes [3] . The following section looks at the relationship between IEC 80001-1 and ISO/IEC 20000.

6 IEC 80001-1 – Relationship with ISO/IEC 20000

6.1 Service Management in the Lifecycle of a Medical Device Network

IEC 80001-1 addresses risk management throughout the life cycle of the Medical IT network. The monitoring of Medical IT networks during operation may reveal the need for a change to the device. Due to the stringent regulation of medical devices, HDOs must follow strictly formal approaches and procedures directly involving the medical device manufacturer when making changes to or performing maintenance activities on medical devices. This establishes an on-going relationship between the manufacturer of the device and the HDO which continues throughout the lifecycle of the Medical IT network. This relationship is constrained by the need on the part of the HDO to change a medical device and the need for the medical device manufacturer to ensure that the changed device continues to be validated. It must be understood by the medical device manufacturer and the HDO that these opposing constraints impact service management [1] . Lifecycle risk management must be performed in a way that allows the HDO to support effective healthcare delivery. In this context, the principles of Service Management outlined in ISO/IEC 20000 have been reviewed to determine their ability to meet the requirements of IEC 80001-1. It should however be noted that compliance with ISO/IEC 20000-1 does not equate to compliance with IEC 80001-1.

6.2 Relationship between IEC 80001-1 and ISO/IEC 20000

IEC 80001-1 applies lifecycle risk management to Medical IT networks. IEC 80001-1 states that "Lifecycle risk management in a medical IT-network needs to be done in the context of the specific operating conditions required to support effective healthcare delivery" [1]. Due to the common lifecycle approach, the concepts of Service Management as described in ISO/IEC 20000-1 and ISO/IEC 20000-2 [11] have been examined for their ability to meet the requirements outlined in IEC 80001-1. The relationship between IEC 80001-1 and ISO/IEC 20000 is described in Annex D of IEC 80001-1. This annex provides a simple overview of the relationship between IEC 80001-1 and ISO/IEC 20000-2 to aid in the investigation of service

Development of a Process Assessment Model for Assessing Medical IT Networks   155

strategies that could address the service needs of a medical IT-network. Figure 1 provides an overview of the areas described in Annex D of IEC 80001-1.

The top portion of the diagram shows areas identified within the standards wherein the terminology may differ but the underlying role, document or the processes are similar e.g. what is referred to in IEC 80001-1 as "Risk Management Process" appears as "Security Risk Assessment Practices" within ISO/IEC 20000, but the underlying process areas are the same.

The lower portion of the diagram shows areas within the lifecycle that are common to both standards. For example IEC 80001-1: Figure 2 shows an overview of the "Overview of life cycle of medical IT-networks including risk management"[1] which shows "Change – Release Management" (including the risk assessment process) through the "Go Live" implementation of the change and to finally "Live Environment Risk Management" (including monitoring of the change and event management). These processes are common to ISO/IEC 20000-1 as shown in Figure D.1 of IEC 80001-1[1] which lists the ISO/IEC 20000-1 processes as Control Processes (including Change Management), Release Processes (including Release Management) and Resolution Processes (including Problem & Incident Management). The additional processes identified in Figure D.1 including Service Delivery Processes and Relationship processes (including Supplier Management) are also common to both standards.

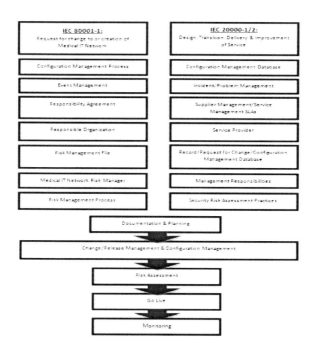

Fig. 1. Provides an overview of the relationship between IEC 80001-1 and ISO/IEC 20000-1:2011 and ISO/IEC 20000-2:2005 showing aligned teminology and common processes

Given the relationship between the standards, our research has focused on assessment frameworks that are currently available to assess against ISO/IEC 20000.

The following section 7 of this paper examines how the TIPA process models were developed to assess against ISO/IEC 20000.

7 TIPA Methodology

This section of the paper examines how the TIPA methodology has combined the requirements expressed in ISO/IEC 15504 and used these requirements to build process models to assess against ISO/IEC 20000 and ITIL. As per ISO15504-2, in order to perform a process assessment, a PAM must be developed with reference to one or more PRMs. The TIPA methodology advocates the use of a transformation process, based on goal-oriented requirements engineering techniques, in order to develop the required PRMs and PAMs [14]. An explanation of the transformation process is given in section 7.1.

The development of the TIPA PAM for ISO/IEC 20000-1 was based on the existing PRM described in ISO/IEC 20000-4. Barafort et al. [14] focussed on developing the PAM using the transformation process outlined within the next section. The TIPA PAM for ISO/IEC 20000 (which was developed using the TIPA methodology) was one of the inputs to ISO/IEC 15504-8 that is further developed in JTC1 ISO/IEC SC7 [15]. ISO/IEC 15504-8 "provides an example of an IT Service Management Process Assessment Model (PAM) for use in performing a conformant assessment in accordance with the requirements of ISO/IEC 15504-2." [15].

In developing the PAM for assessment against ITIL, no PRM existed so a PRM based on ITILv3 and a PAM were developed using the same transformation process. The TIPA transformation process can be used for the development of both PRMs and PAMs. A PAM is formed on the basis of one or more PRMs and the addition of a measurement framework. As the TIPA transformation process can be used for the development of both PRMs and PAMs, this methodology could also be used to develop the PRM and PAM for IEC 80001-1.

7.1 TIPA Transformation Process Overview

As examined in section 6, ISO/IEC 15504 provides a detailed description of the process assessment approach and provides an exemplar PAM in ISO/IEC 15504-5 [10]. ISO/IEC TR 24774:2010 provides guidelines for the formulation of process descriptive elements [9]. However, Barafort et al. identified that a gap exists in that there is no guidance to support the transformation from the input (domain requirements) to the output (process model) [14]. The CRP Henri Tudor has produced a PAM for ISO/IEC 15504 compliant assessment against both ISO/IEC 20000 and ITIL. The TIPA transformation process is as follows [14]:

1. *Identify elementary requirements in a collection of requirements.*
2. *Organise and structure the requirements.*

Development of a Process Assessment Model for Assessing Medical IT Networks 157

3. *Identify common purposes upon those requirements and organise them towards domain goals.*
4. *Identify and factorise outcomes from the common purposes and attach them to the related goals.*
5. *Group activities together under a practice and attach it to the related outcomes.*
6. *Allocate each practice to a specific capability level.*
7. *Phrase outcomes and process purpose. (Apply ISO/IEC TR 24774 guidelines)*
8. *Phrase the Base Practices attached to the Outcomes. (Apply ISO/IEC TR 24774 guidelines)*
9. *Determine Work Products among the inputs and outputs of the practices.*

Based on the transformation process above TIPA PAMs have been developed to assess against ISO/IEC 20000 and ITIL.

Assessment against ISO/IEC 20000 focuses on the processes within 2 process categories: Primary Processes and Organisational Processes. The Primary Processes consist of the following process groups: Service Delivery Process Group, Relationship Process Group, Resolution Process Group, Control Process Group and Release Process Group. The Organisational Processes consists of one process group: Planning and Implementing Service Process Group. Assessment against ITIL focuses on the processes within 2 process category groups of version 2: Service Support Group and Service Delivery Group.

TIPA applies the ISO/IEC 15504 assessment method to IT Service Management as a means to verify the maturity of the process. In applying the requirements expressed in ISO/IEC 15504-2 to build process models for ISO/IEC 20000-1 and ITIL, TIPA provides a means to assess the maturity of IT Service Management processes.

8 How the TIPA Transformation Process May Be Applied to IEC 80001-1

Given the common areas in terms of lifecycle risk management and service management processes between ISO/IEC 20000 and IEC 80001-1 as defined in Section D of the IEC 80001-1 standard, it is clear that a Process Assessment Model could be built using the TIPA transformation process that would provide a framework against which to assess medical IT networks. Using the TIPA transformation process will ensure that the resultant PAM will meet the requirements of process assessment models as outlined in ISO/IEC 15504-2.

The diagram below shows how a PRM and PAM could be developed for assessment against IEC 80001-1 based on the TIPA transformation process.

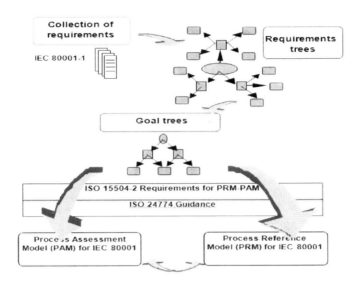

Fig. 2. Shows how the TIPA transformation process may be used to create a process reference model and process assessment to assess medical IT networks against IEC 80001-1

9 Conclusions and Future Work

Traditionally medical devices have functioned as stand-alone products which often meant that there was a need for information from devices to be transcribed or transferred to systems holding patient medical records. Placing a medical device onto the network and transferring the information directly removes the burden of transferring this information and removes the risk of human error in transferring the information impacting on patient care. However, the introduction of medical devices onto non-proprietary networks may risk compromising the safety of the device, the effectiveness of the device in its ability to produce the intended result for the patient or may result in a breach of data and system integrity. IEC 80001-1 seeks to mitigate these risks by applying a lifecycle risk management approach to the establishment or modification of medical device networks.

In order to perform an assessment (which is compliant with ISO/IEC 15504-2) on a Medical IT networks against IEC 80001-1, a Process Assessment Model is required. IEC 80001-1 Annex D shows the relationship between ISO/IEC 20000 and IEC 80001-1. TIPA has been developed as a means of assessing Service Management processes against ISO/IEC 20000-1. Given this overlap in processes and the common lifecycle approach it is proposed that a Process Assessment Model could be developed, using the TIPA transformation process, to assess against IEC 80001-1. This approach would also ensure compliance with ISO/IEC 15504-2.

Future research will focus on the formulation of a Process Reference Model and Process Assessment Model based on the TIPA transformation process. An iterative approach will be followed. Each process will be validated by industry experts and amended according to the consensus. Once the PRM and PAM have been fully developed, the model will then be validated through trials.

Acknowledgements. This research is supported by the Science Foundation Ireland (SFI) Stokes Lectureship Programme, grant number 07/SK/I1299, the SFI Principal Investigator Programme, grant number 08/IN.1/I2030 (the funding of this project was awarded by Science Foundation Ireland under a co-funding initiative by the Irish Government and European Regional Development Fund), and supported in part by Lero - the Irish Software Engineering Research Centre (http://www.lero.ie) grant 10/CE/I1855. ITIL® is a registered trade mark of the Cabinet Office. TIPA® is a Registered Trade Mark of the CRP Henri Tudor.

References

1. IEC, IEC 80001-1 - Application of Risk Management for IT-Networks incorporating Medical Devices - Part 1: Roles, responsibilities and activities. International Electrotechnical Commission, Geneva (2010)
2. ISO/IEC, ISO/IEC 20000-1:2011 - Information technology —Service management Part 1: Service management system requirement, Geneva, Switzerland (2011)
3. Barafort, B., Betry, V., Cortina, S., Picard, M., St Jean, M., Renault, A., Valdés, O., Tudor, P.R.C.H.: ITSM Process Assessment Supporting ITIL: Using TIPA to Assess and Improve your Processes with ISO 15504 and Prepare for ISO 20000 Certification. In: Best Practice, vol. 217. Van Haren, Zaltbommel (2009)
4. ISO/IEC, ISO/IEC 15504-2 - Software engineering — Process assessment — Part 2: Performing an assessment, Geneva, Switzerland (2003)
5. Cooper, T., David, Y., Eagles, S.: Getting Started with IEC 80001: Essential Information for Healthcare Providers Managing Medical IT-Networks, p. 76. Association for the Advancement of Medical Instrumentation (2011)
6. ISO, ISO 14971:2007 - Medical Devices - Application of Risk to Medical Devices. International Organisation for Standardization, Geneva (2007)
7. Cartlidge, A., Hanna, A., Rudd, C., Macfarlane, I., Windebank, J., Rance, S.: An introductory Overview of ITILv3 - A high-level overview of the IT INFRASTRUCTURE LIBRARY. The UK Chapter of the itSMF (2007)
8. Barafort, B., Di Renzo, B., Merlan, O.: Benefits Resulting from the Combined Use of ISO/IEC 15504 with the Information Technology Infrastructure Library (ITIL). In: Oivo, M., Komi-Sirviö, S. (eds.) PROFES 2002. LNCS, vol. 2559, pp. 314–325. Springer, Heidelberg (2002)
9. ISO/IEC, ISO/IEC TR 24774:2010 - Systems and software engineering — Life cycle management — Guidelines for process description, Geneva, Switzerland (2010)
10. ISO/IEC, ISO/IEC 15504-5 - Information technology — Process Assessment — Part 5: An exemplar Process Assessment Model, Geneva, Switzerland (2006)
11. ISO/IEC, ISO/IEC 20000-2:2005 - Information technology – Service management – Part 2: Code of Practice, Geneva, Switzerland (2005)

12. ISO/IEC, ISO/IEC TR 20000-4:2010 - Information technology — Service management - Part 4: Process reference model, Geneva, Switzerland (2010)
13. Dugmore, J., Taylor, S.: (2008) ITILv3 and ISO/IEC 20000 - Alignment White Paper. Best Management Practice for IT Service Management (March 2008)
14. Barafort, B., Renault, A., Picard, M., Cortina, S.: A transformation process for building PRMs and PAMs based on a collection of requirements – Example with ISO/IEC 20000. In: SPICE 2008, Nuremberg, Germany (2008)
15. ISO/IEC, ISO/IEC PDTR 15504-8 - Information technology – Process assessment – Part 8: An exemplar process assessment model for IT service management, Geneva, Switzerland (2011)

Traceability-Why Do It?

Gilbert Regan, Fergal McCaffery, Kevin McDaid, and Derek Flood

Regulated Software Research Group, Department of Computing & Mathematics, Dundalk Institute of Technology & Lero, Dundalk Co. Louth, Ireland
{gilbert.regan,fergal.mccaffery,
kevin.mcdaid,derek.flood}@dkit.ie

Abstract. Traceability of software artifacts, from requirements to design and through implementation and quality assurance, has long been promoted by the research and expert practitioner communities. However, evidence indicates that, with the exception of those operating in the safety critical domain, few software companies choose to implement traceability processes, in the most part due to cost and complexity issues. This paper presents a review of traceability literature including the implementation of traceability in real organizations. Through both analyzing case studies and research published by leading traceability researchers, this paper synthesizes the motivations of the organizations for implementing traceability. Given the importance of traceability in the regulated domain of safety critical software, the paper compares the motivations and benefits for organizations operating inside and outside of this domain. Finally, based on an analysis of the disparate case studies, the paper re-assesses the value of traceability motivators for more widespread adoption by firms outside of the safety critical sector.

Keywords: traceability.

1 Introduction

Software systems are becoming increasingly complex. Artefacts such as test cases, requirements documents, source code, design documents, bug reports etc, and the links between them are created over long periods of time by different people. Creating and maintaining these links is a difficult and expensive task. Therefore most existing software systems lack explicit traceability links between artefacts [1]. Though the importance and role of traceability in supporting systems development have been long recognised, there are wide variations in the quality and usefulness of the practice of traceability [2].

Traceability was initially used to trace requirements from their source to implementation and test, but now plays an increasing role in defect management, change management and project management. Increasingly software development is globally distributed across multiple teams and sites which makes traceability even more relevant [3].

Good traceability information is also important to process improvement. It is fundamental for change impact analysis, requirements validation and regression testing among others. Often the quality of this information is poor, or out of date due to not being properly maintained [4].

Traceability techniques and tools are not widely used in industry [5, 6]. Complexity and cost are two of the reasons why this is the case. Companies who do adopt traceability techniques often adopt inefficient manual traceability methods and tools despite semi-automated and automated approaches becoming available [6].

This paper considers the motivations for implementing traceability. The focus is on detailing the motivators for an organisation to implement traceability and to consider if there is any difference in motivations between the general and safety critical domains.

To achieve this, a literature review including eight case studies was conducted for both generic and safety critical software domains.

This paper is structured as follows: Section 2 describes what is meant by the term traceability while section 3 details considerations when implementing traceability. Section 4 presents the research methodology used in this work. Section 5 presents the findings of this work. Our conclusion is provided in section 6 while section 7 details a future direction for this work.

2 Traceability-What Is It?

There are misconceptions as to what is traceability. Section 2.1 provides a definition of traceability and an explanation of that definition.

2.1 Definition

In engineering terms a trace is comprised of a source artefact, a target artefact and the link between them [7]. Traceability therefore is the ability to establish and use these traces.

A distinction should be made between the terms Requirements traceability, Software traceability and System traceability. Requirements traceability facilitates tasks such as requirements validation and verification and focuses on tracing requirements related artifacts, using links that expose both requirements derivation and coverage [7].

Numerous definitions for traceability exist in the literature but one of the most popular and encompassing is:

> "Requirements traceability refers to the ability to describe and follow the life of a requirement, in both a forwards and backwards direction (i.e., from its origins through its development and specification to its subsequent deployment and use, and through all periods of on-going refinement and iteration in any of these phases" [8].

Tracing can be performed in a forwards or backwards direction. Forwards tracing traces the requirement from its source through specification, implementation and

testing. The main aim of forward tracing is to ensure that the requirement set is complete and that every requirement gets implemented and tested. It ensures that the right product is being built. Backwards tracing is tracing test cases or code back through design to the requirement specification and further onto the origin of the requirement. This can be especially useful for analyzing the impact on a requirement or its origin from a proposed change to a piece of code or test case. It helps to eliminate 'gold plating' i.e. no code or test case is written that doesn't trace to a requirement or that no requirement is written that doesn't trace to a business need, user need, standard etc
It is worth highlighting the term 'iterative' in the above definition. Stakeholders frequently introduce and change requirements therefore the continued maintenance of traces is vitally important.

Software traceability extends the definition to encompass and inter-relate any uniquely identifiable software engineering artifact to any other, extending the lifecycle coverage of the validation and verification activities accordingly. Systems traceability goes further and interrelates systems engineering artifacts to a broad range of systems-level components, such as people, processes and hardware models [7].

In general, traceability is about understanding a design right through from the origin of the requirement to its implementation, test and maintenance. Traceability allows us to understand aspects such as to whether the customers' requirements are being met, the specific requirements that an artefact relates to, and the origins and motivation of a requirement. Traceability helps ensure that 'quality' software is developed.

3   Implementation of Traceability

This section presents the considerations that should be taken into account when implementing traceability. Section 3.1 looks at different aspects to be considered while section 3.2 contemplates the different trace tools available. Finally section 3.3 examines some cost considerations.

3.1   Implementation Considerations

Important considerations when implementing traceability include Pre and Post requirements traceability, non functional requirements (in addition to functional requirements), vertical and horizontal traceability, and whether to trace manually, automatically or semi-automatically.

Pre-Requirements traceability is tracing requirements from their specification to their origin. **Post-Requirements traceability** is tracing requirements from their specification through both its development and maintenance lifecycles [8]. Pre-requirements traceability is used to demonstrate that a product meets the stakeholders' stated requirements, or that it complies with a set of government regulations. Post requirements traceability supports impact analysis and requirements validation.

The tracing of **non functional requirements** i.e. system qualities such as safety, security, and performance, in addition to functional requirements, is another important consideration when implementing traceability. In practice, many organizations either focus their traceability efforts on functional requirements or else entirely fail to implement an effective traceability process. In many organizations non-functional requirements are treated in a rather ad hoc fashion and are rarely traced [9].

Vertical traceability is tracing artefacts at different levels of abstraction, such as tracing requirements to code. Its aim is to accommodate end to end traceability. In contrast **horizontal tracing** is tracing artefacts at the same level of abstraction such as traces between requirements or traces between versions of a particular requirement at different moments in time. This highlights dependencies between requirements [10].

Manual, Automatic or semi-automatic? Traceability can be implemented manually (by a human), automatically (via automated methods and tools) or semi automatically (combination of automated methods, tools and human activities) [1].

Traceability is implemented manually in many organizations [6] due to the cost and complexity of automation, therefore potential of software traceability is often not exploited, particularly in smaller companies.

Automatic traceability is much faster than manual tracing but in reality automatic traceability falters in either producing inexact traces or misses required traces. Traces can be produced after-the-fact or in-lifecycle. After the fact traces are of a "good enough" nature and sometimes not perfectly recovered. For in-lifecycle tracing, manual tracing is time consuming and arduous while fully automated tracing sometimes produces inaccurate traces and human analysts are reluctant to take responsibility for them. Semi-automated tracing therefore would seem to offer the best of both worlds, where human analysts make final traceability decisions.

"When performing semi-automated tracing, human analysts, at a minimum, need to examine the results produced by the automated methods. Additionally, analysts may interact with the tracing software, provide tracing feedback to the software, and ask the tracing software to retrace"[4].

3.2 Tool Options for Traceability

Tool options for traceability fall into three basic categories:

1. Dedicated Requirements Management Tools – which concentrate on supporting the fundamental activities of requirements management and are frequently referred to as traceability tools due to their focused support in this area. The advantage of using a dedicated requirements management tool is that it focuses exclusively on the fundamental requirements management activities and on enabling traceability [7].

2. Lifecycle Tools –support a wide span of the software and systems development lifecycle and manage its broader artifact types. The traceability provided can be more generic in nature than with the dedicated tools, though more encompassing of lifecycle phases, and a single lifecycle tool may provide for a total tooling solution. End-to-end traceability is possible, in theory. There can also be benefits from having fewer tools to learn to use and to handle [7].

3. General-Purpose Tools and Proprietary Development – Text editors, graphic editors, spreadsheet tools, databases and wikis are all general-purpose tools that can all be configured to allow previously manual and paper-based requirements management activities to be carried out with some form of tool support. The advantage here is that general purpose tools are widely available and many people already know how to use them. General purpose tools are most suited for small and short lived projects. There is also the option to develop a proprietary tool completely from scratch. However tool building is not the primary focus of most organizations and is sometimes best left to those with expertise in the area [7].

3.3   Cost Considerations

Cost, as always, is an important factor. An optimal balance of cost and trace quality can be achieved by ranking requirements and refining trace quality as necessary. A traceability strategy can combine tactics such as; varying the granularity of trace links, varying the coverage of trace links, adopting tools where possible to optimize recall or precision, varying the frequency of trace link maintenance [11].

A flexible approach to choosing techniques is prudent. Prioritizing requirements means a selection of techniques can be used thus ensuring the best balance between cost and quality. However *"a 'greedy' approach would result in each requirement using the technique that best supported its own needs. Such an approach could result in the excessive use of links at the project level, and create a non sustainable situation. Individual traceability decisions must therefore be made within the context of project level trace objectives"* [12].

4   Research Methodology

The purpose of this research is to answer the following research questions:

RQ 1: What are the motivators for an organisation to implement traceability?

In addition to examining the motivators, we also decided to investigate any difference in motivations between the general and safety critical domains?

The literature on traceability was surveyed to gather viewpoints from both research experts and industry practitioners regarding the potential motivations of implementing traceability to an organisation.

The portals that facilitated the research were IEEE Xplore digital library, ACM digital library and Google Scholar. Key search words used were *traceability, software+traceability, requirements+traceability, traceability + case + study, traceability+survey, traceability+motivators*. These searches returned more than 150 publications. Each abstract was scanned for relevance to our topic and 45 publications were identified. On further examination of their content, 33 were selected to inform our research, based on their relevance to our search topic. 14 of these were case studies from which we selected 8 of the more recent ones.

The book Software and Systems Traceability 2011 (Gotel, Cleland-Huang and Zisman) informed a great deal of our research. Many of the chapters from this book are referred to throughout this paper.

Details of the Aforementioned Case Studies Are

Klimpke: 2009 [13] interviewed stakeholders in five enterprises (with different backgrounds regarding size, type of software, sector and number of locations)in relation to their experiences of using traceability. The organisations ranged from very large (with 10,000 people working in development and projects of 40,000 requirements) to small (200 people and projects of 50 to 300 requirements).

Panis: 2010 [14] carried out a traceability survey on-line at Teradyne (US manufacturer of ATE). 23 engineers (4 Systems Engineers, 7 Subsystem Engineers, and 12 Design Verification Engineers) responded directly to the survey regarding their experiences with traceability.

Arkley and Riddle: 2006 [15] observed a project, conducted at BAE SYSTEMS Electronics and Integrated Solutions (E&IS) (Plymouth, UK) that developed a requirements traceability system which is integral to their development process. The E&IS operating group of companies designs, develops and manufactures a wide range of electronic systems and subsystems for both military and commercial applications.

Neumuller and Grunbacher: 2006 [6] introduced traceability into a very small Austrian software company (GeDV2), whose main product is a business information system for small and medium-sized enterprises. The product is used by 29 customers; the largest installation supports about 150 concurrent users. To implement traceability GeDV developed a number of customised tools in-house and they also established some fairly simple coding and id conventions.

Mc Caffery: 2011 [16] assessed two SME companies (one in Ireland and one in the UK) who operate in the medical device domain. Both companies develop electronic based medical devices that are marketed in the US and Europe. To sell their products they require compliance with both the FDA and the MDD.
In both organizations the importance traceability plays in medical device software development was understood and a member of the management team was responsible for its implementation. The dual role of tracing requirements and managing risk and hazards were appreciated, but were recognized as complex and difficult to achieve.

Heindl and Biffl: 2005 [17] reports a case study on value-based requirements tracing (VBRT) that systematically supports project managers in tailoring requirements tracing precision and effort, based on the following parameters: stakeholder value, requirements risk/volatility, and tracing costs. The research question to be answered is: To what extent can VBRT reduce requirements tracing efforts (economy of requirements tracing)? The case study project "public transport on demand" is about an improved and more efficient public transportation system in rural areas supported with modern information technologies. The challenge is to stop further deterioration of public transportation access in rural areas with a new traffic model.

Born, Favaro and Kath: 2010 [18] report on experience gained with the application of ISO 26262 (international standard for functional safety of road vehicles) in a pilot project at a German car manufacturer as well as experience from various consultancy projects.

Mader, Gotel and Philippow: 2009 [19] reports on an exploratory study of the traceability practice within ten companies based predominantly in Germany. Only two of the ten practitioners selected were known to have a prior interest in traceability topics. The size of the participating companies included six medium (50–500 employees) and three large (>500 employees) companies. The only small company (<50 employees) actually reported about a consulting project they were undertaking for a large company and the traceability practices therein. "Our cases included a mix of software development offering, including companies who predominantly create end products to sell to a user, who do project development work for other companies supplying a market, or who provide expert advice on processes, techniques and methods. Most worked in the transportation domain (avionics and automotive). The subjects we interviewed held the following positions: three system analysts, two consultants, one requirements engineer and four team or project leaders" [19].

5 Findings

While recognising that there are many obstacles to discourage an organisation from implementing traceability, this section considers the factors/reasons why an organisation would benefit from implementing traceability. This section synthesises industry viewpoints on motivation (taken from the case studies) with those published by established researchers. This section provides an answer to RQ 1: What are the motivators for an organisation to implement traceability?

Regulation: Traceability implementation is mandated in many software development standards as seen in [2, 6, 13, 14, 16, 19-21], and many industries, in particular the safety critical industries e.g. in the US the Federal Drugs Authority states that code must be linked to requirements and test cases. In Europe, a medical device cannot be marketed unless it is developed using processes that comply with the European Council's Medical Device Directive (1993/42/EEC) [22] and amendment MDD (2007/47/EC) [23]. To be marketed in the US, a medical device must be developed using processes that comply with Federal Drugs Authority guidelines. "In both locations medical device companies must be able to produce sufficient evidence to support their compliance"[16].

Safety Case: Safety critical systems must satisfy a number of non-functional requirements e.g. safety, availability and reliability [16, 18]. Regulation normally requires critical systems are certified before entering service. This involves submission of a safety case - a reasoned argument and supporting evidence that such requirements have been met and that the system is acceptably safe" [24]. A safety critical organisation who fails to make a safety case can be fined or have its product recalled. These organisations must employ bi-directional traceability such that the safety case shows full life-cycle traceability between hazards, requirements, design code and test cases [25]. A good safety case encompasses an effective risk mitigation process which is highly dependent on requirements traceability. It should also be noted that a good safety case is useful in defence of any litigation.

Competitive Advantage: Traceability reduces production costs [15, 17] through reuse, error avoidance etc. Traceability also allows for impact analyses (case studies [6, 13-16]and general literature [9, 26, 27]) which in turn allows for cost estimation of any change to a system. A change to any artefact will impact on other artefacts. This is particularly useful during the maintenance phase when the cost proposed changes needed to be communicated to the relevant stakeholders. The cost of achieving each quality goal and the recognition of risk is more completely understood by stakeholders through the ability to trace functional and non-functional requirements [28]. Traceability improves the ability to develop realistic cost proposals and gain competitive advantage in building similar systems due to "savings from using [a] lessons learned database of critical issues and rationale"[2].

Productivity and Quality Gains: Traceability helps facilitate productivity and quality gains [13, 15-17, 19]. Reuse of 'proven' artefacts from design, code or test stage ensure productivity gains as these artefacts don't have to be reproduced, saving both time and effort. As they have already been proven, quality and reliability should be assured [29]. In addition to this there are occasions when a requirement should not be changed. This may be because of regulations; therefore linking requirements to sources can help avoid conflict and rework.

Requirements Validation: Process conformance will be facilitated through traceability as requirements validation [25] will be ensured and the product will satisfy customer requirements [14, 15, 17, 19]. While unidirectional forward tracing facilitates requirements validation, the reverse of this(tracing from code to design and onto requirements) helps mitigate the risk of 'gold-plating' i.e. excess artefacts or functionality [25].

Identification of Stakeholders: Traceability helps project leaders identify the relevant stakeholders [6, 15] to involve when drawing out requirements and makes the requirements negotiation stage easier as backward tracing links requirements to their origin.

Rationale for Decisions: Many critical decisions are taken during the SDLC and the rationale for these decisions [13, 14] can be lost unless they are documented and traced to the corresponding artefacts. This facilitates new members learning (Mc Caffery [16] highlighted training) and is also useful because, after a period of time, developers may not remember the rationale behind decisions. Rationale is helpful for handling major system extensions, refactoring or preparing safety cases [11].

Change Management: Sometimes it is cheaper to build software quickly and change it if it fails to meet requirements [1] (maybe because of volatile requirements) as in the Agile process. Constant change of requirements [13-16, 19] means a greater need for traceability support. It also means greater customer interaction. Traceability can thus allow developers to better manage customer relationships [6, 15]. Traceability tracks requirements (or user stories) to versions [18, 19] i.e. to track exactly which requirement has been implemented in a specific version. Traceability also tracks dependencies between requirement i.e. requirements to requirements [25].

Project and Risk Management: The role traceability plays has expanded and it has become an important tool in the software development activities of project management, risk management, and defect management [14-17]. This is particularly relevant as software development is increasingly globally distributed across multiple teams and sites [3]. It is therefore essential to have an effective traceability process in place as it provides an essential support for developing high quality software systems [3]. Traceability provides confidence [14].

Variability in Product Line Engineering: In PLE traceability helps to understand dependencies among diverse reusable artefacts as well as between the product line and the derived products which often include additional developments and customizations. Traceability in PLE thus helps understanding variability and ensuring the consistency of products. Engineers need traceability support in IDEs when modifying product line artefacts[29].

Other motivators for traceability include the ability to measure test coverage [11], test success [13], project progress [13, 30], reduction in requirements creep [11, 30] easier program understanding [6]. Finally, traceability facilitates code maintenance [6, 17, 31].

Regulation and safety case are the two main differences in motivations between the safety critical domain and general domain. These two motivators are particularly relevant to the safety critical domain. The remaining motivators are relevant to the safety critical and general domains. Organisations operating in the safety critical domain are mandated by regulations to implement traceability. They must provide acceptable evidence that their system is safe and that risks have been mitigated and be able to prove a safety case as failure in a safety critical domain can cause great harm or even loss of life.

6 Conclusions

While we recognise that there are many barriers to implementing traceability (such as cost, tooling issues, trace decay, difficulties in tracing NFRs and lack of implementation guidance), the focus of this paper is on the motivations for an organisation to implement it. The research question which guided this work was: 'What are the motivations for a company to implement traceability?' In addition to that question we also decided to investigate any difference in motivations between the general and safety critical domains.

According to the literature, traceability is beneficial. However its implementation is inconsistent at best, with most companies not implementing it or implementing it in a haphazard manner. As this paper shows, there are many advantages to a company implementing and using traceability with productivity, maintenance and quality gains being chief among them. These benefits, along with reductions in production costs, help give an organisation a competitive advantage. Customer satisfaction is enhanced through requirements validation. Risk is better managed as it is crucial to maintain traceability between the software safety requirements, the decisions taken during design and their actual implementation in the code. Impact analysis allows for better change management which is especially useful when requirements are volatile.

All of the above motivators are important to both the general and safety critical domains. However for the safety critical domain, 'regulation' and 'safety case' are two extremely important motivators.

7 Future Work

While this paper presents the motivations for an organisation to implement traceability, it does not describe the barriers that an organisation might face in implementing traceability. Important future work would be to describe these barriers and how to overcome them.

It is noted that the amount of information in literature regarding traceability implementation is limited. We also plan to analyse the current state of practice for software traceability within Irish companies with a view to providing a framework for the implementation and use of traceability.

Acknowledgements. This research is supported by the Science Foundation Ireland (SFI) Stokes Lectureship Programme, grant number 07/SK/I1299, the SFI Principal Investigator Programme, grant number 08/IN.1/I2030 (the funding of this project was awarded by Science Foundation Ireland under a co-funding initiative by the Irish Government and European Regional Development Fund), and supported in part by Lero - the Irish Software Engineering Research Centre (http://www.lero.ie) grant 10/CE/I1855.

References

[1] Gotel, O., et al.: Software and Systems Traceability. Springer, Heidelberg (2011)
[2] Ramesh, B.: Factors influencing requirements traceability practice. Commun. ACM 41, 37–44 (1998)
[3] McCaffery, F., et al.: Medical Device Software Traceability. In: Gotel, O., et al. (eds.) Software and Systems Traceability. Springer (2011)
[4] Dekhtar, A., Hayes, J.H.: Studying the role of Humans in the Traceability Loop. In: Software and Systems Traceability. Springer (2011)
[5] Gotel, O., et al.: The Grand Challenge of Traceability. In: Software and Systems Traceability. Springer (2011)

[6] Neumuller, C., Grunbacher, P.: Automating Software Traceability in Very Small Companies: A Case Study and Lessons Learne. In: 21st IEEE/ACM International Conference on Automated Software Engineering, ASE 2006, pp. 145–156 (2006)
[7] Gotel, O., Mader, P.: Acquiring Tool Support for Traceability. In: Software and Systems Traceability. Springer (2011)
[8] Gotel, O.C.Z., Finkelstein, C.W.: An analysis of the requirements traceability problem. In: Proceedings of the First International Conference on Requirements Engineering, pp. 94–101 (1994)
[9] Cleland-Huang, J.: Toward improved traceability of non-functional requirements. Presented at the Proceedings of the 3rd International Workshop on Traceability in Emerging forms of Software Engineering, Long Beach, California (2005)
[10] Gotel, O.: Traceability Fundamentals. In: Gotel, O., et al. (eds.) Software and Systems Traceability. Springer (2011)
[11] Ingram, C., Riddle, S.: Cost Benefits of Traceability. In: Software and Systems Traceability. Springer (2011)
[12] Cleland-Huang, J., et al.: A heterogeneous solution for improving the return on investment of requirements traceability. In: Proceedings of 12th IEEE International Requirements Engineering Conference, pp. 230–239 (2004)
[13] Klimpke, L., Hildenbrand, T.: Towards End-to-End Traceability: Insights and Implications from Five Case Studies. Presented at the Proceedings of the 2009 Fourth International Conference on Software Engineering Advances (2009)
[14] Panis, M.C.: Successful Deployment of Requirements Traceability in a Commercial Engineering Organization...Really. In: 2010 18th IEEE International Requirements Engineering Conference (RE), pp. 303–307 (2010)
[15] Arkley, P., Riddle, S.: Tailoring Traceability Information to Business Needs. In: 14th IEEE International Conference on Requirements Engineering, pp. 239–244 (2006)
[16] McCaffery, F., Casey, V.: Med-Trace. In: O'Connor, R.V., Rout, T., McCaffery, F., Dorling, A. (eds.) SPICE 2011. CCIS, vol. 155, pp. 208–211. Springer, Heidelberg (2011)
[17] Heindl, M., Biffl, S.: A case study on value-based requirements tracing. Presented at the Proceedings of the 10th European Software Engineering Conference Held Jointly with 13th ACM SIGSOFT International Symposium on Foundations of Software Engineering, Lisbon, Portugal (2005)
[18] Born, M., et al.: Application of ISO DIS 26262 in Practice. Presented at the CARS, Valencia, Spain (2010)
[19] Mader, P., et al.: Motivation Matters in the Traceability Trenches. Presented at the Proceedings of the 2009 17th IEEE International Requirements Engineering Conference, RE (2009)
[20] McCaffery, F., Casey, V., McHugh, M.: How Can Software SMEs Become Medical Device Software SMEs. In: O'Connor, R.V., Pries-Heje, J., Messnarz, R. (eds.) EuroSPI 2011. CCIS, vol. 172, pp. 247–258. Springer, Heidelberg (2011)
[21] Asuncion, H.U., et al.: An end-to-end industrial software traceability tool. Presented at the Proceedings of the the 6th Joint Meeting of the European Software Engineering Conference and the ACM SIGSOFT Symposium on The Foundations of Software Engineering, Dubrovnik, Croatia (2007)
[22] Council, E.: Council Directive 93/42/EEC of 14 June 1993 concerning medical devices. Official Journal of The European Communities (1993)
[23] Council, E.: Directive 2007/47/EC of the European Parliament and of the Council of 5 September 2007. Official Journal of the European Union (2007)

[24] Mason, P.: On Traceability for Safety Critical Systems Engineering. Presented at the Proceedings of the 12th Asia-Pacific Software Engineering Conference (2005)
[25] Cleland-Huang, J.: Traceability in Agile Projects. In: Software and Systems Traceability. Springer (2011)
[26] Hayes, J.H., et al.: REquirements Tracing On target (RETRO): Improving Software Maintenance through Traceability Recovery (2007)
[27] Antoniol, G., et al.: Recovering Traceability Links between Code and Documentation. IEEE Transactions on Software Engineering 28 (2002)
[28] Kazman, R., et al.: ATAM: Method for Architecture Evaluation. Carnegie Mellon Software Engineering Institute, Pittsburgh (2000)
[29] Heider, W., et al.: Evolution-Driven Trace Acquisition in Eclipse-Based Product Line-Workspaces. In: Software and Systems Traceability. Springer (2011)
[30] Arkley, P., Riddle, S.: Overcoming the Traceability Benefit Problem. Presented at the Proceedings of the 13th IEEE International Conference on Requirements Engineering (2005)
[31] Oliveto, R., et al.: Software Artefact Traceability: the Never-Ending Challenge. In: IEEE International Conference on Software Maintenance, ICSM 2007, pp. 485–488 (2007)

Improving the Tendering Process through the Deployment of PMBOK®

Antònia Mas and Antoni Lluís Mesquida

University of the Balearic Islands, Department of Mathematics and Computer Science,
Cra. de Valldemossa, km 7.5, 07122 Palma de Mallorca (Illes Balears), Spain
{antonia.mas,antoni.mesquida}@uib.es

Abstract. In the adverse economic situation customer requirements for purchasing a new product or service are even greater. Software companies have been forced to improve their tenders to be competitive. The experience and knowledge gained in previous projects is crucial for organizations to prepare accurate and viable tenders. In this paper, two generic processes to support the tendering preparation and the project management according to PMBOK® are presented. These generic processes have been deployed in two software companies involved in an ISO/IEC 15504 SPI initiative. The implementation of these generic processes has facilitated the improvement of some ISO/IEC 15504-5 processes.

Keywords: Software Process Improvement (SPI), Project management, PMBOK®, ISO/IEC 15504 (SPICE), ISO/IEC 12207.

1 Introduction

In a situation of general crisis like the current one, customer requirements are even greater. When a customer wishes to purchase or to provide its organization with a new product or service, several proposals must be requested and comparisons must be performed with the aim of choosing the one that best suit its needs and budget.

The ICT sector is no stranger to this situation. Software companies have also been forced to improve their tenders to compete in today's market and survive in these recessionary conditions. We will use the term tender to refer to: "the document obtained from the initial study of a new business opportunity that proposes a solution for the new system". The tender is made in order to be understood and accepted by the customer and constitute an agreement between both parties.

For an organization to make viable proposals it is often necessary to use the experience and knowledge gained in previous projects. Therefore, it is essential to have a procedure to capture and collect the knowledge gained in each project. The information collected and analyzed throughout the project lifecycle, from the initiation phase to the closing phase, can provide valuable feedback to make more appropriate proposals. In other words, the improvement of the tender lies in conducting an integrated management of the projects in the organisation's portfolio.

It is widely accepted that the project management process is crucial for most software companies, regardless size and kind of applications it develops. Almost all companies committed to process improvement have set as a priority the establishment and deployment of this process. To meet this goal, the adoption of a renowned and tested framework covering the entire project lifecycle is strongly recommended. There are different international standards related to Project Management. One of them is the Project Management Body of Knowledge (PMBOK®) Guide [1] developed by the Project Management Institute (PMI®), which has been used in this work.

This paper presents the research made by the authors during their participation in a R&D project with two software development companies of the Balearic Islands: Brújula and Bizzit. In 2007 these two companies initiated a software processes improvement programme thanks to public subsidies from the Spanish government. Both companies made major internal efforts to adapt some of their processes to the best practices proposed by the ISO/IEC 15504 standard [2, 3, 4], achieving the capability level 2 in some of these processes. Nowadays, these companies remain interested in maintaining and improving the capability of their processes in order to reach a certain maturity level according to this standard. As it was impossible for the companies to launch a complete project to reach ISO/IEC 15504-7 [5] maturity level 3, the efforts were focused on improving the processes related to customer tendering, and therefore also to project management. Even though the research described in this paper was specifically applied to these two companies, the results could be extrapolated to other companies in similar starting positions.

The paper is structured as follows: Section 2 presents a generic tendering process to support the preparation of tenders which includes most of the best practises of the related ISO/IEC 15504-5 processes. Section 3 defines a generic project management process which describes a complete set of activities to cover the PMBOK® good practices for the successful management of projects. Section 4 details the application of these generic processes in two software companies. Finally, Section 5 concludes this paper and opens discussions regarding the results.

2   Definition of a Generic Tendering Process

With the aim of improving the tendering process, the first task of our work was to determine what an offer was from the point of view of the two companies involved in the project. The tenders used by these companies and other tenders from different organizations in our environment were carefully analysed. We evaluated all the sections and aspects included in these tenders and then, with the support of the experienced sales staff, we defined a generic structure and contents for the new tender template, which should be adaptable to any type of organization and useful in a wide variety of projects.

Since the interest of the project also focuses on improving the software lifecycle processes related to the tendering process, and as the main interest of both companies is to progress on the way towards maturity using SPICE, the relations between the proposed tender template and the processes defined in the process dimension of the exemplar Process Assessment Model of ISO/IEC 15504-5:2006 [3] were identified and the best practices of the related processes were incorporated to the new tender template. Table 1 shows the sixteen ISO/IEC 15504-5:2006 processes which results or outputs are related to the developed tender.

Table 1. ISO/IEC 15504-5:2006 processes related to the tender

ISO/IEC 15504-5:2006 Processes	
SPL.1	Supplier tendering
SPL.2	Product release
SPL.3	Product acceptance support
ENG.1	Requirements elicitation
ENG.4	Software requirements analysis
ENG.5	Software design
ENG.11	Software installation
MAN.1	Organizational alignment
MAN.3	Project management
MAN.4	Quality management
MAN.5	Risk management
PIM.1	Process establishment
RIN.1	Human resource management
RIN.4	Infrastructure
SUP.4	Joint review
SUP.7	Documentation

It is important to note that software lifecycle standards have undergone significant changes since the participant companies initiated their SPI programmes in 2007. The most significant changes are:

- A new version of the ISO/IEC 12207 standard for software lifecycle processes came out in 2008.
- A new version of ISO/IEC 15504-5 [4] appeared in January 2012.

Therefore, and due to these changes were taking place simultaneously with this research, it was also found convenient to consider the relations between the obtained tender and the processes of new ISO/IEC 15504-5:2012. Table 2 shows the fifteen ISO/IEC 15504-5:2012 processes which are related to the tender and their correspondence with the ISO/IEC 15504-5:2006 version.

Table 2. ISO/IEC 15504-5:2012 processes related to the tender

ISO/IEC 15504-5:2012 Process		Correspondence with ISO/IEC 15504-5:2006
AGR.2	Supply	SPL.1, SPL.2, SPL.3
ORG.1	Life cycle model management	PIM.1
ORG.2	Infrastructure management	RIN.4
ORG.4	Human resource management	RIN.1
ORG.5	Quality management	MAN.4
ORG.6	Organizational alignment	MAN.1
PRO.1	Project planning	MAN.3
PRO.2	Project assessment and control	MAN.3
PRO.4	Risk management	MAN.5
ENG.1	Stakeholder requirements definition	ENG.1
ENG.7	Software installation	ENG.11
DEV.1	Software requirements analysis	ENG.4
DEV.2	Software architectural design	ENG.5
SUP.1	Software documentation management	SUP.7
SUP.6	Software review	SUP.4

Finally, Table 3 provides the sections and contents of the generic tender developed. This tender has been obtained from the analysis of the proposals used by the companies participating in the project and considers the best practices of the processes listed above in Tables 1 and 2.

Table 3. Generic tender

Section	Contents	Correspondence with ISO/IEC 15504-5:2006
About this document	Table for document verification and approval (With name, position, date and signature) Document purpose and objectives Scope Document identification Access control and distribution Referenced documents Abbreviations and acronyms	SUP.7 Documentation MAN.4 Quality management
About the company	Corporate presentation Advantages of this proposal Mission and vision Expertise Environmental compliance Security	PIM.1 Process establishment MAN.1 Organizational alignment

Table 3. *(Continued)*

Section	Contents	Correspondence with ISO/IEC 15504-5:2006

Technical offer	Project scope and objectives
	Stakeholders
	User and system requirements
	    Functional requirements
	    Non-functional requirements
	Interfaces with other systems
	System design
	    Technological features
	    System architecture
	    Detailed design
	System delivery
	    Installation
	    Training and manuals
	    Approval of deliverables
		ENG.1 Requirements elicitation
		ENG.4 Software requirements analysis
		ENG.5 Software design
		ENG.11 Software installation

Management plan	Work Breakdown Structure
	Effort estimation
	Project team: Profiles, roles and responsibilities
	    Internal team
	    Customer team
	Schedule
	Project control and monitoring
	Identified risks
		MAN.3 Project management
		MAN.5 Risk management
		RIN.1 Human resource management
		SUP.4 Joint review

Financial plan	Budget Commercial terms and conditions	MAN.3 Project management SPL.1 Supplier tendering SPL.2 Product release SPL.3 Product acceptance support
Organizational process assets	Lifecycle Model Methodology Standards to be used Applicable plans and policies	SUP.7 Documentation PIM.1 Process establishment RIN.4 Infrastructure
Appendix: Acceptance sheet	Tender data Customer data Tender acceptance	SPL.2 Product release

3 Definition of a Generic Project Management Process

As previously mentioned in the introduction section, when an organization wants to improve its tenders, it should adequately collect the experience from previous projects and use the all the knowledge gained to prepare accurate, comprehensive and viable proposals. This requires performing an integrated management of the projects carried out in the organization. There exist different frameworks and standards for project management. In this research, PMBOK® was considered as the reference standard. Nevertheless, there are other alternatives as PRINCE2® or IPMA 4-L-C. PRINCE2® is a process-based method for effective project management which was initially developed for managing ICT projects and which has been used since 1989, especially in the United Kingdom. The IPMA 4-L-C (four-level certification) program is based on a competence model which considers the behavioural, contextual and technical competences that must have a project manager.

In order to define the generic project management process which is presented in section 3.3, the PMBOK® Guide project management good practices were carefully analysed. Next, a brief introduction to this standard is presented.

3.1 The Project Management Body of Knowledge, PMBOK®

The Project Management Body of Knowledge (PMBOK®) [1] is a collection of recognised good practices that are widely applied by project management professionals and practitioners for the successful management of projects around the world. The PMBOK® Guide provides guidelines for managing projects within an organization. The PMBOK® Guide also provides and promotes a common vocabulary within the project management profession for discussing, writing, and applying project management concepts.

The PMBOK® Guide project management good practices cover the entire project lifecycle, from proposal to delivery, final acceptance and closing. The standard defines 42 project management processes which are grouped into five categories known as Project Management Process Groups: Initiating, Planning, Executing, Monitoring and Controlling, and Closing. Moreover, the PMBOK® Guide recognises nine project management knowledge areas typical of almost all projects:

- Project integration management (Chapter 4)
- Project scope management (Chapter 5)
- Project time management (Chapter 6)
- Project cost management (Chapter 7)
- Project quality management (Chapter 8)
- Project human resources management (Chapter 9)
- Project communications management (Chapter 10)
- Project risk management (Chapter 11)
- Project procurement management (Chapter 12)

3.2 Project Management in ISO/IEC 15504-5

Since the organizations participating in this research have already reached a certain capability level in some of the implemented ISO/IEC 15504-5:2006 processes, the relations between the PMBOK® Guide processes and the processes of the ISO/IEC 15504-5:2006 standard were analysed. As a result, we could observe that thirteen different ISO/IEC 15504-5:2006 processes were related to project management good practices. These processes are shown in Table 4. If these processes are already implemented in the organization, all the efforts devoted to their implementation may be very useful for deploying project management activities.

Table 4. ISO/IEC 15504-5:2006 processes related to project management activities

ISO/IEC 15504-5:2006 Processes	
ACQ.1	Acquisition preparation
ACQ.2	Supplier selection
ACQ.3	Contract agreement
ACQ.4	Supplier monitoring
SPL.1	Supplier tendering
MAN.2	Organizational management
MAN.3	Project management
MAN.4	Quality management
MAN.5	Risk management
PIM.1	Process establishment
RIN.1	Human resource management
RIN.2	Training
RIN.4	Infrastructure

Table 5. ISO/IEC 15504-5:2012 processes related to project management activities

ISO/IEC 15504-5:2012 Process		Correspondence with ISO/IEC 15504-5:2006
AGR.1	Acquisition	ACQ.1, ACQ.2, ACQ.4
AGR.2	Supply	ACQ.3, SPL.1
ORG.1	Life cycle model management	PIM.1
ORG.2	Infrastructure management	RIN.4
ORG.4	Human resource management	RIN.1, RIN.2
ORG.5	Quality management	MAN.4
ORG.7	Organizational management	MAN.2
PRO.1	Project planning	MAN.3
PRO.2	Project assessment and control	MAN.3
PRO.4	Risk management	MAN.5

Table 5 shows the ten ISO/IEC 15504-5:2012 processes which are related to project management activities and their correspondence with the ISO/IEC 15504-5:2006 processes.

3.3 A Generic Project Management Process

The generic project management process developed covers all the detected business needs and addresses the processes of the five Process Groups of the PMBOK® Guide. In addition, this generic process considers the ISO/IEC 15504-5 base practices related to project management processes listed above in Tables 4 and 5. Due to space limitations, the full process is not presented. Nevertheless, Table 6 shows an extract of the process, detailing solely the activities within the Planning Process Group.

Table 6. Planning activities of the generic project management process

Section	Activities according to PMBOK®	Correspondence with ISO/IEC 15504-5:2006
Project management plan	4.1 Develop Project Charter 4.2 Develop Project Management Plan	MAN.3 Project management
Project scope	5.2 Define Scope	MAN.3 Project management
Project schedule	5.3 Create Work Breakdown Structure 6.1 Define Activities 6.2 Sequence Activities 6.4 Estimate Activity Durations 6.5 Develop Schedule	MAN.3 Project management
Human resource management	9.1 Develop Human Resource Plan 6.3 Estimate Activity Resources 9.2 Acquire Project Team 9.3 Develop Project Team	MAN.3 Project management RIN.1 Human resource management RIN.2 Training
Cost management	7.1 Estimate Costs 7.2 Determine Budget	MAN.3 Project management RIN.4 Infrastructure
Communication management	10.1 Identify Stakeholders 10.2 Plan Communications	MAN.3 Project management MAN.2 Organizational management SPL.1 Supplier tendering PIM.1 Process establishment
Risk management	11.1 Plan Risk Management 11.2 Identify Risks 11.3 Perform Qualitative Analysis 11.4 Perform Quantitative Analysis 11.5 Plan Risk Responses	MAN.3 Project management MAN.5 Risk management RIN.4 Infrastructure

Table 6. *(Continued)*

Section	Activities according to PMBOK®	Correspondence with ISO/IEC 15504-5:2006
Procurement management	12.1 Plan Procurements	MAN.3 Project management ACQ.1 Acquisition preparation ACQ.2 Supplier selection ACQ.3 Contract agreement ACQ.4 Supplier monitoring RIN.4 Infrastructure
Quality management	8.1 Plan Quality	MAN.3 Project management MAN.4 Quality management

4 Application in Software Companies

This section describes the application of the research in the companies involved in the project. Brújula and Bizzit are two Spanish companies based in the Balearic Islands.

4.1 Companies' Overview

Brújula is a Spanish company which began its activity in 2000. Nowadays, Brújula has 82 employees dedicated to the development of Internet-based applications and the implementation of the infrastructure which supports them. The implementation of a quality management system and the ISO 9000 certification obtained by the company in 2002 has become one of the main identity insignias of Brújula as a company: the quality as a management strategy. In 2005 the company introduced the EFQM Excellence Model to its management system and at the end of 2007 began the adaptation of its processes to the ISO/IEC 15504 international standard for software process assessment and improvement. In 2009 the company implemented an information security management system according to ISO/IEC 27001 and got this certification.

Bizzit is a Spanish software development company which began its activity in 2004. The company has performed many projects for both the Balearic Islands civil service and other private organizations of all kind of sectors, especially for the tourism sector. Moreover, it has developed some of its own information systems for internal management. Bizzit has completed more than 400 projects during the last five years. The company is structured in four business units: a software factory, an innovation department, an expansion department and a management department. It has a young team of 30 employees with different professional profiles of the IT sector.

4.2 Starting Point for the Companies

As mentioned in the introduction section, the two companies initiated a process improvement programme thanks to the public subsidies of Plan Avanza. Brújula started the implementation of ISO/IEC 15504-5:2006 in late 2007 and Bizzit in late 2008. Table 7 shows the process capability levels that the companies had reached in late 2009, with respect to processes in the first column. The correspondence of this data with the companies has been omitted for privacy reasons.

Table 7. ISO/IEC 15504 process capability levels of the participant companies

ISO/IEC 15504-5:2006 Process		Capability level in Company A	Capability level in Company B
ACQ.3	Contract agreement	1	
ACQ.4	Supplier monitoring	1	
ACQ.5	Customer acceptance	1	
SPL.2	Product release	2	
ENG.1	Requirements elicitation	1	2
ENG.4	Software requirements analysis	1	2
ENG.5	Software design		1
ENG.8	Software testing	1	1
ENG.11	Software installation	1	
ENG.12	Software and system maintenance	1	
MAN.3	Project management	1	1
MAN.5	Risk management	2	
SUP.1	Quality assurance	2	
SUP.4	Joint review		1
SUP.7	Documentation	2	
SUP.8	Configuration management		1
SUP.9	Problem resolution management	1	1

So far, both companies have carried on working on the improvement of their processes and on the deployment of the two developed generic processes in all the projects within the organization. It is important to note that the adverse economic situation faced by many European Union countries in recent times, and by Spain as well, has made the organizations to redirect their efforts to survive in the market. As a consequence, the interest in improving their process has been shifted to the background. In addition, in recent years the government has reduced or cancelled the majority of public subsidies to improve the enterprise competitiveness through the implementation of process standards.

4.3 Application in Company A

Table 8 shows the ISO/IEC 15504-5:2006 processes already implemented in Company A which are related to the generic tendering process (first column) and to the generic project management process (second column).

Table 8. ISO/IEC 15504-5:2006 processes implemented in Company A

ISO/IEC 15504-5:2006 processes related to the generic tender		ISO/IEC 15504-5:2006 processes related to the generic project management process	
SPL.2	Product release	ACQ.3	Contract agreement
ENG.1	Requirements elicitation	ACQ.4	Supplier monitoring
ENG.4	Software requirements analysis	MAN.3	Project management
ENG.11	Software installation	MAN.5	Risk management
MAN.3	Project management		
MAN.5	Risk management		
SUP.7	Documentation		

4.3.1 Deployment of the Generic Tendering Process

From the analysis of the data contained in Tables 3 and 8, it can be concluded that the process improvement programme according to SPICE initiated in Company A has facilitated the implementation of the generic tendering process in the following ways:

- Having the ENG.1 Requirements elicitation process adequately deployed has led the company to routinely perform the capture of project requirements and therefore, to cover part of the contents in *Technical offer*.
- Having the processes MAN.3 Project management and the MAN.5 Risk Management fully consolidated indicates that the contents of the *Management Plan* section are already addressed by the projects within the organization. However, this section will be even improved by implementing the generic project management process.
- The processes SPL.2 Product release and ENG.11 Software installation have helped the company to better specify the supply and installation conditions of the deliverable products and services described in the tender.
- The SUP.7 Documentation process has allowed the company to have already addressed some aspects of the first section of the generic tender (*About this document*).

On the other hand, and from an analysis of Table 3, there are some ISO/IEC 15504-5:2006 processes which implementation has been considerably facilitated after the deployment of the generic tendering process in Company A:

- By establishing the aspects of the section *Commercial terms and conditions* some of the base practices of the processes SPL.1 Supplier tendering and SPL.3 Product acceptance support have been performed.
- Moreover, the use of the new tender has helped to create *Organizational process assets* and deploy the human resource management processes. Then, the best practices proposed by the processes PIM.1 Process establishment, MAN.1 Organizational alignment, RIN.4 Infrastructure and RIN.1 Human resource management has been implemented. It has to be noted that the first three processes are related to both the tendering process and the generic project management process.

4.3.2 Deployment of the Generic Project Management Process

From the analysis of the data contained in Tables 6 and 8, it can be concluded that the process improvement programme according to SPICE initiated in Company A has also facilitated the implementation of the generic project management process in the organization in the following ways:

- Having the MAN.3 Project management process implemented has had a positive impact on almost all activities of the generic project management process. The MAN.3 process has not reached the capability level 2 yet. However, the Level 1 process attribute is largely achieved (L) and the two Level 2 process attributes are also largely achieved (L). Then, the company could reach capability level 2 in this process with only a little effort.
- Having reached the capability level 2 for the MAN.5 Risk management process has considerably facilitated the implementation of the *Risk management* activities of the generic project management process.
- Having the processes ACQ.3 Contract agreement and ACQ.4 Supplier monitoring implemented has provided a big advantage in *managing acquisitions*.

On the other hand, and from an analysis of Table 6, there are some ISO/IEC 15504-5:2006 processes which implementation has been considerably facilitated after the deployment of the generic project management process:

- By performing the *Human resource management* activities some important steps in the implementation of the processes RIN.1 Human resource management and RIN.2 Training has been implemented.
- By performing the acquisition management activities of the *Procurement management* section a great number of base practices of the processes ACQ.1 Acquisition preparation and ACQ.2 Supplier selection has been implemented.
- The deployment of the *Quality management* activities means that most of the MAN.4 Quality management base practices have been performed.
- Finally, the deployment of the generic project management process has facilitated the implementation of the processes PIM.1 Process establishment, RIN.4 Infrastructure and MAN.2 Organizational management.

5   Conclusion

In this paper two generic procedures have been presented. On the one hand, a tendering process to facilitate the preparation of accurate sales proposals has been detailed. On the other hand, a generic project management process to perform an efficient management of the projects in the organization has been defined. Since this research was supported by a R&D project in cooperation with two software development companies, the results have been applied in these companies. They had already participated in previous software process improvement initiatives led by our research group. The two companies manage some processes and work products and have also standardized many of the organizational process assets. They are fully aware of the need of continually improve their processes in order to remain competitive in today's market, hence the importance of this project for them.

From the analysis of the obtained results, we can conclude that if a company decides to implement the generic tendering process and the generic project management process presented in this paper, it will be implementing at the same time a great number of the best practices recommended by ISO/IEC 15504 processes. As a result, besides of setting up these two procedures within the organization, it could maintain or even increase the capability level of its internal processes according to this standard and then advance to higher maturity levels.

Finally, it is important to note that the deployment of the two generic processes could be considered for a company which has not taken part in any process improvement initiative as the first implicit step on the road to maturity.

Acknowledgments. This research has been supported by CICYT-TIN2010-20057-C03-03 "Simulación aplicada a la gestión de equipos, procesos y servicios", Sim4Gest.

References

1. A Guide to the Project Management Body of Knowledge (PMBOK® Guide), 4th edn. Project Management Institute (2009)
2. ISO/IEC: ISO/IEC 15504-2:2003/Cor 1:2004 Software Engineering - Process Assessment - Part 2: Performing an assessment (2004)
3. ISO/IEC: ISO/IEC 15504-5:2006 Information technology - Process Assessment - Part 5: An exemplar Process Assessment Model (2006)
4. ISO/IEC: ISO/IEC 15504-5:2012 Information technology - Process assessment - Part 5: An exemplar software life cycle process assessment model (2012)
5. ISO/IEC: TR 15504-7:2008 Information technology - Process Assessment - Part 7: Assessment of organizational maturity (2008)

FIRST: Common-Sense Process Scopes for Starting a Process Improvement Program

Luigi Buglione[1,2], Fergal McCaffery[3], Jean Carlo Rossa Hauck[4],
and Christiane Gresse von Wangenheim[4]

[1] Engineering.IT SpA - Via R. Morandi 32, 00185 Rome Italy
[2] Ecole de Technologie Superieure (ETS) – Montréal Canada
[3] Regulated Software Research Group & Lero - Dundalk Institute of Technology – Ireland
[4] Federal University of Santa Catarina (UFSC) – Brazil
luigi.buglione@eng.it, fergal.mccaffery@dkit.ie,
{jeanhauck,gresse}@gmail.com

Abstract. One of the main challenges for ICT organizations is to initiate a well-structured process improvement program. This is particularly the case when adopting a maturity & capability model (MCM) as it brings with it costs associated with internal appraisals, and the realization that in order to achieve a particular maturity level (ML) a number of processes within the Process Reference Model (PRM) will need to be successfully implemented. Some initiatives have been proposed in the last decade, such as the RAPID initiative, but there is still some resistance to adopting MCMs such as CMMI or SPICE (ISO/IEC). This paper will propose the FIRST (Fast Improvement aSsessment sTep) approach, providing a minimum, common-sense set of processes to be appraised during the initial gap analysis which will form the foundation for the design and deployment of an improvement plan, which will be particularly useful for Small-Medium Enterprises (SMEs) and Very Small Entities (VSEs), that are coherent with ISO Management Systems requirements.

Keywords: Process Appraisals, Process Improvement, CMMI, ISO/IEC 15504, FIRST, Appraisal Scope.

1 Introduction

During the '90s some publications such as the CHAOS Report [1] focused upon the success rate of IT projects, reporting how project failure may be avoided and the probability for achieving better results improved through adopting improvement activities. This helped to promote, during the same period, the diffusion of 'maturity models' such as the Sw-CMM [2], the first SPICE (ISO/IEC 15504) technical reports [3] and few other process improvement models and initiatives (e.g. Bootstrap [4] and AMI [5]). Unfortunately, ICT organizations mostly perceived maturity & capability models (**MCM**) as an improvement tool for large companies (even though many of the models and frameworks are specific for SMEs/VSEs[1]) requiring a significant

---
[1] See ISO/IEC 29110 public site: http://profs.etsmtl.ca/claporte/english/VSE/VSE.html

budget for sponsoring such structured initiatives, instead of something simpler based on the continuous improvement quality principle.

Therefore, in order to promote the usage of MCM's there was a need to create appraisals with reduced appraisal scopes, with few premises: low budget, but willing to promote improvement initiatives → limited usage of MCM → design of a reduced scope for process appraisals, focusing upon assessing the 'vital' processes for determining the health of an organization and helping to provide improvement steps based upon the evidence gathered during reduced scope appraisals, moving from the cause-effect relationship of those processes with the other ones described in their own 'full' models/frameworks.

Upon analyzing reduced scope appraisals, some questions arise, such as: 1) is there a unique scope for all companies? 2) are the suggested set of processes the right ones? If not, which modifications could be suggested?

The aim of this paper is to discuss how to improve the usage of MCMs in any type and size of ICT organization, trying to use the 'reduced scope' shortcut as a communication tool for stimulating managers to adopt these models, whilst also proposing a renewed version of such an idea.

The paper is organized as follows: Section 2, shows the most diffused process appraisal methods (PAM), with particular attention to those ones having a reduced appraisal scope and their rationale. Section 3, proposes FIRST (Fast Improvement aSsessment sTep), highlighting the need to have different scopes for different information needs and maturity positioning by ICT organizations. Finally, Section 4 provides some conclusions and the next steps for this work.

2   Process Appraisals: State-of-the-Art

2.1   Process Appraisal Methods (PAMs)

In the ISO world, any MCM has two facets: a PRM (Process Reference Model) and a PAM (Process Assessment Model), the first one describing the processes[2], the second one the detailed model that is used for the actual assessment[3]. For instance, looking at CMMI constellations, each constellation with its technical report (DEV/ACQ/SVC) describes the PRM, while SCAMPI (Standard CMMI Appraisal Method for Process Improvement) is the process based on ARC (Appraisal Requirements for CMMI), representing its PAM. Looking at SPICE (ISO/IEC 15504 standard), ISO 15504-5 contains the PAM that is based upon the PRM for software ISO/IEC 12207.

---

[2] A PRM is "a model comprising definitions of processes in a life cycle described in terms of process purpose and outcomes, together with an architecture describing the relationships between the processes *(ISO/IEC 15504-1:2004 Information technology -- Process assessment -- Part 1: Concepts and vocabulary, 3.48)*".

[3] A PAM is: "a model suitable for the purpose of assessing process capability, based on one or more process reference models *(ISO/IEC 15504-1:2004 Information technology -- Process assessment -- Part 1: Concepts and vocabulary, 3.3)*".

Since those PRMs contain many processes, from the late '90s a number of tailored versions for SMEs/VSEs arose, with the two main drivers for achieving improvements at lower costs were: a) reduce the PRM scope, with lighter PRMs (less processes); b) simplify processes in terms of actions and WPs to be used. Just to name a few, for the SPICE world: MARES [6], MPS.BR[4], MoProSoft[5], SPIRE [7] and FAME [8], etc.; for the Sw-CMM/CMMI world: IPSS [9], Dynamic CMM [10], etc.

2.2 PAM Scope

Irrespective of the appraisal method, the common-sense criteria applied is mostly to design the appraisal scope by prioritizing those processes that – if properly managed and controlled – could enable an organization to obtain valuable information for planning and running focused improvement actions.

For instance, the assessment/appraisal 'scope', in the CMMI world, ARC asks *"The method documentation shall provide requirements and/or guidance for identifying the scope of the model(s) to be investigated in the appraisal, including the process areas and capability levels, as appropriate for the model representation."* (requirement 4.1.3) [11], while for the SPICE world, ISO/IEC 15504-2:2003 states that *"A Process Assessment Model shall declare its scope of coverage in the terms of: a) the selected Process Reference Model(s); b) the selected processes taken from the Process Reference Model(s); c) the capability levels selected from the Measurement Framework."* (Clause 6.3.2.3) [3]

In both cases, there is not a well-established list of criteria for shaping the PRM/PAM scope, leaving each organization to cope with technical constraints and to choose what could be subjectively important for them. Of course, when few organizations following the same criteria this decreases the potential to provide external, competitive benchmarking.

2.3 Reducing the Appraisal Scope: Some Experiences

2.3.1 RAPID

RAPID (Rapid Assessment for Process Improvement for software Development) [12][13] was one of the most diffused methods based on ISO/IEC 15504, applying a reduced appraisal scope. Proposed in 2000, referring to the SPICE TR documents, it was updated lately in 2006 to reflect updates to the 15504 IS (International Standard) references, as described in Table 1. Eight (8) processes are taken into account out of a full set of forty-eight (48) ISO/IEC 15504 processes.

---

[4] http://www.softex.br/mpsbr
[5] http://www.comunidadmoprosoft.org.mx/

FIRST: Common-Sense Process Scopes for Starting a Process Improvement Program   189

Table 1. RAPID processes and process categories

	Process	Process Category	ISO/IEC TR 15504	ISO/IEC IS 15504
RE	Req. Elicitation	Customer-Supplier	CUS.3	ENG.1
SD	Software Development	Engineering	ENG.1	ENG.x
CM	Configuration Mgmt	Support	SUP.2	SUP.8
QA	Quality Assurance	Support	SUP.3	SUP.1
PM	Project Management	Management	MAN.2	MAN.3
PR	Problem Resolution	Support	SUP.8	SUP.9
RM	Risk Management	Management	MAN.4	MAN.5
PE	Process Establishment	Organization	ORG.2.1	PIM.1

2.3.2 Express Process Appraisal (EPA)

The Express Process Appraisal (EPA) method [14] was developed in 2003 to reduce the scope of the CMMI® model [15] to focus upon only the foundational processes that would bring the most benefit to SMEs. The EPA complies with the ARC 1.1 [16] requirements for a class-C methods. The EPA was therefore based upon only 6 process areas of the continuous representation of the CMMI® model as opposed to the full 25 process areas. The processes included in the EPA are listed below in table 2. The EPA does not provide any form of rating. The EPA method was designed to assess software processes within software development companies with little or no previous experience of software process improvement programs, and so it was decided not to assess the generic practices for each of the process areas. Therefore the EPA method is currently limited to appraising the specific practices for each of the process areas mentioned previously.

Table 2. EPA process areas

Process Area		Process Category	Maturity Level
REQM	Requirements Management	Engineering	2
PP	Project Planning	Project Management	2
CM	Configuration Management	Support	2
PMC	Project Monitoring & Control	Project Management	2
PPQA	Process & Product Quality Assurance	Support	2
MA	Measurement & Analysis	Support	2

2.3.3 Adept

The Adept method [17] was developed in 2007 and was based upon the EPA method. It however differed from the EPA in that it extended the scope of the assessment to include 12 process areas (out of 25 processes within the CMMI model) as opposed to 6 process areas. It was developed based upon experiences from the EPA and therefore four of the fundamental process areas that were included in the EPA were deemed to be mandatory and the remaining 8 process areas optional. The Adept method, like the EPA was designed so that 6 process areas could be assessed, with 4 being mandatory this meant that the sponsor company could select 2 of the remaining 8 processes for inclusion within the assessment. The four mandatory processes were those that were deemed to provide the most benefit to companies when the EPA method was implemented [18], these were *Requirements Management; Configuration Management; Project Planning; Project Monitoring & Control*. Table 3 provides details of the Adept process areas.

Table 3. Adept process areas

Process Area		Process Category	Maturity Level	Mandatory/ Optional
REQM	Requirements Management	Engineering	2	**Mandatory**
PP	Project Planning	Project Management	2	**Mandatory**
CM	Configuration Management	Support	2	**Mandatory**
PMC	Project Monitoring & Control	Project Management	2	**Mandatory**
PPQA	Process & Product Quality Assurance	Support	2	*Optional*
MA	Measurement & Analysis	Support	2	*Optional*
RD	Requirements Development	Engineering	3	*Optional*
TS	Technical Solution	Engineering	3	*Optional*
PI	Product Integration	Engineering	3	*Optional*
VER	Verification	Engineering	3	*Optional*
VAL	Validation	Engineering	3	*Optional*
RSKM	Risk Management	Project Management	3	*Optional*

2.3.4 MARES

MARES [6] is an ISO/IEC 15504-conformant assessment method for small software companies developed in 2004. The first version of the method defined a context-process model. Process profile patterns are used to indicate the process capability's relevance to the organization's characteristics and a set of heuristics are used for adapting the patterns to a specific organization. Within the method a SWOT analysis is performed in order to identify strengths and weaknesses by analyzing processes' importance to the organization's context and goals and their estimated capability. Although the initial version of MARES does not provide a minimum set of processes, the experience of its application [19] has led to its extension in 2006 to facilitate VSEs assessments, with the inclusion of a set of 17 processes taken from ISO/IEC 15504-5. Some processes may not be assessed when considered irrelevant to the organizational context, for instance, if a company has not yet reached the stage of providing support.

2.3.5 ISO/IEC TR 15504-7:2008 – Appendix A

Last but not least in this short list of experiences, there is Part 7 of the ISO/IEC 15504 standard, recently released [20]. This technical report describes how to determine organizational maturity, and proposes a predefined sequence of processes by maturity levels (ML), similar to the CMMI staged representation.

FIRST: Common-Sense Process Scopes for Starting a Process Improvement Program 191

Table 4. MARES processes

	Process Area	Process Category	Capability Level	Mandatory/ Optional
SPL.1	Supply	Support	3	*Optional*
SPL.2	Software release	Support	3	*Optional*
SPL.3	Software acceptance support	Support	3	*Optional*
OPE.2	Customer support	Support	3	*Optional*
ENG.4	Software Requirements Analysis	Engineering	3	**Mandatory**
ENG.5	Software Design	Engineering	3	**Mandatory**
ENG.6	Software construction	Engineering	3	**Mandatory**
ENG.7	Software integration	Engineering	3	**Mandatory**
ENG.8	Software test	Engineering	3	**Mandatory**
ENG.11	Software installation	Engineering	3	**Mandatory**
ENG.12	Software Maintenance	Engineering	3	**Mandatory**
CFG.1	Documentation	Support	3	**Mandatory**
CFG.2	Configuration Management	Support	3	**Mandatory**
CFG.4	Change request management	Support	3	**Mandatory**
MAN.3	Project management	Project Management	3	**Mandatory**
MAN.4	Quality Management	Project Management	3	**Mandatory**
MAN.5	Risk Management	Project Management	3	**Mandatory**

Compared to ISO/IEC 15504-5 PRM, the main difference is that there is greater flexibility for selecting the appraisal scope. Appendix A, describes an exemplar organizational maturity model, proposing different sets of processes for each ML: (a) full set, (b) minimum set, (c) eventual additional processes to the minimum set, as shown in Table 5.

Table 5. ISO/IEC TR 15504-7 – Full set, minimum set, additional processes[6] by ML

	ML	Full Set	Minimum Set	Additional processes
Basic processes	1	ENG.1-12 SPL.2	ENG.1, ENG.4, ENG.5, ENG.6, ENG.7, ENG.8, SPL.2	ENG.2, ENG.3, ENG.9, ENG.10, ENG:11, ENG.12
Extended processes	2	SUP.1-4, SUP.7-10 MAN.3, MAN.5, ACQ.3-5, SPL.3	SUP.1-2, SUP.7-10 MAN.3, MAN.5	SUP.3-4, ACQ.3-5, SPL.3
	3	RIN.1-4, PIM.1-3 MAN.2, MAN.4, MAN.6 SUP.5, REU.1-3	RIN.1-4, PIM.1-3 MAN.2, MAN.4, MAN.6, SUP.5	REU.1-3
	4	QNT.1	---	---
	5	QNT.2	---	---

---

[6] Just for sake of paper length, not included in this table the conditions for additional processes.

3 FIRST, Keep It Simple!

FIRST (**F**ast **I**mprovement a**S**sessment s**T**ep) is our proposal for starting an improvement initiative, and it will be described in the following sections.

3.1 (Re)shaping Appraisal Scopes: Criteria

In order to (re)design a possible appraisal scope, the following requirements should be considered:

a) Processes to be included in the appraisal scope: relationships should be determined between other processes in the process model. In this way it may be possible to derive information on related processes without having to assess ALL those processes.
b) Mapping elements: represent mapping tables between two (or more) models (e.g. CMMI-DEV vs ISO 9001:2008). Any model provides a single representation of the intended reality. Thus, at least two descriptions from different viewpoints could complement each other, providing more details and enabling a more realistic and affordable evaluation to be performed, with related corrective and improvement actions.
c) Types and number of appraisal scopes: there is typically more than one single scope, it's a better approach that may adapted according to an organization's current maturity level or their target maturity level. The rationale for the scope of each appraisal should be determined by a causal relationship so that effort and costs could be minimized without impacting t the overall informative value for the assessed organization in terms of WPs that are verified within the organization.
d) Balancing processes by category: a further criterion for selecting a reduced set of processes for appraisal can be their distribution by process category/group [21]. E.g. in CMMI-DEV there are four categories (Process Management, Project Management, Engineering, Support), while in ISO/IEC 15504-5 there are nine groups (from 'Acquisition' to 'Reuse'). In such a way improvement actions will be derived through cross checking objective evidence (OEs). This reduces the probability of making the wrong decision.
e) Map organizational software quality requirements to processes. This consists of discovering the organization's relevant software quality requirements and mapping them to relevant processes. An adapted version of the QFD (Quality Function Deployment) technique may be used to systematically map the organizational quality needs to the relevant processes [22].

3.2 (Re)shaping Appraisal Scopes: Content

In the previous sections two main questions arise: 1) is there a unique scope for all types (and sizes) of companies? 2) are the suggested set of processes the right ones? If not, which modifications could be suggested?

Probably the answer should be 'no' for the first question and it could be 'it depends' for the second one. In the case when we answer 'no' to the second one, it

FIRST: Common-Sense Process Scopes for Starting a Process Improvement Program   193

could be possible to argue that there are at least three main issues for improving the way to design a 'reduced' assessment/appraisal scope, whilst being able to assure retrieval of the useful elements needed for assuring a substantial process improvement, whatever the organizational size, this would be the 'FIRST' step:

- **Project Management is not Measurement** [23]: without assessing the measurement process, it's not possible to determine if what an organization metrics are balanced, correct and fit with its informative needs. Project Management (Planning + Monitoring & Control, in the CMMI model) only plans and tracks project progress, typically against time and cost, but does not determine if we're measuring the right things for that organization. Therefore we feel that the measurement process should be included in the assessment scope[7].

- **Root-Cause Analysis (RCA):** a fundamental criterion for understanding the real thoughts of an organization in relation to improvement is to verify how it performs (or not) root-cause analysis. For example, within the ISO 9000:2005 quality management principles (§0.2) [24], one of the eight principles relates to the "system approach to management", requesting "*identifying, understanding and managing interrelated processes as a system contributes to the organization's effectiveness and efficiency in achieving its objectives*". Since there is a common understanding that an ISO 9001 certified company iapproximately equates to between a CMMI ML2 and ML3 organisation, meaning that such a principle should also be included in a smaller appraisal scope. Observing CMMI-DEV and ISO 9001 [25], there is a well-known and accepted mapping table by Mutafeljia & Stromberg [26] which compares the two models (even if CMMI is a process model, while ISO 9001 is a requirement model). This may be taken into account for translating the '*whats*' (ISO requirements) into the '*hows*' (CMMI processes and related tasks and suggested practices)[8]. Further rationale and details in [27][28] → consequence: include CAR (Causal Analysis & Resolution) (in CMMI) or SUP.5 (in SPICE).

- **Historical data:** another ISO 9000:2005 quality management principle concerns the "factual approach to decision making", where "*effective decisions are based on the analysis of data and information*". Again, such a goal could be satisfied – in CMMI terms – by OPD (Organizational Process Definition) through the so-called 'Process Asset Libraries' (PAL – SP 1.5) and the 'Measurement Repository' (SP 1.4) and MA (Measurement & Analysis) through the setup of those repositories (SG1) and the related data gathering (SG2). In SPICE terms, it requires the assessment also of REU.2 (Reuse Program Management), looking at

---

[7] E.g. MAN.6 (Measurement) is not included and it's not Project Management; being assessed, it'd reveal a plenty of information that would – yet from a ML2 viewpoint – be helpful for suggesting focused and well-pointed improvements knowing the causal relationships among processes in a certain process model (CMMI, SPICE or another one) → consequence: include MAN.6 (or MA in CMMI). See also [28]. Furthermore, it's one of the few ISO 12207 processes deployed as separated standard [34].

[8] An excerpt with mapping tables is available from the CMMI website: http://goo.gl/vG5Rx.

all the data repositories supporting what is required in REU.2.BP7 (Collect and Manage Learning), as well as specific WPs such as the Information and the Experience Repository (related to PA2.1 – Performance Management) and the Knowledge Management System (related to PA2.2 – Process Deployment).

3.3 (Re)shaping Appraisal Scopes: the FIRST Proposal

Applying the criteria (described above) and suggestions for which processes (or some elements) should be included, it is possible to develop at least three different scopes, as shown in Table 6, proposing an instantiation both for CMMI-DEV and for ISO/IEC 15504. This is also shown graphically in Figure 1.

In relation to the mapping between CMMI-DEV v1.3 [30] and ISO/IEC 15504-5:2006, as there is not an 'official' one provided by either ISO and/or SEI, we re-used the SQI 2001 mapping between CMMI v1.0 and ISO/IEC 15504-2:1998. We then applied to the subsequent evolutions for both models until arriving at the current versions for both models [30][9], and also including a more recent 2011 mapping proposed for the Automotive domain using Automotive SPICE [33][10].

Table 6. FIRST scopes, suggested audience and processes

Scope	Suggested audience	CMMI-DEV v1.3	ISO/IEC 15504-5:2006
A	• **Basic** – Crossing MLs, it includes the need of part of the lowest ML plus: ✓ Cause-Effect Analysis – as asked by ISO 9001:2008 principles and requirements ✓ Project Historical Data – as asked still by ISO 9001:2008 §8.4	• 5 (ML2: PP, PMC, MA, ML3: OPD, ML5: CAR)	• 4 (MAN.3, MAN.6, PIM.1, PIM.3)
B	• **Conservative** - for those intended to strictly achieve ML2 (exactly all ML2 processes)	• 7 (ML2: PP, PMC, MA, SAM, PPQA, CM, REQM)	• 7 (MAN.3, MAN.5, MAN.6, ACQ.3, SUP.1, SUP.8, ENG.4)
C	• **Advanced** – for those intended to progress from ML2 towards higher MLs, mainly reinforcing Support processes (the pink ones in the figure) plus historical data and cause-effect analysis as a foundation for better estimates and improvement actions yet from ML2 on.	• 9 (ML2: PP, PMC, MA, SAM, PPQA, CM, REQM; ML3: OPD; ML5: CAR) •	• 9 (MAN.3, MAN.5, MAN.6, ACQ.3, SUP.1, SUP.8, ENG.4, PIM.1, PIM.3)

---

[9] There are some recent papers/publications formally about such 'mapping', but instead proposing other kind of correspondences (e.g.[32].).
[10] See Chapter 5.

FIRST: Common-Sense Process Scopes for Starting a Process Improvement Program   195

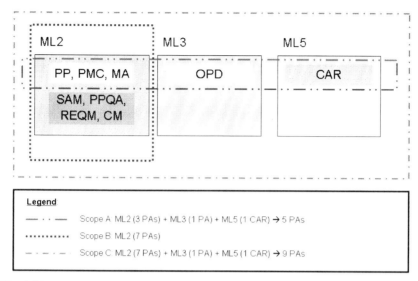

Fig. 1. Three FIRST possible initial process scopes and related PA using the CMMI schema

4   Conclusions and Next Steps

'You cannot control what you cannot measure' is an old, well-known motto which may also be applied to process improvement, in terms of process measurements. Since measurement has a cost (it's not for free), it is not necessary to measure everything (every process) but just what is strictly needed for our own informative goals. Thus, reducing the process scope in appraisals could be feasible and acceptable for speeding up the improvement process and also reducing costs. This would therefore be particularly useful in those organizations with a reduced budget and/or with a medium-small organizational size, and with few resources for performing appraisals.

Different initiatives have been proposed in the past for performing quick process appraisals, but typically each contained just one process scope definition, whatever the type of organization. **FIRST** is our proposal for trying to match this informative need, respecting the allocated budget for process appraisals, but modifying the choice of processes to be assessed based upon priority, in terms of informative value.

Next, we plan to extend this research to pilot our proposal within ICT organizations.

Acknowledgements. This research is supported in part by the Science Foundation Ireland (SFI) Stokes Lectureship Programme, grant number 07/SK/I1299, the SFI Principal Investigator Programme, grant number 08/IN.1/I2030 (the funding of this project was awarded by Science Foundation Ireland under a co-funding initiative by the Irish Government and European Regional Development Fund), and supported in part by Lero (http://www.lero.ie) grant 10/CE/I1855.

This work has been also supported by the CNPq (Conselho Nacional de Desenvolvimento Científico e Tecnológico – www.cnpq.br), an entity of the Brazilian government focused on scientific and technological development.

References

[1] Eveelens, J.L., Verhoef, C.: The Rise and Fall of the CHAOS Report Figures. In: IEEE Software, pp. 30–36 (January/February 2010)
[2] Paulk, M.C., Weber, C.V., Garcia, S.M., Chrissis, M.B., Bush, M.: Key Practices of the Capability Maturity Model Version 1.1, Software Engineering Institute, CMU/SEI-93-TR-025 (February 1993)
[3] ISO/IEC IS 15504-x, Information technology – Process assessment, Parts 1-7, International Organization for Standardization (2001-2007)
[4] Kuvaja, P., Similä, J., Krzanilk, L., Bicego, A., Saukkonen, S., Koch, G.: Software Process Assessment & Improvement. The Bootstrap Approach. Blackwell Publisher (1994)
[5] Pulford, K., Kuntzmann-Combelles, A., Shirlaw, S.: A Quantitative Approach to Software Management. The AMI Handbook. Addison-Wesley (1996) ISBN 0-201-87746-5
[6] Gresse Von Wangenheim, C., Anacleto, A., Salviano, C.F.: MARES - A Methodology for Software Process Assessment in Small Software Companies. Technical Report LQPS001.04E, LQPS - Laboratório de Qualidade e Produtividade de Software. UNIVALI (2004)
[7] CSE, The SPIRE Handbook. Better, Faster, Cheaper Software Development in Small Organisations, The SPIRE Project, Centre for Software Engineering, ESSI Project 23983, ISBN 1-874303-03-7, http://www.cse.dcu.ie/spire/handbook.html
[8] Beitz, A., Jarvinnen, J.: FAME - An approach for software process assessment. Technical Report 001.00/E, Fraunhofer IESE (2000)
[9] Garcia, S.: Thoughts on Applying CMMI in Small Settings, Software Engineering Institute (SEI), Presentation (2005)
[10] Laryd, A., Orci, T.: Dynamic CMM for Small Organizations. In: Proceedings of 1st Argentine Symposium on Software Engineering, ASSE 2000, Tandil, Argentina, pp. 133–149 (September 2000)
[11] SEI, Appraisal Requirements for CMMI, Version 1.3 (ARC, V1.3), Software Engineering Institute, Technical Report, CMU/SEI-2011-TR-006 (April 2011)
[12] Rout, T.P., Tuffley, A., Cahill, B., Hodgen, B.: The RAPID Assessment of Software Process Capability. In: SPICE 2000 Conference, Ireland (June 2000)
[13] Cater-Steel, A., Toleman, M.A., Rout, T.: Process improvement for small firms: An evaluation of the RAPID assessment-based method. Information & Software Technology (IST) Journal 48(5), 323–334 (2006)
[14] Wilkie, F.G., McFall, D., Mc Caffery, F.: The Express Process Appraisal Method. In: Dorling, A., Mayr, H.C., Rout, T. (eds.) Proceedings of the 5th International SPICE Conference on Software Process Assessment and Improvement (SPICE 2005), Klagenfurt, Austria, April 27-30, pp. 27–36. Austrian Computer Society (2005)
[15] SEI, The Capability Maturity Model: Guidelines for Improving the Software Process. Software Engineering Institute, Carnegie Mellon University, Addison Wesley Longman (1994) ISBN 0-201-54664-7

[16] CMMI Product Team, Appraisal Requirements for CMMI, Version 1.1 (ARC, V1.1), Technical Report CMU/SEI-2001-TR-034, Software Engineering Institute, Carnegie Mellon University, Pittsburgh, PA (December 2001)
[17] Mc Caffery, F., Taylor, P.S., Coleman, G.: Adept: A Unified Assessment Method for Small Software Companies. IEEE Software 24(1), 24–31 (2007), doi:10.1109/MS.2007.3
[18] Wilkie, F.G., McFall, D., Mc Caffery, F.: An Evaluation of CMMI Process Areas for Small to Medium Sized Software Development Organisations. Software Process: Improvement and Practice Journal (10), 189–201 (2005)
[19] Gresse Von Wangenheim, C., Anacleto, A., Salviano, C.F.: Helping Small Companies Assess Software Processes. IEEE Software 23(1) (January/February 2006)
[20] ISO/IEC TR 15504-7:2008, Information Technology – Process Assessment – Part 7: Assessment of Organizational Maturity, International Organization for Standardization, Geneve (November 2008)
[21] Buglione, L.: The Metric Cards. A Balanced Set of Measures ISO/IEC 15504 Compliant. In: Presentazione, Automotive SPIN Meeting, Milano
[22] Richardson, I.: Quality Function Deployment: A Software Process Tool? In: 3rd Annual International QFD Symposium, Linkoping, Sweden (October 1997); Matook, S., Indulska, M.: Improving the Quality of Process Reference Models: A Quality Function Deployment-Based Approach. Decision Support Systems 47 (2009)
[23] Buglione, L.: Project Management & Measurement. What Relationship? Presentation, Universidade Federal de Santa Catarina (UFSC), Florianopolis (Brasile) (September 16, 2010)
[24] ISO IS 9000:2005, Quality management systems – Fundamentals & Vocabular. International Organization for Standardization (December 2005)
[25] ISO IS 9001:2008, Quality management systems – Requirements. International Organization for Standardization (December 2008)
[26] Mutafelija, B., Stromberg, H.: Process Improvement with CMMI v1.2 and ISO Standards, Auerbach (2008) ISBN 978-1420052831
[27] Buglione, L., Abran, A.: Introducing Root-Cause Analysis and Orthogonal Defect Classification at Lower CMMI Maturity Levels. In: Proceedings of MENSURA 2006, Cadiz (Spain), November 6-8, pp. 29–40 (2006) ISBN 978-84-9828-101-9
[28] Buglione, L.: Strengthening CMMI Maturity Levels with a Quantitative Approach to Root-Cause Analysis. In: Proceedings of the 5th Software Measurement European Forum (SMEF 2008), Milan (Italy), May 28-30, pp. 67–82 (2008) ISBN 9-788870-909999
[29] Buglione, L., Lami, G.: A proposal for a new common process scope for Automotive SPICE: Six reasons for adding the MAN.6 process. In: 1st AutomotiveSYS Conference, Berlin (Germany), July 4-6 (2011), http://www.vda-qmc.de/sys5w
[30] CMMI Product Team, CMMI-DEV (CMMI for Development) v1.3, Technical Report, CMU/SEI-2010-TR-033. Software Engineering Institute (November 2010)
[31] Rout, T., Tuffley, A., Cahill, B.: CMMI Evalutation – Capability Maturity Model Integration Mapping to ISO/IEC 15504-2:1998. Technical Report. Defense Material Organization (DMO)
[32] Peldzius, S., Ragaisis, S.: Comparison of Maturity Levels in CMMI-DEV and ISO/IEC 15504. In: Proceedings of the "Applications of Mathematics and Computer Engineering" (CEMATH 2011) Conference, pp. 117–122 (2011) ISBN: 978-960-474-270-7
[33] Sabar, S.: Software Process Improvement and Lifecycle Models in Automotive Industry. Final thesis. Linkopings Universitet, Sweden (June 2011)
[34] ISO/IEC IS 15939:2007, Systems and software engineering – Measurement process, International Organization for Standardization (July 2007)

A Systematic Approach to the Comparison of Roles in the Software Development Processes

Murat Yilmaz[1], Rory V. O'Connor[2], and Paul Clarke[1]

[1] Lero Graduate School in Software Engineering, Dublin City University, Ireland
[2] Lero, the Irish Software Engineering Research Centre, Dublin City University
{murat.yilmaz,roconnor,pclarke}@computing.dcu.ie

Abstract. The vision of building a successful software product requires teams of individuals equipped with a wide range of social and technical skills. Furthermore, by combining these skills with appropriate job roles, we should be able to improve the productivity of a software organization. In order to identify and compare different roles in software development activities, we conduct a systematic comparison of software development models, covering traditional approaches through to agile techniques. To compare the roles in the literature with industrial software landscapes, we use data from a survey conducted on 266 software practitioners to ascertain job roles in two middle size software companies, one of which uses traditional methods and in particular ISO/IEC 12207 for managing their software development activities while other uses a tailored agile methodology. In light of our interviews, we found that based on project specific needs, the roles used in industry vary significantly from the roles defined in literature.

1 Introduction

Software development is a complex socio-technical activity, which relies on teams of individuals working harmoniously. Therefore, individuals should be able to cope with challenges embedded in software development tasks. These tasks, however, should be performed as teamwork to accomplish a particular contract with stakeholders [1]. During these activities, the socio-technical skills of individuals are an important consideration when forming teams. As mentioned in every software development methodology, there are job roles for individuals to be assigned. A role is a series of expectations from an individual mostly for team-based activities that are defined in a social context or a situation.

Furthermore, from an industrial perspective, the actual success of customizing a methodology not only depends on the methods we choose but also the roles that are included in a software development method. Therefore, understanding these roles and systematically selecting a set of suitable roles for a proposed methodology has several merits. Firstly, the role selection process helps us to control the flow of information to manage the activities in a software company. Consequently, roles convey a value to the development methodology [2]. Software development is not easy, it needs dedicated personnel. However, evidence suggests that individuals should be more effective in settings such that roles are well-defined [3]. Secondly, role selection can be used for stimulating individuals. Agile methods cause alterations in several roles or job titles previously defined in traditional software development. This realignment has weakened some of the traditional roles to some extent: therefore even some practitioners think that agile reduces the ability of managers to command their teams [4]. Thirdly, organizing the roles for the software development methodology can be considered as a form of software quality assurance activity in order to improve the product quality [5].

In this paper, we constitute a systematic comparison framework based on actualized roles and defined roles in the software development processes. We formalize our research question as: "*In practice, do software development roles differ from the role definitions provided by the software development process methodologies?*" To this end, we review the literature to single out the set of defined roles for the selected software development processes and systematically compare them with the roles that are used in industrial settings. Based on a case study with two middle size software companies, we first use the data collected on our surveys to understand the working roles or titles in an industrial software organization, and secondly we interview software practitioners to validate our results.

The remainder of this paper is structured as follows: In section two, we introduce our research viewpoint, which defines our systematic approach that enables the comparison of different roles. The following section reviews the roles identified in literature for the different software development processes. The next section evaluates our approach by analyzing of data gathered from the case studies we conducted in two middle size software companies. The last section will conclude the paper with a brief summary of contributions.

2 Research Overview

The first part of our systematic approach starts with constructing our research goal to evaluate whether there is a significant amount of difference in previously identified roles and their actualizations especially when tailoring a role-based task assignment in software development. Next, we survey the literature for the roles for both traditional and agile methodologies that are mentioned in software development literature. We selectively chose software methodologies and processes and work on the roles that are defined by these approaches. In technical terms, we conduct a thematic content analysis (i.e. descriptive presentation of this literature review) based on roles as the units of analysis. After identifying software development roles in the literature, secondly we conduct a focus group study with one of our industrial partners, where we seek opinions about actual roles that are used in their company. We initiate the focus group conversation by using some parts on our previously conducted survey, in which we ask participants about their organizational roles and experience levels on that role (see figure 1). Secondly, we interview team leaders and development managers about how accurate the actualization of the job roles.

Content analysis is an organized study of characteristics found in a content of any type of communication, such as books, websites, newspapers, etc [6]. Our approach uses the content analysis technique for making interpretations to create a role selection schema based on literature of roles in software development methodologies. Based on the survey data collected previously, these roles will be systematically compared to their industrial actualizations. To this end, we first collect data from literature and consult industry about the defined roles frequently used in software engineering settings. Secondly, we conduct a focus group, where we record the session and a content analysis was performed on participants' definition of roles that are actualized in software development landscapes.

We form a number of acronyms based on the roles that are found from the literature. Here, we are making partial use of a coding mechanism to construct a role-based schema with the defined roles from the literature. The coding aims to create variables based on the roles defined in software development. It is done for easy comparison of roles by constructing a unique key for each role found from the literature. Our coding schema allows us to observe the commonalities and differences between software engineering roles. It helps us to investigate cause-effect relationships, interrelationships, and situational conditions for each role category. Here, we design several questions to seek validity for our coding in the defined categories, and analysis of identified roles from the literature.

- Is this role the same as a role in the other categories?
- Are there any duplicated role codings in a category?
- In which context do these roles emerge?
- What kind of roles have changed or evolved in emerging methods?
- Is there any observable change for other roles when a role evolved to an other form (i.e. covariance between categories)?

The *objective coding* [7] is a technique to review a collection of documents for extracting and indexing the information so as to form a new perspective on representing the data. We use an objective coding scheme on the collected information of roles. This coding should be helpful for visually comparing actualized roles systematically with the ones cited in the literature. In addition, a diagram is drawn to support the development of the relationship among roles (see Figure 1).

Finally, we aim to formulate a framework for software practitioners, which enable them to select proper roles for their software development methodologies. Consequently, by using such a framework, a software practitioner may easily choose or customize the necessary roles for his or her development activities.

3 Roles in Software Development Processes

Many different variants of development models and methodologies have been created. In this section, we survey the roles that are defined in the literature starting from traditional software development and working through ISO/IEC 12207, and agile methodologies such as extreme programming (XP), scrum and feature driven development (FDD).

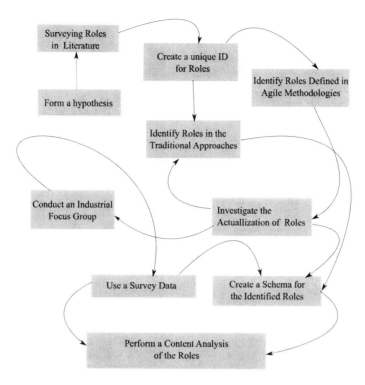

Fig. 1. Our Systematic Approach for Investigating the Roles in Software Development Environments

3.1 Roles in Traditional Software Development

Software engineering teams address the complex problems of software development by sharing the tasks among its members with respect to their roles. Roles are the descriptions of duties or assignments and competence for participants that are required to achieve a defined tasks and activities of software development [8]. In his essay, *The Cathedral and the Bazaar*, Raymond states that because of the strict roles defined in traditional software development, traditional approach is similar to building a cathedral, where a small team of people working in an isolated environment [9]. Therefore, this could be considered as a drawback because several artifacts are only visible for a limited number of individuals in this setting.

Traditional roles include: *Project manager* who is responsible for allocation of resources, project expenditures, and responsible from the general objectives of a software project. Another typical role in the development processes is the role of a developer. A *software developer* is responsible for designing and maintaining the software programs, whereas a *software tester* is responsible for creating test plans and testing the developed programs. In many cases *user interface designers* (design screen interfaces), *database designers* (design database schema) and the *software architects* (design technical blueprints) are also included as a generic software practitioner category.

Table 1. Traditional Software Development Roles

Code	Role Name	Primary Type of Value
PM	Project Manager	Resource Allocation and Budgeting
SD	Software Developer	Development Activities
UID	User Interface Designer	Design Screen Interfaces
DD	Database Designers	Data Modeling
SA	Software Architects	Software Modeling
BA	Business Analyst	Stakeholder Management
RE	Requirement Engineer	Gathering Requirements
SQA	Software Quality Assurance	Creating and Maintaining Quality
SAN	System Analyst	Construction of a System

A business analyst is not only responsible for solving the problems by regulating the connections between the business and the technical people but also for documenting several parts (e.g. requirement documents) of a software project. In addition to these roles some others can also be seen regarding several needs; e.g. requirements engineer, systems analyst, software quality assurance engineer (see Table 1).

Table 2. Systems Engineering Roles and their values from [10]

Code	Role Name	Primary Type of Value
RO	Requirements Owner	Understanding Need
SD	System Designer	Accomplishing work
SA	System Analysis	Reducing Risks
VV	Validation & Verification	Mitigating Risks
LO	Logistics and Operations	Understanding need
G	Glue among the subsystems	Accomplishing work, Reducing Risks
CI	Customer Interface	Understanding the Need
TM	Technical Manager	Technical Management
IM	Information Manager	Knowledge Management
PE	Process Engineer	Managing and Understanding Needs
CO	Coordinator	Organizational Management
CA	Classified Ads SE	Accomplishing Work (assumed)

Sheard [11] identifies twelve roles (see Table 2) of development from system engineering viewpoint while investigating the relationship between the roles and their importance for creating a value. This work not only suggests that the value is asserted in qualitative terms and it should be quantified in further research but it also claims that it should be observed as a requested improvement within a product by better (i) definition of the requirements, (ii) management strategies, (iii) ways for mitigating risks, (see [10] for details).

3.2 Roles in ISO/IEC 12207

ISO/IEC 12207 [12] has three main groups of roles for its participants. The first group consists of the principal roles are the *acquirer*, who is a form of stakeholder that obtains products or services from *supplier*, who is an individual or another organization agree on providing a software products or services. *Implementer* executes development tasks, while the *maintainer* can be either an organization or an individual who performs the upkeep of developed software), and *operator* is responsible for the execution of a system [12]. The second category consists of configuration and supporting roles; the *configurator* is responsible for the establishment and transformation of the information needed by an individual or a group, *evaluator* tests and measure a software process or a product by using the data collected during the actual tasks that are performed, the *auditor* investigates the products and processes are compatible with the agreements, the *usability specialist* deals with the demands and needs of the stakeholders such as the design activities based on human factors and skills and their fulfillment [12].

Table 3. Roles in ISO/IEC 12207 (adapted from [12,13])

Code	Role Name	Primary Type of Value
AC	Acquirer	Software Client or User or Product Owner
SU	Supplier	Software Producer, Product Seller
IMP	Implementer	Realization of Development Tasks
MN	Maintainer	Maintain the Software
OP	Operator	System Execution
CON	Configurator	Accomplishing Work, Reducing Risks
EV	Evaluator	Test & Measure a Process or a Product
AU	Auditor	Contract Management
US	Usability Specialist	Problems Regarding to People Factors
MA	Manager	Managing
AM	Asset Manager	Managing Assets
CM	Knowledge Manager	Knowledge Management
RA	Reuse Administrator	Seeking for Reusable Parts

The third group has the organizational roles, the *manager* identifies and manages the state of the play (i.e. condition and progression of the project) with respects to project constraints (e.g. objectives, budget, schedules), the *asset manager* is a type of manager deals with the management and optimization of the assets regarding to the plan he or she prepared, the *knowledge manager* role works on the collection of particular knowledge and skills throughout the organization and used for improvement for the products and services. The *reuse program administrator* seeks to find favorable or advantageous circumstances for reusable parts of a product or a service. Unlike the other two subfields of software engineering (i.e. requirements engineering and software development), *domain engineer* is a form responsible for designing the domain models (i.e. software models) and domain descriptions for a software system (see Table 3).

3.3 Roles in Extreme Programming

According to Beck [14], the participants and their roles are as follows; *Programmers* are the individuals who need to have good communication and collaboration skills for both team and individual levels. They are responsible for developing, maintaining and testing the software. One of their main responsibilities is to ensure that their work is clean and lean. The technical decisions are made by programmers. *Customers* form the steering teams in business terms and in particular in requirement satisfaction decisions. *Testers* help customers to write functional test cases. Business decisions are made by customers [14]. The *tracker* role composes a trace and feedback mechanism in XP. The estimations, goals and iterations made by teams are controlled by a tracker, who provides feedback. The *tracker* is also responsible for measuring constraints such as scarce resources and delivery times versus goal evaluation. The *coach* is the role which is accountable for XP project who needs to understand the problems occurring during the process to instruct team members and transfer the information or sometimes experience among teams and individuals. Finally, the *manager* is responsible for final decisions, and also an aim of this role is to recognize problems likely occur during the development life-cycle (see table 4).

Table 4. Roles in XP (adapted from [14,15])

Code	Role Name	Primary Type of Value
PRG	Programmers	Maintaining and Testing Software
CU	Customers	Managing Business Decisions
TST	Testers	Helps Costumers for Functional Test Cases
TRC	Tracker	Feedbacks and Estimations
CO	Coach	Supervise Team
CON	Consultant	Guides the Team for Problem Solving
MA	Manager	Management

3.4 Roles in Scrum

Schwaber and Beedle [16] single out six roles for the participants of Scrum. The *Scrum Master* is a type of management role specific to Scrum, who is responsible for the alignment of practices and rules as they have organized. This role interacts not only with project team but also customer and management. Its aim is to maximize productivity by practicing the agile and scrum values and monitoring the team to avoid any kind of complications. The *Product Owner* is the role which is responsible for exercising the project management and control activities. Additionally, this role is also responsible for transforming the product backlog into product features. *Scrum Team* should be considered as a self organizing structure to produce a working piece of a product, where its main goal is to achieve time targeted objectives of each sprint. The *customer* role will continuously evaluate the backlog items, and helps the selection for a sprint. The *management* role is responsible for implementing the proper standards for the software development process. Additionally, this role encompasses decision making activities and finalizing them at different stages of development process such as evaluating goals, gathering requirements, etc. (see Table 5).

Table 5. Roles in SCRUM (adapted from [16])

Code	Role Name	Primary Type of Value
SM	Scrum Master	Managing Scrum Team
PO	Product Owner	Product Management Decisions
CUS	Customer	Evaluation of backlog items
ST	Scrum Team	Organized itself for time boxed goals
MNG	Management	Evaluate Decisions and Goals
USR	User	Evaluate System Functionalities

3.5 Roles in FDD

FDD has the most comprehensive role description with a flexibility of roles [17]. For example, an individual can play multiple roles, or either a role can be shared by multiple persons [15]. The three main categories of roles, which are: *key, supporting and additional* roles. The key roles are *project manager*, who administers the entire project and maintains the work settings of the software team, the *lead software architect* is the role which makes the appropriate decisions for software development, the *software development manager* is a role which focuses on daily activities and team negotiations during the software development activities. The *lead programmer, the class owner and the domain expert* are the three roles used in FDD. The supporting roles includes; *manager (release), knowledge expert, build process engineer, toolsmith* and *system administrator*. Moreover, *testers, technical document expert* and *software deployment personnel* are the other roles used in this practices [17](see table 6).

Table 6. Roles in FDD (adapted from [17,15])

Code	Role Name	Primary Type of Value
PM	Project Manager	Resource Management
LSA	Lead Software Architect	Architectural Decisions
DEM	Development Manager	Evaluation of backlog items
LP	Lead Programmer	Organized itself for time boxed goals
CO	Class Owner	Form Teams for Implementing Features
DE	Domain Expert	Inform Teams for Adequate Features
RM	Release Manager	Managing the development process
DM	Domain Manager	Managing Domain Experts
LG	Language Guru	Acquiring a Knowledge on Technology
BE	Build Engineer	Executing a Build Process
TA	Toolsmith	Creating Utilities for project
SYA	System Administrator	Administration of Work Systems
TE	Testing	Verifying the Actualization of a System
DEP	Deployer	Release of Feature Deployment
TEW	Technical Writer	The Documentation for Users

4 Evaluation of Roles from Industrial Settings

As a part of a survey, we asked 266 participants from two different software companies about their roles in their applied settings in order to identify the commonality of meaning in the different roles. One of the software companies (with a staff about 400 personnel) is working in telecommunication sector, which composes solutions for large-scale e-government projects. The other company supplies turn key software solutions to telecommunications operators and mobile service providers. It has a staff of about 40 personnel. By creating a list of roles based on the roles mentioned in the literature, we conduct a focus group in one of the companies about the actualization of roles in development environments. This brings individuals together to debate about software development roles in their company and their actualizations with respect to their experiences. Next, we ask our research question to a selection of people mostly to the individuals from the management teams.

Company A is using the traditional software development approaches to define the roles: PM, SD, UID, SA, BA, SQA, where DD is embedded in SD, and RE role is somehow split with BA and SD. The role of system analyst provides the requirement engineering processes.

> ***Interview quotation:*** *"During our development activities, we observe lots of overlapping roles, which sometimes hinder our ability to handle some development tasks. For example, some of our teams have key players with overlapping roles and some individuals perform more than one role by the nature of our development process. We found it interesting to have a big picture of the roles in the different software development processes."*

Company A uses ISO/IEC 12207 combined with an iterative development schema and a customized role selection based on the traditional viewpoint for developing and maintaining software project. However the roles defined by ISO/IEC 12207 are not fully used to profile the personnel. Instead, they use the role names (see Table 1) that are traditionally used in software development.

> ***Interview quotation:*** *"We use approximately 14 out of 43 processes, 60 out of 95 activities, 180 out of 406 tasks from ISO/IEC 12207. We believe that assigning suitable roles to teams and individuals is very important for our success. A review of roles in different methodologies is useful from an industrial perspective. All type of roles should be visible to everyone in the company, and they should be defined in a simple language to provide a way of ensuring everyone understands them. Therefore, we are not using the role names provided by ISO/IEC 12207. I would say, we mostly use the classical role names you have mentioned."*

According to the management team of Company A, the role of team leader should not dictate anything to teammates but communicated the vision of a company or a project. Therefore, maintaining a friendship and trust is more important than dictating the facts to software teams.

> ***Interview quotation:*** *"People usually trust other people to some extent. There are always problems, when it comes to role assignment as well as delegations based on these roles. I personally observed several situations, where improper delegation did cause lots of conflicts and tensions. I would strongly suggest that role tailoring should not be taken lightly."*

Company B uses a customized agile methodology, which relies on XP and Scrum. They use agile methodology so as to cope with dynamically challenging requirements and to fulfill the request of their customer for continuous integration with small increments. They use all roles defined by scrum (i.e. SM, PO, CUS, ST, MNG, USR) and a tester role (TST) and a progress tracker (TRC) role from XP.

Interview quotation: *"There is the notion of tailoring methodologies, how about the roles? It is always a problem for us to select the suitable roles for our customized methodology. Therefore, broader view of roles in software development activities are very important for us. However, just as there is no one-size-fits-all methodology for developing applications in software development, there should not be a one-size-fits-all approach to role selection."*

Finally, Company B highlights the importance of face to face communication for agile landscapes, and therefore selection of suitable roles for development activities becomes more important.

Interview quotation: *"The process of customization of roles is very important particularly in agile development environments. A summary with roles contained in different agile approaches is very helpful for us to see the suitable roles for our process."*

5 Conclusions

In this paper, we highlight how roles in literature and their actualizations on industrial environments vary for both plan driven and agile methodologies. Software development is a collaborative endeavor that depends on its development methodology. However, selection of a proper methodology is not enough for achieving goals of a software organization. The evidence suggests that we should also tailor the necessary roles depending on development activities.

After analyzing the defined categories in light of the questions above, we confirmed that several roles presented in older methods are emerged with a different name, with similar responsibilities in newer approaches. Some of the roles, however, have their responsibilities changed while revealing in different software development organizations. Most frequently, the role definitions that an organization uses based on a domain and a set of circumstances.

Here, we present role orientations for the selected software development methodologies as shown in Table 7. We identify four types of role orientations: Actor-based, activity-based, artifact-based and methodologies with extended role definitions based on a previously defined role. For example, both Scrum and FDD have actor-based roles, in which the skills of an individual are defined by the role characteristics such as product owner or a class owner. In addition, all methodologies have activity-based roles

Table 7. Comparison of roles for the selected development methodologies

Models		Actor Based	Activity Based	Artifact Based	Extended
	Traditional		✓		
	System Engineering		✓		✓
	ISO/IEC 12207		✓		
	XP	✓	✓	✓	
	Scrum		✓	✓	
	FDD	✓	✓	✓	✓

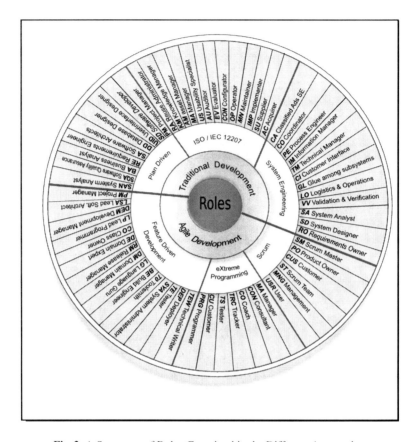

Fig. 2. A Summary of Roles Contained in the Different Approaches

such as software developer, a software tester, etc. We also consider roles that are based on a creation of an artifact, which are highlighted by the agile methodologies. Finally, extended roles are the roles that can be integrated or shared among the individuals such as the roles like the domain expert role, which somehow comprises the technical writer role in FDD.

Our study exhibits that a role-based schema can be useful for a tailoring process of roles regarding to the organizational needs. Furthermore, we argue that a software development organization should customize their own roles suitable for their social structure, where we suggest that our role based construct (see Figure 2) will be beneficial for such activities. In other words, it enables them to select proper roles for their software development methodologies. Consequently, by using such a framework, a software teams may easily choose or customize the necessary roles based on their activities.

Analysis of identified roles from the literature is portrayed in Figure 2. We can confirm that several roles presented in older methods are emerged with a different name with similar responsibilities in newer approaches. The roles, however, mostly have their responsibilities changed and reappeared as another form while revealing in different software development organizations. Most frequently, the role definitions that an organization uses based on a domain and a set of circumstances. Moreover, it is important to choose roles, based on the social structure of an organization and required interactions. These customized roles are found to be organizational centric, which also clearly supports the notion of *separation of concerns* [18].

Acknowledgments. This work is supported, in part, by Science Foundation Ireland grant number 03/CE2/I303-1 to Lero, the Irish Software Engineering Research Centre (www.lero.ie).

References

1. Humphrey, W.: Introduction to the team software process (sm). Addison-Wesley Professional (2000)
2. Hazzan, O., Dubinsky, Y.: Agile Software Engineering. Undergraduate Topics in Computer Science. Springer (2008)
3. Cooper, D., Sutter, M.: Role selection and team performance. In: Working Papers in Economics and Statistics. University of Innsbruck (2011)
4. Larman, C.: Agile and iterative development: a manager's guide. Addison-Wesley Professional (2004)
5. Pressman, R.S., Ince, D.: Software engineering. McGraw-Hill (2000)
6. Krippendorff, K.: Content analysis: An introduction to its methodology. Sage Publications, Inc. (2004)
7. Glaser, B., Strauss, A.: The discovery of grounded theory: Strategies for qualitative research. Aldine Transaction (2007)
8. Sommerville, I.: Software Engineering, 9th edn. Addison Wesley (2009)
9. Raymond, E.: The cathedral and the bazaar. Knowledge, Technology & Policy 12, 23–49 (1999)
10. Sheard, S.: The value of Twelve systems engineering roles. In: Proceedings of INCOSE. Citeseer (1996)
11. Sheard, S.: Twelve systems engineering roles. In: Proceedings of INCOSE. Citeseer (1996)
12. ISO/IEC: Amendment to ISO/IEC 12207-2008 - Systems and software engineering Software life cycle processes (2008)
13. Acuna, S.T., Juristo, N., Moreno, A.M., Mon, A.: A Software Process Model Handbook for Incorporating People's Capabilities. Springer (2005)
14. Beck, K.: Extreme programming explained. Addison-Wesley (2000)
15. Abrahamsson, P., Salo, O., Ronkainen, J., Warsta, J.: Agile software development methods: Review and Analysis. VTT Publications 478. Technical Research Centre of Finland (2002)
16. Schwaber, K., Beedle, M.: Agile Software Development with SCRUM. Prentice Hall (2002)
17. Palmer, S.R., Felsing, J.M.: A practical guide to feature-driven development. Prentice Hall PTR (2002)
18. Dijkstra, E.W.: On the role of scientific thought. In: Selected Writings on Computing: A Personal Perspective, pp. 60–66. Springer (1982)

Framework for Usage of Multiple Software Process Models

Stasys Peldzius and Saulius Ragaisis

Software Engineering Department, Faculty of Mathematics and
Informatics, Vilnius University, Naugarduko Str. 24, LT-03225 Vilnius Lithuania
{Stasys.Peldzius,Saulius.Ragaisis}@mif.vu.lt

Abstract. The most popular Software Process Models worldwide are ISO/IEC 15504 and CMMI. It is desirable for organizations to have assessments according to both these models but every assessment is expensive both financially and time-wise, and furthermore new assessments are required when a new models version is released. In order to define and/or to improve their software process, organizations choose different Software Development Methodologies. It is important for the organization to know what capability/maturity of the process a chosen methodology could ensure. In order to solve these problems we propose Transitional Software Process Model (TSPM). It enables the transformation of results of an assessment according to one Process Model to other models and determines what capability/maturity according to different Process Models a chosen methodology could ensure. Also, TSPM ensures transition of the existing assessment results to a new version of the model without reassessment. The principles of TSPM implementation are given in this article.

Keywords: CMMI, ISO/IEC 15504, Agile methodologies, models mapping, transitional software process model.

1 Introduction

Investigations in software process maturity provide a deep insight into software activities and introduced various software process models which helped assess and improve both software process capability, and the maturity of organizations producing software. The research achievements are noticeable but the problems related to software projects are very real. Organizations seek to obtain benefit from different software process models that stimulate harmonization of the models and investigation of process improvement in multi-model environments [1, 2, 3, 4, 5 and 6].

The most popular Software Process Models worldwide are ISO/IEC 15504 and CMMI. It is desirable for organizations to have assessments according to both these models but every assessment is expensive both financially and time-wise.

In order for organizations to improve their software process, they should choose from one of the many different Software Development Methodologies, for example, XP, Scrum, DSDM, RUP. There are many and various methodologies, so it is important for the organization to know how it could benefit from their chosen methodology. It is also important to harmonize the methodologies with process models. The choice of methodology should depend on what it can achieve for the organization It is desirable to determine software process capability/maturity according to different software process models. When a new version of the model is released the organizations needs to know their capability/maturity according the newest version preferably without making the new assessment.

We propose the Transitional Software Process Model (TSPM) which would help organizations to tackle problems related to multiple software process models and the evaluation of software development methodologies. The principles of TSPM implementation are given in this article.

2   Background and Related Works

This chapter provides the motivation for the mapping between the models and development methodologies assessment. The research performed is presented and explained in the following chapters.

A software process model defines the standard process that provides the basis for an organization's process assessment and improvement. It should ensure the usage of the same concepts and maintain relevance with the best software engineering practices and compatibility with internationally accepted standards.

All software process models summarize the best practices of software development and services worldwide. But although the source is almost the same, the resulting models are different. Therefore, organizations face the double problem of selection in that they need to choose both the process model and the software development methodology that is most suitable for their business goals. The solution is made further complicated because organizations want the benefit of the advantages of different models, but they do not know what methodology can achieve these advantages. Therefore research that establishes the relationships between software process models and software development methodologies is important. That is why mapping between the models and methodologies, which help to solve this problem, are developed.

Fundamental ideas of CMMI and ISO/IEC 15504 mapping have been proposed in [7]. Mappings of the current versions of the models are presented in [8]. They show how CMMI maturity levels can be expressed by ISO/IEC 15504 processes capability profiles and vice versa. Mappings show what is common in the models and how they differ. These mappings will be used for TSPM development.

Also it is important to track the changes in different versions of the same process model. An approach for the control of model evolution and compliance maintenance is proposed in [9]. The organization may want to have assessments by several models in the hope of achieving the respective benefits of each model. It is important for organizations to efficiently implement and assess multiple reference models and benefit from synergy effects [10]. It is significant for organizations to have assessments according both CMMI and ISO/IEC 15504. For example, many organizations drive their process improvement on the basis of CMMI. However, their customers require process capability ratings determined on the basis of ISO/IEC 15504. An approach that enables organizations performing internal process improvement on the basis of CMMI to survive SPICE assessments with relatively small efforts is presented in [11]. As it is important for organizations to be aware of their process capability, it has become important for methodologies to determine what capability they could ensure. There are many articles published, that analyze what capability/ maturity could ensure popular Agile methodologies [12, 13, and 14]. It is important to emphasize that all these works investigate CMMI only.

3 Transitional Software Process Model

The Transitional Software Process Model (TSPM) could solve the problems discussed in the previous chapters. It enables the transformation of results of an assessment according to one process model to other models and also deals with the transition to a new version of the model. Also, it provides the means to determine what capability/maturity according to different process models such as Agile and other software engineering methodologies could ensure. The relationship between the TSPM and other Process Models and Software Development Methodologies is given in Fig. 1.

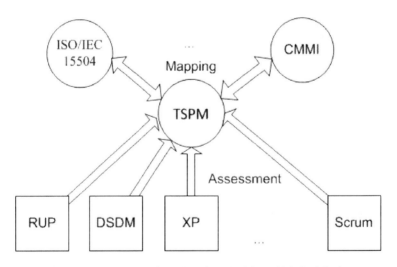

Fig. 1. TSPM relationships with other Models and Methodologies

Furthermore, the methodology showing how to extend the transitional model is provided. It covers the following cases: inclusion of a new software process model, transition to a new version of existing software process model, and addition of a software development methodology.

An organization's assessment according to TSPM and/or transformation of existing assessment's results through TSPM could not lead to any official certificate but it provides enough exact capability profiles and maturity levels according both CMMI and ISO/IEC 15504, as well as other software process models included in TSPM.

4 Requirements of Transitional Software Process Model

The requirements of the Transitional Software Process Model themselves have been presented in [15]. The following sections describe the principles for each of these requirements implementation.

4.1 Ontology of TSPM

The ambiguities occur when we try to introduce or describe common characteristics of the organizations activities. It is not clear what terms should be used because the same terms are referred to differently in ISO/IEC 15504 and CMMI. For example, ISO/IEC 15504 uses term process when CMMI refers it as process area. That is why it is constantly necessary to specify on which terms the model description is based. It is not always possible to determine unambiguously an equivalent of one model's concept in another model. This is an unsatisfying situation so it is a must to create the ontology in such a way that it would be possible to relate the terminology of different software process models. Mapping of the main concepts applied in the CMMI and Automotive SPICE is presented in [5].

In order to add/integrate a new model into TSPM, first it is necessary to align the concepts of a new model with TSPM ontology. If they correspond this means that a new model is compatible with the existing ones. The main concepts are discussed further.

An Organizational Process describes a set of activities, which are carried out developing software products or providing services. The Organizational Process consists of the set of Named Processes. The Organizational Process corresponds to the Process in CMMI. The Process according CMMI is a set of interrelated activities, which transform inputs into outputs, to achieve a given purpose [16]. ISO/IEC 15504 does not have a corresponding concept because from the beginning it was process model of continuous representation.

A Named Process describes a reusable cluster of activities related to the purposes of software product or service life cycle. A Named Process shall be described in terms of its Process Purpose and Outcomes. A Purpose statement describes the purpose of the Named Process. The Outcome describes the unique characteristics that must be presented to satisfy the Named Process. The Outcomes are achieved by Practices. The implemented Practice increases the achievement of the Named Process Outcomes. The Outcome corresponds the Specific Goal in CMMI. The Specific Goal is a required model component that describes the unique characteristics that must be present to satisfy the process area (Named Process). The Goal and the Outcome are not identically the same, but their essence is the same.

The Generic Properties are concepts of a Named Process that can be evaluated on a scale of achievement. They are applicable to all Named Process. Generic Property meets ISO/IEC 15504 concept of Process Attribute. The Generic Practices are activities and provide guidance on the implementation of the Generic Properties characteristics.

Each Process Area in CMMI has Specific Goals and it is implemented by Specific Practices. A Specific Goal is a required CMMI model component and it is used in appraisals to determine whether a Process Area is satisfied [16]. A Process Area is satisfied, if all Specific Goals are satisfied. Implementing the Specific Practices of the Process Area is sufficient to achieve all Specific Goals of the Process Area.

ISO/IEC 15504 Process is described in terms of its Purpose and Outcomes. The set of Process Outcomes is necessary and sufficient to achieve the Purpose of the Process. Implementing the Base Practices of the Process should achieve the Outcomes that reflect the Process Purpose.

TSPM Outcome is necessary and sufficient to achieve the Process Purpose of the corresponding Named Process. Both Outcomes and Process Purposes are required components of TSPM model. TSPM Practices help to increase achievement of the corresponding Process Purpose. They are not required but expected components of TSPM model. This means that alternative achievement of the Process Purpose and Outcomes is possible.

TSPM is a continuous model so it is necessary to define the dimension of the capability. The dimension of the capability consists of Generic Properties and every Generic Property is made of several Generic Practices. The Capability levels comparison is given in table 1.

Table 1. Comparison of capability levels

Level	TSPM	ISO/IEC 15504	CMMI
0	Incomplete	Incomplete	Incomplete
1	Performed	Performed	Performed
2	Managed	Managed	Managed
3	Established	Established	Defined
4	Predictable	Predictable	Quantitative Managed[1]
5	Optimizing	Optimizing	Optimizing[1]

Though CMMI General Goal and ISO/IEC 15504 Process Attribute are not equivalent concepts, they are essentially the same. In CMMI-DEV 1.3, General Goals of levels 4 and 5 and their practices were eliminated as well as Capability Levels 4 and 5. The capability levels in TSPM coincide with ISO/IEC 15504 because this one is an international standard and it was the continuous model with six capability levels from the beginning.

In general, the performance of all Generic Practices is expected for full achievement of the Process Attribute in ISO/IEC 15504. Implementation of the General Practices is sufficient to achieve General Goals in CMMI. It is sufficient to implement the Generic Practices for achievement of Generic Properties in TSPM.

---

[1] Capability levels 4 and 5 are from CMMI-DEV 1.2. They were eliminated in CMMI-DEV 1.3.

When the matches between terms of the models are determined it is necessary to make models' description structures corresponding as well. All the models must be transcribed according to the defined ontology so they will become structurally equal and it will facilitate the mapping between them. Table 2 shows the ontology of TSPM.

Table 2. The ontology of TSPM

TSPM	ISO/IEC 15004	CMMI
Organizational Process	-	Process
Named Process	Process	Process Area
Process Purpose	Purpose Statement	Process Purpose
Outcome	Process Outcome	Specific Goal
Practice	Base Practice	Specific Practice
Generic Property	Process Attribute	General Goal
Generic Practice	Generic Practice	General Practice

4.2 Formalized Description of the Model

Software & Systems Process Engineering Meta-Model (SPEM) is chosen for the definition of Transitional Software Process Model. As an alternative approach the Resource Description Framework (RDF) has also been evaluated. In [9], it is proposed for expressing the models. RDF has come to be used as a general method for conceptual description or modeling of information that is implemented in web resources, using a variety of syntax formats. SPEM is used to define software and systems development processes and their components. Choice of SPEM as the base notation for description of the models and their comparison is made, because SPEM is defined as the processes Meta-Model while RDF is a language for representing information about resources in the World Wide Web.

Table 3. The relationships between TSPM concepts and SPEM

TSPM	SPEM	Icon
Organizational Process	Process	
Named Process	Process Pattern	
Process Purpose	Process Purpose	n/a
Outcome	Outcome	
Practice	Practice	
Generic Property	Task Definition	
Generic Practice	Step	

The next step was mapping of the TSPM Ontology with SPEM stereotypes. RUP modeling using SPEM is presented in [17]. The proposed mapping of TSPM concepts to SPEM terms and icons [18] are presented in table 3.

The TSPM and other models will be represented in SPEM according to the relationships presented in table 3. In order to equalize a new process model with TSPM, it is necessary to match the components of a new model to the TSPM ontology and then to SPEM stereotypes. If it is impossible to match it means that a new model is not a model of the software process, or its structure is completely different from the structure of TSPM, something that is very unlikely.

4.3 Scope of the Model

We now need to determine the scope of the TSPM. Different models can include different activities, so each model could have specific areas that are not presented in other models.

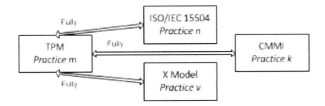

Fig. 2. Relationship between practices of the Models (Full Coverage rule)

TSPM includes all the different outcomes and practices from included models (yet ISO/IEC 15504 and CMMI). When new model will be included, TSPM is added with new outcomes and practices or existing ones will be updated. The same will be done, when a new version of an included model is released. The Full Coverage rule as shown in Fig. 2 should always be fulfilled: each TSPM practice should be covered fully by one or more practices of included models.

This section presents how TSPM practices are developed. First of all, all ISO/IEC 15504 practices are included in to TSPM, because ISO/IEC 15504 is de jure international standard. Later the TSPM practices have been adjusted/added in four ways presented in Fig. 3. The grey shaded areas represent new practices or modified existing practices. These four variants can be combined with each other. Practices of TSPM always have a priority versus other models, because ISO/IEC 15504 is the primary source of these practices.

Now, in order to include the CMMI into TSPM it is necessary to follow the rules shown in Fig. 3. Further application of each rule is discussed more detailed.

Based on the results of [8] where mapping between ISO/IEC 15504 and CMMI-DEV is presented first of all the rule of first variant will be applied: CMMI practices that are not covered in TSPM (ISO/IEC 15504) will be included in to TSPM. The table 4 shows some examples of such practices. In this case unique CMMI practices will simply become new TSPM practices.

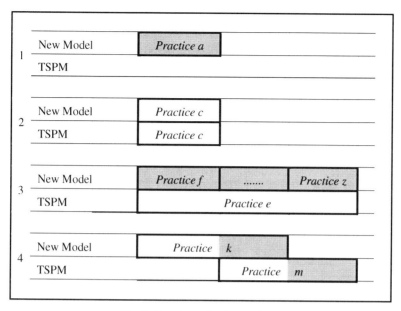

Fig. 3. Practices selection variants

Table 4. Examples of unique CMMI practices

New TSPM practice	CMMI
Identify Alternative Solutions Identify alternative solutions to address issues.	DAR SP 1.3
Select Suppliers Select suppliers based on an evaluation of their ability to meet the specified requirements and established criteria.	SAM SP 1.2

Table 5. Examples of substantially the same practices in both models

TSPM	TSPM practices source	New model practices
Develop configuration management strategy. Determine configuration management strategy, including configuration management activities and schedule for performing these activities.	ISO/IEC 15504 SUP.8.BP1	CMMI CM SP 1.1
Agree on requirements. Obtain agreement across teams on the customer requirements, obtaining the appropriate sign-offs by representatives of all teams and other parties contractually bound to work to these requirements.	ISO/IEC 15504 ENG.1.BP3	CMMI REQM SP 1.2

There are some practices that are essentially the same in both models (second variant). Table 5 shows some examples of such practices. In this case, no new practices are included in to TSPM. It should be noted that the practices (their descriptions) are not perfectly equal in the different models. However, if practices cover each other fully (i.e. ratings are the same, if there are no significant weaknesses in any of these practices) there is no need to include the same practice in to TSPM.

The third case is when the practices of the new model are more detailed than practice of TSPM. Even if some more detailed practices together match one practice of TSPM, the Full Coverage rule is violated and the corresponding TSPM practice should be adjusted. Therefore, the corresponding *practice e* (see Fig. 3) is taken out of TSPM and it is replaced by more detailed *practices f...z*. The descriptions of new practices are modified in order to correspond the terms which are used in TSPM (e.g. change CMMI stakeholder in to customer where it means the same). In this way, the integrity of TSPM will be preserved and the Full Coverage rule will be fulfilled. Table 6 shows an example of such a case.

Table 6. Example of more detailed practices in CMMI

TSPM practice	CMMI practice	New TSPM practices
Ensure consistency. ISO/IEC 15504 ENG.7.BP5	PI SP 2.2 **Manage Interfaces** Manage internal and external interface definitions, designs, and changes for products and product components.	Ensure consistency of software design to software integration.
	PI SP 2.1 **Review Interface Descriptions for Completeness** Review interface descriptions for coverage and completeness.	Consistency is supported by establishing and maintaining traceability between software design and the software items when needed.

The last case is when the practice of the new model partially covers the existing practices of TSPM. It should be noted that this case is the most common and complicated. In this case it is necessary to divide both existing TSPM practice and the practice of the new model. As a result the TSPM practice will be replaced by two practices combining parts of the initial practice and the new model's practices and this should be further investigated according all four rules.

It should be emphasized that these four rules are enough for inclusion of all practices of a new model.

The same rules are used when a new version of the model already included in TSPM is released. In this case it is important to preserve the versions of TSPM and to track the changes made. The relations between the new and old practices should be kept to enable transition of an assessment's results to the new models version. Of course, pure new practices will have no ratings but the complete reassessment will not be needed.

4.4 Process Assessment Model

As it is described in the section 4.1, TSPM has a capability dimension with six capability levels. The Named Process achieves capability level N, when it implements 1 to N Generic Properties. The Generic Property is rated by scale presented in Table 7. This scale is based on the ISO/IEC 15504 process attributes rating and SCAMPI [19]. The SCAMPI rating do not provide percentage scale but the descriptions basically coincide.

Table 7. Generic Properties rating scale

Value	Percentage scale of achievement	Description
N – Not achieved	0 to 15 %	Insufficient objective evidence exists to state that the practice is implemented.
P – Partially achieved	> 15 % to 50 %	Some artifacts are absent or judged to be inadequate. One or more weaknesses are noted.
L – Largely achieved	> 50 % to 85 %	Sufficient artifacts are present and judged to be adequate. One or more weaknesses are noted.
F – Fully achieved	> 85 % to 100 %	Sufficient artifacts are present and judged to be adequate. No weaknesses are noted.

The TSPM Generic Properties and Generic Practices correspond ISO/IEC 15504 Process Attributes (PA) and Generic Practices. General Goals (GG) from CMMI are not included in TSPM, because PA full covers GG in accordance with [20].

4.5 Transformation of Assessment Results

The TSPM Assessment Model is compatible with included process models (ISO/IEC 15504 and CMMI). This means that their structure is the same and the relations between practices are established. Therefore, multiple assessments are avoided in order to get capability profiles of processes according to different assessment models. There is now a framework to unambiguously transform the organization's and/or software development methodology's assessment results into results of the assessment according another process model. For instance, an organization has its assessment results according to CMMI and wants to find out the process capability profile according ISO/IEC 15504. In this case the organization would transform CMMI assessment results into TSPM using established practices relationships and then into the results of assessment according ISO/IEC 15504. In such a way the organization should assess its processes according to only one model and the assessments according other models could be obtained through TSPM. Of course, the unique practices of the destination model should be rated additionally but the scope of such additional rating will be very small compared with new assessment. So, the main goal of TSPM will be achieved: the organization will not need to do the complete assessment of the process by different model more than once.

When TSPM is renewed by including a new model or when a new version of included model appears, the previous assessment will be automatically updated. It will be necessary to reconsider only those new practices which have appeared in a model because they have not been covered earlier.

4.6 Empirical and Descriptive

It is necessary to be aware of two requirements while creating new TSPM practices. The TSPM practice must be such that it defines an organized and benchmarked software process system and that it incorporates best practices captured and elicited from the software industry. The TSPM practices must describe "what to do", leaving the methodologies to answer "how to do it"[22]. All the practices will come into the TSPM from the models included, but not from the side. As ISO/IEC 15504 and CMMI are aware of these requirements TSPM answers this requirement as well.

5 Conclusions

The ontology proposed in this paper could contribute the future development of the process models as the essential ambiguities have been resolved.

The principles described ensure the creation of TSPM that enables the transformation of the results of an assessment according to one Process Model to the results of other models and thereby determining what capability/maturity according to different Process Models a software engineering methodology could ensure. These principals have been proved on engineering processes of ISO/IEC 15504 and CMMI.

Further, complete ISO/IEC 15504 and CMMI will be defined by SPEM stereotypes. Then TSPM will be created according the principals defined. Also some popular Software Development Methodologies will be included into TSPM and their capability profiles according ISO/IEC 15504 and CMMI will be determined. To verify the correctness these capability profiles will be compared with the results of other research that evaluate the methodologies directly according CMMI and ISO/IEC 15504.

References

[1] Ferreira, A., Machado, R.: Software Process Improvement in Multimodel Environments. In: Fourth International Conference on Software Engineering Advances, pp. 512–517 (2009)

[2] Khoshgoftar, M., Osman, O.: Comparison of maturity models. In: 2nd IEEE International Conference on Computer Science and Information Technology, pp. 297–301 (2009)

[3] Garcia, I., Pacheco, C., Coronel, N.: Learn from Practice: Defining an Alternative Model for Software Engineering Education in Mexican Universities for Reducing the Breach between Industry and Academia. In: Proceedings of the International Conference on Applied Computer Science, Malta, pp. 120–124 (2010)
[4] Wu, C.-H.: An Exploration of the Relationship between Organizational Learning and Software Development Process Maturity. In: Proceedings of the 6th WSEAS International Conference on Applied Computer Science, Hangzhou, China, pp. 301–305 (2007)
[5] Vanamali, B., Bella, F., Hormann, K.: From CMMI to SPICE – Experiences on How to Survive a SPICE Assessment Having Already Implemented CMMI. In: 32nd Annual IEEE International Computer Software and Applications, COMPSAC 2008, pp. 1045–1052 (2008)
[6] Wang, Y., King, G., Dorling, A., Wickberg, H.: A Unified Framework for the Software Engineering Process System Standards and Models. In: ISESS 1999 Proceedings of the 4th IEEE International Symposium and Forum on Software Engineering Standards, pp. 132–141 (1999)
[7] Rout, T.P., Tuffley, A., Cahill, B.: CMMI Evaluation: Capability Maturity Model Integration Mapping to ISO/IEC 15504 2:1998. Software Quality Institute, Griffith University, Brisbane (2001)
[8] Peldzius, S., Ragaisis, S.: Investigation Correspondence between CMMI-DEV and ISO/IEC 15504. International Journal of Education and Information Technologies 5(4), 361–368 (2011)
[9] Soto, M., Münch, J.: Using Model Comparison to Maintain Model-to-Standard Compliance. In: CVSM 2008 Proceedings of the 2008 International Workshop on Comparison and Versioning of Software Models, pp. 35–40 (2008)
[10] Pricope, S., Lichter, H., Rosenkranz, C.G.: Efficient Adoption and Assessment of Multiple Reference Models. In: 5th IFIP TC2 Central and Eastern European Conference on Software Engineering Techniques, Debrecen, Hungary, August 25-26 (2011)
[11] Vanamali, B., Bella, F., Hörmann, K.: From CMMI to SPICE – Experiences on How to Survive a SPICE Assessment Having Already Implemented CMMI. In: 32nd Annual IEEE International Computer Software and Applications, COMPSAC 2008, pp. 1045–1052 (2008)
[12] Cohan, S., Glazer, H.: An Agile Development Team's Quest for CMMI® Maturity Level 5. In: 2009 Agile Conference, pp. 201–206 (2009)
[13] Baker, S.: Formalizing Agility, Part 2: How an Agile Organization Embraced the CMMI. In: Proceeding AGILE 2006 Proceedings of the Conference on AGILE, pp. 147–154 (2006)
[14] Mikulėnas, G., Butleris, R., Nemuraitė, L.: An approach for the metamodel of the framework for a partial agile method adaptation. Information Technology and Control 40(1), 71–82 (2011)
[15] Peldžius, S., Ragaišis, S.: Requirements of Transitional Software Process Model. Information Sciences 56, 138–145 (2011) (in Lithuanian)
[16] CMMI® for Development, Version 1.3, Improving processes for developing better products and services, CMU/SEI-2010-TR-033. Software Engineering Institute (2010)
[17] Schuppenies, R., Steinhauer, S.: Software Process Engineering Metamodel. Components (2006), http://www.omg.org/technology/documents/formal/spem.html
[18] Software & Systems Process Engineering Meta-Model Specification, Version 2.0 (2008)
[19] Standard CMMI® Appraisal Method for Process Improvement (SCAMPISM) A, Version 1.3: Method Definition Document (2011)
[20] Rout, T.P., Tuffley, A.: Harmonizing ISO/IEC 15504 AND CMMI. Software Process Improvement and Practice 12, 361–371 (2007)

Self-assessment Model and Review Technique for SPICE: SMART SPICE

Sharmistha Kar[1], Satyabrata Das[2], Amiya Kumar Rath[3], and Subrata Kumar Kar[4]

[1] ITER, Siksha O Anusandhan University, Bhubaneswar, India
jana_sharmistha@yahoo.com
[2] Trident Academy of Technology, BPUT, Bhubaneswar, India
sb_das@hotmail.com
[3] DRIEMS, Bhubaneswar, BPUT, Cuttack, India
amiyaamiya@rediffmail.com
[4] CES Technologies, Kolkata, India
subratkar23@gmail.com

Abstract. Self-assessment to understand the capability of any organization or "Where we Stand" is the key objective of this paper. It enhances the software engineering practices in the context of the quality of products. Software Process Improvement Assessment frameworks like CMMI and ISO/IEC 15504 –SPICE does assessment by the experts and professional involving high cost resulting many SMEs refrain from adapting the standard models for assessment. Perceived need observed to have a Self-assessment model, which will enable the organization using indigenous model for assessment following standards. The proposed model will address the issues of strength and weak-ness and to take appropriate measure for software process improvement thus enhancing organization's capability. It is a well disciplined and well targeted assessment framework based on basic and simple questionnaires that covers the whole organization diversified activities and success stories to arrive at conclusion and establishing improvement initiatives.

Keywords: SPI, SPICE., CMMI.

1 Introduction

Globalization is the defining fact in the 21st Century and the Software Organizations play a significant role in the process. Many global economic activities such as transport, communication etc. is largely associated to Information Technology (IT). In the largest and fastest growing sector of Information technology, it has fostered the need for sustainability in the global competition for the Software Organizations. The Small and Medium Enterprises (SMEs) having employees between 50-150 employees constitute the majority of the software organizations around the world and it is very important to encourage them growing for their large contribution to economy [1]. As many of these SMEs produce many significant and quality products, good and plausible engineering practices and its improvement is needed constantly. Also over the years the software development process has evolved as a well-defined and self-managed tool of many of the software organization out of their long experiences to develop software product more efficiently in terms of quality and quantity with respect to limited resources. However the scenario as mentioned above is not same for all the software organization across the globe. The various Software processes being followed for development ought to maintain its quality and standard as well. It is a well known fact that product developed through standard and quality process will definitely result in quality product and hence process needs to be continuously measured so as to understand how effectively it is accomplishing the objectives and identifying the shortfalls for improvement [2]. Non adaptation to measurement tools to assess the standard and quality of the process, consequences into poor outcome with less efficiency in long run for many of the SMEs reluctant to process assessment. Further, the credibility of the organizations is at stake, if the products delivered are not considered of standard that best suited to client requirement. Capability Assessment of these small and medium level organizations is highly essential not only to put-forth the quality outcome also enabling the authorities in identifying the strength and weakness of the organization and to take appropriate measures.

The quality and process capability are evaluated by the standard Software Process Improvement (SPI) framework. Many sophisticated and easy to use SPIs frameworks have evolved since 1980s and gained popularity for its significant contribution in retaining the good practices and deliverable of good products. Its objectives is not only to enhance quality of product but also to increase productivity reducing cost and development time[3]. The most suited software process improvement model developed are Capability Maturity Model Integration and SPICE which focuses on defining and measuring processes and practices to achieve quality. They also guide in process improvement in the entire organization [3]. But it is observed to be limited to greater extent in the large companies only and has failed to acquire favor from small organization due its overhead assessment procedure [5].

This paper presents an attempt to identify the reasons for not adopting the formal SPIs by many of the SMEs and includes the results of a survey conducted to understand and to create awareness of the application of SPIs among the SMEs. It focuses on the international standardized SPIs SO/IEC 15504 - SPICE that is flexible and applicable for all processes. The authors analyses the current scenario and requirement for sustaining globally and suggests a simplified assessment procedure by proposing a SMART SPICE Model for self assessment by the organization itself to know its status and then apply for international standardization benchmarking.

2 Literature Review

In Software development three major components determines the quality of product: The people that develop a software system, technology employed by them, and the process of development. The development process is the key to success for the growth of software organizations [16]. The SPI, particularly asses the process to evaluate the methods, tools and practices that are used in the developing the software and identify the strength, weakness and associated risk of the process [3]. The overall outcome of these SPIs is analyzed to focus on the weakness and then suggest for plan for making the organizational change resulting to improvement. This continuous process improvement custom leads to the development of more established approaches to the software engineering reducing time, labor and cost of the project in an organization and standard development of quality product that helps the organization to be well recognized and acquire more business with prospective clients. So it leads to holistic enhancement of the organization [3].

The SPI framework is adapted in various Software Development Organizations for defining and measuring the process and practices enhancing the overall growth in productivity in terms of quantity and quality of process and organizations as well. SPI involves understanding existing process and evaluates its maturity to determine the capability. So the Software intensive organization strives to adopt the standardized process to achieve maximum maturity level and higher capability and to realize the best outcome. It adopts the continuous software process improvement by performing compulsive procedures including the re-use of software process artifacts and with corresponding domain knowledge.

A number of SPIs models has emerged since its inception in the last two decades and is implemented sporadically in different organization to large extent. But most of the SPI don't show much adoption among Small and Medium Scale Enterprises (SMEs) due to various reasons. It is mainly due to ignorance of the available model, rigorous procedures, constraints of budget and schedule, risk of being assessed in low level hampering business, a substantial overhead that make organizations reluctant to adopt SPI reference models. Another reason for limited success in many SPI programs is consulting companies that sometimes ignore organizational culture facing practitioners' resistance to change. Also this standardize model are too cost effective to be implemented in Small and medium sized organization which has a large recognizable contribution in global economy. The assessment procedure turns to be heavy on SMEs, as it requires sufficient established documents and rigorous procedures, the SMEs hardly follows the stringent policies, thus hesitant to adopt SPI models. But process assessment cannot be ruled out in the SMEs since it not only evaluate the process maturity but also specifies the status or the capability of the organization by identifying strength and weakness suggesting improvement measures [1-5,16].

There is also an emerging standard ISO/IEC 29110 "Software Engineering - Lifecycle Profiles for Very Small Entities (VSE) of 25 employees" an ISO initiative to provide Very Small Entities (VSE) with a suitable set of profiles for Process Assessment and Process Improvement conforming to ISO 15504 model of process capability. With this approach VSE entities can have their own software process model and can conform to process assessments resulting process improvement. But it too has limitations as its address the characteristics of Size in terms of number of employees only but not the factors like Business Models (commercial, contracting, in-house development, etc.); Situational factors (such as criticality, uncertainty environment, etc.); and Risk Levels. The standards don't provide a clear defined profile for assessment of any particular organization of combinations of various dimensions. These may lead to its poor adaptation.

Apart from these models, two well-known software product oriented standards worldwide accepted are CMMI and ISO/IEC 15504-SPICE which can be applicable to organizations of all size. Both the models provide a framework to assess and improve software processes based on different models of maturity levels by and validating the practices implemented and recommend techniques and process requirement for improvement, the sole objective to enhance quality and business.

But it is more applicable to large industries as it has rigorous procedure of accessing and involves high cost and time. Most of the large enterprisers undertake this assessment, as they understand the importance of the performance assessment, which is essential for substantial growth of the organization. However this model is challenging for the small and medium scale organizations since it involve high cost, time and efforts. Besides, low publicity of the efficacy of the framework also leads minimum usage. It is highly essential to promote the SPICE framework-the international standard, establishing improved marketing system so as to reach to the potential clients with informative module.

The literature review revealed the importance of SPI initiatives to improve organizations maturity and limitations of existing SPI reference models. Little attention has been paid to the effective implementation of SPI models in small and medium organization, which has resulted in limited success for many SPI programs. In last couple of decades various SPI framework has been emerged but with little success to address the process assessment for the small and medium organizations. It is also revealed that ignorance of the available model, rigidity, budgetary constraints, risk of being assessed in low level hampering business, that make organizations reluctant to adopt SPI reference models. Very little attention has been made to explore short, simple and flexible SPI model, which can be effectively implemented in the small organizations.

3   Survey Work

The standard Software Process Improvisation following the Standard Capability Assessment Framework is the key for the sustainability of the various small and medium enterprises operational. Adding value to its importance, a detailed survey was conducted on five local SMEs in India to understand their awareness on SPI.

The survey conducted indicated that most of the SMEs does not follow any capability determination model for software process improvement. Further analysis implicates that the organization do not follow standard "Capability Determination Model" for assessment mostly due to ignorance, its cost and many other stringent requirement. Besides, the authorities of the SMEs also apprehend that the assessment of organizations with the application of the Capability Determination Models of CMMI, SPICE and other international SPIs might defame their organization for poor quality in terms of products and processes. Most of them also responded that these international models are mostly demonstrated for the risk and safety critical projects such as spacecraft, finance and medical industry. But the process assessment is the ultimate for overall organizational growth and quality enhancement.

Thus there is necessity of a simplified approach for assessing the organization's capability for benefiting in large of SMEs. The model proposed is a "Self Assessment Model" for these organizations to maintain the quality in term of processes and products delivered following the similar framework of international standard as SPICE. This would enable the authorities to understand "Where they are", to what extent the standards being followed, it strengths and weakness. The outcome of self assessment would enable them to take immediate measures for process improvement and thus ensuring the quality products. So a Self-assessment model and Review Technique for Software Process Improvement and Capability Evaluation (SMART SPICE) a simple and manageable review technique is suggested following the basic framework of SPICE that would definitely benefit the potential software intensive industries with all basic information. Nevertheless Self-assessment model would be persuading factor for adapting the SPICE model to ensure standard software engineering processes in an organization.

4   Proposed SMART SPICE Model: An Innovative Tool

Benchmarking on product and performance is essential for all the SMEs to sustain in the market. This entails, that all organizations be of small and large need to undertake process assessment of initial levels, which would enable them to understand the maturity & capability level. The Simplified evaluation approach proposed would ensure initial assessment of software development practices by the organization it-self without much investment. The rational of proposed model are three fold: enabling the Small & Medium level enterprises for timely assessment,: understand the strength & weakness of their organization : and potential improvement can be planned based on the assessment feedback received.

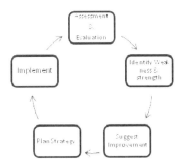

Fig. 1. SMART SPICE Assessment Framework

The proposed model suggests a step-by-step approach for self assessment of the organization. This model assesses the performance level and determines the organization capability by the organization itself. This model mainly focuses on the weakness then giving more importance to its strength. This assessment not only makes them understand the progress of the organization in terms of breadth & depth of their coverage but also enable them to take appropriate action to attain continuous improvement (Figure 1), in order to survive the competition of "survival of fittest". Taking into consideration of all factors, a simple "Self-assessment Model and Review Techniques" for SPICE is designed.

4.1 Framework of the Proposed Assessment Model and Its Features

The features of model are: Adaption of SPICE framework in simple form: Step by step Self Assessment procedure for initial levels: Cost effective and less stringent requirement to adopt the model: Easy to adapt the assessment technique by the authorities. The framework of Self Assessment model for Process Assessment & Capability Evaluation has been inspired from SPICE Model. In order to popularize the SPICE model, a simple method of Self Assessment model is proposed.

Process Assessment framework under the SMART model covers only the basic initial process dimension areas not the complete assessment model as covered in SPICE Framework. However, the basic initial process dimensions of SMART model have been derived following the Process Reference Model (PRM) as envisaged in SPICE: The outcome of continuous process assessment in the initial phases triggers for capability determination of the SMEs in each segment with respect to PRM model of SPICE. The proposed framework identifies the strength and weakness in each stage and guides the authorities to augment timely action for appropriate improvement in the areas of lacunas identified reducing risk.

4.2 Methodology

Framework of SMART SPICE, a Self Assessment model consists of three Process Dimensions as Engineering, Organizational and Management (Table 1). Each Process Dimension Framework has been divided in to 5 numbers of Areas of Operation based on actual requirement for assessment. Individual area of assessment would be characterized by five relevant questions to access the processes followed. Scoring would be taken up for each question answered from scoring scale 0-5. The best-rated process will be awarded with "Five" score and the least will be with "Zero". Once all the questions are covered, than the total score in each "Process Dimension" will be evaluated and the total score would bring the range of performance of each Process Dimension.

4.3 Scoring

Altogether there would be 3 Process Dimension, in each process dimension, there are five "areas" and each area is further characterized by 5 questions relating to the processes are being covered in respective phases. As each question is awarded with score range 0-5, based on the response, so the maximum score could be "125" point and least score could be "0". The total score obtained in each process dimension, determines the capability of the SME. Further the scoring table has been grouped in five categories i.e well established, established, average & manageable, fair and poor, based on the score obtained. The score from 0 to 50% rated poor,: 51% to 65% rated fair,: 66% to 80% rated average & manageable,: 81% to 90% rated established : and above 90% rated well established. This scoring chat would enable to establish their capability status.

Table 1. Process Dimensions and its Process Areas

Organization	Management	Engineering
Governance	Planning	Requirement management
Human recourse	Implementation	Design
Finance	Monitoring	Implementation
Infrastructure	Convergence	Testing
Inter Organization Link	Documentation	Maintenance

4.4 Capability Determination

Each questionnaire used for assessment of processes would further be elaborated for qualitative analysis following an assessment scale, which would enable to assess the core functioning of the organization. For example: one question to assess the process part in governance area of a SME: if the Byelaw, guideline are formulated or not. The answer would be "Yes, No, or In Process of development". But to evaluate the capability assessment of the SME in different phases, the qualitative aspects of these dimensions are further elaborated, which cover the qualitative aspects such as efficiency of the bye-law, clarity, flexibility, timeliness etc. The process will be rated as per the attainment of the process such as 0-Not attained at all, 1- poorly attained, 2- fairly attained, 3- attained averagely 4-Largely attained, 5- completely attained.

4.5 Technical Aspects and Implementation Modalities

SMART SPICE has been designed following the SPICE framework for process assessment of initial levels of the SMEs for capability determination. This model follows the Process Assessment Model (PAM) as referred in SPICE for process assessment. The assessment of initial phases can also be rated as rapid appraisal of the SMEs following Standard Process assessment Framework.

SPICE framework of Software Process Improvement is a comprehensive assessment model and covers each and every dimensions of execution of SMEs. However the proposed SMART SPICE is limited to the initial phases only. But the process assessment framework under the SMART SPICE is more simplified versions from other assessment framework like SPICE, ISO / IEC 29910 following the PRMs of ISO 12207.

It is envisaged that the selected officials of the SMEs will be oriented thoroughly on the SMART SPICE framework for self-assessment. Initial hands on support to be augmented to the SMEs for assessment and later on they can access of their own. This process would ensure continuous assessment by the SMEs following the basic framework derived from ISO / IEC – 15504 - SPICE following the ISO 12207.

5 Implementation

The framework of Self Assessment model for Process Assessment & Capability Evaluation has been implemented in one of the small software organization having about 50 employees. The organization is established for more than 15 years and is associated in developing different software for various clients with due credibility. Inspite of long experience and expertise, it has not adapted CMMI or SPICE assessment to know the organizational capabilities. It only follows the standard process for development as mentioned in the guidelines. It was also ascertained that, the authorities have good understanding on the various process improvisation tools but they are reluctant to adapt either of the tool, as the evaluation through the international standard may lose the credibility of the organization status, which may lead to client loss. However, it was open to implement the proposed self-assessment model, which is largely adapted following SPICE model. The implemented framework was in one of the process area Organization (Table 2, 3).

Table 2. SPI Framework for Organization Dimension

Questions for each Process Areas	Ratings (0-5)	Tot
Governance		23
1. Is the Organisation registered?	4	5
2. Do the Organisation has Bi-Law/ Guideline?	4	5
3. Do the Organisation has well defined Goals & Objective?	3	4
4. Do the Organisation has established Finance Module?	3	4
5. Do the Organisation has HR Manual?	4	5
Human Resource		19
1. Do the Organisation has defined HR Manual?	3	3
2. Availability of established Recruitment Processes?	3	3
3. What is the skill level?	3	4
4. Do you follow strategy on performance appraisal of staff?	4	5
5. Strategic Leadership?	3	4
Finance		11
1. Does the Organisation have defined Finance Manual?	3	3
2. Is there sufficient flow of finance?	2	2
3. Does the Organisation have flexibility in Finance Management?	2	2
4. Does the Organisation has established Auditing system?	2	2
5. What is the profit level?	2	2
Infrastructure		12
1 Office Building: Own / Rented, Sft	3	3
2. Availability of required infrastructure support	3	3
3. Budgeting flexibility for Infrastructure development	2	2
4. Provision of maintenance of infrastructure / assets	2	2
5 Is it updated regularly?	2	2
Inter Organizational Link		20
1. Well Defined strategy for Partnership & Convergence	4	5
2. Availability / flexibility budget line for Convergence Programme	3	4
3. Established Communication Strategy	2	3
4 Frequency of client communication.	4	4
5 Customer and Supplier Dealings	4	4
Total Organizational Score		**85**

Table 3. SPI Framework for Engineering Dimension

Questions for each Process Areas	Ratings 0	1	2	3	4	5	Tot
Requirement Management							16
1. Is the system requirement collected through prescribed framework?				●			3
2. Is there any provision to accommodate the changes required?					●		4
3. Is any written policy for requirement management?				●			3
4. Are the people are adequately trained for managing the allocated requirement.				●			3
5. Are the requirement activities reviewed periodically?				●			3
Design							21
1. Does the organization follow specific Design format?						●	5
2. Does the System Design match the functional requirement?					●		4
3. Does the Organization follow the sequential processes for System design?					●		4
4. Product Component Design Prepared?					●		4
5. Does the System design is verified?					●		4
Implementation							20
1. Does the organization define coding standards?					●		4
2. Are the engineers trained as per client's need					●		4
3. Do you follow any policy for coding?						●	5
4. Product Integration compatibility				●			3
5. Is the implementation application automated?					●		4
Testing							16
1. Are all the units verified?					●		4
2. Flexibility of changes and quick adaptability?				●			3
3. Peer review performed?			●				2
4. Do you have standard Compatibility Check procedure application and hardware system				●			3
5. Is the testing application automated?					●		4
Operation and Maintenance							16
1. Status of Implementation Support?				●			3
2. Implementation Manual Book prepared and supplied?				●			3
3. Compiled to Cyber Security Audit for hosting?				●			3
4. Support for hosting the application?				●			3
5. AMC Support Augmented?					●		4
Total Engineering Score							89

5.1 Results and Analysis

The result is analyzed. The total score obtained under Organizational dimension of the organization was 85 out of 125, which is about 68%. : Score obtained for Organizational Governance, Human Resource Management and Linking with External Organization is 80%, which is rated as average and is manageable. : Score Obtained for Finance Management and Infrastructure Management is less than 45% and rated poor in financial strength, Suggestion:- need improvement. Overall performance of the firm observed to be about 68%, which is rated as average and manageable and needs enhancement in organizational change.

Similarly under the Engineering Dimension, the result is analyzed: The total score obtained under Engineering dimension of the organization was 89 out of 125, which is about 71%. This score come under the category of average and manageable. : Score obtained for Requirement Analysis & Specification is only 64%, which is rated as fair and need improvement. : Score Obtained for System design and Implementation is more than 80% and rated average and manageable. : Score obtained in System Testing and Implementation is about 68% and rated average and manageable. The overall engineering performance of the firm observed to be about 64%, which is rated was fair and needs SPI for immediate improvement. Similarly the management process dimensions can be assessed and evaluated but was not much discussed in detail, as it is the internal matter that cannot be disclosed.

It is observed that the authorities of the organization, where the proposed model implemented are quite comfortable to follow the Process Assessment Framework for self-assessment. While acknowledging the need for SPI Certification, the organization, which is quite old and have excellent reputation in the local market, didn't adopt any SPI framework for several reasons. The SMART SPICE framework observed to be well accepted and gained confidence to the organization for obtaining certification by using SPI Model like SPICE. So it reiterates that the self-assessment model not only helps the SMEs in identifying the shortcomings for necessary improvement, it also motivate the SMEs for continued assessment through the standard SPI framework like SPICE.

5.2 Challenges

The Self Assessment Model perceived found observed to be effective tool for Software Process Improvement in the small and medium level organization. However, it is considered that the low-grade certification of process assessment would adversely affect the business of the organization. This compels the authorities to refrain from simple Software Process Improvisation assessment. Besides implementation of Self Assessment model require authorization from SPICE, which then require professionals to be oriented on the model for Process Improvement Assessment for the interested organizations. It is simple assessment framework, which may not cover all the assessment parameters for comprehensive assessment of any organization.

6 Conclusions

SMART Self Assessment tool has been proposed with a strategy to have better promotion of SPICE globally. It is a simple, user friendly, cost effective and specific to purpose model that would definitely bring improvement in the organization.

References

1. Laporte, C.Y., Alexandre, S., O'Connor, R.: A Software Engineering Lifecycle Standard for Very Small Enterprises. In: O'Connor, R.V., Baddoo, N., Smolander, K., Messnarz, R. (eds.) EuroSPI 2008. CCIS, vol. 16, pp. 129–141. Springer, Heidelberg (2008)

2. Ehsan, N., Pertwaiz, A., Arif, J., Mirza, E., Ishaque, A.: CMMI/SPICE based process Improvement. In: Proceedings of the 2010 IEEE ICMI (2010)
3. Shih, C.-C., Hung, S.-J.: Exploring the relationship between organizational culture and software process improvement deployment. Information and Management 47, 271–281 (2010)
4. Kalpana, A.M., Ebenezer Jeyakumar, A.: Software Process Improvization Framework based on Fuzzy logic approach for optimizing Indial Small Scale Software Organization. International Journal of Multimedia and Ubiquitous Engineering 6(1) (2011)
5. Habra, N., Alexandre, S., Desharnais, J.-M., Laporte, C.Y., Renaul, A.: Initiating software Process Improvement in very small enterprises experience with light assessment tool. Information and Software Technology 50, 763–771 (2008)
6. Pettersson, F., Ivarsson, M., Gorschek, T., Ohman, P.: A practitioner's Guide to light weight software Process assessment and Improvement Planning. The Journal of System and Software 81, 972–995 (2008)
7. Salvano, C.F., Martinez, M.R.M., Zoucs, A.A., Thirty, M.: Practices and Techniques for Engineering process Capability Models. Cele Electronic Journal 13(1), paper 3 (2010)
8. Kim, J.A., Choi, S.Y., Kim, T.-H.: Management Environment for software Process Improvement. In: International IEEE Symposium on Computer Science and its Applications (2008)
9. Greif, N., Parkin, G.: Development of an international guide for measurement software. Measurement 43, 694–701 (2010)
10. Malzahn, D.: Assessing- Learning-Improving, and integrated approach for self assessment and process improvement system. In: Fourth IEEE international Conference on Systems (2009)
11. Von Wangenheim, C.G., Hauck, J.C.R., Salvino, C.F., Von Wangenheim, A.: Systematic Literature Review of Software Process Capability/ Maturity Models. In: Proceedings of International Conference on Software Process Improvement and Capabity dEtermination (SPICE), Pisa, Italy (2010)
12. Varkoi, T.K., Makinen, T.K.: Case study of CMM and SPICE comparison in Software Process assessment. In: IEEE IEMC (1998)
13. Jung, H.-W.: Evaluating the ordering of the SPICE Capability levels: an Empirical Study. Information and Software Technology 47, 141–149 (2005)
14. Muller, S.D., Mathiassen, L., Balshoj, H.H.: Software Process Improvement as organizational change: A metaphorical analysis of the literature. The Journal of Systems and Software 83, 2128–2146 (2010)
15. Wu, M., Ying, J., Yu, C.: A methodology and its Support Environment for Bench mark-based Adapatable Software Process improvement. In: IEEE International Conference on Systems, Man and Cybernetics, pp. 5183–5188
16. Seyyedi, M.A., Shams, F., Teshnehlab, M.: A new method for measuring Software Process Within Software Capability Maturity Model Based on the Fuzzy Multi Agent Measurements. World Academy of Science, Engineering and Technology 4, 250–255 (2005)
17. Staples, M., Niazi, M., Jeffery, R., Abrahams, A., Byatt, P., Murphy, R.: An exploratory study of Why organization do not adopt CMMI. The Journal of Systems and Software, Science Direct (2006)
18. Baldassarre, M.T., Piattini, M., Pino, F.J., Visaggi, G.: Comparing ISO/IEC 12207 and CMMI-DEV: Towards a mapping of ISO/IEC 15504-7. In: IEEE ICSE Workshop, pp. 59–64 (2009)

Bayesian Network Based Bug-fix Effort Prediction Model

Bharathi V., Udaya Shastry, and Joseph Raj

Wipro Technologies, 53/1, Ganapa Towers, Madiwala, Bangalore, 560068, India
{bharathi.kumar,udaya.shatry,joseph.raj}@wipro.com

Abstract. Development and use of prediction model (process performance models, PPM) are the primary requirements of high maturity practices. PPMs are useful tools for project management and process management. They help project managers to predict process performance with a known level of confidence thereby enabling them identify the risk and take actions. Over a last few years, Bayesian Belief Networks (BBN) have received a great deal of attention as prediction models, since they provide better solution to some of the problems found in Software Engineering when compared with traditional statistical models. In this paper, we are presenting our experience of using BBN for bug-fix effort prediction.

Keywords: Process performance model, BBN, effort prediction.

1 Introduction

In this information era of intense competition, increased cost of software development and raising customer's expectations, it is important that the project management shifts from reactive mode to pro-active mode. It has become essential for the project managers to employ the prediction models to identify the problems, which will help them take the actions quickly and meet the client's expectations consistently.

Implementation and effective usage of prediction models is also driven by the industry standards like CMMI [1] and Automotive SPICE® [2]. As a result, organizations are adapting these techniques to establish process predictability, thus enabling better project planning and management.

Traditionally, regression is the most widely used tool for prediction. This method works with the underlying assumptions of normality and linearity. However, the data sets derived from software engineering do not always adhere to this assumption [3].

Over the last few years, the Bayesian networks have become exceedingly popular and have been applied in diverse fields like medical diagnostics, finance, mechanical engineering, space operations [4].

The main reasons for such a wide acceptance are:

- They are capable of solving complex and non-linear relationships
- They aid visual representation of causal relationships
- They facilitate the combination of domain knowledge and data
- They can handle large number of predictors

In this paper we present our experience of employing BBN technique for bug-fix effort prediction.

2   Bayesian Belief Networks

Bayesian Belief networks or Bayesian networks are the type of expert systems that have evolved through research at the intersection of probability, statistics, and artificial intelligence. They are probabilistic graphical model that represents a set of random variables and their conditional dependencies through a directed acyclic graph (DAG). They can serve as decision support systems while dealing with uncertainty. In software engineering, it is a challenge to predict exact values for quality estimations. It is usually sufficient to deal with ranges or intervals of parameters. BBNs allow us to represent the parameters with the values that indicate the intervals. Also the visual support further helps in understanding the causal effects [5].

Bayesian networks are based on Bayes' theorem of probabilistic inference. Mathematically, the theorem gives the relationship between the probabilities of A and B, $P(A)$ and $P(B)$, and the conditional probabilities of A given B and B given A, $P(A \mid B)$ and $P(B \mid A)$. In its most common form, it is:

Where $P(B) \neq 0$,

$$P(A|B) = \frac{P(B|A)\,P(A)}{P(B)}. \qquad (1)$$

The typical structure of a BBN network is as shown in the figure 1.

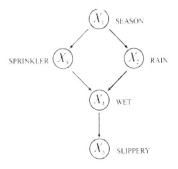

Fig. 1. Structure of a BBN network

Variables are represented by nodes. The arcs represent causal/influential relationships between variables [6]. Each variable has a finite set of mutually exclusive states.

3   Case Study

We applied Bayesian network for the development of bug-fix effort prediction model in a corrective maintenance project. Process-performance models are employed to represent past and current process performance of the project. Projects use these models for estimating, analyzing, and predicting the process performance for the defined processes.

The Critical-to-Quality specified by our client for this project includes the resolution effort required for bug fixes. Critical-to-Quality represent the characteristic of a product or a service. It is a measure of what is important to a customer. With software maintenance accounting for an excess of 50% of the total programming effort [7], accurate effort estimation becomes very essential. To meet the resolution norms set by the client consistently, we wanted to employ a prediction method which not only supports in decision making but also allows the practitioners to apply the domain expertise in model building and what-if analysis. What–if analysis is a method of determining what things can go wrong and assessing the likelihood and consequences of those events.

3.1   Data Analysis and Pre-processing

The first step in the development of a PPM is preliminary analysis and data selection. The data set used in this study belongs to telematics area of Automotive domain. The data set contain the information on effort spent on bug-fix, complexity of the bug, experience of the engineers and analysis effort. The bug –fix resolution effort in terms of effort in person-hours, was chosen as response. Attributes like defect complexity, experience of the engineers and analysis effort were chosen as predictors.

Resolution effort = f (Defect complexity, Experience of the engineers, Analysis effort)   (2)

In the above attribute set, experience of engineers and analysis effort are controllable factors. During project execution, above factors can be varied. But defect complexity is an un-controllable factor as complexity is intrinsic to a defect.

We discretized the each attribute into two levels. Discretization is a method through which numeric attribute is transformed into a nominal or categorical data. We used the equal-width binning method for the predictor variables. Equal-width binning divides the range of possible values into N sub ranges of the same size. The response variable was categorized as {Met, Not met}.

Secondly, the above data set was partitioned into two sections – learning data and test data. This was done to guard against overtraining and to improve generalizability. So far, there has been no universal rule to determine the ratio of the size of learning and testing data set. Normally the 70:30 or 80:20 rules are employed. We selected the latter.

3.2 Model Construction

The second step of PPM development is building the model. We modeled the above data set using the tool GeNIe 2.0, Copyright (c) 1996-2003, developed by Decision Systems Laboratory, University of Pittsburgh.

The learning data set was fed into the tool. We created the network using the PC algorithm [8]. We studied the causal- effect relationship among the nodes projected by the directed acyclic graph. Based on our knowledge and domain experience, we re-defined some of the nodal relationships. Then the network was made to learn the parameters. The resulting model is as shown in the figure 2.

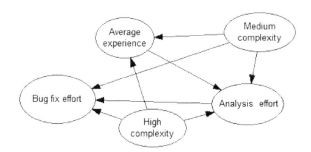

Fig. 2. BBN model for bug-fix effort prediction

3.3 Model Verification

The final step of PPM development is verification of the model.

The goodness of a model is determined by how well it can perform when presented with the data it has not seen before. We applied the predictors of the test data set to the constructed model and noted the response shown. We evaluated the model using the confusion matrix [9]. Confusion matrix is a table lay-out used to evaluate the performance of the classification system. It contains the information about actual and predicted classifications performed by a classification system. It allows detailed analysis than mere measurement of correctness of prediction. Performance of the model was measured using the two metrics viz., 1. Accuracy 2. Sensitivity

$$Accuracy = \frac{TP + TN}{TP + TN + FP + FN} \quad (3)$$

$$Sensitivity = \frac{TP}{TP + FN} \quad (4)$$

Where:

TP=Number of True Positives, TN=Number of True Negatives, FP=Number of False Positives, FN=Number of False Negatives

In the confusion matrix, low values of False Negative (FN) and False Positive represent a good model. For a perfect model, all the response data points should fall in the True Positive (TP) or True Negative (TN) region.

4 Results and Discussions

The confusion matrix obtained is as shown in the table 1. Classification is represented in percentage.

Table 1. Confusion matrix Actual Predicted

Resolution norm	Not met	Met
Not met	25%	12.5%
Met	12.5%	50%

Referring to the table 1, the sum total of True Positive and True negative cases is 75%. That means, model is able to predict 75% cases correctly.

There are False Positive cases. Though actually norm is 'met', model is predicting as 'not met'. This is a false alarm. There are False Negative cases. Though the norm is 'not met' actually, model is predicting as 'met'. This is a gap. Corresponding to the confusion matrix of Table 1, the accuracy is 75%. Sensitivity is 67%.

From practitioner's point of view, we believe that this model is good enough to start with.

We carried out the what-if analysis with the above model. Details are as follows.

- We were able to meet the resolution norm with experienced team for low complexity defects with minimum level of analysis effort.
- If certain level of analysis effort was maintained, we were able to meet the resolution norm even for the high complex defects. But, the level of analysis effort varied between experienced and less experienced team. Comparatively, more effort was required for less experienced team.
- In the cases where the level of analysis effort was not maintained, we were not able to meet the resolution norm irrespective of the experience of the team.

The above output from what-if analysis is inline with our observations. Analysis effort is the major contributor for the consistent meeting of resolution norm.

Above analysis helped us estimate the effort and allocate the resources effectively.

5 Conclusion and Future Work

In this paper, we have presented our experiment of applying BBN for the development of a bug-fix effort prediction model. The accuracy and sensitivity we obtained from this model for initial data set are good and encouraging. What-if analysis output is also in line with our observations.

Our future plan is to refine the model further. Firstly, we want to collect more data points and enhance the model. Secondly, we want to employ more efficient techniques like dynamic discretization during pre-processing phase. With this, we expect to achieve a higher value of accuracy and sensitivity.

Acknowledgement. The model described in this paper was created using the GeNIe modeling environment developed by the Decision Systems Laboratory of the University of Pittsburgh (http://dsl.sis.pitt.edu).

The core of our implementation is based on the SMILE reasoning engine for graphical probabilistic models, contributed to the community by the Decision Systems Laboratory of the University of Pittsburgh (http://dsl.sis.pitt.edu)."

References

1. CMMI Product Team, CMMI® for Development, Version 1.3, Software Engineering Institute (2010)
2. Automotive SIG, Automotive SPICE© Process Assessment Model (v2.5) and Process Reference Model V4.5 (2010)
3. Kitchenham, B., Pickard, L.: Towards a constructive quality model part ii, Statistical techniques for modeling software quality in the esprit request project. Software Engineering Journal 2(4), 114–126 (1987)
4. Heckerman, D., Mamdani, A., Wellman, M.P.: Real-World Applications of Bayesian networks. Communications of the ACM 38(3) (March 1995)
5. Rodriguez, D., Harrison, R., Satpathy, M.: An Investigation of Prediction Models for Project Management. In: IEEE COMPSAC 2002 (2002)
6. BBN online Tutorial,
   `http://www.eecs.qmul.ac.uk/~norman/BBNs/BBNs.html`
7. Sarkar, S., Sindhgatta, R., Poolooth, K.: A Collaborative Platform for Application Knowledge Management in Software Maintenance Projects. In: Compute 2008, Bangalore, Karnataka, India, January 18-20. ACM (2008) ISBN 978-1-59593-950-0/08/01
8. Spirtes, P., Glymour, C., Scheines, R.: Causation, Prediction, and Search. Lecture Notes in Statistics, vol. 81. Springer, New York (1993) ISBN 0-262-19440-6P
9. `http://faculty.smu.edu/tfomby/eco5385/lecture/Confusion%20Matrix.pdf`

A State of Art of Software Improvement Implementation Support Tools in SMEs

Mirna Muñoz[1], Antonio De Amescua[1], Jezreel Mejia[2], Jose A. Calvo-Manzano[3], Gonzalo Cuevas[3], and Tomás San Feliu[3]

[1] Departamento de Informatica, Universidad Carlos III de Madrid
Avda. de la Universidad no. 30, 28911 Leganés, Madrid, Spain
mirna.munozm@gmail.com, amescua@inf.uc3m.es
[2] Centro de Investigación en Matemáticas
Av. Universidad no 222, 98068 Zacatecas, México
jmejia@cimat.mx
[3] Departamento Lenguajes y Sistemas Informáticos e Ingeniería de Software
Universidad Politécnica de Madrid, Facultad de Informática
28660 Boadilla del Monte, Madrid, España
{joseantonio.calvomanzano,gonzalo.cuevas,tomas.sanfeliu}@upm.es

Abstract. Nowadays becoming competitive is a critical challenge for organizations and software process improvement is an obvious and logical way to address this increasing need in the software industry, unfortunately not all software process improvements have the expected results, because of the lack of knowledge on how to do it and the lack of support available for organizations specially SMEs. This paper presents a state of art of research focused on software tools which help organizations in performing a successful implementation of software process improvements initiatives.

Keywords: SPI, software tools, systematic review, small and medium enterprises, SMEs.

1 Introduction

In the past 20 years Small and Medium Enterprises (SMEs) are becoming an important piece in the worldwide industry economy. SMEs covers small enterprises, which are companies with fewer than 50 employees, and medium enterprises, which are companies with have between 50 and 249 employees. These kinds of companies, especially in software development industry has emerged, grown and become strong. Therefore, they represent a major economic activity throughout many nations in the word [1][2].

However, software projects often have problems in time excess, budget, effort and poor quality. As a result, they are not able to meet customer requirements [3]. In this context, software product quality is largely dependent on the process that is used to create it [4]. Therefore, SMEs are more and more concerned about software process improvement (SPI), since it has been identified as a mechanism to boost the competitiveness and efficiency in software industry[4][5][6].

Unfortunately, software process improvement initiatives are not successfully implemented [7] or have a limited success [8]. Specially in SMEs where this problem is potentiated because of their very limited resources, budgets and time that they have in order to improve their software processes [1][3][4][9][10].

As a result, it is necessary to introduce the elements to address a successful SPI. In this context it is important to develop and provide software tools that support SMEs in the implementation of software process improvements initiatives.

The goal of this paper is to analyze existing SPI tools which support SMEs in the implementation of software process improvements initiatives and establish a state of the art. This paper is structured as follows: section 2 introduce to software process improvements in SMEs, section 3 shows the results and finally, section 4 presents the future work and conclusions.

2 Software Process Improvement in SMEs

SMEs are very important as a key part to the economic growth. On the one hand, there is an increasingly growing of SMEs as a key component in the industrial profile of many countries [3]; on the other hand, they constitute the majority of software development organizations around the world [10].

Due to its importance, since 2002 there has been increasing interest in SMEs [1]. Therefore, organizations such the Software Engineering Institute (SEI) and International Organization for Standardization (ISO) have been addressed their efforts in SMEs in order to achieve that theirs models and standards such as CMMI, ISO 12207 and ISO 15504 respectively, can be successfully applied in SMEs [10].

Unfortunately, the obtained results are far from the expected one. This is because the main motivation why SMEs implement software process improvement initiatives is not to obtain a certificate, but it is to making more efficient and effective organizations [1][4][6]. Therefore, SMEs are not able to invest in the implementation of expensive programs [6]. Besides, due to its nature the implementation of software process improvements in SMEs become harder and most of the times chaotic [4][6][11]. Then, there is an increasing need of providing software support tools which enables SMEs to implement successful SPI initiatives.

3 State of Art of SMEs' Software Tools for Software Process Improvement

Systematic review summary: the state of art of SMEs' tools for software process improvement was established after analyzing the obtained results of carrying out a systematic review. Table 1 summarizes the analysis done in order to select primary studies.

Table 1. Results derived from each source

Source	Search date	Found	Repeated	Relevant	Primary	%
ACM	23-30/06/2011	353	18	8	7	12
IEEE	20-21/10/2011	625	18	43	37	60
ISI Web	4-18/10/2011	15	10	5	5	8
Springer	25-27/10/2011	15	4	6	5	8
Science	28/10/2011	36	14	8	7	12
TOTAL		**1045**	**64**	**70**	**61**	**100%**

Results Summary: This section shows the obtained results of analyzing primary studies as follows: Figure 1 (a) shows studies trends and (b) studies classification and Figure 2 shows the studies by country.

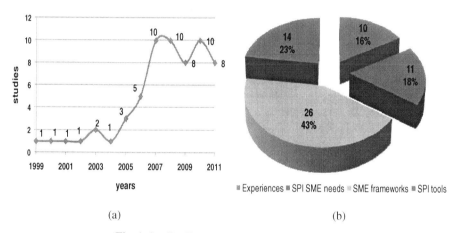

Fig. 1. Studies Trends and studies classification

Figure1 (a) shows three types of trends, between 1999 and 2003, there is a constant linear trend because the studies by years are one per year; from 2004 to 2007 data have a linear trend because the studies increased at a constant rate and; from 2007 to 2011 there is a polynomial trend of order 2 because data fluctuates along the graphic. This shows that has been an increasing interest in software tools for SPI. Unfortunately, the research effort in this topic is low.

Figure 1(b) shows the results of the studies classification in four categories as follows: 16% are focus on showing experiences and lesson learned in the implementation of SPI at SMEs; 18% are focus on highlighting key factors and needs in order implement a successfully SPI in SMEs; 43% are related to frameworks which make light versions of large organizations' models and standards; and 23% shows approaches of assessment software tools, which only support SMEs at beginning of SPI implementation.

Finally but not less important Figure 2 shows primary studies by country. As figure shows Mexico, Spain and Brazil are countries which have more research in software tools for SMEs' SPI.

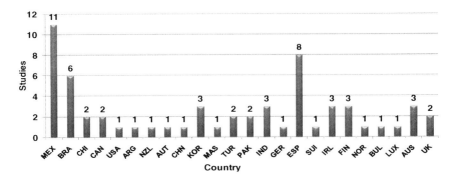

Fig. 2. Studies by country

4 Conclusions

This paper shows the first results of a research focus on establish the requirements of software tools which helps SMEs in the implementation, monitoring and control of SPI. Based on the obtained results of performing the systematic review four conclusions are derived: 1) most of the analyzed studies are related to make an adequacy of large companies' actual models and standards in SMEs; 2) analyzed studies which include software tools for SPI are focused on assessment phase; 3) Mexico, Spain and Brazil are countries with have focused on this research; and 4) there is a lack of research in software tools which helps SMEs during the implementation, monitoring and control of SPI. This highlights that even when frameworks to implement improvements in SMEs have been developed they don´t provide software tools which could enable organizations to have better results in the implementation, monitoring and control of software process improvement initiatives.

Acknowledgments. This work is sponsored by CONACyT México and the Polytechnic University of Madrid, through the Software Process Improvement Research Group for Spain and Latin American Region.

References

1. Pino, J.F., García, F., Piattini, M.: Software process improvement in small and medium software enterprises: a systematic review. SQJournal 16, 237–261 (2008)
2. Garcia, I., Pacheco, C., Cruz, D.: Adopting an RIA-based tool for supporting assessment, implementation and learning in software in software process improvement under the NMX-I-059/02-NYCE-2005 standard in small software enterprises. In: Eighth ACIS International Conference on Software Engineering Research, Management and Application (2010)

3. McCaffery, F., Pikkarainen, M., Richardson, I.: Ahaa –agile, hybrid assessment method for automotive, safety critical SMEs. In: ACM/IEEE 30th International Conference on Software Engineering, ICSE 2008, pp. 551–560 (2008)
4. Mishra, D., Mishra, A.: Software Process Improvement in SMEs: A Comparative View. Computer Science and Information Systems 6(1), 111–140 (2009)
5. Oktaba, H., Garcia, F., Piattini, M., Ruiz, F., Pino, F.J., Alquicira, C.: Software Process Improvement: The Competisoft Project. Computer 40, 21–28 (2007)
6. Goldenson, D.: Performance Outcomes from Process Improvement -Tech Views. Software Tech. 10 (2007)
7. Conradi, H., Fuggetta, A.: Improving software process improvement. IEEE Software 19, 92 (2002)
8. Dyba, T.: An empirical investigation on the key factors for success in software process improvement. IEEE Transactions on Software Engineering 31 (2005)
9. Garcia, I., Pacheco, C.: Toward Automated Support for Software Process Improvement Initiatives in Small and Medium Size Enterprises. In: Lee, R., Ishii, N. (eds.) Soft. Eng. Research, Manage. & Appli. 2009. SCI, vol. 253, pp. 51–58. Springer, Heidelberg (2009)
10. Pino, F.J., Pardo, C., García, F., Piattini, M.: Assessment methodology for software process improvement in small organizations. Inf. Softw. Technol. 52, 1044–1061 (2010)
11. García, I., Pacheco, C.: A Web-based Tool for Automatizing the Software Process Improvement Initiatives in Small Software Enterprises. IEEE Latin America Transactions (Revista IEEE America Latina) 8, 685–694 (2010)

Adaptive Process Improvement Approaches

Ravindra Joshi

Infiniti, Bangalore, India
ravindrabjoshi@gmail.com

Abstract. There are many practices for organizational process improvement in order to achieve various business objectives. Most of such take form of time capped initiatives or drives to bring focus & energy. These intense team efforts are characterized by implementation of guidance based on standard process reference models. It is observed that majority of the cases, though the intent starts from business objectives, most of the processes outcomes and evidences start aligning to requirements of standards, than business impact so are not sustained. This paper compares summary of existing popular methodologies and proposes few mix-n-match approaches to bring process performance closer to ongoing business goals and objectives. Also discussed are related topics: keeping the processes lightweight & dynamic, leveraging simple tools & techniques, re-calibrating the processes based on changing business trends and importance of teamwork (people & passion). Though majority of this observation is based on automotive, can be applied across industries.

Keywords: adaptive process improvement, organizational change management, process optimization.

1 Introduction to Process Improvements

There has been steadily increasing interest over last few years for Process improvement across industries globally – and more so in outsourced IT industries which leverage the knowledge professionals' expertise through offshored work practices. When the workforce is remote and mainly accessed thru communication such as e-mails, teleconferences and video calls – it's a challenge that the work practices need to be not only uniformly consistent but understood & implemented throughout global work locations. The competitive market dynamics calls for service organizations to implement processes of higher maturities and thus there is increased emphasis for relying on standards i.e. set of collective global best improvement practices.

The paper explores few key issues on observations & lessons gathered from automotive supplier practices. It further delves into quick understanding & comparisons of underlying improvement methodologies. It ends up demonstrating how to be adaptable in maintaining as well as sustaining improvements by selecting & utilizing underlying improvement techniques.

2 Context and Relevance of Process Improvements

As a matter of providing assurance to OEMSs, the supplier organizations benchmark the capability of varied work practices as per the standard models like CMMi, SPICE etc. Then they go ahead in obtaining a certification as testimonial from a well known accredited third party assessment agency. Such benchmarking initiatives often take own shape & form, some cases what typically happens is a structured time-bound exercise of

- mapping the work practices to model,
- identification of process gaps and bridging them at QMS/process level
- selecting candidate projects & making them aware of the model,
- collating evidences to conform to various clauses
- project teams to showcase various the adherence to model clauses during assessment defense

The real challenge is observed afterwards to sustain the advantages in coming months or years by maintaining its relation to business outcomes, not just sufficing to documentation i.e. work products as per the standard reference models. The key is to leverage right improvement technique or methodology to make it work for the business as a competitive advantage. Main key lies in implementation as ongoing basis.

3 Improvement Methodologies

There are many prevailing techniques for business process improvements esp in manufacturing / automotive. Few key & popular ones are

Kaizen
- Definition: Philosophy of gradual, incremental, and orderly continuous improvement, creating more value and less waste; emphasis on process improvement and process control; it is a Japanese word meaning "ongoing improvement"
- Objective: Small improvements by optimizing existing systems
- Requires:
    - Taking action on obvious problems and deviations to maintain process control
    - Establishing control through Standard Operating Procedures (SOPs)
    - Duration : 1-10 days

Lean
- Definition: Focus on speed, efficiency, and elimination of waste
- Objective: Maximizing process speed (cycle time) by reducing waste
- Requires:
    - Elimination of waste: Defects, overproduction, inventories, unnecessary processing, unnecessary movement of people,

unnecessary transport of goods, waiting, designing goods and services that don't meet customers' needs
- Value stream mapping: Map process and focus on elimination of non-value add activities
  - Ask what activities the customer is willing to pay for
  - Focus on process standardization

Six-Sigma
- Defined: Data-driven methodology focusing on reducing defects and variability
  - 6 σ = 3.4 defects per million (Motorola Shift)
  - σ = Sigma = Standard deviation
- Objective: Reduce variability through continuous process improvement
- Requires:
  - Processes must be in place
  - The processes must be predictable (in statistical control with normal distribution)
  - The processes must be improved by reducing variation (continuous improvement)
  - Data availability
  - Focus on understanding customer requirements

Another quick way of looking at a glance as follows

Quality Improvement Methodology	Six Sigma	Lean	Theory of Constraints
Theory	Reduce variation	Remove waste	Manage constraints
Focus	Problems	Work Flow	Systems constraints
Applications / Guidelines	Define; Measure; Analyze; Improve; Control.	Identify value; Identify value stream; Flow; Pull; Perfection.	Identify constraint; Exploit constraint; Subordinate processes; Elevate constraint. Repeat cycle
Assumptions	A problem exists; Fast throughput; Less inventory; Fluctuation-performance measures for managers; Improved quality.	Waste removal will improve business performance; Many small improvements are better then systems analysis.	Emphasis on speed and volume; Uses existing systems; Process interdependence.

Primary impact	Uniform process output	Reduced flow time	Fast throughput
Key effects	Less waste; Fast throughput; Less inventory; Fluctuation-performance measure for managers.	Less variation; Uniform output; Less inventory; New accounting system; Flow-performance measures for managers Improved.	Less inventory/waste; Throughput cost accounting; Throughput-performance measurement system; Improved quality.
Criticisms	System interaction not considered; Process improved independently.	Statistical or system analysis not valued;	Minimal worker input; Data analysis not valued;

Following are few quick examples just to get idea about relevance of various implementations (de-referenced due to confidentiality)

a. Issue : Producing multiple variants of a basic design drawing - Six-sigma implemented resulting in re-use of base design and reduction in time to produce multiple variants
b. Issue: improving productivity & bonding in long duration projects involving shifts – Kaizen was used to gather suggestions and after review team building activities arranged boosting morale & customer orientation of personnel
c. Issue : automation of code testing – Lean/agile principles applied to expedite the testing time
d. Issue: new technology services introduced without immediate supply of trained resources – combination of six-sigma and lean was used to re-skill legacy technology resources in fulfilling the demand. Also people and change management techniques like team building & training used
e. Issue : tedious supply chain & stack up of inventory in Stores TOC (distribution) leveraged for storage & distribution PCs
f. Issue: long wait time to deploy new hires on live project - combination of Lean (hiring just in time as per project pipeline) and TOC (distribution) was used to streamline the deployment process. Also people and change management techniques like mentoring used to enhance timely effectiveness of newly inducted resources

By above samples we can see - when it comes to deciding relevant technique or methodology -

- depends on the needs, supply, priorities and current state of organization
- it may be stand-alone or a combination of methodologies

- When an organization has successfully piloted or used Six Sigma – it is also likely that it is ready for Lean or other methodologies like TOC as the culture is already sensitized and supportive of improvements as work ethic

4   Conclusions

After a certain organizational maturity has been assessed via external assessment, few key process improvement areas need to be identified & iteratively improved further, whereas rest of the processes need to be maintained at certain capability. There is need to focus & scope the improvement efforts such that the progress and outcomes are traceable to respective contexts: organization vision, long term mission and short term business objectives by utilizing relevant techniques or methodology.

In summary following are the takeaways for Adaptive process improvement:

- Aligning practices to business objectives, in line with the Senior Management's guidance for strategic direction of the organization
- Choosing right methodology & piloting as well as institutionalizing successful examples
- Managing organizational change – do it early, do it often, communicate across well to sensitize teams about relevance and importance of change
- Allocate appropriate staff and time, Train staff in applicable techniques. Encourage creativity, inclusive participation by recognition of achievements
- Eliminate process variation over & beyond established capability levels, so the improvements are sustained as well as positively progressive

References

1. Handbook for Basic Process Improvement (May 1996)
2. Wang, Y., King, G.: Philosophies and Approaches to Software Process Improvement (EuroSPI 1999) (1999)
3. Various resources on world wide web

Improving Risk Management Practices with Success Driver Analysis

Ernest Wallmüller

Qualität & Informatik
wallmueller@itq.ch

Abstract. In a complex network in Switzerland project risk management and the evaluation of success driver has helped the project leader and key stakeholders to achieve the goals and to quickly find clear improvements. This paper presents the experience with the success driver analysis method, which extends and improves the classical risk management approach and inspires a discussion about potential benefits in complex projects and programs.

Keywords: Success Driver Analysis, Risk Management.

1 Introduction

The case study present the experiences in a large infrastructure project in Switzerland with goal of setting up a new common network with different security zones. More than 630 existing IT services had to be migrated and more than 2700 server systems were affected. The project management model was PRINCE2, altogether more than 450 people were involved.

The project had started in 2008. The actual migration was supposed to start in November 2010 and to be concluded one year later. In early 2011 the crisis occurred, which led to the replacement of the existing risk management. Subsequently, the method of Success Driver Analysis (see [1], [2]) was used to refocus and to re-initiate the project.

The result was that the project could be finished on time and within the agreed scope.

2 Risk Management with Success Drivers

A project is defined as a collection of interrelated work tasks or activities that achieves a specific result. It includes all tasks, policies, procedures, organizations, people, technologies, tools, data, inputs, and outputs required to achieve a specific, predefined set of objectives. Such objectives are often in conflict with each other.

A key objective is a vital outcome intended to be achieved in the future; it provides a benchmark against which success will be judged. Typically the focus lies on product, cost, and schedule, where "product" refers to technical objectives such as the system's functionality and performance characteristics. Focusing solely on such objectives limits the context within which the project outcome is viewed. Further considerations, such as whether the system effectively supports operations and whether people can use and maintain the system, are frequently left out.

The project is subject to constraints. Most prominent are budget, as project management has limited funds at their disposal, and schedule, as delivery date is normally pre-set. Such constraints must be considered alongside the project objectives. They are key factors for management decisions.

2.1 Drivers

A driver is a factor within the project context that has a strong influence on the outcome and the extent the results can be achieved. Each driver is characterized by four attributes.

Table 1. Example of an Attribute Table for a Driver ([1])

Attribute	Description	Example
Name	A concise label that describes the basic nature of the driver	Process
Success State	A driver exerts a positive influence on the outcome	The process being used to develop and deploy the system is sufficient.
Failure State	A driver exerts a negative influence on the outcome	The process being used to develop and deploy the system is insufficient.
Category	The category to which the driver belongs	Preparation

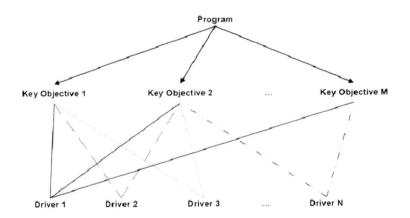

Fig. 1. Relationship between Key Objectives and Drivers ([1])

The two driver states indicate if the project factor under consideration rather drives the project towards reaching its objectives ("success state") or not ("failure state").

There is a set of 20 standard success drivers (see [1]) which can be found in any project, such as e.g. plan, process, requirements or operational preparedness. On top the project's specific nature could give rise to specific drivers, which should be identified and assessed.

The complete set of standard and specific project drivers, or driver profile, indicates where efforts should be concentrated in order to assure the project success, namely on the ones in "failure state".

A risk is a potential event that might occur and jeopardize the project outcome. Tactical risk management is focused on the handling of such threats (see [3], [4]). From the previous section it is clear that risks and success drivers are closely related, since every driver in a "failure state" is an area where risks are hidden. success driver analysis is therefore a tool for the systematic identification of project risks.

3 Application of the Method

In order to assess the project state an initial assessment of the 20 standard drivers was done by different stakeholder groups from both within and outside the project. In a questionnaire each person had to qualify the driver on a 5-level-scale

- Almost certainly in its success state
- Most likely in its success state
- Equally likely in its success or failure states
- Most likely in its failure state
- Almost certainly in its failure state.

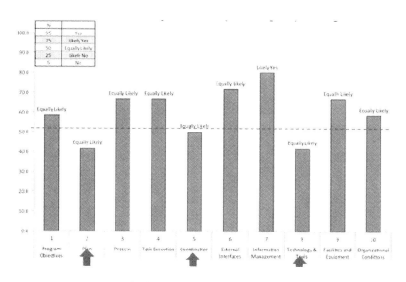

Fig. 2. Initial success driver profile

The combination of the answers has led to the initial success driver profile of Fig. 2. The drivers which a majority has seen to be in a failure state were marked for further investigation on risks: Plan, Coordination and Tools.

The success driver analysis and subsequent risk identification and risk treatment sessions where repeated several times.

4 Conclusions

The usage of a risk management together with a success driver analysis has various advantages. First of all, it is easy to identify which success driver are in success state or in a failure state. The discussion of success driver also triggers common understanding of risks, mitigation actions within project team. It supports the focus on goals and future states to be achieved, which are under the influence of a certain success driver. Another important aspect of this approach is the easiness of reaching an "overall picture" of the situation of a (complex) project. This enables the agreement on measures for improvement.

References

1. Alberts, C.J., Dorofee, A.J.: A Framework for Categorizing Key Drivers of Risk, CMU/SEI-2009-TR-007
2. Alberts, C.J., Dorofee, A.J., Marino, L.: Executive Overview of SEI MOSAIC: Managing for Success Using a Risk-Based Approach, CMU/SEI-2007-TN-008
3. Wallmüller, E.: Software Quality Engineering - Ein Leitfaden für bessere Software-Qualität, Hanser (2011)
4. Wallmüller, E.: Risikomanagement für IT- und Software-Projekte - Ein Leitfaden für die Umsetzung in der Praxis, Hanser (May/June 2004)

Software Engineering Process and Quality Assurance Framework for Automotive Product Engineering Outsourcing

Manfred Schedl[1], Eugene Nebrat[2], and Lyudmila Matveeva[2]

[1] Harman Automotive Division, Ulm, Germany
Manfred.Schedl@harman.com
[2] Luxoft, Automotive Practice, Kyiv, Ukraine
{ENebrat,lmatveeva}@luxoft.com

Abstract. Outsourcing of software development and maintenance is among the most effective ways to cut costs, to get state-of-the-art R&D and engineering solutions without the extra expenses on in-house team developing. Customer and outsourcing service provider have to establish and ensure sufficient and transparent quality assurance framework. This work presents a method to define outsourcing partner's process capability profiles. These profiles constitute quality goals and correspond to business model and projects' specifics.

Keywords: process profile, software development outsourcing, ASPICE standard.

1 Introduction

To sustain margins and market place providers of Automotive Systems and Software have to use global outsourcing models. Today for many businesses it's rather about survival than sustainability. Nowadays, players of Automotive Systems and Software market often face following business issues:

— Major stake of fixed costs is generated by in-house R&D or engineering, and is hard to reduce;
— Market of Automotive electronics and in-vehicle software is being developed rapidly, causing time-to-market expectations to shorten, companies to scale up and down engineering resources very quickly and marketing strategies to consider indeed specific emerging markets.

Issues above could be resolved with further implementation of outsourcing model. This requires handing over parts of product engineering processes considered as core-functions before. Such shift triggers outsourcing quality issue projected to the product, final customer and end user. Outsourcing provider thus steps into the industry specific process environment, and both Customer and Supplier have to define and ensure sufficient and transparent quality assurance framework.

2 Software Process and Quality Assurance Framework as Part of Business Design

Many factors, both generic and automotive specific, influence definition of software engineering processes (SEP) and quality assurance (QA) framework for the mixed in-house and outsourced product engineering environment[1]:

— Chosen outsourcing model (staff augmentation, out-tasking, project based, managed services),
— Customer's process maturity, corporate culture, outsourcing experience, company design and business volume,
— Requirements from final customer (OEM) to provide transparent quality management system through suppliers chain for assessments.

Staff augmentation (AG) model is transparent to assess, but requires Customer to micro-manage Supplier resources, deploy Customer's SEP outside, extend QA service to cover Supplier as well. AG requires significant communications, sensitive to Supplier personnel, creates considerable overheads both management and quality related on Customer side. AG (similar to out-tasking) works well for small or pilot engagements, but has limited efficiency and does not allow leverage quality. We do not consider this engagement.

Managed services are on the opposite extreme, fit well for technology and innovations consulting and joint prospective R&D. On delivery side they are close to direct procurement of finished goods, relay completely on Supplier's quality standards and trust to the partner. Thus, we do not consider this engagement either.

Luxoft experience shows project-based (or managed delivery) as a most efficient model to support wide spectrum from small/medium size Tier 2 technology providers up to big or global Tier 1 automotive solution vendors. Mature sustainable project-based outsourcing product engineering engagement must provide common quality framework to meet following requirements:

— Integrity. Each required practice, process or activity should be explicitly assigned to Customer or/and Supplier.
— Transparency. Whole project setup must allow internal or external assessor to audit the project against chosen quality model and in terms and language of that model.
— Scalability. If required by business, Supplier delivery organization must be able to scale framework without any threat.
— Flexibility. Differences between projects must be organically responded by the framework.

---

[1] While more and more software and system components are "commoditized" and could be purchased directly from niche solution providers, many efforts in automotive projects remain project/platform specific and are purchased as service contracts with outsourcing partners. Here we consider only service contracts.

Luxoft has developed and offers approach to fulfill requirements listed above. Common quality framework has been defined to meet Customer needs, to adapt the software process with respect to projects specificity and in order to assist in the positive projects' outcome.

3 Process Adaptation by Means of Process Capability Profiles

Software engineering process implemented by Luxoft Automotive Practice Delivery Center (AP DC) is based on Automotive SPICE (HIS scope) standard [1]. Each project conducted within AP DC is expected to tailor the organization process to meet the project's particular needs. Tailoring requirements can be sourced from:

— Project goals,
— Statement of Work (SOW) planned for the project,
— Specific Customer's requirements for the project.

ASPICE standard is very generic; it doesn't intend to cover specific context of each project. A project's specific characteristics should be considered in order to establish proper practices. So, Luxoft AP DC process is deployed in the projects with respect to projects process capability profiles. The process profile is two-dimensional goal for a project's process capability, namely it constitutes the process quality goal for the project (example is presented in Fig. 1).

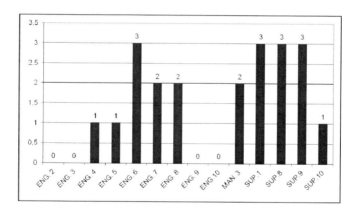

Fig. 1. Example of a project process profiles, along X-axis – ASPICE HIS processes, along Y-axis – process capability levels

Project process profiles are lined up with the specific characteristics of projects driven by end-customer, time, internal customer, constraints, etc. We propose following characteristics that may affect the project process profile preparation or selection:

— scope and purpose of a project,
— life-cycle model,

- restrictions and assumptions,
- commercial model (fix-price, time and material, etc.),
- risk levels.

The process profile is doubled as the tool for process self-assessment in projects. Process self-assessment is a form of internal process quality audit, which is conducted by the Quality Assurance and Process Engineering team. Important function of the process profile diagram here is to ensure the shared vision on what to be evaluated and what should be improved. The profiles development method that assists to obtain process profiles is composed of following main steps.

1. Identify the relevant characteristics of a project, its expected outcomes.
2. Scoping step. Select processes subset applicable for the project. Map the practices and work products of ASPICE HIS according to information related to the identified characteristics. The aim is to analyze the processes to validate the applicability of each base practice and work product for the project. Selected processes form the profile.
3. Scoring step. Define the target capability levels of the selected processes and adjust derived profile to fit projects needs. It is necessary to adjust the levels of capability of each process of the project to suit them a) to business goals of the company and b) to Customer quality requirements for the given project.
4. Review the profile with all relevant stakeholders. Document profile in the project management plan as process quality goal.

The Project Manager is responsible for these steps implementation. Senior manager and the customer representative approve this profile. It is audited regularly if the project team utilizes an approved process to guide software development and/or maintenance, and if the project' quality goal defined by the process profile is achieved.

4 Conclusion

This paper presents the method that can be used to adapt outsourcing partner's software process, which is based on ASPICE standard, relative to projects specificity and in order to assist in the positive projects' outcome. Process capability profile lined up with business model and project's specifics is defined for the project. We will continue to refine the profile development method based on the experience gained in undertaking Luxoft process self-assessments and future external (conducted by Customer) process quality audits.

Reference

1. ISO/IEC 15504-2, Information technology – Process assessment – Performing an Assessment (2003)

Applying Kaizen for Improving Productivity in Automotive Software Projects

Smitha Bhandary, Balaji Ramachandran, and Basavaraj Betageri

Wipro Technologies, Bangalore
{smitha.saikumar,balaji.ramachandran,
basavaraj.betageri}@wipro.com

Abstract. Automotive software industry today is living in an increasingly tougher competitive climate where there is no room for inefficiency. Reducing time to market with improved quality and productivity supported by an efficient process is the need of the hour. To reduce inefficiencies and eliminate waste is a constant challenge faced by the suppliers. Therefore in Automotive software industry any innovative way of streamlining the supply chain which constitutes the OEM, Tier-1and their suppliers is critical for time to market. In this paper we present the actual case study of application of Kaizen in an automotive software project and how it helped improve defect fix productivity.

Keywords: Kaizen, Automotive Software, Case Study.

1 Introduction

Automotive Software Industry today is facing new challenges due to globalization, customization and increased competition. Companies that find new and innovative ways to create value have a fair chance to prosper. New production concepts need to be developed to reduce the cycle time and eliminate waste by reducing inefficiencies. Kaizen philosophy is not new to Automotive Industry as they have been practiced in Japanese Automotive industry for past few decades. Kaizen is small incremental changes made for improving productivity and minimizing waste. Adopting Kaizen helps in the following

- Reduction in waste
- Reduction in cycle time
- Improvement in productivity

2 Background

Kaizen strategy is the single most important concept in Japanese management. Basically Kai means change or actions to correct. Zen means good. Masaaki Imai is known as the developer of Kaizen [1] [3]. The approach is highly result focused. Double it or halve it. Our case study is based on the below two Kaizen principles:

1. Consider the process and the results
2. Look at the entire process of the job at hand and evaluate the job as to identify the best way to get the job done

This process of ongoing or continuous improvement opens up methods to reduce cycle time, reduce inefficiency and increase productivity as mentioned by standards such as Automotive SPICE [2].

3   Case Study

During the project execution the major challenges were that the

1. Defect fix productivity was not on par with customer expectations.
2. Customer was not confident about the ability of the project team to manage the inflow rising out of in-vehicle testing prior to start of production.

The challenge for the project team was to showcase improvements in defect fix productivity within four to six months time to win the customer confidence and to meet the OEM's start of production deadline. Team felt that Kaizen [3] event was best suited for this continuous improvement initiative as it was expected to generate quick measureable results and help the team sustain improvements .The following tenets were decided to be used during the kick off of the 5 day Kaizen event.

Table 1. Kaizen Tenets used

Tenet	Reason for Selection
Value Stream Mapping	To understand as is defect fixing process
Visual Controls	To improve planning and monitoring through visual aids
Knowledge management	To share knowledge among the team

3.1   Value Stream Mapping

Value stream mapping technique [3] was used to identify steps which had no value or was inefficient and could be immediately avoidable. The project applied value stream mapping on the defect fixing life cycle. The entire set of activities of the defect life cycle was examined in detail. Team identified Pre-event time taken for each activity and selected those activities that could be improved. For example the lead time to get the hardware for reproduction of issues (Activity no 5 in the below figure) was easily avoidable by ensuring availability of hardware with the project team. The team then brainstormed to identify new ways of doing the activities in a much more optimal way. The Post- Event time for each selected activity was then clocked. Given below are a few activities selected from the entire set of activities where significant improvements were achieved.

Driver Measure	Pre-Event	Objective	Post-Event	% Improved
Defect fix productivity improvement	2.2 defects / Person Week	3.0 defects / Person week	2.92 defects / Person week	32.7%

#	Impact Measures	Pre-Event	Objective	Post-Event	% Improved
1	Time taken to understand the use case flow in the source code and identify the error scenario in the log	8 hrs	4 hrs	4 hrs	50%
2	Clone/reject the defects which does not belong to Presentation Control Layer	5 hrs	3 hrs	3.2 hrs	36%
3	Reproducing the issue by Wipro	3 hrs	2 hrs	0 hrs	100%
4	Lead time for reproduction of defects by customer QT team	3 days	1 day	0.5 day	83.33%
5	Lead time to the get hardware to reproduce the issues by Wipro team	4 hrs	0 hrs	0 hrs	100%
6	Lead time for code review by onsite team	1 day	2 hrs	1 hrs	87.50%

Fig. 1. Activity List

3.2 Visual Controls

Visual controls were deployed to showcase the following:

1. Top priority defects that were being processed
1. Defect distribution among the each of the modules and their status
2. Monthly recognition of top performers
3. Goal and defects status for each of the modules for the current week

The advantages of using the Visual controls were that the entire team gets to know the alerts and updates visually which results in immediate actions.

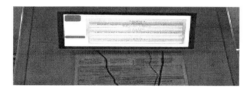

Fig. 2. Visual Control

3.3 Knowledge Management

A knowledge management portal was developed consisting of online training materials, videos and documents. Any new hires could go through the training material. This helped new team members to get started from Day one. Helped in build up and retention of product knowledge by engaging current team in regular trainings by experts

3.4 Benefits

Month on month the defect fix productivity data was measured. After six months it was found that the defect fix productivity increased from 2.2 to 3.5 defects per person week. This helped in gaining the customer confidence and repeat business from the customer. Team morale improved as their suggestions helped in productivity improvements and subsequent recognition from customer.

Table 2. Kaizen Benefits

Month	Defect Fix Productivity	Improvement (%)
Month-1	2.87	30.45
Month-3	2.92	32.73
Month-6	3.50	59

4 Conclusions

In this paper we have presented the experience of application of few Kaizen principles on automotive software projects. By adopting Kaizen, we noticed that overall it reduces waste, improves defect fix productivity, and delivers value.

References

1. Shingo, S.: Kaizen and the Art of Creative Thinking; The Scientific Thinking Mechanism. Hakuto-Shoba Publishing Company, Tokyo
2. Automotive SIG, Automotive SPICE© Process Assessment Model (v2.5) and Process Reference Model (V4.5) (2010)
3. Womack, J.P., Jones, D.T.: Lean Thinking. Banish Waste and Create Wealth in Your Corporation

Best Practices for Achieving Automotive SPICE Capability Level 3

Anna Orecka, Sebastian Dawid, and Rafał Dzianach

Tieto Poland
{Anna.Orecka,Sebastian.Dawid,Rafal.Dzianach}@tieto.com

Abstract. Automotive SPICE is a standard commonly used among car manufacturers all over the world. Many suppliers use it as the means for the process improvement and as a requirement from the clients. This paper will present a case study on the best practices and lessons learnt from the ASPICE implementation up to level three in Tieto Poland. It will deal with such aspects as implementation and lessons learned, deployment of the processes and process improvement.

Keywords: Automotive SPICE, ISO/IEC 15504, Process, Improvement.

1 Introduction

Automotive SPICE is a standard based on ISO/IEC 15504 and is used as a common framework for the assessment of suppliers in the Automotive Industry. For many suppliers it is not only a requirement from their clients, but also a strategy for managing process improvement and assuring successful deliveries. Therefore many companies nowadays strive for a higher capability level. Although some say that for big corporations it should be easier to improve processes, we encountered a lot of challenges on the way to reach Automotive SPICE capability level 3. After almost three years of hard work we are proud with what we achieved and ready to share our observations.

1.1 ASPICE Capability Level 1

What is needed at level 1 (performed process) are work products evidences as outputs of the base practices fulfilment. Although it sounds easy, in fact it might be the most challenging part of working on the processes. It is also the most important step, as without a thorough implementation of level 1, any higher capabilities are unachievable.

Companies implementing level 1 usually have little practical knowledge about SPICE and can face many problems. Our experience shows that at this point it is crucial to underline the importance of the capability development. Engineers might treat it as an overhead, something that does not bring any profit. That is why the team should be made aware that the extra effort spent on assuring work products evidence is not meaningless. They will be more willing to cooperate when they understand "the story" behind it and do not treat quality requirements as enforced.

Since a work product is a key item at this level, it is also very important to develop a well organised document workflow. What might help here could be the assignment of a devoted Configuration Manager to deal with configuration and document workflows. Of course, even the most experienced CM won't be successful if he has no tools. That is why at this moment the management must make a decision about a toolchain. A good tool can take off a lot of burden from the project team focused on satisfying ASPICE requirements. What should be remembered when taking a decision? One of the most important concepts in ASPICE is traceability in all aspects. The changes made to the work products must be recordable, verifiable and traceable - so does the flow between the requirements, implementation and test cases.

On top of that, in the situation of the dynamic growth, organizations should remember to assure that every new team member is trained to work according to the standard and knows the processes in force. The knowledge should be transferred in advance, before the new person starts working in the project. This applies for people new to the whole organization, as well as experienced employees who are just changing a project.

2 ASPICE Capability Level 2

When the organization achieves a performed process, the managed one comes next in line. Earlier on work products evidence was needed, now it is the process evidence that is essential. This means that achievement of the process outcomes is the result of planned and tracked activities, leaving little possibility for coincidence. In our business unit we found useful a bottom-up approach in order to reach capability level 2. Since the performed process is in place, what needs to be done is to write it down. Having done that, the authentic, real-life process description is created. The advantage of such a solution is that in general, no huge change is being introduced to the project.

Of course, it takes time to describe the processes, so another lesson that we learned is: assure the time for process development activities. Although it may seem banal, the organizational issues play an important role in capability development. Who should perform the work? When? What is the effort for that? To answer some of these questions: the work could be done by the so-called process owners who with authorities to propose solutions and introduce them into the living processes. Good practice would be to assign them from the people who do the actual work in the project, who know the process inside-out from their work experience. There are of course shortcomings of such a solution. First of all, the PO's project time is being limited (it must be planned and agreed by the Project Manager). Even with the PM's support there is a risk that the Process Owner will be a subject to what we called "preemption effect" - a situation when a given person has a fixed effort for project work of $x\%$, but in the remaining time they are still doing the project work because it's of higher priority. A lesson learned from that: set up a fixed time for the POs to work on the capability development, assure that they meet in one place all together, so that the information exchange is fast and easy and no one from the "real project" interrupts the capability development work.

Another issue that has already been mentioned in the previous paragraph – there is no process improvement without the management commitment. By management are meant Project Managers as well as business owners. Those groups must actively support quality improvements across the organisation, otherwise it could be difficult to facilitate improvements and process changes.

Last but not least, even the most motivated group of Process Owners will not achieve capability level 2 if they do not know how to do it. Theoretical knowledge may turn out to be insufficient, so the competency of the development team needs to be assured by some training, external or internal.

3 ASPICE Capability Level 3

Finally, after satisfying all previous requirements, level 3 appears on the horizon. What should organisations remember now? First of all, a standard process needs to be defined. A common mistake can be defining too broad a scope. Companies tend to think that if something is "standard" it needs to apply to all possible projects within their business, whereas it is not the case. A standard process can be defined on the basis of the selection of the projects that have something in common, e.g. automotive domain projects.

Once a standard process is defined, the tailoring for the specific projects should be done. Here another common misunderstanding. Tailoring does not mean cutting off. Imagine a chubby lady asking a tailor to redo her dress from the early years when she was fit. Will the tailor make the dress smaller or larger? And then imagine the same lady coming to him after finishing the miracle diet (since it is "miracle" we assume it is successful). What will he do – add the material or cut it down? On this simple example can be seen that tailoring must address the needs of the given process and it can be both: extending and shrinking. And remember - "old habits die hard" – which means that people must be trained from the scope of the new, tailored process.

Another thing that is crucial at level 3 is process data collection and process change management (not to be misunderstood with project change management). Establishing a reliable and systematic change procedure enables easy access to data needed for level 3 process improvement. It is advised to think about this issue from the very beginning of the level 3 implementation, because at the early phases of the standard and tailored process definition most often there are a lot of changes which should be managed and recorded for the future use. In case dedicated actions for change management are not in place there is a risk of a valuable data loss.

Last but not least, something that should be remembered throughout the whole of the capability development cycle is to use the dedicated tools. Water can be boiled on a frying pan but everyone will agree that a kettle is of better use in this case. By analogy, every process can be described in a text editor but is this really a good choice? An alternative to that would be a tool that was designed for process engineering that surely can save the time and nerves spent on achieving Automotive SPICE compliance.

4 Deployment

Every process improvement venture can be decomposed into two phases: development and deployment. One cannot undervalue the meaning of any of them. Managers quite often strive with the reluctance to change among the project team. This might be a huge obstacle when introducing process improvements and implementing ASPICE. One of a theory from the sociology field called "critical mass" could help to overcome the unwillingness for the innovations. It's a theory stating that after achieving a so-called "tipping point", the innovation becomes self-sustaining and does not need special activities to facilitate. In practice, this means that it is enough to persuade to "the new" a specific amount of people to put the change into practice.

In real life this might be done by identifying the "agents of change" group. These must be the project team member with a specific set of character traits. In every group of people there is a spectrum of characters – people reluctant to any change, indifferent and keen on the innovations. It is important to identify the agents of change from the latter. It must be a group who will eagerly and with engagement undergo the change process. On top of that, it is crucial that those agents of change should have authority among the whole team. Most often these would be the more experienced engineers or managers who enjoy respect among others. These features are important because after engaging the members of this group into change process, they should spread their commitment across the organization.

Last question that arises: how could this group be engaged into change process? An example method would be a roll-out of dedicated trainings on the changed procedures/tools and feedback collection. Another idea would be organizing workshops before identifying the change, in order to make the people come up with the idea for improvement themselves. The commitment of the team will be surprisingly high provided that they have an influence on the way the change is being identified and implemented.

5 Summary and Conclusions

The road to Automotive SPICE level 3 is not an easy one. Each level has its own requirements and specifics which should be taken into account when implementing the standard. After going through this road, we identified a couple of lessons learnt and best practices. The main ones are as follows: it's better to describe the reality when writing down the processes and introducing the changes into the projects, not on the paper; commitment of all involved parties is crucial – without it the capability development might face a lot of obstacles; deployment of the processes and changes is as important as their development; tool choice can save a lot of trouble when implementing ASPICE practices, so it is advised to analyze the needs and then selecting a most suitable instrument for development.

Development of the Medi SPICE PRM

Valentine Casey and Fergal McCaffery

Regulated Software Research Group,
Dundalk Institute of Technology & Lero, Dundalk, Co Louth, Ireland
{Val.Casey,Fergal.McCaffery}@dkit.ie

Abstract. As the importance and complexity of medical device software continues to increase there is growing demand for effective process assessment and improvement in this domain. To address this need the Medi SPICE process assessment and improvement model is being developed. Regulatory compliance is both an important and challenging aspect of medical device software development. Particularly as new regulations are being released and existing standards revised due to the attention that software is receiving within the health domain. To comply with these latest developments the Medi SPICE Process Reference Model (PRM) is being developed to conform with ISO/IEC 12207:2008 and the forthcoming release of ISO/IEC 15504-5 (currently under ballot). This paper outlines the development of the Medi SPICE PRM. It also provides details of the schedule for the full release of the Medi SPICE model.

Keywords: Medical Device Software, Software Process Improvement, SPI, ISO/IEC 15504-5:2006, SPICE, ISO/IEC12207:2008, IEC 62304:2006.

1 Introduction

Today software plays a key role in the diagnosis, treatment and care of patients in the healthcare sector. As a result the functionality, complexity and role of medical device software has increased substantially over the last few years. This is acknowledged by the European Union (EU) who in their latest amendment to the Medical Device Directive (MDD) (2007/47/EC) [1] recognize that standalone software can now be classed as an active medical device. As a result of all these changes the complexity of developing medical device software has increased. This is coupled with the necessity to meet the regulatory requirements of the location where the medical device is to be marketed. In the United States the regulatory and approval body is the Food and Drug Administration (FDA). In the EU medical devices must comply with the MDD and receive a CE mark before they can be marketed. To achieve compliance with national regulatory requirements conformance with a number of international standards, technical reports and guidance documents are recommended by the relevant auditing bodies. In addition to the release of new regulations the revision of existing standards and the publication of new guidance documents is ongoing. These include IEC/TR 80002-1:2009 [2], ISO/IEC 12207:2008 [3], FDA guidance regarding medical device data systems [4] FDA draft guidance in relation to mobile applications [5] and EU guidance for the qualification and classification of standalone software MEDDEV 2.1/6 [6].

Despite the regulatory bodies outlining the necessary regulations, standards and guidance documents, no specific methods for performing the required activities to achieve regulatory approval have been provided. In these circumstances medical device organizations have been compliance centric in their approach to software development and there has been very limited adoption of software process improvement within this domain. While previously this was not a vital issue due to the limited proportion of software contained in medical devices, this is no longer the case. There is now a particular requirement for highly effective and efficient software development processes to facilitate medical device software development [7]. To address this need Medi SPICE is currently being developed.

2 Medi SPICE

The objective of Medi SPICE is to provide a software process assessment and improvement model that meets the specific requirements of the medical device domain [7]. The results of a Medi SPICE assessment may be used to indicate the current state of a medical device supplier's software practices in relation to the regulatory requirements of the industry and identify areas for improvement. It may also be used by medical device software organizations to assess and improve their software development processes. Medi SPICE is being developed in line with the requirements of ISO/IEC 15504-2 [8] and contains a PRM and Process Assessment Model (PAM). It also incorporates the requirements of the relevant medical device regulations and standards. IEC 62304:2006 is a key standard for medical device software development and is based on ISO/IEC 12207:1995 [9] AMD 1[10] & AMD 2 [11], as is ISO/IEC 15504-5:2006 [12]. Both IEC 62304 and IEC 15504-5 are currently being revised and as a result of the release of ISO/IEC 12207:2008 the changes it introduced are being incorporated into these revisions. Medi SPICE is also being developed to conform with these changes.

3 The Development of the Medi SPICE PRM

The Medi SPICE PRM is currently under development. It was originally decided to base the structure of Medi SPICE on ISO/IEC 15504-5:2006 and IEC 62304:2006. Given the importance of conformance to the latest standards this approach was reviewed with the release of ISO/IEC 12207:2008. This resulted in the decision to develop the Medi SPICE PRM in line with this standard and the next release of ISO/IEC 15504-5 (currently under ballot). The structure of ISO/IEC 12207:2008 is considerably different from the previous version of the standard. This is the outcome of an extensive revision of ISO/IEC 12207:1995 AMD 1 & AMD 2 which took place in parallel with the revision of ISO/IEC 15288:2002. The focus of ISO/IEC 12207:2008 is no longer just the software engineering processes life cycle it now addresses the system engineering processes as well.

The first step in the development of the Medi SPICE PRM was the selection of relevant processes. In order to achieve this objective two key requirements needed to be consider: 1) provide effective life cycle processes and 2) facilitate conformance to the necessary medical device regulations, standards and guidance documents. The structure of ISO/IEC 12207:2008, and the next release of ISO/IEC 15504-5 were both reviewed in detail. Analysis of the relevant medical device regulations, standards and guidance documents were also undertaken. Based on this work 42 Medi SPICE processes and 15 subprocesses were defined and released for review by interested parties from the SPICE User Group and industry experts. Following their approval the Medi SPICE PRM was structured as follows:

- The System Life Cycle Processes contains:
    - 3 Agreement Processes and 7 Subprocesses;
    - 6 Organizational Project - Enabling Processes and 6 Subprocesses;
    - 7 Project Processes;
    - 10 Technical Processes and 2 Subprocesses.
- The Software Life Cycle Processes contains:
    - 6 Software Implementation Processes;
    - 1 Supplementary Process and 9 Software Support Processes which includes a medical device specific process Hazard Mitigation.

Having defined the structure and processes of the PRM the developers of Medi SPICE were invited to participate in the current revision of IEC 62304. To both assist with the alignment of IEC 62304 with ISO/IEC 12207:2008 and also to provide details to the medical device community of the relationship between IEC 62304 and other medical device standards and guidelines. The decision was also taken that the next release of IEC 62304 will contain a subset of the Medi SPICE PRM.

Work then commenced on the development of the contents of the Medi SPICE PRM processes. The initial focus was on the IEC 62304 relevant processes. In line with the requirements of ISO 15504-2 each process was assigned an ID and name, with a process purpose also being defined. Based on the process purpose outcomes were identified. The purpose and outcomes addressed the requirements for an effective process and those of the medical device standards and regulations. The regulatory aspects were addressed by undertaking a detailed analysis of the standards, regulations and guidance documents with reference to each process. In addition to the normal content of a PRM the Medi SPICE PRM records the source of each outcome and where relevant an outcome is given a safety classification.

4 Current Status

The development of Medi SPICE has been warmly welcomed by the medical device industry and its release is keenly anticipated. The 14 processes which constitute the subset of the Medi SPICE PRM for inclusion in the next release of IEC 62304 have been completed. These are currently being reviewed by interested parties from the SPICE User Group, industry experts and the IEC SC62A JWG3 Standards working group (the IEC 62304 development team). It is planned that this subset of the Medi SPICE PRM will be included in the Appendix of the forthcoming release of IEC 62304. The development of the remaining Medi SPICE PRM processes is currently under way. A draft version of the Medi SPICE PRM is scheduled for released in September 2012. This will be followed by the release of the Medi SPICE PAM by the end of December 2012. The release of the complete Medi SPICE model is planned for January 2013.

Acknowledgments. This research is supported by the Science Foundation Ireland (SFI) Stokes Lectureship Programme, grant number 07/SK/I1299, the SFI Principal Investigator Programme, grant number 08/IN.1/I2030 (the funding of this project was awarded by Science Foundation Ireland under a co-funding initiative by the Irish Government and European Regional Development Fund), and supported in part by Lero - the Irish Software Engineering Research Centre (http://www.lero.ie) grant 10/CE/I1855.

References

1. European Council, Council Directive 2007/47/EC (Amendment). Official Journal of the European Union: Luxembourg (2007)
2. IEC/TR 80002-1:2009, Medical device software Part 1: Guidance on the application of ISO 14971 to medical device software. BSI, London (2009)
3. ISO/IEC 12207:2008, Systems and software engineering - Software life cycle processes. ISO, Geneva (2008)
4. US FDA, 21 CFR Part 880 Medical Devices; Medical Device Data Systems Final Rule. Federal Register 76(31), 8637–8649 (2011)
5. US FDA, Draft Guidance for Industry and Food and Drug Administration Staff Mobile Medical Applications (July 21, 2011),
   http://www.fda.gov/downloads/MedicalDevices/
   DeviceRegulationandGuidance/GuidanceDocuments/UCM263366.pdf
   (accessed February 20, 2012)
6. European Commission, MEDICAL DEVICES: Guidance document- Qualification and Classification of stand alone software (MEDDEV 2.1/6), Brussels, Belgium (2012)
7. Mc Caffery, F., Dorling, A.: Medi SPICE Development. Software Process Maintenance and Evolution: Improvement and Practice Journal 22(4), 255–268 (2010)
8. ISO/IEC 15504-2:2003, Software engineering - Process assessment - Part 2: Performing an assessment. ISO, Geneva (2003)
9. ISO/IEC 12207:1995, Information Technology — Software life Cycle Processes. ISO, Geneva (1995)
10. ISO/IEC 12207:1995/Amd.1, Information Technology — Software life Cycle Processes Amendment 1. ISO, Geneva (2002)
11. ISO/IEC 12207:1995/Amd.2, Information Technology — Software life Cycle Processes Amendment 2. ISO, Geneva (2004)
12. ISO/IEC 15504-5:2006, Information technology - Process Assessment - Part 5: An Exemplar Process Assessment Model. ISO, Geneva (2006)

Concrete, Steel and ISO 15288

Han van Loon

Leistungs Consult GmbH. Switzerland
welcome@lc-stars.com

Abstract. Construction and process life cycle standards were anathema. However in the Netherlands, the ministry responsible for construction of public works, the Rijkswaterstaat, is now specifying ISO standards like ISO 15288 for large infrastructure construction projects. This paper looks at how this is specified and applied, and experience in its use.

1 Background in the Foreground

The construction industry is one of the foundations for a country's well being. It provides the infrastructure upon which all other endeavours build. Without roads, railways and buildings, and even sewage works, society cannot even start to think about commerce, manufacturing and esoteric things like writing software. Construction people think in very concrete terms; e.g. digging holes, building foundations, laying down a road, constructing a bridge or tunnel. The work approach is very item specific, e.g. "what do I need to do to build a bridge?" Even the designers think in terms of the work item, rather than the process of design. Lead designers rely greatly upon accumulated knowledge and experience. Although civil engineers have the civil engineering code - a set of rules and standards for building something, this is very work item specific. The code describes aspects like the sizing of load-bearing beams and columns, what materials to use, etc. So the focus on the work item is in the foreground for any construction project person.

Rijkswaterstaat staff are often civil engineers with in-depth construction experience. They have a world-wide reputation for construction excellence. Projects like the Delta plan on the mouth of the Rhine set world best practice in waterway-estuary construction in the 1980s. The adjustable water barrier construction in the Delta plan is 5 times larger than the Thames barrier in England. The Netherlands government is transforming the Rijkswaterstaat from a construction expert into a construction contract manager. Against this background of item specific work, imposing a process lifecycle standard like ISO 15288 introduces a novel challenge in an industry that has never used process life cycle standards.

2 Best Practice Specification

The Rijkswaterstaat has tendered several highway construction projects in 2011. The two largest projects are for parts of the A-12 and A-15 highways. A-12 runs inland near Utrecht. The A-15 project is a 30 kilometre highway running from Vaanplain, south of Rotterdam, to the new Maasvlakte port in the north sea area of the port of Rotterdam. The highway when completed will consist of 5 road lanes in each direction, a new road bridge and tunnel (Botlek) also 5 lanes wide, multiple crossovers and connections to existing roads and thousand of electrical installations. It will have state of the art signalling and traffic controls.

As part of the request for tender, Rijkswaterstaat has specified thousands of requirements, including several hundred around the management systems of the winning constructor. These range from specifying the use of ISO standards including ISO9001, ISO14400 and ISO15288, to local Health and Occupational Safety standards, and even making the fulfilment of requirements meet SMART (pecific, Measurable, Attainable, Relevant, Timely) criteria. Competing consortia worked 6 to 12 months in the bidding process, which continually refined the tender requirements as well as the tender responses.

3 Leistungs Consult and Enterprise Based Business Design Improvement

Leistungs Consult was involved in helping to define the management system part of the tender response. A-Lanes committed to designing their management system to fully meet the ISO 9001, ISO 14400 and ISO 15288 standards. Leistungs Consult ran workshops with the A-Lanes tender team, which would become part of the core A-15 project management team. Initially the workshops focused on explaining what the ISO 15288 system lifecycle standard meant, and then how it could be applied to the construction industry. For many of the participants this was their first introduction to such a standard, so their level of understanding was low.

Leistungs Consult then worked with A-Lanes persons to define the overall shape and application of the standard to the proposed A-Lanes management system. Due to the nature of the contract, which covers design, build, finance and maintain (so-called DBFM contract), A-Lanes consortia decided to set up 3 companies, one for design, one for construction and one for maintenance. The advantage of this structure is that each company only needs to exist for a specific time, e.g. the design company needs to operate for 4 years, while the maintenance company needs to operate for 20 years, as they will maintain the highway once it is constructed.

The next workshop focused on tailoring the generic process descriptions in the ISO 15288 standard into activities and work products that had real meaning and application for construction industry work. It was agreed to follow Leistung Consult's Enterprise Based Business Design Improvement (EBBDI) method to tailor and deliver the process descriptions and process implementation plans. EBBDI is a design first approach that takes into account the need to later perform process assessment using ISO 15504. This was combined with creating target process profiles using Practical Process Profiles that focussed on reducing risk for A-Lanes and Rijkswaterstaat.

A-Lanes implemented all the required processes within the contract mobilization phase, well ahead of schedule. There has been continual training as the project team ramp-up occurs, with new staff being trained on a regular basis. The team is growing from the 15 core team members to over 300 persons in a period of little over a year.

4 EBBDI Tailoring: Integration and Implementation Process Examples

A-Lanes is the overall engineering company. It designs and specifies how construction work will be performed, but does not do the construction work. The construction work will be contracted using a limited competitive tendering approach among the consortium partners. Therefore the way ISO 15288 specifies the implementation process does not apply per se to A-Lanes. Using EBBDI, this process was tailored together with the Integration process to create a combined project and industry specific process. The process has three main instantiations, one for civil construction (e.g. tunnels, etc.), one for the road construction and one for traffic installations (e.g. signalling, etc.).

To highlight some of the unusual aspects of implementation that a construction industry company faces, one of the process activities includes the removal of bombs found at the work site. Due to the nature of the terrain, which is very soft ground and in places marshy. It is not unusual to find unexploded bombs from the Second World War buried in various parts of the highway corridor. Already one bomb has been unearthed by backhoe. There are specific procedures for disarming and removing bombs, using specialist personnel.

To minimize the possibility of accident due to unexploded bombs, part of the stakeholder requirements definition process includes reaching out to local communities, and particularly older citizens who may remember where bombs dropped. This has already successfully identified and located another two unexploded bombs.

Integration activities include the coordination of the three main work streams, namely roads, civil and traffic installations, as well as coordination with the industrial stakeholder works. For example there are literally hundreds of cable and pipe corridors between port facilities and users such as the Shell refinery. When these adjoin or cross the highway corridor, there needs to be specific integration activities to ensure the corridor constructions are usable 'as is' or moved if needed. Naturally these cannot be damaged or simply ignored as they are usually in operation, so any change requires specific coordination with the affected stakeholders during the construction phases.

5 Example of EBBDI Tailoring: Maintenance Process

The maintenance process takes into account various types of planned highway maintenance, including regular and heavy maintenance. Heavy maintenance is an activity where part of the highway would be closed for a longer period of time, for example in order to re-lay the road surface. Regular maintenance includes work like line marking, servicing of the thousands of electrical installations along the highway (e.g. road lighting, signalling systems, automated toll collection systems for trucks, etc.) and other work that do not require major road closure.

The maintenance process also needs to take into account the work environment – imagine working on the highway as trucks whizz by at 100 kmh! So safety of personnel is paramount. Other aspects include when to work without lane closures; how to divert traffic temporarily using lane closure and lane re-opening coordinated with signalling; getting maintenance vehicles, materials and personnel onsite; all while minimizing traffic disturbance.

The maintenance process will also perform a very significant quantity of measurements, both static and dynamic. Measurement includes the number of vehicles using the highway per day and the types of vehicles and loads; rate of wear on the road surface; using weighing stations on a temporary basis; as well as sophisticated measurement approaches like dynamic weight measurement of trucks travelling on the highway with related road deflection measurement. This latter measurement requires data collection from various sources (e.g. stress sensors built into road structures) as well as remote sensing (e.g. laser tracking of truck movement).

There are contractual requirements on minimizing traffic disturbance, with penalties based upon aspects like traffic delays and reduced traffic capacity at peak versus slack times. It is therefore in A-Lanes interest to minimize traffic disturbance while not compromising safety of maintenance personnel. Based upon the goals of minimizing life cycle cost of maintenance and related risks to this goal, the EBBDI method identified specific activities for the maintenance process and combined with use of Practical Process Profiles specified the required process capability level.

6   Summary and Results

Using the Enterprise Based Business Design Improvement method from Leistungs Consult has allowed A-Lanes to define a management system suitable for a construction industry company and fully meet the requirements of ISO 15288. The method has also allowed A-Lanes to incorporate best practice solutions to project specific challenges (e.g. bomb removal). The ability of A-Lanes to put a management system in place early in the life time of the project has been positively received by the client. A-Lanes are already reaping the rewards of their pro-active definition of the management system in terms of lower risk and the ability to bring new people into the project with a minimum of disturbance and training. Specific process owners are finding that following the process is more efficient and effective than the usual construction industry approach, hence they are seeing savings already, even in the early phases of the project. In particular the maintenance process owner has recognized greater potential for savings in maintenance through using the tailored maintenance process in the design phase of the project.

DEFT – A Test Framework to Aid Decision Making

Gerry Crines, Sarah Salahuddin, and Donald Mackinnon

Lloyds Banking Group,
69 Morrison Street, Edinburgh, EH3 8YF, UK
{gerry.crines,sarah.salahuddin,
donald.mackinnon}@scottishwidows.co.uk

Abstract. Testing can benefit greatly if there are ways to predict the defects that will be detected during a phase of the software development lifecycle and none more so than during the System testing phase itself. There are several examples of defect prediction models in the literature [1]. These have been derived, used and also critically evaluated. However, they are not the easiest to use due to the dependencies on the data and metrics required for these models; as they take into account several variables. This paper describes a **D**efect **E**ffort **F**ix & **T**est (DEFT) framework that was developed to provide an end date for testing for a challenging programme.

Keywords: Software test execution, Defect prediction.

1 Introduction

Testing can only prove the presence of defects [2]; however when there is a greater than expected presence it can start to impact the confidence levels and increase the nervousness about the delivery of the application. Add to this the finite amount of time available and any programme would find itself in a challenging position requiring a Go/No Go decision to be made.

This was the situation that led to the development of the framework described in this paper. The Defect Effort Fix & Test (DEFT) Framework has been developed to aid the main purpose of testing - provide information [3]. The purpose of the DEFT framework is to provide sufficient information to senior management to help them in making a decision. It uses historic data from the project to predict the number of defects expected against the outstanding number of tests along with the expected rate of fixing and results in an indicative end date for the testing.

The framework was developed out of necessity; however, this also generated an interest to explore models that already existed. The defect prediction model developed to feed into the framework was one of the main components that allowed for the objective to be achieved. There is a considerably large literature available that covers numerous software metrics and the statistical models that have been developed. Most of the prediction models use size and complexity metrics to predict defects, whereas others use test data or take a multivariate approach. Our model would fall under the multivariate approach; however, since the framework is in the early stages of development derived from a very small data set, more work is needed to refine it.

The next section describes the DEFT framework and the concluding section summarizes the approach and the further work that is required to refine the framework.

2 The DEFT Framework

This framework was born out of necessity. The testing team was requested to provide a plan for completing the testing but the intention was to run all planned tests at least once. Achieving the original end date seemed highly unlikely, and therefore for a decision to be made regarding the project delivery as part of the last release of the year it was essential for testing team to indicate a date when all tests could be run and passed with most defects fixed. To aid this, it was agreed that the process for arriving at an indicative end date would only take into account critical and high priority defects; and all medium and lows would be deferred. With this steer, we had the challenge to come up with a framework that would provide a plan for test execution, along with predicting the number of critical and high defects and taking into account a predicted rate of fixing. Therefore, the three main inputs to the framework were identified as the defect prediction model, testing effort model and defect fixing model. These models used the numbers from the programme and relied on the data that had already been captured for the 10 weeks of testing of the code being developed.

2.1 Defect Prediction Model

The purpose of the defect prediction model was to provide a number of critical and high defects from the point of running the model to the point of test completion where all tests had been executed. The tables below describe the input parameters and outputs of this model which are required for the framework.

Table 1. Input parameters for the Defect Prediction Model

Ref.	Input Parameter	Value
DIP1	No. of Critical and High (C&H) Defects outstanding	Actual number for the project in testing.
DIP2	No. of Test Scripts still to be executed	Number of documented test scripts not executed.
DIP3	Rate of C&H defect on first execution (%)	Based on the metrics for the project.
DIP4	Rate of C&H defect on retest (%)	
DIP5	Rate of C&H defect on script with defect (%)	
DIP6	No. of C&H defects from exploratory testing	

Table 2. Output for the Defect Prediction Model

Ref.	Output	Value
DOP1	No. of C&H defects from 1st execution	DIP2*DIP3/100
DOP2	No. of C&H defects from defect fixes testing	DIP1*DIP4/100
DOP3	No. of C&H defects from scripts with defects	DIP1*DIP5/100
DOP4	No. of C&H defects from retest of additional defects	(DOP1+DOP2+DOP3+DIP6)*DIP4/100
DOP5	Total no. of C&H predicted defects.	DOP1+DOP2+DOP3+DIP6+DOP4

2.2 Testing Effort Model

The Defect Prediction model is then used to derive the Testing Effort model to calculate the total time required to run all planned tests and complete the re-testing of the defects. The tables below describe the input parameters and outputs of this model, which are required for the framework.

Table 3. Input parameters for the Testing Effort Model

Ref.	Input Parameter	Value
EIP1	Average time required to retest a defect (mins)	Based on the metrics for the project.
EIP2	Average time required to execute a test script (mins)	

Table 4. Output for the Testing Effort Model

Ref.	Output Parameter	Value
EOP1	Time to complete testing of all scripts	DIP2*EIP2
EOP2	Time to retest current C&H defect fixes	DP1*EIP1
EOP3	Time to retest additional C&H defect fixes	DOP5*EIP1
EOP4	Contingency	As appropriate
EOP4	Total time required to complete the testing	EOP1+EOP2+EOP3+EOP4

The Output of the model is Total time required for the testing. This effort model is then mapped across to a day by day projection taking into account the rate of defect fixing so that an end date for testing can be obtained with minimal outstanding critical and high defects.

2.3 Defect Fixing Model

To derive the effort required for fixing the defects being reported by the testing team, a classification was needed for these defects. This was based on classifying defects by functional areas and complexity. For each functional area and the associated complexity the effort to fix defects was estimated. The second input was the effort available in terms of man hours taking into account evening and weekend working options. This model is then used to provide a delivery schedule for delivery of fixes for defects into testing which is an input for the combined test execution and completion schedule.

Table 5. Input parameters for the Defect Fixing Model

Ref.	Input Parameter	Value
FIP1	New defects predicted	DOP5
FIP2	Effort required to fix a defect by complexity and functional area (days)	Classification for complexity and functional area based on the project metrics.
FIP3	Effort available taking into account evening and weekend working options	Based on the availability of resources, holidays and their project allocations.

Table 6. Output for the Defect Fixing Model

Ref.	Output	Value
FOP1	Total effort required to fix the defects	Obtained using FIP1, FIP2 and FIP3

2.4 Test Schedule to Completion

The outputs obtained from the three models above are used to populate the test schedule to completion to show when testing can be completed dependent on when the outstanding number of defects approaches zero. The test schedule monitors the planned versus actual numbers for tests execution each day, the number of defects being fixed and new defects predicted against the execution. As the testing progresses the aim is to execute all outstanding tests and retest the defects found. Under the circumstances in which the model was developed the first iteration of this model allowed a detailed conversation with senior management where additional options of resource stretch were considered to bring the schedule in. The model was then revised using real project metrics to adjust variables to be ready to fix defects quicker and accelerate the test execution process.

3 Conclusion

While the Framework served its purpose and was successful in achieving the immediate objectives of the programme, more work needs to be done to adopt its use widely.

Developing this framework was indeed a challenge; however, it also highlighted the importance of capturing relevant data during test execution and how it could be used to predict future trends and assist in providing input to decision making. It would now be useful to extend this framework formally and evaluate the models more rigorously to provide a more robust yet flexible framework to be used across various testing phases.

References

1. Fenton, N.E., Neil, M.: A Critique of Software Defect Prediction Models. IEEE Transactions on Software Engineering 25(5), 675–689 (1999)
2. Dijkstra, E.W.: Notes on Structured Programming. Academic Press, London (1972)
3. Wienberg, G.: Perfect Software: And Other Illusions about Testing (2008) ISBN 0932633692

Evaluating Management Sentiment towards ISO/IEC 29110 in Very Small Software Development Companies

Rory V. O'Connor[1,2]

[1] School of Computing, Dublin City University, Ireland
[2] Lero, the Irish Software Engineering Research Centre, Ireland
roconnor@computing.dcu.ie

Abstract. This paper presents the results of a set of interviews with senior management in a series of very small software development companies, which were conducted to gauge their opinion, attitude and sentiment towards the of new standard, ISO/IEC 29110 Life Cycle Profiles for Very Small Entities (VSEs). This paper serves as a roadmap for both researchers wishing to understand the issues of process standards adoption by very small companies and also for the software process standards community.

Keywords: SPI, VSE, process standards, ISO/IEC 29110.

1 Introduction

Very Small Entities (VSEs) - *an enterprise, organization, department or project having up to 25 people* - [1] have unique characteristics, which make their business styles different to SMEs. Their constraints in financial and resource terms impact on process infrastructures such as limited training allocation, limited allocation in performing process improvement and may other constraints. Moreover due to the small number of people employed most of the management processes are performed through an informal way and less documented manner [2].

A new process lifecycle standard has been developed by ISO/IEC JTC1/SC7 known as ISO/IEC 29110 "Lifecycle profiles for Very Small Entities" [3]. This is aimed at addressing the specific needs of VSEs [4]. The overall objective of this new standard is to assist and encourage small software organization in assessing and improving their software process and it is predicted that this new standard could encourage and assist small software companies in assessing their software development process. The approach [5] used to develop ISO/IEC 29110 started with the pre-existing international standards ISO/IEC 12207 and ISO/IEC 15504.

This paper is concerned with understanding VSEs issues regarding the adoption of process lifecycle standards, their needs from process lifecycle standards and their willingness to engage with the new published ISO/IEC 29110 standards' in particular. To this end we are interested in eliciting from senior management of VSEs their opinion, attitude and sentiment towards the potential introduction ISO/IEC 29110 in their organization.

2 The Research Process

The context for this research has limited in scope to software product companies whose primary business is software development and for practical purposes was also confined the to the Irish geographical region. A total of ten VSEs participated in this study, with individuals holding job titles such as CEO, COO, Managing Director, and Managing Partner, where nine the participants was also the owner or co-owner of the company.

A semi-structured interview approach consisting of both open-ended and specific questions was used in this study in order to discuss the topics in depth and to get respondents' candid discussion on the topic. The qualitative contents analysis method of Grounded Theory [6] data coding process was employed to analyse all collected data in a manner. The main code categories are show in figure 1 and the findings discussed in section 3.

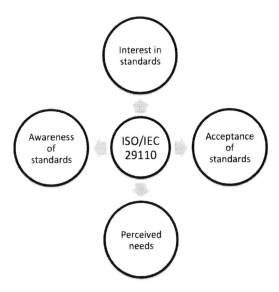

Fig. 1. Study Core Categories

3 Study Findings

In terms of *acceptance of standards* among VSEs, none of the VSEs are or have plans to adopt any particular standard in their software development process. Interview data analysis identified several reasons, which have been divided to 2 subcategories *Low Acceptance* and *Low Priority*. Low acceptance issues were predominately due the perception that process standards are overly complicated, lacking in detailed implementation guidance and would require additional [unavailable] resources.

Participants also believed that the processes as generally described in software standards are not easy to actually tailor and implement in their organizations. In addition, the analysis also indicates that the lack of requirement from the market in general and their customer in particular has contributed to low acceptance of such standards. Examples of interviewee opinion illustrating these would be: *"In a company of our size they [standards] would not necessarily add value... we would only need more sophisticated process if we were a larger company"* and *"Our developers are busy with coding, we don't have resources to do that [standards compliance]"*.

The interview analysis indicated that a software lifecycle standard is *a low priority* issue for multiple reasons including: low to no demand for standards compliance from clients; the view of standards as a 'sales tool' only; and the perception that the software lifecycle standards are designed for the big companies rather than for VSEs. Examples of interviewee opinion exemplifying this includes: *"We had never had a problem selling our stuff or not selling our stuff because we don't follow an ISO standard"* and *"I think a lot of process in quality standard are nonsense. Some standards tell you to do XYZ steps but they are not beneficial to our business"*.

Two related major categories are the level of *interest in standards* and *awareness of standards*. These explain VSEs level of interest and awareness regarding software lifecycle standards and ISO/IEC 29110 in particular. Even though VSEs have shown low acceptance and priority level regarding standards, our analysis has also shown that there is an indicator that VSEs are interested and are aware about software process and quality standards and the potential benefits from having a quality standard, and in particular ISO accreditation. Leading to a quality product, creating consistency, improving company image, creating consistency in development work, improving work process and 'good for business' are the main points that the interviewees gave about the potential benefits of standards compliance. Supporting interview extracts from one company is: *"It would be great to have them [standards accreditation] in order to have a consistent process up and running that can always be relied on"*; and another quote from a VSE about to enter into a period of planned growth *"We need to put those processes in place so when grow, we have a good platform upon which to sustain the growth and train people in what we do"*.

Finally, in order to understand more about VSEs *perceived needs* from lifecycle standards, we asked the interviewees the criteria they considered important in a software lifecycle standard. The main criteria were:

- Align with current development process style
- Provide detailed guidelines and assistances
- Provide clear templates
- Provide workshop and/or training on how to actually apply it

In lightweight process subcategory, interviewees have proposed several criteria as:

- Minimum documentation requirement
- Easy to administer

- Less change from current development process
- Minimum overhead in terms of cost and resources

In business and technical process subcategory, interviewees have proposed several criteria below:

- Align with company existing business and development process.
- Align with others specific software technical standard and process.

4 Conclusions

As we discussed above, the standards issues in VSEs can be divided into 3 categories: *interest*, *awareness* and *acceptance* of process lifecycle standards. Our detailed interview analysis revealed that the acceptance level of any type or model of software quality or lifecycle standard in VSEs is a very low priority item, but the level of awareness of standards and potential benefits was high.

The study showed the main reason for not adopting standards was a lack customer requirement, a lack of resources and the perceived difficulties in defining an organizational process. Furthermore, our analysis reveals a pattern that indicates that the acceptance level of quality standard such as ISO among VSEs are still low even though the staff and management are knowledgeable and aware the benefit of adopting such standards. The main reasons are more related to the lack of the customer requirement and the limited resources in the company. In addition the perception a heavyweight process especially in terms of documentation, cost and non-alignment with current development process are among the reasons why the companies did not plan to adopt a lifecycle standard in the short to medium term. However from the analysis, VSEs may still be interested in lifecycle standards if certain important criteria are met and such standards are closely related to their needs.

Acknowledgments. This work is supported, in part, by Science Foundation Ireland grant 03/CE2/I303_1 to Lero, the Irish Software Engineering Research Centre (www.lero.ie).

References

1. Laporte, C.Y., Alexandre, S., O'Connor, R.: A Software Engineering Lifecycle Standard for Very Small Enterprises. In: O'Connor, R.V., Baddoo, N., Smolander, K., Messnarz, R. (eds.) EuroSPI 2008. CCIS, vol. 16, pp. 129–141. Springer, Heidelberg (2008)
2. O'Connor, R.V., Basri, S., Coleman, G.: Exploring Managerial Commitment towards SPI in Small and Very Small Enterprises. In: Riel, A., O'Connor, R., Tichkiewitch, S., Messnarz, R. (eds.) EuroSPI 2010. CCIS, vol. 99, pp. 268–279. Springer, Heidelberg (2010)
3. International Organization for Standardization (ISO): ISO/IEC TR 29110-5-1-2 Software Engineering - Lifecycle Profiles for Very Small Entities (VSEs) – Management and Engineering guide: Generic profile group: Basic Profile, Geneva (2011)

4. O'Connor, R.V., Laporte, C.Y.: Deploying Lifecycle Profiles for Very Small Entities: An Early Stage Industry View. In: O'Connor, R.V., Rout, T., McCaffery, F., Dorling, A. (eds.) SPICE 2011. CCIS, vol. 155, pp. 227–230. Springer, Heidelberg (2011)
5. O'Connor, R.V., Laporte, C.Y.: Using ISO/IEC 29110 to Harness Process Improvement in Very Small Entities. In: O'Connor, R.V., Pries-Heje, J., Messnarz, R. (eds.) EuroSPI 2011. CCIS, vol. 172, pp. 225–235. Springer, Heidelberg (2011)
6. Coleman, G., O'Connor, R.: Using grounded theory to understand software process improvement: A study of Irish software product companies. Journal of Information and Software Technology 49(6), 531–694 (2007)

Using Process Assessment Models Based on Multiple Process Reference Models in a Capability Determination Context

Terry Rout

Software Quality Institute, Griffith University, Queensland, Australia
T.Rout@griffith.edu.au

Abstract. Two cases are presented where the use of Process Assessment Models based on multiple Process Reference Models was found to be successful. It is suggested that this approach can be of particular help when the purpose of the assessment involves the determination of process-related risk – Process Capability Determination.

Keywords: Process assessment, ISO/IEC 15504, Process capability determination.

1 Introduction

ISO/IEC 15504 [1] defines an approach to Process Assessment where the capability of processes implemented in an organization is assessed by comparing objective evidence collected in the organization to indicators of performance and capability specified in a Process Assessment Model. The Process Assessment Model is based on an appropriate Process Reference Model, which contains the definitions of the process entities to be assessed, in combination with a specified framework for measurement of process capability, based on a series of defined Levels of Capability.

The Standard contains provisions for Process Assessment Models to be based upon multiple different Process Reference Models, but there have been few reports on the application of this flexibility. This report provides information on the development of an Assessment Model based on multiple Reference Models, and its application in the context of Process Capability Determination [2].

2 Case Study

The context for this assessment was the determination of comparative risks associated with two different options for the development and delivery of a suite of services in a large government organization. Units within the organization were involved with both development and delivery of the services, and it was clear that a simple assessment of service management capability alone would not suffice; in addition, it became clear, in the initial scoping of the exercise, that governance issues were of considerable importance, and were not adequately covered by the process models most commonly available.

Following detailed discussions with the sponsoring organization, and with representatives of the units subject to the assessment, the Process Scope for the assessment was determined. It was decided initially to combine processes from two available Assessment Models – ISO/IEC 15504-5 (Software Life Cycle Processes) [3], and the Committee Draft version of ISO/IEC 15504-8 (IT Service Management) [5]. Having regard to the management practices in the organization to be assessed, it was decided that the bulk of the management and support processes to be evaluated would be drawn from ISO/IEC 15504-5. However, the processes for budgeting and business relationship management were taken from ISO/IEC 15504-8. Core engineering processes came form ISO/IEC 15504-5; fundamental service management processes from ISO/IEC 15504-8. The process scope initially determined for the assessment thus comprised the following processes:

ISO/IEC 15504-5
> ENG.1 Requirements elicitation
> ENG.3 Systems architectural design
> ENG.9 Systems integration
> ENG.10 Systems testing
> SPL.3 Product acceptance
> MAN.3 Project management
> MAN.5 Risk management
> SUP.8 Configuration management
> SUP.9 Problem resolution management
> SUP.10 Change request management

ISO/IEC 15504-8 (PDTR)
> 5.2 Budgeting and accounting of IT services
> 5.3 Business relationship management
> 5.9 Incident management and request fulfillment
> 5.16 Release and deployment management
> 5.24 Service transition

Review of this draft scope with the organization identified the issue (mentioned above) relating to the need to address overall governance. This was resolved by selecting a suitable process from the Val IT model – Investment Management [6]. It was necessary to construct a Reference Model definition for this process from the content of the Val IT document, and to identify assessment indicators consistent with those employed in the ISO/IEC 15504 models. The full process scope for the assessment this covered 16 processes, drawn from 3 different process models.

The Capability Dimension scope for the assessment was determined by examining the levels of potential risk broadly across the organization. Major management processes were scoped to Capability Level 3; the remainder of the scope was to Capability Level 2.

The assessment was conducted following the requirements of ISO/IEC 15504-2, and ratings of Process Attribute Achievement were determined for all processes. There were few significant issues in the conduct of the assessment, as the wording of the Practice Indicators were generally consistent. Managing the Work Product indicators was more complex, as the classification scheme was different in the two principal models (15504-5 and 15504-8); the complexity was however manageable.

Application of the Capability Determination approach defined in ISO/IEC 15504-4 proved highly successful in identifying potential risks associated with the two proposed strategies, and enabled clear and justified recommendations to be provided. The overall results of the assessment were regarded as highly successful by the Sponsor.

3 Further Application

Since the conduct of this exercise, a draft Process Assessment Model has become available as part of COBIT V4.1 [7]. In a separate exercise to the principal one

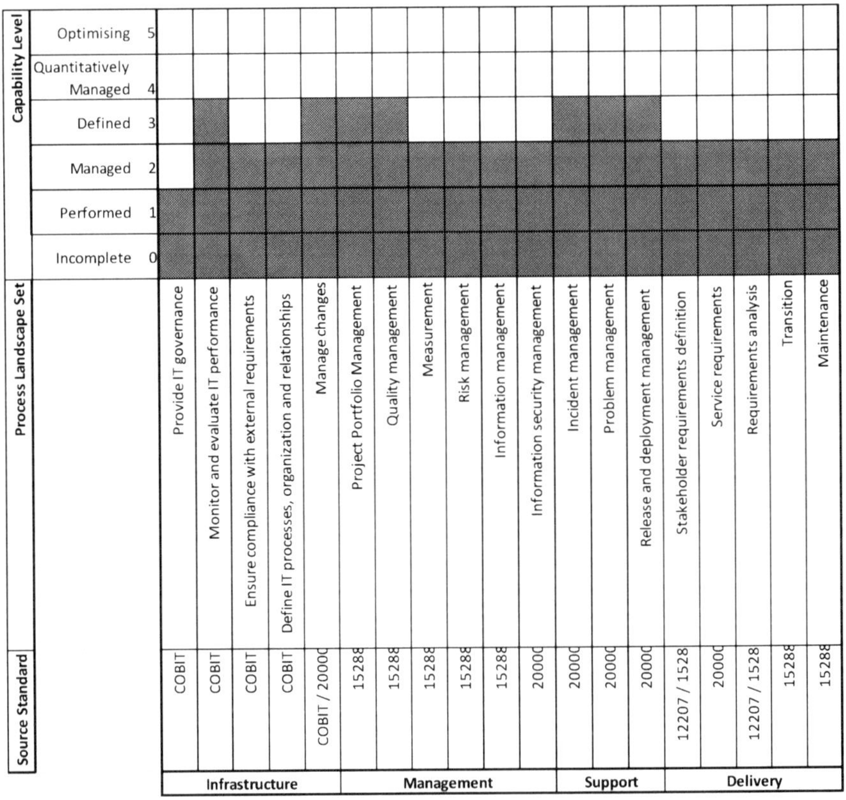

Fig. 1. Target Process Profile, Organization B

described above, a Target Profile was determined for risk management purposes in another organization; on this occasion, processes from four separate models were chosen – System Life Cycle processes (drawn from ISO/IEC 15504-6 [4]) were seen as relevant, and COBIT replaced Val IT as a source of governance content. A target profile covering 19 processes was defined, and is shown above, in Figure 1.

At this stage, the assessment for this organization has not been completed; however, the determination of Process Scope again showed the value, in addressing the Sponsor's concerns, of being able to employ multiple different process models.

It is suggested that in the revision of ISO/IEC 15504 (as ISO/IEC 330xx) the assessment framework should facilitate the use of multiple models in a single assessment, particularly where the determination of process-related risk is an aim for the assessment.

References

1. ISO/IEC 15504-2: Information technology – Process assessment – Part 2: Performing an assessment (2003)
2. ISO/IEC 15504-4: Information technology – Process assessment – Part 4: Guidance on use for process improvement and process capability determination (2004)
3. ISO/IEC 15504-5: Information technology – Process assessment – Part 5: An exemplar Process Assessment Model (2008)
4. ISO/IEC 15504-6: Information technology – Process assessment – Part 6: An exemplar system life cycle process assessment model (2008)
5. ISO/IEC 15504-8: Information technology – Process assessment – Part 8: An exemplar process assessment model for IT service management (2008)
6. IT Governance Institute, Enterprise value: Governance of IT Investments – The Val IT Framework 2.0 (2008)
7. ISACA, COBIT Process Assessment Model (PAM), Using COBIT 4.1 (2011)

Using Target Process Profiles in the Real World

Han van Loon

Leistungs Consult GmbH, Switzerland
Reijer v.d. Eijk, A-Lanes-A15, Netherlands
welcome@lc-stars.com

Abstract. In 2011, ISO TS 15504 part 9 was published after over three years of standardization work. How does using it look like in reality? This paper looks at real application in the construction industry of Target Process Profiles using the Practical Process Profiles method of Leistungs Consult.

Keywords: Target Process Profile, Practical Process Profile.

1 Setting the Scene

The Dutch ministry responsible for construction projects, the Rijkswaterstaat, has adopted a new approach to construction projects. This includes a shift from performing projects themselves to assessing project performance. The winning construction consortia are now responsible for design, build, finance and maintenance, commonly referred to as a DBFM contract.

The largest contract awarded to date went to A-Lanes, a consortium of finance and construction companies. This is for the A-15 highway in the port of Rotterdam for a highway of 5 lanes in each direction. The A-15 weaves its way through mostly industrial areas. It needs to handle the massive amounts of heavy freight transport originating and ending at the port of Rotterdam. The level of project complexity is high.

2 Laying the Foundations

During the tendering process, Rijkswaterstaat specified thousands of requirements. This is necessary for such a complex project but also increases project risk due to the amount of details that have to be handled.

One requirement is that the winning consortium had to have a management system that met multiple ISO standards including ISO9001, ISO14400 and ISO 15288. Another was that the management system would need to reach increasing levels of process capability over time.

Leistungs Consult worked with the consortium team during the tendering and proposal stages with the goal to optimize the management system approach. As part of this cooperation, it became clear that setting a set of target process profiles could help reduce risk. A-Lanes agreed to use Leistungs Consult's Practical Process Profiles method to set the target process profiles.

3 What Are Target Process Profiles?

According to the standard, a Target Process Profile provides a desired target for the purpose of selecting suppliers for specific projects, programmes and product types, and for targeting improvement of processes to meet defined business needs. The application is called risk based process capability optimization in the diagram.

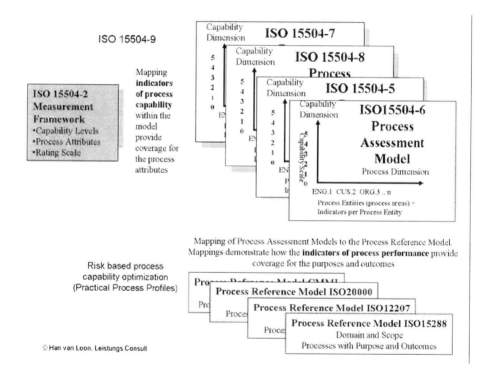

4 The Practical Process Profiles Method

Leistungs Consult created a fully compliant method for creating target process profiles called Practical Process Profiles. In brief the method, defines a set of target process profiles, in the following steps:

- Define the purpose of the target process profile = improvement target to reduce process related risk
- Select the community of use = A-Lanes consortium
- Define the business requirements = construction project management

- Define the domain of application = ISO15288 oriented management system
- Define categories for the domain of application = single management category
- Define target process profile factors used to convert the intended use into process attributes = project risk
- Define criteria for data and information collection = individual and collective risk analysis
- Select business processes and practices, PRM and PAM = ISO 15288, ISO 15504-6
- Define target process profile output content and format = risk oriented profiles
- Define target capability statement = set of target process profiles and management system application related to risk reduction.

5 The Result – Lower Risk and Reduced Costs

A-Lanes demonstrated during the tender proposal phase that they could offer a superior management system than competing consortia. This was one of the main differentiators that led to winning the A-15 contract.

A-Lanes have implemented the management system with the guidance of Leistungs Consult. It is focussed on the proceses that bring the most benefit in terms of project performnce and reduced risk.

A-Lanes successfully achieved the required Rijkswaterstaat capability determination process assessment result three months before scheduled in 2011. In fact, A-Lanes exceeded the required target capability for the assessment. Rijkswaterstaat has a high level of confidence that A-Lanes has a superior management system in place.

More importantly, A-Lanes has already started reaping benefits in term of reduced risks and an associated reduction in the cost of managing the A-15 project.

Agile Maturity Model: Oxymoron or the Next Level of Understanding

Tomas Schweigert[1], Risto Nevalainen[2], Detlef Vohwinkel[1],
Morten Korsaa[3], and Miklos Biro[4]

[1] SQS Cologne, Germany
tomas.schweigert@sqs.com, Detlef.vohwinkel@sqs.com
[2] FiSMA (Finnish Software Measurement Association), Helsinki, Finland
risto.nevalainen@fisma.fi
[3] Delta, Copenhagen, Denmark
MKO@delta.dk
[4] Software Competence Center Hagenberg GmbH, Hagenberg, Austria
miklos.biro@scch.at

Abstract. From the agile camp you can hear someone to say that CMMI is the big American waterfall model monster, and is outright contra productive to agile methods. From the CMMI camp you can hear someone to say that agile methods is hackers from hell that uses the agile paradigm to enjoy anarchy with no rules. You can also hear some say that agile works the best in CMMI level 5 companies. The context of the dilemma however is slightly awkward. CMMI describes characteristics of good development practices, and agile is a lifecycle concept. So from a meta point of view they can easily co-exist. We would like to state that they do, and that you need both to support the best development performance. Starting in December 2011 three surveys were launched to get an idea about what could an agile maturity model deliver and what might be its added value. 67 Participants from several agile or/and CMMI® related LinkedIn Groups contributed to the survey. This article explains the survey results and proposes further research topics and harmonization actions.

Keywords: Agile, CMMI, Maturity models.

1 The Current Discussion of Agile Maturity Models

There are several types of agile maturity models published in the Internet. There are also some principle thoughts about agile maturity published. The discussion is somehow influenced from ideas of the CMMI® Model. So it seems to be adequate to group the published agile maturity models in those who are close to the level structure of CMMI, those who have a level structure and those who don't use explicit levels.

Here is a list of some proposed staged models that are close to CMMI (CMMI influenced models):

CMMI (1)	Initial	Managed	Defined	Quantitatively managed	Optimising
Patels (9)	Initial	Explored	Defined	Improved	Sustained
Anderson (3)	Analysis Ability	End to End Traceability	Stabilize System Metrics	System thinking and a learning organization	Anticipated ROI and the Failure tolerant Organization
Humble & Russell (6)	Regressive	Repeatable	Consistent	Quantitatively managed	Optimizing

A different than CMMI but level based or staged approach is in many proposed agility value driven Maturity Models. Here some examples:

Ambler (2)		Rhetorical stage	Certified stage	Plausible stage	Respectable stage	Measured stage
Proulx (10)		Team Level Maturity	Department Level Maturity	Business Level Maturity	Project Management Level Maturity	Management Level Maturity
Jarajay (7)	Regressive	Neutral or Chaotic	Collaborative	Operating	Adaptive	Innovating
Benefields (5)		Emergent Engineering Best Practices	Continuous Practices at Component Level	Cross Component Continuous Integration	Cross Journey Continuous Integration	On Demand Just in Time Releases

These Agile Maturity Models use maturity levels. But even if they use the level names of CMMI their content is different. To analyze the detailed structure of these models will be a future research task.

A large number of experts propose an agile model or set of principles that have individual structures. Some of them might also be considered as collections of requirements for agile software development. In this article we do not present them, because they are very different. The world of software engineering has always had a large number of collections, and agile world does not make an exception.

2 Results of the Agile Maturity Model Survey

The survey done by Tomas Schweigert was aimed to analyze the thinking about some base principles of agile maturity. There are some other surveys that address a more technical perspective. The questions of the survey were asked as follows:

- Do you think an "Agile Maturity Model" makes sense at all?
- What do you think should be the main focus of an agile maturity model?
- What do you think could be possible sources for an agile maturity model?
- What you think about the Agile Manifesto?
- What is the best approach to manage multiple agile teams?
- If an organisation undergoes an audit/appraisal/assessment what should be the main focus?
- Please give a first global opinion about Agile Maturity Models
- Considering, that each Agile Maturity Model might have a roadmap: Which roadmap to agile maturity would you prefer:
- Thinking at a reference model for Agile Maturity: How should it be defined?
- What would the best thing to use an Agile Maturity Approach for?
- What would be the best frequency of Agile Maturity Assessments?
- What would be the best approach for Agile Maturity Improvement?

In this section we show survey results of some selected questions. The whole survey will be documented also separately as a technical paper.

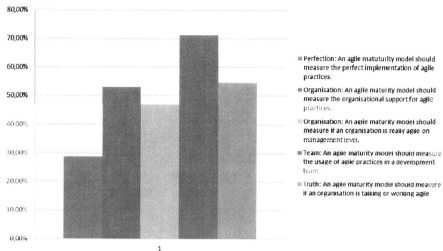

What do you think should be the main focus of an agile maturity model?

- Perfection: An agile matuturity model should measure the perfect implementation of agile practices.
- Organisation: An agile maturity model should measure the organisational support for agile practices.
- Organisation: An agile maturity model should measure if an organisation is really agile on management level.
- Team: An agile maturity model should measure the usage of agile practices in a development team.
- Truth: An agile maturity model should measure if an organisation is talking or working agile.

The result shows that there is only a little support for using the agile maturity approach for measuring agile perfection All currently described Agile Maturity Models describe new capability or maturity levels. But most of the participants think that the Agile Manifesto contains an implementation guideline for common development processes.

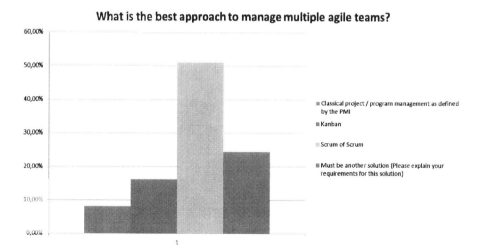

What is the best approach to manage multiple agile teams?

- Classical project / program management as defined by the PMI
- Kanban
- Scrum of Scrum
- Must be another solution (Please explain your requirements for this solution)

There is a substantial need for a new idea how to manage multiple agile teams.

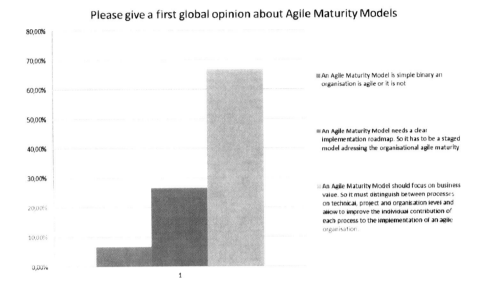

As expected most of the participants state that an Agile Maturity Model must focus on delivery of business value. But even is if this is one of the core principles of the SPI Manifesto the SPI Manifesto is not known in the agile community.

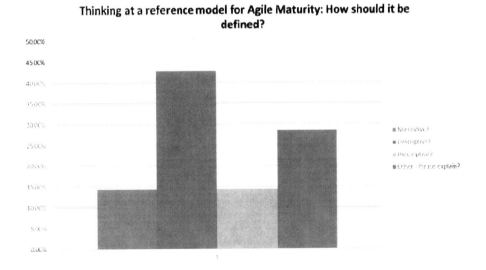

Most of the participants prefer a descriptive model.

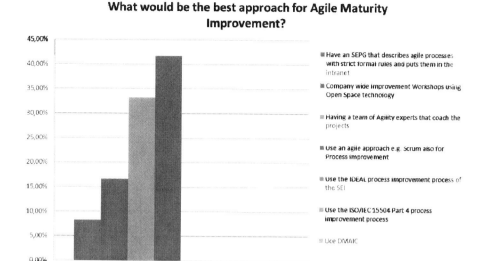

As we can see, there is complete ignorance of all experience of process improvement models in the agile community.

3 Conclusions

Currently we cannot find a common accepted Agile Maturity Model. Similar to the beginning of SPICE and BOOTSTRAP (8), there are lots of incomparable models in the market.

To prepare a commonly accepted Agile Maturity Model, some intensive research has to be done. There are estimated about 500 Outcomes in all the models mentioned at chapter 1 and about 50 outcomes that have common relevance. We also see a multidimensional ground model. It will cost some effort to make agile maturity to something that is explainable to the management.

An important question is then what value a specific agile maturity model will bring to the community. The alternative roadmap would be to improve existing SPICE and CMMI models to focus on the characteristics of good agile practices, and cover those inside the established process framework.

The question is also who should perform the Agile Maturity Model Assessments? Gurus, understanding only one model that is incomparable to the rest of the world or trained certified and experienced assessors, who are used to deal with different reference and assessment models?

References

1. CMMI Product Team. CMMI for development, version 1.3. Software Engineering Institute, CMU/SEI- TR-2010- 033, Pittsburgh, PA, USA (2010)

2. Ambler, S.: The Agile Maturity Model (AMM) (web publishing),
http://drdobbs.com/architecture-and-design/224201005
3. Anderson, D.J.: Agile Management for Software Engineering, Applying the theory of constraints for business results. Prentice Hall (2004) (web publishing)
4. Banerjee, U.: Agile Maturity Model – Three Different Approaches (web publishing)
5. Benefield, R.: Seven Dimensions of Agile Maturity in the Global Enterprise: A Case Study. In: Proceedings of the 43rd Hawaii International Conference on System Sciences – 2010 (2010) (web publishing)
6. Humble, J., Russell, R.: The Agile Maturity Model Applied to Building and Releasing Software. ThoughtWorks White Paper (web publishing)
7. Jayaraj, S.: The Agile Maturity Model (web Publishing)
8. Kuvaja, P., Simila, J., Krzanik, L., Bicego, A., Saukkonen, S., Koch, G.: Software Process Assessment & Improvement, The BOOTSTRAP Approach. Blackwell, Oxford (1994)
9. Patel, C., Ramachandran, M.: Agile Maturity Model (AMM): A Software Process Improvement framework for Agile Software Development Practices. Int. J. of Software Engineering, IJSE 2(1), 3–28 (2009)
10. Proulx, M.: Yet Another Agile Maturity Model (AMM) – The 5 Levels of Maturity (web publishing)

The Gamification of SPICE

Alec Dorling[1] and Fergal McCaffery[2]

[2] Regulated Software Research Group,
Dundalk Institute of Technology & Lero, Dundalk, Co Louth, Ireland
[1] Volvo Group, Goteborg, Sweden and Impronova AB, Lindome, Sweden
Fergal.McCaffery@dkit.ie,
alec.dorling@impronova.com

Abstract. Process Improvement has been used for decades as a means to become better and more efficient. Whilst many organizations have used considerable resources for process improvement, investments in process improvement have not always led to changes and improvements expected. One most important aspects of management is to motivate the work force. However, management often fails to deliver. In fact, because management often uses extrinsic incentives to motivate their work force, it often ends up decreasing people's intrinsic motivation to work. The transformational moment has arrived where we need to re-think the traditional ways to foster engagement in process improvement. Gamification offers a solution for transformational change. By using game psychology and the principles of gamification it is possible to translate the traditional enthusiasm for play and social media engagement into the workplace as a basis for both succeeding with and accelerating the uptake of improvement. Gamification as a solution offers the opportunity for better user engagement, faster feedback of achievement and more visible progress indicators of process improvement.

Keywords: Gamification, Game Mechanics, Engagement, Software Process Improvement, SPI, SPICE, ISO/IEC 15504.

1 Introduction

Process Improvement has been used for decades as a means to become better and more efficient. Whilst many organizations have used considerable resources for process improvement, investments in process improvement have not always led to changes and improvements expected [27]. In a large study of organizations that had invested in process improvement 26% of organisations agreed that nothing had changed much, and 49% declared themselves disillusioned due to lack of improvements [19].

There has however been useful learning from process improvement experiences over the last few decades [20] [21] [22] [26]. Companies have made significant progress toward understanding how to measure, consistently and quantitatively, their software development processes, the density of errors in their products as well as the programmers´ productivity.

Process improvement initiatives are beginning to take effect, experience of implementing process improvement is growing and change is occurring - but we are still left wanting. There are still huge differences at different levels of an organization in relation to goals, perspective and success, which means that the wrong arguments are being used at the different levels in an organization and it is difficult to get into step. Organizational factors and barriers to SPI success often quoted include [19].

Organizational factors

- Senior management monitoring of SPI
- Compensated SPI responsibilities
- SPI goals well understood
- Technical staff involved in SPI
- SPI people well respected
- Staff time/resources dedicated to process improvement

Barriers

- Discouragements about SPI prospects
- SPI gets in the way of 'real work'
- 'Turf guarding' inhibits SPI
- Existence of organizational politics
- Assessment recommendations too ambitious
- Need guidance about how to improve
- Need more mentoring and assistance

One most important aspects of management is to motivate the work force. To be successful one needs to establish top management commitment [24] [25]. However, management fails to deliver on this promise [23]. In fact, because management often uses extrinsic incentives to motivate their work force, it often ends up decreasing people's intrinsic motivation to work [7].

Since the introduction of process assessment and process improvement models such as CMM [28], CMMI [29] and ISO 15504 (SPICE) [30] in the 1990s, there has been a generational change in the workforce coupled with the onset of the social media revolution.

Generation Y today is the fastest growing segment of the workforce. Generation Y are tech-savvy, family-centric, achievement-oriented, team-oriented and attention-craving. The Generation Y is confident, ambitious and achievement-oriented. They value teamwork and seek the input and affirmation of others. They crave attention in the forms of feedback and guidance [11]. Generation Y expects clear goals, trackable progress, shareable status, social visibility and reward schedules [10].

The transformational moment has arrived where we need to re-think the traditional ways to foster engagement in process improvement. A new approach for a new generation is needed. Gamification offers that solution for transformational change.

The remainder of this paper is structured as follows: Section 2 provides an introduction to Gamification; Section 3 describes the role of Game Mechanics within Gamification; Section 4 explains how Engagement is a key component of Gamificaction; and finally the Conclusions are presented in Section 5.

2   Gamification

Gamification is the concept of applying game-design thinking through the use of game mechanics to drive game-like player behavior to non-game applications to make them more fun and engaging [1].

Gamification is all about injecting fun, recognition and/or competition into otherwise normal work activities using game-like techniques to engage and motivate employees and management to help reach goals [4]. Examples of game-like player behavior include engagement, interaction, addiction, competition, collaboration, awareness, learning, and/or any other observed player behavior during game play.

Gamification is not itself a game. Gamification and serious games are however related because both try to leverage aspects of games to achieve something more. A serious game does it through an actual game, but gamification does it through a broader set of tools (e.g. game mechanics/dynamics, game design, gaming psychology, etc.).

Gamification has been called one of the most important trends in technology by several industry experts. Gamification can potentially be applied to any industry and almost anything to create fun and engaging experiences [5].

Gamification is a certainly a hot topic. Gamification recently made its debut on the Gartner's Hype Cycle 2011 chart, an infographic designed to show the potential real-world success of emerging technology. Gamification sits right alongside 3D printing, social analytics and group buying, and, according to its positioning, is just about to hit its high point on the peak of inflated expectations [15]. Gamification also made it into Oxford's Short List for Word of the Year 2011 [16] [17].

Gartner predicts that by 2015, more than 50% of the organization will gamify their innovation processes. By 2014, a gamified service for consumer goods marketing and customer retention will become as important as Facebook, eBay or Amazon, and more than 70 percent of Global 2000 organizations will have at least one gamified application [6]. M2 Research also reports that the market for gamification will grow to $1.6 billion in 2015, from $100 million in 2011 [14].

3   Game Mechanics

Game Mechanics are the principles, rules, and/or mechanisms that govern a behavior through a system of incentives, feedback, and rewards with a reasonably predictable outcome [9]. Game mechanics are the building blocks that can be applied and combined to gamify any non-game application [5].

Game mechanics can be used to drive almost any user behavior. They have the potential to tap into the full range of human emotions and motivate a wide range of behaviors. That's the beauty and value proposition of game mechanics [12].

Game mechanics often motivate people by providing positive feedback, such as the accumulation of points, obtaining badges, increased visibility of status, recognition of progress, customization, pleasant surprises, etc. In theory, negative feedback can also be useful, but it is less effective in practice. Negative feedback mechanisms can lead to the complete abandonment of the gamified activity, unless the users are extremely motivated, or used in a social/communal context [8].

There are many game mechanics, with new ones being discovered and constructed by game designers every day. There is a slight distinction between game mechanics and game dynamics. Point and achievement are game mechanics used to motivate behaviors, but how and precisely when the badges are unlocked over time and the precise reward schedule are gaming dynamics. Gaming dynamics are created by combining various game mechanics over time to make game play more interesting and engaging [9].

Gamification.org on its gamification wiki has compiled a list of well know game mechanics [5], but there are myriad, as humans can be motivated in practically infinite numbers of ways.

Some of the key game mechanics that are relevant in the context of process improvement are:

- **Points:** A device used for scoring or counting. Points allow one to keep track of user activities and to shape user behavior. Points encourage engagement.
- **Badges:** Badges provide the ability to create demonstrable social rewards for specific, parallel or tangential activities. Badges can be obtained for goal achievement or for points earned and can be easily showcased. Everyone likes to know that they have value. For some, status in their community is an incredible motivator.
- **Leaderboards:** Leaderboards are a universal way to convey success. Leaderboards provide users with an easy way to show their score and how they compare against others.
- **Levels:** Levels are the perfect solution for creating a constant sense of forward motion. Points and badges can be integrated into levels. Users are encouraged to return to complete tasks, achieve goals and much more whilst in the pursuit of achieving the next 'level'. Rewards can be given in greater increments as they achieve new "levels" of status.
- **Awards:** Awards are granted as merited or due. Users can show off the awards they earn.

Research has shown that employees (and people in general) are motivated by autonomy, mastery, purpose, progress and recognition. Games provide all of these aspects and through them motivate people leaning forward, engaged, and working individually and collectively toward their goals [3].

So the question is - how can we leverage game mechanics to engage and motivate people in the work place towards process improvement? How can we use game mechanics for the gamification of SPICE?

SPICE [31] is an international initiative to support the International Standard ISO/IEC 15504 for Process Assessment however industry has generally adopted the term SPICE for the international standard ISO/IEC 15504. SPICE however has itself spawned many other initiatives and process assessment models such as Automotive SPICE® [32] Medi SPICE [33] and Enterprise SPICE [34].

4 Engagement

Games it seems are perfectly tuned to give out rewards that engage the brain and keep us questing for more. Engagement occurs when the brain is rewarded, and that for something to be perceived as rewarding, it must evoke positive emotions in a person. Essentially, there are two components to the perception of something being rewarding: wanting and liking [1].

Games are generally structured so that players have various **"layers" of goals**. That is, they have the long-term goal of completing the game, the medium-term goal of completing the levels in the game, and the short-term goal of completing the missions in the levels.

As part of any game play **frequent feedback** is given at all times. An important part of providing feedback to users in games is to let them know how much progress they've made. It's also important to **measure progress** at multiple levels.

Even though it takes no extraordinary effort on the part of the user to make progress, people generally want to be acknowledged for their work. And if it's presented in a way which is interesting, people feel rewarded, and thus, engaged. One hundred small rewards are better than one big one. **Reward effort (not just success).** Rewards should be scaled in proportion to the effort, or risk, that it takes to get the reward.

A **reward schedule** is the timeframe and delivery mechanism through which rewards are delivered. Within any game, multiple types of reward schedules can be utilized either throughout. There are two primary types of reward schedules. Interval Reward Schedules are rewards given based on time. Ratio Reward Schedules are rewards given after a number of actions are completed. Rewards are generally classed as momentary and persistent. Momentary rewards are given immediately upon completing the prerequisite of the reward, and are not tracked. Persistent rewards are tracked over the entire time. Currently, there is a trend to use collectible badges or achievements as a persistent reward.

Perhaps the most effective motivator is **peer motivation** through the approval of our fellows. Especially, when these people are those we respect. The makers of social media games have based their entire business on this powerful motivating force.

5 Conclusion

By using game psychology and the principles of gamification the prospect is available to translate the traditional enthusiasm for play and social media engagement into the workplace as a basis for succeeding with and accelerating the uptake of improvement.

This would mean a change in the way that we view current capability and maturity models. A progressive measurement scale would be overlaid on the current continuous and staged models. This would involve using a system of goal challenges and points awards to attain badges and levels along the path to obtaining traditional process capability and organizational maturity levels that are the currently the target.

Gamification as a solution offers the opportunity for better user engagement, faster feedback of achievement and more visible progress indicators of process improvement.

Acknowledgments. This research is supported by the Science Foundation Ireland (SFI) Stokes Lectureship Programme, grant number 07/SK/I1299, the SFI Principal Investigator Programme, grant number 08/IN.1/I2030 (the funding of this project was awarded by Science Foundation Ireland under a co-funding initiative by the Irish Government and European Regional Development Fund), and supported in part by Lero - the Irish Software Engineering Research Centre (http://www.lero.ie) grant 10/CE/I1855.

References

1. Raymer, R.: Gamification: Using Game Mechanics to Enhance eLearning (September 2011), http://elearnmag.acm.org/featured.cfm?aid=2031772#.T1KMoq8mZPY.twitter
2. Chatfield, T.: 7 ways games reward the brain. TED Global (July 2010), http://www.ted.com/talks/tom_chatfield_7_ways_games_reward_the_brain.html
3. Kittle, M.: Motivating Employees: Gamification at Work. VP Digital Strategy, Bunchball, http://schedule.sxsw.com/2012/events/event_IAP13069
4. Julia: Make It a Game: Using Gamification to Build Your Business. Small Businesses (January 18, 2012), https://www.odesk.com/blog/2012/01/make-it-a-game-using-gamification-to-build-your-business/
5. Game Mechanics. Gamification Wiki, http://gamification.org/wiki/Game_Mechanics#Achievements
6. Newsroom, G.: Gartner Says By 2015. More Than 50 Percent of Organizations That Manage Innovation Processes Will Gamify Those Processes (April 12, 2011), https://www.gartner.com/it/page.jsp?id=1629214
7. Pries-Heje, J., Johansen, J.: ImproveIT: A book for improving software projects, DELTA (2007) ISBN 978-87-7398-086-6
8. Wu, M.: The Magic Potion of Game Dynamics. Lithium Technologies Inc. (February 02, 2011), http://lithosphere.lithium.com/t5/Building-Community-the-Platform/The-Magic-Potion-of-Game-Dynamics/ba-p/19260
9. Wu, M.: Gamification from a Company of Pro Gamers. Lithium Technologies Inc. (February 02, 2011), http://lithosphere.lithium.com/t5/Building-Community-the-Platform/Gamification-from-a-Company-of-Pro-Gamers/ba-p/19258
10. Beresford, T.: 5 game mechanics Gen Y now demands from every marketer. Gamification Theory (October 21, 2011), http://gamificationofwork.com/2011/10/5-game-mechanics-gen-y-now-demands-from-every-marketer/
11. Generation Y, http://legalcareers.about.com/od/practicetips/a/GenerationY.htm
12. Snow, S.: HOW TO: Use Game Mechanics to Power Your Business (July 13, 2010), http://mashable.com/2010/07/13/game-mechanics-business/

13. Johnson, M.: Gamification Is More Than Just Fun and Games, How companies can use game dynamics to improve loyalty marketing efforts. Expert Opinion (December 7, 2011), http://www.1to1media.com/view.aspx?docid=33011
14. Gamified Engagement: M2 Research shows Enterprise Demand Skyrocketing for Gamification. Gamification Summit (September 15, 2011), http://www.m2research.com/gamification.htm
15. Gartner: Gamification's hype is about to reach its peak. Libe Goad (August 14, 2011), http://www.zdnet.com/blog/gamification/gartner-gamifications-hype-is-about-to-reach-its-peak/583
16. Gamification Almost in the Oxford Dictionary — Is it the Next Big Thing? (Infographic), http://socialtimes.com/gamification-almost-in-the-oxford-dictionary-is-it-the-next-big-thing-infographic_b86491
17. Brockmeier, J.: Gartner Adds Big Data, Gamification, and Internet of Things to Its Hype Cycle (August 11, 2011), http://www.readwriteweb.com/enterprise/2011/08/gartner-adds-big-data-gamifica.php#.TkQnteaJQi8.twitter
18. Zichermann, G.: Top 5 Ways to Make Your Site More Fun (April 08, 2010), http://mashable.com/2010/04/07/funware-game-mechanics/
19. Goldenson, D.R., Herbsleb, J.D.: After the appraisal: a systematic survey of process improvement, its benefits and factors that influence success CMU/SEI-95-TR-009, SEI (1995), http://www.sei.cmu.edu/reports/95tr009.pdf
20. O'Hara, F.: European experiences with software process improvement. In: Proceeding ICSE 2000 Proceedings of the 22nd International Conference on Software Engineering. ACM, New York (2000) ISBN:1-58113-206-9
21. VASIE Best Practice Repository, The European Comission, DG III Industry, EPSRIT program, http://www.esi.es/VASIE
22. SPIRE project and handbook, The European Commission, ESPRIT/ESSI 23873, http://www.cse.dcu.ie/spire
23. Abrahamsson, P., Jokela, T.: Development of Management Commitment to Software Process Improvement (2000), http://citeseerx.ist.psu.edu/viewdoc/summary?doi=10.1.1.103.7664
24. Stelzer, D., Mellis, W.: Success Factors of Organizational Change in Software Process Improvement. Software Process Improvement and Practice (1999)
25. Diaz, M., Sligo, J.: How Software Process Improvement Helped Motorola. IEEE Software (1997)
26. EC ESSI Office: The Business Benefits of Software Best Practice: Pilot case studies
27. Christainsen, M., Johansen, J.: Improvability guidelines for low maturity organisations. Software Process: Improvement and Practice 13(4), 319–325 (2008)
28. Capability Maturity Model (CMM), http://en.wikipedia.org/wiki/Capability_Maturity_Model
29. Capability Maturity Model Integration (CMMI), http://www.sei.cmu.edu/cmmi/
30. ISO/IEC 15504 Information Technology - Process Assessment Parts 1-10. International Standard Organisation ISO, http://www.iso.org
31. Software Process Improvement and capability dEtermination (SPICE), http://www.spiceusergroup.org/page/903579:Page:12672
32. AutomotiveSPICE, http://ww.automotivespice.com
33. MediSPICE, http://www.medispice.com
34. EnterpriseSPICE, http://www.enterprisespice.com

Author Index

Adedjouma, Morayo 107
Alarifi, Abdulrahman 51
Alchieri, João Carlos 118
Alvarez, Amalia 85

Barafort, Béatrix 129
Bayona, Sussy 1
Bellotti, Marco 118
Besson, Jeremy 75
Betageri, Basavaraj 257
Bhandary, Smitha 257
Bharathi, V. 233
Biro, Miklos 289
Boronowsky, Michael 75
Buglione, Luigi 186

Calvo-Manzano, Jose A. 1, 239
Casey, Valentine 141, 265
Cassiers, Grégory 51
Clarke, Paul 62, 198
Crines, Gerry 273
Cuevas, Gonzalo 239

Das, Satyabrata 222
Dawid, Sebastian 261
De Amescua, Antonio 239
Demirörs, Onur 26
Desharnais, Jean-Marc 51
Dorling, Alec 295
Dubois, Eric 129
Dubois, Hubert 107
Dzianach, Rafał 261

Eagles, Sherman 148

Flood, Derek 161

Garcia, Maria Antonieta 118

Habra, Naji 51
Hauck, Jean Carlo Rossa 186
Heymans, Patrick 129

Joshi, Ravindra 244

Kar, Sharmistha 222
Kar, Subrata Kumar 222
Karpištšenko, André 13
Keenan, Frank 148
Kitouni, Tarek 107
Korsaa, Morten 289
Kumar Rath, Amiya 222

Lepmets, Marion 13, 148

Mackinnon, Donald 273
MacMahon, Silvana Togneri 148
Mangin, Olivier 129
Mas, Antònia 173
Matalonga, Santiago 85
Matveeva, Lyudmila 253
McCaffery, Fergal 141, 148, 161, 186, 265, 295
McDaid, Kevin 161
McHugh, Martin 141
Mejia, Jezreel 239
Mesquida, Antoni Lluís 173
Mitasiunas, Antanas 75
Muñoz, Mirna 239

Nebrat, Eugene 253
Neumann, Robert 93
Nevalainen, Risto 289

O'Connor, Rory V. 62, 198, 277
Orecka, Anna 261

Peldzius, Stasys 210

Ragaisis, Saulius 210
Raj, Joseph 233
Ramachandran, Balaji 257
Regan, Gilbert 161
Renault, Alain 148
Robaeys, Antoine 51
Rout, Terry 38, 282

Salahuddin, Sarah 273
San Feliu, Tomás 1, 85, 239
Schedl, Manfred 253
Schweigert, Tomas 289

Author Index

Shastry, Udaya   233
Stallinger, Fritz   93

Terrier, François   107
Tuisk, Anneli   13

Uskarcı, Algan   26

van Loon, Han   269, 286
Viale, Ernesto   118

Vohwinkel, Detlef   289
von Wangenheim, Christiane Gresse   186

Wallmüller, Ernest   249
Wen, Lian   38
Woronowicz, Tanja   75

Yilmaz, Murat   62, 198

Zarour, Mohammad   51